"Scrupulous, impressive and irrefutable. No one can read this damning historical portrait without wondering why we allow such grotesque gaps — seldom related to merit or social worth — to continue. An utterly necessary book."
David Kynaston, author of *Austerity Britain*

"An important and illuminating book, an essential antidote to the outdated and iniquitous idea that some people are worth more than others."
Kate Pickett, co-author of *The Spirit Level*

"A readable and illuminating context to our present-day extreme inequalities, exposing the narratives that justify these persistent conditions and the folly of ignoring them."
Chuck Collins, Institute for Policy Studies

THE RICHER, THE POORER

How Britain Enriched the Few and Failed the Poor

A 200-YEAR HISTORY

Stewart Lansley

First published in Great Britain in 2022 by

Policy Press, an imprint of
Bristol University Press
University of Bristol
1-9 Old Park Hill
Bristol
BS2 8BB
UK
t: +44 (0)117 954 5940
e: bup-info@bristol.ac.uk

Details of international sales and distribution partners are available at
policy.bristoluniversitypress.co.uk

British Library Cataloguing in Publication Data
A catalogue record for this book is available from the British Library

ISBN 978-1-4473-6320-0 hardcover
ISBN 978-1-4473-6321-7 paperback
ISBN 978-1-4473-6323-1 ePdf
ISBN 978-1-4473-6322-4 ePub

Cover design: Liam Roberts
Front cover image: iStock/jamielawton
Bristol University Press and Policy Press use environmentally responsible print partners.
Printed and bound in Great Britain by CMP, Poole

Also by Stewart Lansley

Poverty and Progress in Britain (with G.C. Fiegehen and A.D. Smith)
Housing and Public Policy
Poor Britain (with Joanna Mack)
Beyond Our Ken (with Andy Forrester and Robin Pauley)
After the Gold Rush
Top Man: How Philip Green Built His High Street Empire (with
Andy Forrester)
Rich Britain: The Rise and Rise of the New Super-Wealthy
The Cost of Inequality
Breadline Britain, The Rise of Mass Poverty (with Joanna Mack)
A Sharing Economy
It's Basic Income, The Global Debate (editor, with Amy Downes)

I'd like to dedicate the book to the memories of
Peter Townsend, David Donnison, Tony Atkinson,
John Veit-Wilson and John Hills.

'The art of making yourself rich is equally and necessarily the art of keeping your neighbour poor.'

John Ruskin, 1860

'What thoughtful people call the problem of poverty, thoughtful poor people call with equal justice, a problem of riches.'

R.H. Tawney, 1913

'The poor stay poor, the rich get rich. That's how it goes, everybody knows.'

Leonard Cohen,
'Everybody Knows', *I'm Your Man*, 1988

Contents

List of figures

Preface and acknowledgements

There are several studies which have chronicled, separately, the sweeping history of inequality, of wealth and of poverty. By telling the story of impoverishment and enrichment side by side, *The Richer, The Poorer* explores the extent to which the apparently separate fates of rich and poor have been critically linked. What impact, the book asks, has the process of personal enrichment by the few had on the livelihoods, life chances and incomes of the many? Has it been right for policymakers to treat poverty over most of this period as a largely distinct condition, independent of the structural forces that determine how the economic cake is sliced?

As with all books, this is the product of collaboration. I would like to thank the scores of families who have been willing to share their experiences of living on low-paid and insecure work and grappling with a complex and often coercive benefit system. Many of their testimonies, collected over different time periods, have been used as case studies in the post-1970s sections of the book. Each of them illustrate, in different ways, not just the constant struggle to get by but also the failures of policy over time.

A big thank you to co-researchers and the many students and friends from whom I have accumulated a mountain of debt over many years. A special thanks to Joanna Mack. We worked together on the two ITV *Breadline Britain* series shown in 1983 and 1990, co-authored *Poor Britain* in 1985 and *Breadline Britain* in 2015, which set out the methodology and findings of successive 'consensual' surveys on poverty, and helped develop the website Poverty.ac.uk. I would also like to thank the team behind the 2012 *Poverty and Social Exclusion Study* – the last and most in-depth of the four surveys – and especially its project lead, David Gordon. Thanks too to the Friends Provident Foundation for supporting a study on ways of giving all citizens an equal stake in the economy, and to my colleagues on the study, Duncan McCann and Steve Schifferes; and to the Joseph Rowntree Foundation for funding a study on the feasibility of a guaranteed income floor. A special thanks to Howard Reed – we have worked together on several projects – and to the think tank Compass, and its director Neal Lawson; and to colleagues on the council of the Progressive Economy Forum.

A huge thanks to David Webster, Howard Reed, John Brown, Lee Gregory, Michael Orton, Alison Rooper and Peter Sloman, who generously poured over large chunks of early drafts and offered a stream of very helpful – and sometimes sceptical – comments. Thanks too to Adrian Sinfield for guidance through the maze of the 'corporate welfare state', to Peter Scott and Andy Summers for permission to draw on unpublished papers and to three anonymous referees for helpful comments on a first draft. It has been a pleasure to work with the team at Policy Press, especially Laura

Vickers-Rendall, Caroline Astley and Kathryn King. A special thanks to Anne Rannie for help with research at key stages of the project, for being my sternest critic and for providing a constant source of sanity in the bewildering events of the last eighteen months.

Additional thanks are due to the following for their kind permission to reproduce the images used in the book: to Thomas Forsyth for 'The Landlord's Game' (landlordsgame.info); to the Mary Evans Picture Library for the Whitechapel workhouse; to TopFoto for the cartoon 'I smell the blood of a plutocrat' (*Punch*, 28 April 1909); to Glasgow Museums for the 'Glasgow rent strike'; to Mirrorpix/Reach Licensing for the Jarrow March image first published in *The Mirror* (October, 1936); to the LSE Library for the Beveridge plan poster; to The People's History Museum for the 1945 Labour election poster; to Susannah Gibbard for the Les Gibbard cartoon, 'The Unacceptable Face of Capitalism'; to its designer, Iain Lanyon, and the V&A Museum, for the 'Serious Money' poster; to Andrew Moore for the photo of the poll tax riot; to Grizelda Grizlingham for her cartoon, 'After three years of cuts, I'm a leaner, more efficient poor person'; and to Church Action on Poverty for the 'Britain Isn't Eating' poster. Thanks too to Jonathan Lynn for permission to quote from an episode of *Yes, Minister*, to the Alan Brodie Agency for permission to reproduce part of Noel Coward's adaptation of 'The Homes of England' and to the Wylie Agency LLC for permission to use a line from 'Everybody Knows' from *Stranger Music* by Leonard Cohen.

The book has drawn on a treasure trove of documentation, archive material, personal testimony and on the work of generations of social and economic historians, campaigners and reformers who have helped shape the future while shedding light on the past. Our understanding of the twists and turns of the history of poverty, inequality and wealth has been dependent on painstaking statistical groundwork by independent scholars and official statisticians. The data sets used include the annual *Households Below Average Incomes Series* published by the Department for Work and Pensions, the Office for National Statistics' *Wealth and Assets Survey*, and a number of series produced by the Institute for Fiscal Studies, the authors of the *World Inequality Database* and Thomas Piketty.[1] The book also draws on the archives of several national newspapers, published diaries and reports of the National Audit Office, the House of Commons Library and Parliamentary select committees.

I am grateful for assistance throughout from staff at the British Library, Her Majesty's Revenue and Customs and the National Archives. A particular thanks to Dominic Webber at the Office for National Statistics and statisticians at the Department for Work and Pensions for help with the provision and interpretation of official data. Thanks too for feedback from seminars and conferences at which some of the ideas in the book have been aired.

Most studies of political economy have involved value judgments, some made more explicit than others. This is as true of anti-equality texts as it is of critiques of heightened income and wealth gaps. The outcome of the clashes between such contrasting ideological positions have had a profound influence on the way economies and societies have been shaped, and thus on the life chances available to different sections of society.

The book examines the forces that have driven Britain's 'high-inequality, high-poverty cycle'. It takes as a starting point the call by the French economist Thomas Piketty, that 'Every human society must justify its inequalities.'[2] There is a growing body of historical and contemporary evidence that highly unequal societies have serious negative consequences. A key litmus test of a successful democracy must be the way it treats citizens across the income divide, how power and the fruits of progress are shared, and the strength of social well-being.

The book concentrates on income and wealth gaps rather than other sources of inequality related to gender, race, disability and sexuality, important as these are. The term 'the poor' is used throughout to describe those who obtain too small a share of the national cake to be able to enjoy even the most basic of contemporary living standards, while 'the super-rich' are those who sit at the pinnacle of the income and wealth ladder. Both groups are far from homogenous, and the terms should be seen as shorthand descriptions. Although the top 1 per cent is widely used as a 'rich line', this is a simplification, and the most significant of the wealthy power elites over time have been drawn from smaller mega-rich groups.

Over time, descriptions of poverty have been used in ways that too often package, stereotype or marginalise those on low incomes. There have certainly been a lot of labels. A striking cartoon by the American satirist Jules Feiffer once portrayed two 'down and outs' philosophising: 'We used to be poor, then disadvantaged, then deprived, then discriminated against, then socially excluded. We have not got any more money, but we do have a lot of labels.'[3] 'The poor', like 'the rich', are a diverse and far from monolithic group, and a long way from being the passive citizens implied by the use of that term. It is, of course, difficult to write a book on poverty and inequality that avoids the multiple labels and descriptions used over time. Some of the generalisations inevitably involved therefore come with a health warning.

A great variety of labels have also been used to describe different models of capitalism over the last two centuries. The system in place in the Victorian and interwar years has variously been depicted as 'industrial capitalism', 'market capitalism' or 'rentier capitalism'. A markedly different model of 'welfare capitalism', 'social capitalism' or 'regulated capitalism' emerged in the post-war years, only to give way during the 1980s to 'neoliberal capitalism', 'monopoly capitalism', 'corporate capitalism' or 'hyper-capitalism'. These post-1980s' terms, slippery as they are, have been used largely interchangeably to describe a system built around weak state regulation, high concentrations of corporate power, regressive taxation and high levels of inequality.

The term 'extractive capitalism' is used throughout to define an economic model that is heavily geared to enrichment of the few via mechanisms that extract an excessive share of the gains from existing corporate and financial wealth, and from the creation of new wealth, in ways which have significant economic, social and community side-effects. The upwards transfer of wealth has been widely used by over-empowered elites to secure an excessive slice of the national cake using business practices which have profound implications both for economic dynamism and for the level of poverty and the life chances of the many. Such methods were used during the Victorian and Edwardian eras. While the extent of extraction lessened during the post-war era, it then resurfaced from the 1980s.

The broad direction of change required to break Britain's long 'high-inequality, high-poverty' cycle, one directly linked to the power and extent of extraction, is sketched out in the final chapter. The story is taken up to the beginning of 2020. It therefore ends before the outbreak of COVID-19, but with a brief afterword on the key impact of the pandemic on these issues.

Stewart Lansley
April, 2021

Introduction: Knighthoods for the rich, penalties for the poor

In February 2019, a campaigning American entrepreneur, Yarron Brook, arrived for his third successive annual speaking tour of Britain. Chair of the California-based, pro-market and anti-state Ayn Rand Institute, and the co-author of *Equal is Unfair: America's Misguided Fight against Income Inequality*, Brook was a determined critic of the global calls for more equal societies.[1] During these visits, he spoke to thousands of students at universities and top public schools, from Harrow to Westminster, on the virtues of free markets and the merits of inequality. To a crowded lecture room of sixth formers and teachers at Eton College, he outlined Ayn Rand's philosophy of unbridled capitalism spelled out in her 1957 fantasy novel of godlike tycoons, *Atlas Shrugged*. The 2008 global meltdown, he explained, was caused, not by out-of-control financiers but by "too much statism". The rich, he declared, "deserve their wealth" and "everything we are told about inequality is wrong".[2]

While Brook was lecturing Britain's most privileged young people, official statistics showed almost one in three children – 4.2 million – to be in poverty, a figure close to record post-war levels. Over the previous four decades, Britain had moved from being one of the most equal to one of the most unequal of rich nations, while the poorest fifth of Britons are now poorer than the comparable group in many countries with lower overall inequality.[3]

While Brook's pro-rich ideology went against the grain of a growing national and global concern about inequality, his views were shared in influential political circles. A year after the 2008 global financial crisis, Lord Griffiths, a former adviser to Mrs Thatcher and the vice-chair of Goldman Sachs International, told an audience at London's St Paul's Cathedral that the public has to "tolerate inequality as the price to be paid for prosperity".[4] When he was London mayor, and just a few years before he moved into Downing Street, Boris Johnson, giving the third Margaret Thatcher lecture, told his audience that the top 10 per cent should be feted with "automatic knighthoods".[5]

Wealth and poverty: the umbilical link

The Richer, The Poorer traces the remarkable story of wealth and poverty over the last two centuries. It charts the impact of the often bitter ideological

1

and policy rifts on the separate paths taken by those at the extremes of the income and wealth ladder. It asks why rich and poor citizens are still judged, as in the past, by very different standards and expectations? Why too does a 'cycle of privilege' that perpetuates wealth at the top and disadvantage at the bottom remain as embedded today as in the distant past?

Inequality and poverty are distinct but interlocking concepts. Inequality describes the divide in resources, opportunities and assets across society. Poverty arises when sections of society are unable to afford a minimal acceptable material and social living standard, with its scale ultimately determined by – as the economist J.M. Keynes once put it – how the cake is cut.[6] Despite this link, poverty has mostly been treated as a standalone condition, independent of the extent of the overall income and wealth gap.

Interviewed in the run up to the 2001 general election, the prime minister, Tony Blair, dismissed the importance of what was happening at the top. "If you end up going after those people who are the most wealthy in society, what you actually end up doing is in fact not even helping those at the bottom end."[7] The changing fortunes of 'the rich' and 'the poor' over time can be viewed as quite separate. But is it possible to understand the lot of the poorest while ignoring the actions of those who own and control economic resources and the methods they use to build personal fortunes?

The course of poverty and inequality is ultimately the outcome of the conflict over the spoils of economic activity and of the interplay between rich elites, governments and societal pressure. In 1821, one of the pioneers of classical economics, David Ricardo, despite his opposition to state action, acknowledged that 'The principal problem in Political Economy' is to determine how 'the produce of the earth ... is divided among ... the proprietor of the land, the owner of the stock of capital necessary for its cultivation and the labourers by whose industry it is cultivated'.[8]

How the 'distribution question' has been settled has been the central driver of the changing positions of rich and poor. As the distinguished economist and expert on inequality Sir Tony Atkinson wrote nearly 200 years after Ricardo, 'What happens at the top of the distribution affects those at the bottom.' We must ask, he continued, 'whether countries can achieve low rates of poverty at the same time as having high top income shares'.[9]

For most of the last two centuries, wealthy elites have won the 'battle for share'. Although there are a handful of exceptions to the overall pattern, levels of poverty and inequality have followed a largely parallel path.[10] Up to the 1930s, poverty rates in Britain were persistently high, while acute poverty was widespread, because the portion of national income secured by the poorest third of society was low. When that share rose during and after the War, poverty fell. From the end of the 1970s, both poverty rates and the income and wealth gap rose sharply as a powerful financial and corporate elite slowly recaptured the elevated slice of national income its predecessors had reluctantly conceded in the post-war years. For only one brief period over the last 200 years – the three decades after the Second World War – has the distribution question been settled in the interests of those outside the circle of the rich and most affluent. Historically significant as this shift was, it was to prove shallow and temporary.

For the early social reformers, tackling poverty meant targeting inequality. As the eminent historian and Christian Socialist R.H. Tawney declared in 1913, the student of poverty needs to start 'much higher up the stream than the point he wishes to reach. … What thoughtful people call the problem of poverty, thoughtful poor people call with equal justice, a problem of riches.'[11] 'In the long run', George Orwell warned in his dystopian novel *1984*, published in 1949, 'a hierarchical society was only possible on a basis of poverty and ignorance'.[12] Across large chunks of history, however, the question of how to cut the cake has been dismissed as irrelevant. Few have put it quite as bluntly as Robert E. Lucas, the Chicago-based economist and one of the high priests of the post-1980s market revolution. 'Of the tendencies that are harmful to sound economics', he wrote in 2003, 'the most poisonous is to focus on questions of distribution.'[13]

This book examines the multiple and changing mechanisms that link wealth and poverty. These links have shifted in line with the model of capitalism in place, the strength of democratic structures and societal pressure, the restraints imposed on the owners of capital and the lengths to which business and financial elites have been prepared to go to preserve their wealth, power and privileges.

Through much of the nineteenth century, wealth was synonymous with political power. Britain was a near-plutocracy, a society run by and mostly for the richest sections of society who were able to firewall their wealth and status. Some concessions on working conditions and welfare were granted, if only because of fear of the consequences of inaction. The dominant philosophy – a belief in individual liberty, free markets and limited democracy – showed little concern with the lot of the governed. Ricardo's distribution question was to be settled by the outcome of the play of market forces. The question of help for the losers from economic change was considered by mainstream thinking to be a matter of conscience and of private benevolence.

The great personal wealth boom of the nineteenth century was built largely off the back of a cheap and weakly organised labour force. Unrestrained industrial capitalism, eventually tempered by the rise of trade unions, new pressure groups and investment in social infrastructure, did deliver improvements in average living standards, but this was an uneven path. Social progress for most was slow and hard fought, and lagged behind the economic gains enjoyed by the financial, landowning and professional classes.

From 1906, a new Liberal government introduced a fledgling social security system along with bitterly fought higher, if modest, taxes on top income groups. Although extended in the 1920s, the new benefit system was ill-equipped for the upheaval and mass joblessness of the interwar years. While the pain of the slump of the 1930s was borne most heavily by the vulnerable, for the rich it was largely, if not wholly, business as usual.

The years during and immediately following the War were a watershed moment in the history of poverty, wealth and inequality and their interconnections. With the ideological battle of ideas finally won by a pro-equality school of thinkers, a more comprehensive welfare state was born out of the memories of the 1930s, the devastation of war and mass pressure for change. A dramatic change in gear, the post-war reforms brought a softer edge to the British model of capitalism. In the 1950s it seemed, against the odds, that the hunger marches of the 1930s, the misery of the dole queue and the fear of the hated means test had been finally banished.

A temporary truce

For a while, the wealthy classes were forced to give ground, and poverty levels fell. But what had been initiated, it turned out, was a temporary truce between capital and labour and rich and poor. Concessions were made, but largely on capital's terms. Cracks in the new welfare system soon appeared, while the egalitarian push eventually stalled.

With the waning of the social democratic ascendency in the 1970s, egalitarian voices were displaced by those of a small group of once marginalised pro-market evangelists. The distribution question was once again written out of the policy script and the process of equalisation set in reverse. It was a counter-revolution that took the UK, the US and eventually much of the rich world back to pre-war thinking. With the lessons of that earlier era forgotten, an audacious experiment in unequal market capitalism was launched, with the promise that the great prize for a widening gap would be faster growth and a new economic dynamism that would raise living standards for all.

Yet far from greater economic stability and accelerated social progress, the experiment delivered a surge in the level of inequality and poverty. It was the poorest sections of society who ended up on the wrong side of the unending upheavals of the time. The expectation that the tremors of the 2008 meltdown would trigger another major turning point in the direction of post-war history failed to materialise. Instead, the pro-inequality model of political economy, dysfunctional as it had been, proved remarkably resilient.

The last 200 years can be divided into three separate eras. The first 'anti-poor, pro-inequality' era prevailed until 1939. The second 'pro-poor, pro-equality' post-1945 era lasted little more than a single generation. An apparently historic blip, it was replaced by a return to past levels of inequality and a jump in the risk of poverty. That third era is still in place. This is not to deny the wider progress over this long period. The absolute material living standards of the poorest are much higher today than in the past. But measured in relation to contemporary standards not much has changed.

Just as a century earlier, poverty and inequality have become institutionalised, built into an economic and social system which works heavily in the interests of a small financial elite and, to a lesser extent, the affluent professional classes. Despite two hundred years of change, the inequality debate remains highly charged, while official attitudes towards the poorest are not much softer than in the era of the Poor Law. In contrast, wealthy elites, with occasional exceptions, get an easy ride from government, media and the public, leaving them largely free to leverage a share of national wealth out of proportion to their contribution. Britain's governing philosophy is now one that offers 'knighthoods for the privileged and penalties for the poor'.

With the exception of the post-1945 decades, a significant minority has had to make do with the proportion of the proceeds of economic activity consistent with the needs of capital, wider political expediency and the self-interest of the wealthiest classes. 'The poor have been a nuisance, a threat and a financial burden throughout history' writes the social policy academic Peter Golding.[14] Just as the winners have employed multiple ways to justify their position at the top, governments have adopted a long line of explanations – or excuses – for inaction: that poverty is the natural God-given order, the result of natural selection or the product of individual failure; that a certain degree of poverty is necessary to encourage a work ethic; that too much redistribution drains the entrepreneurial spirit.

Britain is a country where disparities in income and assets have long been weakly related to differences in effort and social contributions. Today, as in the past, it is a comfortable society in which to be rich, but not one in which to be poor.

PART I

1800–1939

1

Hierarchical discipline

It was the high summer of 1939. In July, weeks away from the outbreak of war, a thousand people gathered at Holland House in Kensington in West London to celebrate the eighteenth birthday of the debutante Rosalind Cubitt. Rosalind was the granddaughter of Alice Keppel, the mistress of Edward VII. Her mother, Sonia Keppel, had married Roland Cubitt, later the 3rd Baron Ashcombe, heir to the giant global building firm. Camilla Parker Bowles, who later married Charles, the prince of Wales, is Rosalind's daughter.

Set in seventy acres of landscaped gardens and parkland, the sixteenth-century Holland House was one of Britain's pre-eminent private mansions, long the centre of political and society intrigue, and once described as a 'temple of luxury'.[1] Loaned for the occasion by its owner the 6th Earl of Ilchester, the palace played host to one of the most memorable parties of 'the season', when Britain's wealthiest classes came together in a whirl of social and sporting events. The guest list was a roll call of the leading members of Britain's wealthy elite. King George VI and Queen Elizabeth together with Queen Eva of Spain and the playwright Noël Coward mingled with the country's political and literary figures, foreign ambassadors, press barons, financiers and popular entertainers.

Despite the wider privations and the deepening shadow of war, what one insider dubbed the 'ornamental class' showed no inclination for restraint.[2] Across Britain, the champagne continued to flow at lavish social gatherings and traditional aristocratic pastimes – polo, fox hunting and shooting. 'Chips' Channon, Conservative MP and part of a small, privileged orbit which circled many of the most exclusive social and political events of the time, described the summer of 1939 in his diary as 'a feverish season when night after night we went to balls and fetes, each one more splendid and sumptuous than the others'.[3]

Britain's social elite was not just immensely rich, it continued to possess 'power utterly disproportionate to its numbers'.[4] It was a group that included an eclectic mix of aristocratic grandees, scions of the Victorian commercial, industrial and trading barons, names like Lord Vesty and Lord Pilkington and members of banking dynasties such as the Barings and Schroders. Outsiders peering in would have seen an apparently plutocratic paradise, a country heavily skewed in the power and money stakes. A few thousand people – a tiny proportion of the population – lived gilded lives and between them owned large chunks of the nation's most valuable land, industrial wealth and the most celebrated of its historic palaces and mansions. Many of them still sat in the House of Commons as well as the Lords: a third of Conservative cabinets between 1935 and 1955 consisted of aristocrats.[5]

God's will

Until the second half of the nineteenth century, Britain was effectively ruled by a land-owning aristocracy which not only owned much of Britain, and had done for centuries, but still packed both houses of parliament. They controlled the law, the judiciary, the military, the church, the top ranks of the civil service and most of local government.[6] Parliament saw its role as preserving the status quo, or as the duke of Wellington, prime minister from 1828–30, described it, ensuring 'hierarchical discipline' with the mass of society ruled by the enlightened, propertied and educated classes.[7]

The impact of Britain's plutocratic power and the industrial revolution on working-class living standards and the course of inequality during the nineteenth century has long been a matter of debate among historians. So too has been the question of whether the often inhuman conditions imposed on workers during market-led industrialisation were really necessary to economic success.[8] What is not in doubt is that, despite long-lasting innovations from the construction of a vast and transformative railway network to new manufacturing techniques, piecemeal social reforms and a gradual rise in average living standards, divorcing the functioning of the economy from its impact on society meant that Britain remained a deeply riven society.

Poverty throughout the eighteenth and much of the nineteenth century was widely viewed, conveniently, as 'natural', as 'God's will', determined by providence. In the eighteenth century, the preacher Robert Moss instructed 'the poor to rest contented with that state or condition in which it hath pleased God to rank him'.[9] Others pointed to a failure of character or moral weakness, with poor families complicit in their own fate. While hunger was often seen as beneficial, as a motivation to seek work, wealth was welcomed as the product of merit and hard work.

'The poor are like the shadows in a painting: they provide the necessary contrast', wrote the French doctor and moralist Philippe Hecquet in 1740.[10] 'Poverty is a most necessary and indispensable ingredient in society', declared Patrick Colquhoun, the founder of the police force in England in 1800, 'it is the source of wealth, since without poverty there would be *no labour*, and without *labour* there could be *no riches*, no *refinement*, no *comfort*, no benefits to those who may be possessed of wealth'.[11] The poor, then, were necessary to provide labour, preserve the status quo and sustain elite power.

While such views were challenged by social critics, some of them from the ranks of the gentry themselves, less extreme versions have continued to be aired to this day. That poverty was driven by the structural forces of unemployment, intermittent and low-paid work and slum-induced ill health was mostly dismissed by those in power. Apart from the old and sick and the 'good poor' ('those who did not join trades unions or engage in Chartist plotting'), the poor were dismissed by officialdom as a 'residuum'.[12]

This thinking was most potently expressed in the Poor Law Amendment Act of 1834. This set out to end the Speenhamland system of 'out relief'. While variably applied across the country, this form of relief had topped up wages to bare subsistence levels and helped ensure the supply of labour that the new industrial capitalism depended on. The new Act placed the workhouse at the centre of provision, with a central guiding principle of 'less eligibility' – that workhouse conditions should be worse than the lowest living standards available to a working labourer. The moral shame attached to seeking relief under the Act – those receiving help were known as 'paupers' and had no rights – was a deliberate attempt at deterrence and minimising the cost of relief. Workhouse conditions were often, if not always, draconian – with the separation of couples, bad food, strict discipline and attempts to improve moral character.[13]

The aim of the 1834 Act was to prevent starvation, not poverty, and to promote the Victorian ideology of individual responsibility and self-help. Those at risk went to considerable lengths to avoid the taint of pauperism associated with claiming public relief. The new Poor Law contributed to growing disorder in the 1830s and 1840s and new protest movements, from the Anti-Corn Law League to the Chartists. It spawned a glut of novels by authors as varied as Elisabeth Gaskell, Charles Kingsley, Charles Dickens and Benjamin Disraeli, twice a Conservative prime minister. Dickens' second novel, *Oliver Twist*, was an undisguised attack on the new law. These 'condition of England' novels exposed the reality of mass squalor to their middle-class readers, who began to ask why endemic social distress was tolerated in the world's leading industrial nation.

Scattered letters and testimonies assembled by historians give voice to the impact on ordinary workers. John Hawker, born in 1836, spoke of how his wage as a child for a seven-day week was only enough to buy a single loaf. The penalties imposed on those caught pilfering wood or poaching game were severe, including deportation. Some, John recalled, 'steal to be sent away … when I was old enough, I crept into the wood by the light of the moon, and once brought out five pheasants to keep my father, mother, brothers and sisters from starving'. Deep hunger was a common thread. Edwin Cook's 'first recollection of hunger' was when he was five. 'My sister took me to the cabbage bed and pulled up some of the old stalks and peeled off the outer rind and the centre we ate for our dinner, and many times after we did the same.' 'How to exist and keep honest – this was the mistery that confronted my parents; final result it could not be done', recalled

Edwin, who was born in 1844. In 1855, when bread prices soared, Edwin's father was working in a gravel pit owned by a local squire. When he and some men boasted in the village pub that they 'were independent of the Esquire', they were all sacked. 'He now tramped from farm to farm, but no work could be obtained. He arrived home one evening and declared he would take us all to the workhouse. "Never! We would all die rather than go there", declared my mother.'[14]

The age of capital

The nineteenth century was, as the Marxist historian and critic of industrialisation Eric Hobsbawm described, 'the age of capital', the high point of economic liberalism and of near full-blooded free enterprise.[15] Classical economics at the time held that free markets were fully self-adjusting and would deliver superior economies. The state should not interfere with the bargain on pay and conditions struck between master and man.

Before industrialisation, economies were based only partially on free markets. 'Economies used multiple distributive systems, with markets typically playing auxiliary roles to distributive systems based on reciprocity and redistribution. The paradox for 19th-century Britain was that the expansion of the market produced unparalleled wealth on one hand, but a cascade of poverty and social dislocations on the other.'[16]

Britain's free market experiment depended on a compliant and mass industrial workforce, one that was large enough to suppress wage levels, thus boosting returns to capital owners. The share of national income received in profits, rent, dividends and interest stood at close to 40 per cent throughout most of the nineteenth century, only falling slightly in favour of wages in the final quarter. Capital's share then fell in the middle of the twentieth century before rising again from the 1980s.[17] Attempts to deliver a sufficient supply of labour over time involved various forms of enforcement. During industrialisation, the necessary army of labour – capitalism's key raw material – was assembled through population growth, a punitive system of unemployment relief and rural depopulation.

The migration to the mills, factories and mines was driven by a process of 'enclosure' which eroded traditional rights to 'the commons'. Despite popular revolts, there had already been a steady erosion of the entrenched 'right of access' to much of Britain's land, heaths and woods – the source of livelihood, subsistence and community living for farming communities for centuries.[18] This process continued from the closing years of the eighteenth century, with over five thousand acts of parliament sanctioning the mass appropriation of the rights of commoners by land owners. This long struggle over rights to a primary natural resource was won almost entirely by the landed classes, while Britain's extraordinary concentration of land ownership at the time barely changed in the next two hundred years.[19] It is today still possible to travel through the heartland of rural Britain and pass for mile after mile through land owned by a single family.

Although life in pre-industrial times was often grim and unforgiving, there was a strong sense, if unwritten and far from universal, of mutuality – with the granting of certain rights, such as the occupation of land in return for work, and with custom imposing limits on the exploitation of workers. Rights of access to 'the Commons' had been granted to citizens in the 1217 Charter of the Forest, the companion to the better known Magna Carta, but these rights were eroded through centuries of confiscation and encroachment. Justified by the landowning classes as an economic imperative, the loss of common land and rapid industrialisation wrecked long-standing systems of mutual support found in closely bound communities. The trends imposed the mass displacement of millions of commoners, often enforced with brutality, with large numbers of the landless and impoverished forced to turn to industrial labour. As the Northamptonshire peasant poet John Clare put it in his poem 'The Mores' in 1820:

Inclosure came and trampled on the grave
Of labour's rights and left the poor a slave ...
and birds and trees and flowers without a name
All sighed when lawless law's inclosure came.

In the highlands of Scotland, the 'clearances' of small tenant holdings from the late eighteenth century in order to introduce more profitable agricultural systems devastated the livelihoods of local communities and ultimately brought famine.[20] In one case in 1820, Lord Bossmore, an aristocrat and MP, invited villagers living in a village on his inherited estate in the Isle of Arran to a party. When they returned they discovered that Bossmore had razed the village, largely because he found their dwellings unsightly. The villagers were moved a mile away to the coast, where they had no land to till. The annexation of common land was an early case of 'wealth extraction' that enabled the landed classes and others to boost the returns from their ownership of natural assets.

The most widely used justification for the precedence given to private interests and the property rights of the few over those of ordinary people was, and has continued to be, the prospect of a better future for all. The higher agricultural returns from enclosure were used in part to invest in the new industrialisation, but also to finance lavish lifestyles.

The Austrian-Hungarian political economist Karl Polanyi later described the enforced social transformation as 'an economic earthquake that transformed ... vast masses of the English countryside from settled folk into shiftless migrants'.[21] The winners from the 'earthquake' were the titled, the new financial and merchant classes and, sitting well below them but well above the labouring classes, a growing group of professionals – shopkeepers, lawyers, doctors and government officials. Through the nineteenth century each generation of the manual labour force would pay the price for economic progress enjoyed disproportionately by those who ruled them. 'Thus deprived of independence, the private reduces the freedom of the majority, all those without access to sufficient capital, to the narrow choices provided by the marketplace in service of private property.'[22] The appropriation of commonly used natural resources and the dominance of private ownership became an embedded feature of future economic systems based on weakly regulated models of capitalism.

The patrician control of parliament ensured that wealthy and hereditary elites ran the country largely in their interest. The 1815 Corn Law kept wheat prices high by restricting imports. On the day it was passed, troops were called to deal with public protests outside parliament. By forcing up the price of bread, the law came at great cost to the wider population, while further enriching the largest landowning dynasties, such as the Westminster and Bedford families who still own much of the most valuable land in central London. With successive attempts to repeal the measure defeated by a parliament full of landowners, it was only repealed in 1846 in response to the Irish Famine, in which more than a million people died, in large part because of the impact of import controls on grain.

Industrialisation eventually raised average wages, at least for men, and material living standards, but only with a long lag and at a huge cost to the first wave of factory labour crammed into congested and insanitary urban areas.[23] The influential left historian E.P. Thompson, in his account of the power of an industrial 'master-class', controversially dismissed the material improvements of the industrial revolution as 'more potatoes, a few articles of cotton clothing for his family, soap and candles, some tea and sugar, and a great many articles in the *Economic History Review*'.[24]

Fluctuating wages and the high rents ensured by scarcity meant that urban overcrowding – a key cause of high infant mortality – was the norm.[25] In Bethnal Green in the 1840s, the average lifespan was sixteen years, a third of that enjoyed by 'gentlemen and professionals'.[26] One of the many forms of exploitation of wage earners was the hated 'truck system' vividly described in Disraeli's 1845 novel *Sybil, or The Two Nations*, with workers paid in vouchers for exchange in company 'tommy-shops' at higher-than-market prices. 'Free markets' made the market more free for some only by making it less free for others.

To avoid starvation, and desperate to keep out of the workhouse, families turned to self-supporting charities, friendly societies, loans, casual work, begging, petty crime and local pawnbrokers – known as the 'pop shop'. Items pawned were typically basic essentials, from bedding to clothes. In the mid-century, some twenty-six urban-based 'Ragged Schools' provided basic education, meals and medical help for those excluded from regular schools. These were run by volunteers, often founded by people of humble origins and were reliant on donations. Many pupils had run away from home and lived by begging. Many never slept in beds. Barefooted children were donated clogs embossed with the message: 'not to be pawned'.[27] Although the age of economic laissez-faire also spawned a range of self-help and mutual institutions, charitable help was often highly discriminating. The influential Charity Organisation Society, established in 1869, maintained that poverty was self-inflicted, and gave support only to the 'industrious' poor, determined after exhaustive investigation.[28]

Social dislocation and slum-induced disease in the first half of the century did provoke change, but reform was slow. There were long gaps in the extension of the franchise, which was granted through gritted teeth. The two main political parties certainly feared the political consequences of universal suffrage. As Benjamin Disraeli told MPs on the passing of the 1867 Reform Act – which extended the vote to urban workers – it must "never be the fate of this country to live under a democracy."[29] In 1865, 76 per cent of members of parliament were still titled aristocrats or members of the landed gentry.[30] The vote was extended to rural workers in 1884 (though a third of men could still not vote), adding slowly to a more diverse group of MPs. Women, however, could not legally vote in parliamentary

Figure 1.1: Vagrant's ward, Whitechapel workhouse, East London, 1902. The men are picking oakum – teasing lumps of old rope apart into raw fibres.

Source: Mary Evans Picture Library

elections until almost eighteen years after Queen Victoria's death, when voting was extended to women over thirty with sufficient property and to all men over twenty-one. These moves tripled the electorate from seven to over twenty million.

New popular movements and a growing sense of political obligation eventually brought tougher factory legislation along with local government investment in clean water and sewage disposal, while some industrialists built 'model villages' for their workers. Such moves softened the raw impact of unrestrained capitalism. Schooling was mostly provided by charities and religious institutions, and had become compulsory and free for children of primary age by the 1880s. The century's closing decades saw the first TB sanatorium and the first garden city. Although the middle-class conscience was at work, progress, as with the vote, was conceded to defuse social pressure and the fear of pandemic. While most of the victims of tuberculosis were from overcrowded slums, there were also a number of high-profile casualties, from John Keats to Emily Brontë. The social measures were also designed, as the historian of the welfare state Pat Thane has argued, to create 'the conditions in which self-help and independence could be attained rather than to redistribute wealth and opportunities from rich to poor'.[31]

The practice of the Poor Law also evolved, while the ban on 'outdoor relief' – through cash or food handouts – of the pre-1834 system was never fully enforced, if often only because of the lack of space in workhouses. For the elderly, help in cash or in kind had largely replaced the workhouse by the end of the century. Despite resistance from some local guardians, there were moves to cut costs – which were met by a regressive system of local rates – through more stringent rules of entitlement. It was a move echoed throughout the history of social support. Mothers on outdoor relief, for example, were to be pressed to put their children in the workhouse so that they could support themselves by work.[32]

Despite gradual improvements in urban conditions, work for the unskilled and semi-skilled remained intermittent, insecure and badly paid. Although there were regular outbreaks of industrial protest, labour was relatively unorganised. Less than three-quarters of a million workers were members of a union in 1870. Even at the end of the century, despite an improvement in nutrition on average, class differences could be seen in variations in height and weight, with fourteen-year-old boys from the professional classes an average 3.5 inches taller than working-class children.[33] Escape from hunger and early death did not become a reality for many ordinary people until well into the twentieth century.

2

Britain's gilded age

A vast gulf in living standards prevailed through and beyond the Victorian era. 'There is ignorance, and coarse brutality, and sullen hopelessness, and haggard wretchedness, far beyond what there ought to be in the midst of such beauties and blessings', declared Elizur Wright, an American businessman and social reformer. Visiting Britain on a fact-finding journey a decade after the Poor Law Amendment Act, Wright was unimpressed by the rich classes. Meeting the elderly and influential romantic poet, William Wordsworth, who had drifted from the radicalism of his younger days, Wright argued firmly against the poet's belief that America, like Britain, should have 'a class of gentlemen ... born to such large property that they could devote themselves entirely to literary pursuits, and be above sordid interests'. 'The longer I stay here', declared Wright, 'the more this class of independent hereditary gentlemen seems to me like a perpetual devouring curse of locusts.'[1]

While the data sources are imperfect, the evidence is that the UK *income* gap widened through the first six decades of the nineteenth century. Real wages rose slowly in the last decades of the Victorian era, while the income gap narrowed slightly.[2] Industrial capitalism produced vast wealth, but only for the few, creating a *wealth* gap that was even greater than that for incomes. In 1859, the wealthiest sixty-seven estates accounted for 22 per cent of all property left in that year.[3] On the death of Queen Victoria in 1901, the top 1 per cent owned an estimated 70 per cent of all private property – land, property and financial assets – while the top tenth owned 93 per cent. The vast majority owned more or less nothing.[4]

Extractive capitalism

Victorian political ideology embraced the same survival-of-the-fittest social Darwinism that helped to drive the runaway personal fortunes being amassed across the Atlantic, even if wealth in the United States was then slightly less unequally distributed than in the UK.[5] For some, the towering riches being accumulated were a just reward 'for the United States becoming the richest and mightiest nation'.[6] For others, the new tycoons were dismissed as 'robber barons' for their ruthless industrial tactics and the harsh conditions they imposed on workers. The oil magnate John D. Rockefeller – the world's first dollar billionaire – was denounced as the 'most hated man in America' because of the way he treated his workers and the methods by which he accumulated his wealth.[7] As in the UK, colossal wealth sat beside crushing poverty. For years the poet Walt Whitman had written optimistic paeans to American society. He then changed his tune. If the United States grows 'vast crops of poor, desperate, dissatisfied, nomadic, miserably-waged populations', he warned in 1879, 'then our republican experiment, notwithstanding all its surface-successes, is at heart an unhealthy failure'.[8]

In the nineteenth century, in both the US and the UK, a model of 'extractive capitalism' was constructed with the opportunities created by rapid industrialisation added to the exploitation of the private ownership of land and other natural resources. Such extraction takes place when the owners of capital are able to use their economic and political muscle to secure an excessive share of the fruits of economic activity. Although there was nothing new about the power to extract, the upheavals in place – from enclosure to the industrial revolution - brought the potential of higher personal rates of return from both the use of existing assets and from the new financial and business practices. These leveraged gains were the primary source of the great wealth boom of the century, and of the vast personal fortunes being accumulated by landowners and the new financiers and industrialists.

A combination of plutocratic power, concentrated ownership of land and property, a largely powerless labour force and a hands-off state were perfect conditions for building vast fortunes. Some of this new wealth was a justified reward for innovation and risk-taking which boosted the underlying strength of the economy. But while some of it was ploughed back to finance progress and expansion, much of it paid for the lavish and often bohemian lifestyles enjoyed by the 'leisured classes' living off the rent, interest and dividends their assets, nearly always gifted, yielded. R.H. Tawney satirised the group as a 'class of pensioners upon industry'.[9]

A number of leading economic and social thinkers of the time were highly critical of the processes underlying much of this personal fortune building. The inflated returns intensified inequality because the assets from which they derived were very narrowly owned, while nineteenth century economists drew a clear distinction between productive and unproductive activity. The critic of orthodox economics, J.A. Hobson, distinguished between 'property' and 'improperty', while Tawney called assets used simply to extract payments from others, and not to perform a positive role, property 'without function'.[10]

Pro-market thinkers also questioned the nature and extent of extraction. Wealthy landlords getting rich by charging their much poorer tenants inflated rents came to be known as 'rentiers'. The early classical economists argued that these rents were greater than the landowners' contribution to economic gain. The patron saint of economics, Adam Smith, in his immensely influential 1776 work *The Wealth of Nations* warned that scarcity and the private ownership of land, one of the principal natural resources, enabled landlords to extract an excessive share of the earnings from its use: 'The landlords, like all other men, love to reap where they never sowed, and demand a rent even for its natural produce.'[11] David Ricardo – a landlord himself – was equally critical of the surplus 'rent' over and above productive effort – 'money for nothing' – demanded by landlords.[12] As the Victorian philosopher John Stuart Mill said of landlords, they

> grow rich in their sleep without working, risking or economising. … If some of us grow rich in our sleep, where do we think this wealth is coming from? It doesn't materialize out of thin air. It doesn't come without costing someone, another human being. It comes from the fruits of others' labours, which they don't receive.[13]

The term 'rentier capitalism' – originally associated with the higher returns from a lack of competition – later came to be used more widely to describe activities wherein economic muscle drives excessive and unwarranted rewards. This book uses the term 'extractive capitalism' as a more generic description of economies that allow an elite of capital owners and executives to secure an excessive slice of the economic cake. Such extraction, a kind of private tax on the industry of others, reduces the resources available for wages, investment and innovation. Extractive activity was widespread during the industrial revolution, notably through the treatment of the workforce, became less prevalent post-1945, but then returned in multiple forms from the closing decades of the twentieth century.

Such extractive power delivers disproportionate rewards at the expense of others, from ordinary workers and local communities to small businesses and taxpayers, often by steering economic resources into unproductive use, with no or limited addition to economic value. 'The efforts of men are utilized in two different ways', declared the influential Italian economist Vilfredo Pareto in 1896. 'They are directed to the production or transformation of economic goods, or else to the appropriation of goods produced by others.'[14] Such 'appropriation' benefits those who 'have' rather than 'do', and also 'crowds out' activity that would yield more productive and social value. It has come to be associated not just with the concentrated returns from land but with exploitation across a wider range of economic activity.[15]

Extraction has been the primary cause of one of the most enduring features of Britain's political economy over the last 200 years: its high-inequality, high-poverty cycle. While capitalism's business cycle, a 'natural' pattern of economic expansion and contraction, or 'boom and bust', has tended to last for periods of between ten and twenty years, the inequality-poverty cycle has proved much more enduring. For the period covered in this book, the first wave of this long cycle lasted nearly a century and a half, only softening slightly in its later stages and finally drawing to an end with the outbreak of war in 1939. There then followed a period of much lower inequality and poverty, a more forgiving wave, but one that lasted little longer than a single generation. This was short of a golden age – levels were still widely considered to be too high – but the best Britain has been able to achieve. This period then gave way to a second prolonged wave of high inequality and poverty that has so far lasted around four decades, and shows no sign of abating.

Unlike the business cycle which is endemic to the processes of capitalism and common across capitalist-based societies, the inequality-poverty cycle is neither natural, nor universal. It is an artifact determined by the pattern and distribution of the structures of power and the ebb and flow of economic and social regulation and intervention. The two extreme waves of the past 200 years have coincided with periods of high economic extraction. They occur when power is loaded in favour of self-serving elite groups who are able to resist attempts at correction for sustained periods.

How the gains from economic activity are shared between profits and wages, for example, is ultimately dictated by the power balance between capital and labour. When bargaining power is heavily skewed upwards, labour pays a high price. Those extended periods where aggregate wages have been suppressed, and where workforces, and local communities, have been forced to take an excessive share of the risks of economic change, represent a form of large-scale, comprehensive extraction that has exerted downward pressure on living standards and undermined household and community resilience.

The last 200 years have seen the use of multiple and gradually more sophisticated and obscure forms of extraction that have not just undermined wider life chances, but also exacerbated the natural business cycle. In the nineteenth century, the exploitation of a largely unorganised labour force enabled the mass upward distribution of the gains from industrialism and the growing demand for land. From the earliest days of state attempts to levy higher tax rates on the rich, tax avoidance became a new mechanism of large-scale extraction from society at large. From the 1960s, a new breed of financier developed new and always opaque mechanisms for transferring existing wealth. Other examples of extraction have included the boosting of profits through monopolisation, the rigging of product and financial markets, the application of excessive fees on savings and pension products, the manipulation of corporate balance sheets to boost executive earnings and the skimming of returns from financial transactions. City traders in recent years have coined a variety of labels – from 'the croupier's take' to the 'bunce' – for the surpluses they have been able to cream off of trading activity.

State action has the capacity to limit such extraction. Yet for large periods of recent history governments have either facilitated or turned a blind eye to the exploitative muscle of over-empowered capital. The state adopted a largely hands-off role until the last decades of the nineteenth century. For large chunks of the twentieth century it largely ignored the growth of extractive business practices. Too often the state has been an agent of inequality, sometimes by design, sometimes by accident, often knowingly. The policy responses of government in areas from overall economic management to interventions in housing, planning and regulation have often fuelled opportunities for extraction, thus adding to other pro-inequality forces. The transfer of publically owned assets – from land to state-owned enterprises – into private ownership from the 1980s onwards, for example, eroded the principle of common ownership of key natural and created resources, while delivering another extended and largely unearned bonanza for the already wealthy.

In 1886, the social reformer Sidney Webb – the co-founder, with Beatrice Webb, of the London School of Economics and Political Science and the left-of-centre weekly the *New Statesman* – wrote that nothing is done 'without the consent of a small intellectual yet practical class ... not two thousand in number'.[16] The political struggles of the time, less confrontational in many ways than those on the European continent where social upheaval was widespread, ended in overwhelming victory of this 'class' through a form of collective monopoly power over wider society.

While a tiny class of the 'idle' and 'active rich' lived in extravagance from 'unearned income', large numbers lived at, just above or below subsistence. The gilded classes defended the lack of progress on social reform on the grounds that it would undermine the natural laws of economics. Even calls for modest public intervention were widely opposed. Workers and bosses, it was claimed, simply received what each deserved, while tampering with free markets would inflict severe economic damage. As the American economist John Bates Clark, who developed the theory of 'marginal productivity', explained in 1899, 'It is the purpose of this work to show that the distribution of income to society is controlled by a natural law, and that this law ... would give to every agent of production the amount of wealth which that agent creates.'[17]

The 'marginal revolution' was a key innovation in the shift from classical to neoclassical economics at the end of the nineteenth century. Its claim that price equates to value offered a convenient theoretical defence of the persistence of poverty alongside immense wealth and abundance. The idea that the intrinsic value of all 'commodities', including labour, was to be determined by their market price plugged a hole in the framework of classical economics which never had a well worked-out theory of how rewards should be distributed. It helped provide the ideological basis for the way economic activity – including the employment of labour – came to be seen as essentially transactional. 'No assessment of wages, no relief for the able-bodied unemployed, but no minimum wages either, nor a safeguarding of the right to live', wrote Karl Polanyi. 'Labor should be dealt with ... as a commodity that must find its price in the market.'[18]

Workers, according to the headmaster of Rugby School Dr Matthew Arnold, were viewed as 'hands – not as heads, hearts or souls'.[19] The

Victorian economy had created a 'cash nexus of man to man', declared the high-profile writer, historian and philosopher Thomas Carlyle.[20] The way workers were reduced to 'costs of production' became a recurring theme in the subsequent history of economic change.

At the end of the nineteenth century, a Liberal MP was speaking in his Manchester constituency. Asked if he would support the growing campaign for public authorities to pay a minimum wage for unskilled workers, he said no. 'It was the bounden duty of government', he declared, 'to buy its labour in the cheapest market.'[21] As E.P. Thompson later explained, the 'injury' of market societies was to 'define human relations primarily as economic'.[22]

The vast personal fortunes accumulated in the nineteenth century depended on a 'double bluff or deception', argued the leading British economist John Maynard Keynes:

> On the one hand, the labouring classes accepted from ignorance or powerlessness ... a situation in which they could call their own very little of the cake that they and Nature and the capitalists were co-operating to produce. And on the other, the capitalist classes were allowed to call the best part of the cake theirs ... on the tacit underlying condition that they consumed very little of it in practice.[23]

As a result, Keynes added, labour was not able 'to consume in immediate enjoyment the full equivalent of its efforts'. The Victorian values of prudence were exploited to justify high profits and low wages, necessary, it was claimed, to finance growth, but which were also the source of extravagant lifestyles.[24] This 'deception' was not finally exposed and countered until after the Second World War with the creation, if temporary, of a more even balance of power between landlord and tenant, factory owner and workforce, government and citizen.

An ideological counter-offensive

For centuries thinkers had warned of the corrosive impact of too great a divide between rulers and ruled, while the history of inequality can be seen as the outcome of the clash between free market ideologues and those demanding a moderation of its social impact. The former defended the side effects of early industrialism – child labour, slums and sweatshops – as the necessary birth pangs of eventual social progress. Reformers argued that the model of unrestrained capitalism was incompatible with social justice and that progress could have been achieved at less social cost. Polanyi described the process of change in the UK as a 'double movement' in which attempts to expand markets were met by renewed attempts to protect society from those markets.[25]

The most trenchant critique of industrial capitalism, and challenge to the reformist movement, came from the political theorist Karl Marx. The exploitation of labour by industrialists and a class of financial 'parasites' were central themes of his laws of economics. For him, capitalism could not survive without the exploitation and 'pauperisation' of large parts of the workforce.[26] Profit depended on inadequately paid labour. Marx's thinking was summed up in the sweeping opening line of the sixty-four-page *Communist Manifesto* (co-authored with the German industrialist, and funder of Marx's research, Friedrich Engels, and still a global bestseller): 'The history of all hitherto existing society is the history of class struggles.'

For Marx, the struggle between classes was the fundamental determinant of history. If labour had been paid collectively its due contribution, he argued, the capitalist system would have collapsed. While reformism could win concessions, he claimed, these would never be enough to ensure a just division of productive output. A fair society depended on a socialist system in which capital was collectively owned and power equally shared. Since capitalists would not vote for their own downfall, Marx insisted, capitalism's fundamental contradictions would lead to its self-destruction through political revolution, with the industrial working class the agent of this process.

Although large parts of his teachings were shared by other critics, Marx's ideas had only a weak influence on the development of change in Britain at the time. Only eleven mourners attended his funeral on 17 March 1883 in Highgate, North London. The history of the next century, in contrast, was heavily shaped by his followers. A hundred years on from his death, close to half the world's population lived in states ruled by leaders who professed Marxism as their primary philosophy, even if these rulers greatly distorted his teachings and presided over authoritarian and deeply oppressed societies.

In the UK, it was the reformist movement that had the biggest influence on the extent and pace of change. Although prominent reformers shared much of the Marxist critique, they differed profoundly with him on the way forward. The early founders of the Labour Party owed as much to Methodism as to Marxism. With some exceptions, Marxist ideas have never carried more than a marginal or temporary influence on the broad British left. One of those exceptions came during the profound economic crisis of the 1930s. 'The fight for Labour's soul in the thirties', declared the Conservative MP David Howell, could be seen as a contest 'between Marx and Keynes'.[27] It was Keynes, born three months after Marx's death, who won the contest.

While the issue of class conflict came to be defused and a good deal more complex over time, greater equality remained a central goal on the political left. The case against inequality came to take a variety of forms: that too great a divide threatened economic efficiency and stability, weakened social resilience and undermined the democratic process. In 1900, the objections were primarily ethical and humanitarian. Inequality was seen as the source of working-class insecurity and impoverishment, and the outcome of their dependency on employers and lack of opportunity for self-development. Poverty, it was held, was rooted in a distorted view of what the economy was for, and was critically linked to the process of wealth accumulation. As the prominent social thinker, art critic and philanthropist John Ruskin argued in 1860, 'The art of making yourself rich is equally and necessarily the art of keeping your neighbour poor.'[28] Adam Smith, an adviser to governments like John Maynard Keynes and William Beveridge after him, also emphasised that the economic and social were equally vital to a good society, and that markets needed to be tempered by wider questions of morality.[29] For the moral critics, Britain had succumbed to a dehumanised model of political economy. Poverty could not be tackled by self-help, hard work and benevolence alone. For Tawney, society needed to 'rearrange its scale of values' with economic activity 'put in a subordination to the social purpose for which it is carried on'.[30]

The immense divisions of Victorian society stemmed, the reformers claimed, from the way the governing and industrial classes were able to secure a disproportionate share of the economic gains from industrialism. With higher wages and improved working and social conditions, poverty levels would have fallen without any tangible negative effect on economic progress. While the dominant political philosophy of the time continued to canonise the rich, the political tide did begin to turn. The Lancashire cotton famine in the 1860s, when cotton mills closed and soup kitchens mushroomed, the depression-linked turbulence of the 1870s and the unemployment spikes of the 1880s raised deeper questions about the sustainability of 'the age of capital'. Indeed, it was not until that decade that the term 'unemployment' was first used. Aided by high-profile strikes by Bryant and May matchgirls and casualised London dockers against poor working conditions and low pay, the orthodoxy that existing inequality levels were natural and fair began to be more effectively challenged.

In 1883, a widely publicised pamphlet by the Congregational Union, 'The Bitter Cry of Outcast London', revealed the scale of squalor in London's jerry-built tenements. In 1884, the Fabian Society was founded to press for a more equal society through gradual reform. Its first tract – *Why Are the Many Poor?* – sold one hundred thousand copies. In 1890, the leading classical economist Alfred Marshall asked in his *Principles of Economics*, still in print today, 'May we not outgrow the belief that poverty is necessary?'[31]

By the end of the century, the risk of poverty had also spread to farmers, small traders and artisans. Letters to the establishment newspaper the *Times* in the opening years of the new century revealed growing concern about the plight of the educated jobless. 'I speak of the well-bred, well-educated, well-travelled, much experienced man who, through no fault of his own, finds himself in the prime of life penniless, with a family, no employment, and apparently no chance of getting any.' The letter was signed: 'One of them'.[32]

Another letter listed the kind of families being supported by the London-based Sisters of Charity:

A young man very ill with heart disease, a long time out of work, has a wife and child to support. A baker with an excellent character, for many weeks out of work. Wife and three children. Could turn his hand to anything which would pay the rent and support his children. Man dying of diabetes and nearly blind. Formerly in a good position. Wife slaving herself to death to procure necessary food for him ...

Two very respectable women, formerly in good position, now starving on needlework, which they can rarely obtain. An elderly crippled man and his wife, both unable to work. Very respectable, but starving.[33]

The talk of widespread impoverishment was dismissed by leading business and political figures. The wealthy Victorian shipping magnate Charles Booth described them as 'grossly exaggerated'.[34] Determined to test the claims, he embarked on a monumental piece of social investigation, a painstaking, house by house survey of nearly the whole of London. This was the first systematic investigation of poverty in Britain, and a pioneering step in the discipline of social science.

The study – published as *The Life and Labour of the People of London* in stages up to 1903 – found that 30 per cent of London's population fell below Booth's frugal measure of poverty, imprecise as that estimate undoubtedly was.[35] Booth's ground-breaking study – his street-by-street maps of the pattern of poverty in Central London are still widely used today – found that even many in full-time work were scarcely able to feed their families. While Booth accepted that fecklessness, drink and gambling contributed to destitution, they played but a minor part. The study, a stark picture of slum housing, intense overcrowding and meagre work opportunities, concluded that poverty was rooted not in behaviour but in low pay – especially among women – unemployment and irregular work, old age and widowhood. Tackling it required much more than voluntary effort, good works, character improvement and the more humane administration of the Poor Law.[36]

One of those inspired by Booth's work was the industrialist and social reformer Seebohm Rowntree. Seebohm was the second son of the Victorian industrialist and Quaker Joseph Rowntree, founder of the successful confectionary empire. Not all business leaders throughout the nineteenth century put profit above the humanisation of work. Seebohm helped run the family firm, and along with his father and other industrialists such as George Cadbury and George Peabody, was an early pioneer of business philanthropy. Believing, against the grain of business thinking, that owners had responsibility for the mass of former agricultural labourers now working in their factories, the Rowntree family were among the first industrialists to set up an occupational pension scheme and introduce a work's doctor.

Seebohm Rowntree conducted his own smaller study of 11,500 working-class households in the historic town of York in 1899. He developed a more precise and less ambiguous measure of a subsistence poverty standard than the one used by Booth. While Booth's poverty line was linked to class and status rather than income and he made no attempt to draw up a minimum based on need, Rowntree based his on an estimate of the lowest cost of a minimum level of food, clothing, shelter, light and fuel. It was the most meagre of survival standards that allowed nothing other than the mere basics of physical life. He found 28 per cent of the working-class population to be poor, similar to Booth's figure for London, with the primary cause low earnings.[37] The two studies confirmed that subsistence poverty was rife across Britain and delivered the hard evidence that poverty was being driven mostly by structural forces outside individual control – the maldistribution of work, incomes and opportunities. Escaping poverty was way beyond the capacity of individual will.

The studies' authors, motivated by curiosity and moral duty, were influential members of wealthy, intellectual and philanthropic networks. Although the findings were attacked in some circles for failing to admonish the poor, they also touched a nerve.[38] Those influenced by the studies included Clement Attlee, David Lloyd George and Winston Churchill. 'I have been reading a book that has fairly made my hair stand on end', wrote Churchill, the young Conservative MP, of Rowntree's study. 'That I call a terrible and shocking thing, people who have only the workhouse or prison as the only venues of change ... I see little glory in an Empire which can rule the waves and is unable to flush its sewers.'[39]

For most of the nineteenth century, the distribution question was marginal to the political agenda. The social reforms were more than token. They were sufficient to stave off widespread discontent, but were never strong enough to challenge the fundamental sources of poverty or unsettle the existing social order. As the Swedish economist Per Molander later explained, 'Without an active distribution policy, society moves relentlessly toward the inequality limit [where a small elite control the entire economic surplus].'[40]

Public penury and private ostentation

The opening years of the new century brought growing unease about the social state of Britain. In 1903, the American writer Jack London – in *The People of the Abyss* – described the crushing poverty that he witnessed among the slum dwellers of Whitechapel as a 'national sickness'.[1] Raw capitalism and its innovative power may have helped make Britain, for a while, the world's leading industrial nation. But – it was now increasingly asked – were business leaders and landlords demanding too high a price from workers and tenants? In 1903, the American political activist and game designer, Elizabeth Magie, invented a board game she called The Landlord's Game. A forerunner of Monopoly, it was designed to show the consequences of the monopoly ownership of land and had two outcomes, one in which a single landlord secures all the land, and one in which it is equally shared.

Lowering poverty levels, reformers insisted, required the material gains from industrialisation to be shared more evenly through better wages and working conditions, an improved urban environment, an end to the inhumane Poor Law and more. Tackling poverty, wrote Seebohm Rowntree, involved 'larger questions dealing with land tenure, with the relative duties and powers of the state and of the individual towards legislation affecting the aggregation and distribution of wealth'.[2]

Clement Attlee, who became prime minister in 1945, had witnessed the dehumanising power of everyday life working as a volunteer in the East End of London, and was another early convert to the anti-inequality cause. 'I soon began to realize the curse of casual labour. I got to know what slum landlords, and sweating, meant. I understood why the Poor Law was so hated.'[3] Along with Labour's early leaders, he was inspired by the vision of thinkers like Richard Tawney. His aim was to tackle 'the exploitation of the mass of the people in the interests of a small rich class', he declared in his electoral address as the Labour candidate for Limehouse in the 1922 general election.[4] These were bold promises, but, despite the calls from some sections of the left that the solution lay in an intensified 'class struggle', Attlee aligned himself with the reformist wing of the growing Labour movement, one that rejected what he later called 'vague utopian dreams'.[5]

In 1905, the Conservative prime minister Arthur James Balfour appointed a Royal Commission on the Poor Laws. Although there were examples of good practice in well managed workhouses, the commission's findings painted a largely bleak picture of overcrowded, dirty and badly managed institutions. 'There is little or nothing to be said in praise of this house', one investigator

Figure 3.1: The Landlord's Game, 1903

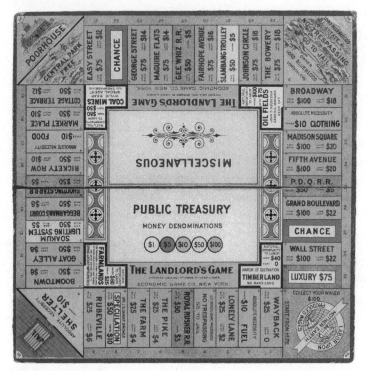

Source: Thomas Forsyth

reported. 'The sanitary arrangements were disgraceful, the laundry was in a state of chaos, and the accommodation in the tramp wards was primitive.'[6] With children often separated from their mothers, and with regular outbreaks of measles and whooping cough, there were high rates of infant mortality. 'The Workhouse and everything within its walls is anathema', announced a medical investigator in evidence to the commission. It is 'the supreme dread of the poor.'[7]

The temper of the time is captured by the radical Liberal MP Charles Masterman. In *The Condition of England*, he highlighted the daily grind of sweatshops, child labour and vagrancy.[8] A similar picture was painted by Robert Tressell's *The Ragged Trousered Philanthropist*, an epic semi-autobiographical novel of a house painter's efforts to find work, to avoid the workhouse, and of the institutionalised corruption of power he encountered in Edwardian times. Tressell died – before his novel was published – of the very social neglect experienced by his characters. The juxtaposition of stark poverty and extreme wealth, or of what Masterman called 'public penury and private ostentation' and the American radical political economist Henry George had earlier called 'The House of Have and the House of Want', was to become an enduring theme of future social debate.[9]

The 'undeserving rich' and the 'deserving poor'

Despite the evident flaws in the Poor Law system the commissioners were deeply divided over their response. When asked whether the Poor Law's treatment of those without work because of a lack of jobs was fair, J.S. Davy, a senior manager, echoing similar sentiments in the Report of the 1834 Poor Law Commission, replied that the unemployed labourer 'must stand by his accidents; he must suffer for the general good of the body politic'.[10]

While the majority report, published in 1909, noted the system's weaknesses, it concluded that tackling poverty should remain the responsibility of individuals and voluntary organisations, and that the state should maintain its distance. It was left to a group of four, led by the economist, labour historian and socialist campaigner Beatrice Webb, to publish a minority report dissociating themselves from the majority findings. Webb was a cousin of Charles Booth and had worked on his surveys. The minority report came to be viewed as a seminal moment in the history of social policy. Its promotion of a radical, state-backed plan for comprehensive welfare provision also had a significant influence on an infant Labour Party's thinking.

Central to Webb's argument was the idea of entitlement to a 'national minimum of civilised life', that there was a minimum level of wages and of quality of life to which all were entitled as part of a common citizenship. For her and other reformers, strengthening the rights of citizenship was a way of rebalancing a system heavily rigged in favour of the few. Guaranteeing such a minimum meant that charity's role should be 'minimised', with a much greater role for the state through provision that is 'universal, as an attribute of citizenship'.[11] This idea of a 'guaranteed social floor' – a minimum income along with access to decent education, health and housing – was to have a powerful influence in future debates, even if it has never come close to full implementation. The idea of a social minimum raised a number of key questions, including about how generous it should be and what to do about the top. This ran in parallel to the debate on how to draw a poverty line, between those who favoured one based on very basic, essentially subsistence needs – 'a sufficiency minimum' – and those arguing for one based on a fuller set of social needs that recognised wider norms – 'a civic minimum'.[12]

Before the Poor Law Commission reported, a Liberal government was elected in 1906 with a large majority. In response to the extension of the franchise, the Liberal Party had reframed itself to appeal to the middle and working classes. It launched a process of profound social reform. After years of popular campaigning, the Old-Age Pensions Act of 1908 introduced non-contributory pensions based on the principle of help as the right of a citizen. If pensions had been made dependent on contributions – and eventual self-funding was intended – there would have been no meaningful payouts for decades. On the day the scheme opened, post offices were overwhelmed by long queues to register, and in Birmingham and elsewhere, ran out of forms. From 1909, some 490,000 pensioners started to receive a means-tested payment – a maximum of five shillings a week – for those aged seventy and over, even though average life expectancy was fifty for women and forty-eight for men. Some groups were excluded from this 'right', including those with a history of imprisonment, even for minor offences, and those with an 'habitual failure to work'. A distinction between the deserving and the undeserving pensioner was therefore built into the new scheme. This was to prevent – as one influential charity figure argued – the undermining of the 'morality, character and self-respect of the poorer classes'.[13] Although a significant step forward, the new scheme still meant a somewhat patchy, minimalist and morally weighted pensioner safety net.

Outside of the Poor Law, perhaps the first tentative step towards social security had come with the Workmen's Compensation Act of 1897, which enshrined the right of a person injured at work to compensation. In 1911, a fuller, if means-tested and basic, system of national insurance was introduced for about a quarter of the labour force, mostly covering male occupations. This brought a statutory right to help for the unemployed and the sick, alongside the aged, aimed at removing the Poor Law stigma from social support. It was a form of collective help, largely self-financed – outside of the new pensions scheme – by workers and employers, if through new flat-rate contributions rather than through 'general' taxation. Despite the continuation of dependency on the Poor Law for those not entitled, and the lack of wider measures to tackle the causes of unemployment and poverty, these were still highly significant reforms, a first step towards liberating people from what the historian Asa Briggs called 'the centuries-old tyranny of fate'.[14] The foundation stones of the modern, amelioratory welfare state were finally being laid, even if they fell well short of the vision outlined in the *Minority Report*.

There were also radical reforms of the tax system, including a higher rate of income tax for 'unearned income' such as that from property. In the 'People's Budget' of 1909, the chancellor David Lloyd George introduced a tax surcharge on around eleven thousand taxpayers on higher incomes. This was the first attempt to implement the principle, bitterly opposed by the wealthy and professional classes, that a fair tax system should be progressively related to 'ability to pay'.

The 1909 Budget also targeted the *wealth* holdings of the rich. Lloyd George, one of the great orators of the time, liked to depict the landed elite as 'idle, greedy, parasitical, self-interested profiteers, as men who enjoyed wealth they did not create while begrudging help to those less fortunate whose labours had helped to make them rich.'[15] The new measures – which offered plenty of material for cartoonists to parody the plight of the rich – included a new capital gains tax of 2 per cent on unearned increments in land values and a doubling of the estate duty first introduced in 1894 at modest rates. The reforms softened the pro-inequality structures of the previous century,

Figure 3.2: 'Fee, Fi, Fo, Fat, I smell the blood of a plutocrat; Be he alive or be he dead, I'll grind his bones to make my bread,' *Punch*, 28 April 1909

RICH FARE.

THE GIANT LLOYD-GORGIBUSTER: "FEE, FI, FO, FAT,
I SMELL THE BLOOD OF A PLUTOCRAT;
BE HE ALIVE OR BE HE DEAD,
I'LL GRIND HIS BONES TO MAKE MY BREAD."

Source: TopFoto

and established the principle of redistribution through taxation – even if at modest rates. They also drew a distinction, if implicit, between 'deserving' and 'undeserving' wealth.

The reforms reflected the view, promoted by some economists including David Ricardo, that rentier income, such as that from 'functionless wealth', should be taxed more highly than wage income. Both Liberal and Labour thinkers favoured at least some socialisation of wealth, especially that arising from the use of natural resources. Some new Liberal activists, such as Leonard Hobhouse, Britain's first professor of sociology and briefly a Liberal MP, argued that taxation should be used to break up the deep concentration of wealth and also to share the gains from that element of wealth creation which is the product of social effort. 'Wealth', he argued, cannot be created on a desert island. 'Some forms of wealth, such as ground rents in and about cities, are substantially the creation of society, and it is only through the misfeasance of government in times past that such wealth has been allowed to fall into private hands.'[16]

Evidence also began to emerge of new forms of extraction by a new generation of business and finance leaders – 'hardheaded genuine plutocrats untouched by moral scruple', as the Edwardian radical Arthur Ponsonby described them.[17] From the last decades of the nineteenth century, these 'plutocrats' created ways of further boosting profits, and pocketing the rewards, not through technical innovation, competitive edge and the development of new skills but by a mix of deal making and price and market manipulation. A much-used technique was that of company acquisition designed to swallow competitors while offering big rewards to the financiers and executives involved. Similar techniques were used in the United States and became the source of quick fortunes without the risks of traditional entrepreneurialism.

Such extraction fuelled an orgy of spending that reached 'elephantine proportions', greatly distorting the pattern of consumption, and contributing to a lack of 'non-luxury' demand in the economy.[18] The American economist Thorstein Veblen, condemning the 'wasteful consumption' by the new plutocrats, described these new extractive devices as forms of market 'sabotage'. Similar techniques designed to undermine competitive forces came to be an obstinate feature of capitalism, contributing in the process to the economic turbulence that followed periodically over the century.[19]

While the Liberal changes were supported by reformers, there were disagreements on the speed, extent and philosophy of change. Liberal leaders mostly saw national insurance as a way of heading off more radical reforms of the whole distribution. As Churchill, who crossed the floor of the Commons to become a Liberal MP in 1904, explained, 'Socialism wants to pull down wealth; Liberalism seeks to raise up poverty.'[20] For more radical reformers they were merely the first step of a rolling process of reform. Progressive thinkers were edging towards the idea of a social minimum to be delivered by a mix of cash support, decent wages and affordable rents. Proposals for a more concerted attack on the crisis- and inequality-driving structures of capitalism included a legally enforceable minimum wage, a shorter working week, free social services and the public ownership of key industries. 'They are but a clearing of the decks for action, a caring for the sick and wounded, before entering upon the battle royal', wrote Keir Hardie, one of the founding members and then leader of the Labour Party, of the Liberal reforms.[21] First elected to parliament in 1893, the ex-miner was carried to Westminster by supporters, one with a trumpet playing 'La Marseillaise'.

A plutocratic playground

Just as the earlier Factory Acts had been bitterly opposed by industrialists, those affected by some of the Liberal reforms fought tooth and nail to defend the status quo. Conservative MPs opposed what they dismissed as a 'nanny and bureaucratic state'. Parts of the medical profession were hostile to health insurance, while the friendly societies and insurance companies, which had sprung up over the previous hundred years, saw national insurance as a threat to their role.

Pensions and unemployment benefit were less controversial, though some unions opposed workers paying for insurance from wages and the additional burden on the low paid and were concerned about the potential level of state intrusion involved, a fear that turned out to be well founded. Benefits for the unemployed came to be used periodically as a form of coercion, both to ensure an adequate supply of labour and to limit costs. The strongest opposition came from what Masterman called a 'vulgarised' plutocracy who were outraged by the proposals for higher rates of income and inheritance tax. When estate duty was first levied in 1894, it was described by one MP as 'throwing into the shade everything that had ever been done in the way of highway robbery'.[22]

While Lloyd George made rabble-rousing speeches mocking the 'Goliath of the aristocracy', the wealthy Earl of Rosebery, prime minister from 1894 to 1895, denounced the changes as a 'social and political revolution of the first magnitude'.[23] The Finance Bill passed through the Commons, but was thrown out by the Conservative dominated and hereditary House of Lords. It was a move that brought a 'peers against the people' general election, a minority Liberal government, and in 1911, a new Parliament Act severely reducing the powers of the Lords.

Various political motives were at work in this first parliamentary attempt at redistribution from the 'undeserving rich' to the 'deserving poor'. The reforms were in part a response to growing public pressure, including demonstrations by the unemployed in the early years of the new century, and the softening mood towards poverty. There was also a sense that, as captured in Ford Madox Ford's much analysed 1915 novel *The Good Soldier*, it was time for some sacrifice by the 'old order'. Then there was the Liberal Party's need to neutralise the electoral threat from the Labour Representation Committee. The group won twenty-nine seats in 1906 and changed its name to the Labour Party.

Another concern was the health of the nation. A third of army volunteers for the 1899–1902 Boer War were rejected because of poor health, the result of poor housing and nutrition.[24] Then there was Britain's deteriorating economic position, with its status as the world's leading industrial power challenged by the United States and Germany. Lloyd George was impressed with the welfare system introduced by the German chancellor Otto von Bismarck, and believed that Germany's economic success was linked to its better-educated and protected, and therefore more productive, workforce.

By the outbreak of war in 1914, the landowning classes had already given some way in the money and power leagues to those who had built huge personal fortunes in manufacturing, but especially in trade and finance. Despite Britain's role as the pioneer of industrialisation, non-landed wealth came to be concentrated among financiers and the new commercial barons rather than among northern industrialists and manufacturers. By 1914, the proportion of millionaires who were landowners had fallen sharply compared with a century earlier. The richest were now more likely to be working as bankers, merchants or shipowners, those like the City financier Lord Swaythling or the shipbuilder Lord Pirrie.[25] As their wealth piles grew, the new banking and property barons started to ape the lifestyles of the landed rich with country seats, ostentatious weekends and shooting parties. 'Instead of being a patrician preserve', described the historian of class David Cannadine, 'the countryside was becoming a plutocratic playground.'[26] In the House of Commons in 1924, the Conservative MP, Edward Wood, the First Earl of Halifax, spoke of 'a silent revolution … the gradual disappearance of the old landed classes.'[27] While that class had been losing its former monopoly on politics, high society and genteel living – they formed only thirteen of ninety-three new peers during the 1920s[28] – aristocratic grandees found new ways of maintaining their influence and income. The half-century up to the Second World War saw a surge in the number of landowners joining company boards.[29]

The war years also helped to initiate a dramatic new trend, a slow process of equalisation that continued for the next half-century. There were new controls over industry, a hike in public spending, new price controls and rationing. To support wartime spending, the standard rate of income tax rose fivefold to 30 per cent. Because of the need for labour, wages rose in key professions. Aided by nursery provision and the mass mobilisation of women into the workforce – though still paid less than the men they replaced – living standards improved. Other changes, including lower pay differentials between professionals and manual labourers, a more redistributive tax system (the 1911 £5000 threshold for supertax was lowered in stages to £2000 by 1921), flat income from land and the breaking up of some landed estates contributed to a further, if limited, narrowing of the income gap.[30] Voting rights (40 per cent of British troops didn't have the vote) were finally extended in 1918 to all men over twenty-one and to 8.5 million women (those over thirty with a property qualification). These changes brought a threefold rise in the number entitled to vote.

There were also a number of domestic conflicts, including rent strikes and protests against landlords raising rents and evicting tenants. In Glasgow in 1915, twenty thousand tenants living in grossly overcrowded tenements launched a protest against landlords, while small children carried placards with captions such as 'While my father is a prisoner in Germany, the landlord is attacking our home.'[31] Fearing that such exploitation would cool public

Figure 3.3: Rent strike, Glasgow, 1915

Source: © CSG CIC Glasgow Museums Collection

support for the war, Lloyd George, head of the coalition government from 1916, rushed through a bill freezing rents at pre-war levels.

The war years were a powerful illustration of the pro-equality impact of the shifts in economic and social policy of the time. Yet, despite full employment, buoyant wages, more progressive taxation and greater state regulation, Britain remained a deeply divided society in 1918, if a little less so than five years earlier. Wealth concentration at the top had fallen a little since 1900.[32] Significant numbers not covered by the new benefits continued to depend on the still-hated system of poor relief. Although an excess duty on profits above a pre-war standard was introduced for industries such as armaments benefiting from the war effort, the wealthy and the professional middle classes were able to make decent returns from their purchase of the war loans issued to pay for the war.[33]

4

A roller-coaster ride

Despite a short-lived boom, the early post-war years brought economic turbulence and recession. There was not a single year from 1921 to 1938 when the dole queue fell below one million.[1] With large numbers of ex-serviceman still unemployed eighteen months after the war and in an 'ugly mood', and establishment and middle class fears of the spread of Bolshevism, the cabinet was warned repeatedly of the risk of unrest.[2]

In January 1919, sixty thousand strikers in Glasgow, many wearing their war medals, clashed with police, with a panicked London cabinet sending in troops. Marches against unemployment were also broken up, often with violence, by foot and mounted police. A central issue in Glasgow was the length of the working week, with demobbed soldiers calling for shorter hours so that work could be shared. Strikers claimed that manufacturers wanted to maintain a local pool – 'a reserve army' – of obedient available labour. The strikers had some success, while one of the organisers – the seaman's leader, Manny Shinwell, later a member of Clement Attlee's 1945 cabinet – was jailed for five months for inciting riot. The 'Red Clydesiders', as the strikers became known, won ten out of fifteen Glasgow constituencies for the Independent Labour Party in the 1922 general election.

The War and its sacrifices raised expectations about the obligations of the state to wider society. While Lloyd George formed a coalition government in 1919, the new parliament was light on members committed to social reform, with an influx of 'new money' businessmen (they were all men) committed to the status quo. They included sixty-one insurance directors, 138 manufacturers, 115 landowners and twenty-eight bankers. 'A lot of hard faced men who look as if they had done very well out of the war', is how Stanley Baldwin, a moderately wealthy Worcestershire ironmaster and the new financial secretary to the treasury, famously described the new House of Commons.[3] Baldwin, who became prime minister on three separate occasions, donated a fifth of his firm's profits towards paying off Britain's War Debt a move that was far from widely followed.

A conscription of riches

The end of the War brought calls for a new levy on 'war wealth' as a way of paying off war debts and recognising the disparity in sacrifice between those at the front and those at home. Drawing a distinction between the 'landed gentry [who] had given their sons nobly and freely with the industrial classes', and 'the capitalist class [who] were sitting at home in comfort and security behind the bodies of better men than themselves', the trade union leader Ben Tillett called for 'a conscription of riches' as an acknowledgement of the sacrifices of those who had joined the armed forces.[4] There was similar outrage in the United States over war profiteering that greatly boosted the number of millionaires.[5] The case for a wealth levy – which would have been accompanied by the withdrawal of the excess profits duty introduced during the War – was backed by some coalition cabinet members, including the chancellor of the exchequer Austen Chamberlain, though largely to counter the risk of wider public outrage. 'The wealth has come to men too rapidly and they have waxed fat while the mass have grown poorer', as Chamberlain wrote in a private letter, though with a warning about the financial lobby: 'The child would scream itself into fits.'[6] The idea was eventually dropped.

Because of their numbers, the new business politicians were able to use their political muscle to serve their commercial interests. According to the historian Bentley Gilbert, they mocked 'the war-time hope by reviving Edwardian opulence and privilege without any vestige of aristocratic sense of duty'.[7] Lloyd George took a different view. The newspaper proprietor Lord Riddell claimed that the prime minister was full of praise for the 'captains of industry and defends the propriety of a large share of profits they take'. The prime minister, he added, believed that 'one Leverhulme or Ellerman [leading industrialists], is worth more to the world than 10,000 sea captains or 20,000 engine drivers'.[8]

The bitterly fought nine-day general strike of 1926 – which ended in defeat for the strikers – exposed Britain's still badly torn society. On one side stood the anger felt by large sections of the working class; on the other the 'antagonism that so many of the upper and middle classes felt towards the labourers, shop workers and factory workers who served them'.[9] There were also prolonged clashes over the extension of the franchise to all women – over 1000 suffragettes had been jailed for breaches of the peace in the fifteen years before they finally achieved their goal in 1928.

Despite pockets of severe unemployment and the waning of the strife-ridden Liberals, a still-young Labour Party enjoyed only two brief periods of undistinguished minority government during the 1920s, both under Ramsey McDonald. The election of the Labour government in 1924 unsettled the establishment. Before the election, Lloyd's of London had offered insurance against the impact of Labour policies. Should Labour win a majority, recorded Chips Channon, 'I see nothing for it but civil war.'[10] Perhaps Labour's key achievement in their first taste of government was the Wheatley Housing Act, which, by raising the state subsidy level introduced in 1919, helped to further expand municipal housing. In power, but not in control, two of the party's goals, to raise more revenue from wealth taxation and secure greater social value from the development of land, came to nothing.[11]

The interwar years did bring social improvements, including a continuing fall in infant mortality rates, improved access to hospitals, a boost to housebuilding and a slight fall in working hours. For many in work, especially those employed in the newly emerging mass consumer industries producing automobiles, radios and the new labour-saving devices such as vacuum cleaners, there was rising prosperity. But the 'roaring twenties', with its growing demand for the trappings of the new consumerism, was much more muted in Britain than in the United States, and was never a party open to many. Large numbers continued to live in little better than overcrowded slum terraces. Northern regions suffered most from the decline of the traditional cotton, shipbuilding, steel and coal industries, while parts of the South East, the home to the new industries, prospered. Married women, despite their role in the war years, were discouraged from working. The husband, it was argued, should be the breadwinner, while after the war, a marriage bar was widely operated by employers, forcing women to resign after marriage.

The benefit system took a roller-coaster ride. With poverty in old age only slightly alleviated by state pensions, the age of qualification was lowered to sixty-five and a new widow's benefit launched. In 1925, a contributory insurance system was introduced for pensions, while wider support continued to be provided by trade unions, friendly societies and an extensive system of support for injured veterans and widows. The Poor Law, with its taint of grudging charity and intrusive administration, was still viewed with hostility. Before the War, unemployment protests would be full of banners declaring: 'Curse your charity: we want work.'

There were repeated policy U-turns in the provision of help for the jobless. In 1920, unemployment benefit, initially limited to a small number of trades including shipbuilding and engineering, was extended to manual workers, though some groups such as agricultural labourers were still excluded. Allowances were also introduced for dependents. Over the 1920s, benefit levels – and contributions – were raised in real terms, but were kept below wage rises to maintain work incentives and the Poor Law principle of 'less eligibility'.

Ill-equipped for mass unemployment, the principle of national insurance was effectively suspended in the early 1920s, while the National Insurance Fund – which held contributions made by employers and employees – turned from a surplus after the war to a growing deficit. For most of its life it has been a fund in name only, rarely large enough to meet the full cost of benefit payments. In a series of ad hoc and near-panic measures from 1922 to deal with spreading militancy and a lack of jobs, temporary top-ups for benefits called 'out-of-work donations' were introduced for demobbed soldiers and civilians without contributions. These means-tested additions required a greatly expanded bureaucracy to administer them. They clashed with the contributory principle of entitlement, while unemployment benefit did not return to a clear insurance basis until the mid-1930s. These measures – together known as 'the dole' – were, wrote Derek Fraser in his history of the welfare state, less the result of a new national social solidarity than 'an expedient for the defence of capitalism'.[12]

Despite the 1911 principle of 'entitlement', help for the unemployed has always been applied with varying levels of conditionality on work availability as a way of maintaining the Protestant work ethic and maximising the size of the labour force. Under the Poor Laws this control was exercised with some force for the able-bodied.[13] In the early 1920s, new, stringently administered restrictions were imposed on the receipt of unemployment benefit. Presented as a way of preventing 'scrounging', despite the unavailability of work in many areas, these included a new 'genuinely seeking work test'.[14]

The degree of 'conditionality' applied to the receipt of benefits has continued to be a running sore throughout the history of social security, raising questions about the way the principle of entitlement and reciprocity – the idea that rights should go hand in hand with obligations – has been applied. Between 1925 and 1928, 1.7 million applicants were refused benefits, while the unemployed again came to hate the way they were treated by officials. 'They treat you like a lump of dirt they do' was a typical view.[15] Most of those disallowed benefit were forced onto poor relief, with a surge in the numbers receiving help with coal and food, or ending up in a workhouse.[16]

The economic strategy pursued through the 1920s conformed to the claims of classical economists that markets would automatically adjust economies to achieve full employment and economic efficiency, and to the contention that stability required state budgets to be in balance, with spending matched fully by tax revenue. An overriding goal was to return Britain to the gold standard at its 1914 parity with the dollar, a policy aimed at enforcing the balanced budgets and economic discipline deemed necessary for prosperity. This was to be achieved by a package of contractionary measures aimed at deflating prices to their pre-war level and boosting the value of sterling. It was a counter-productive economic package which cut investment and further deepened the economic downturn. The instruments used favoured the City and maintained profits in finance, but were bad news for entrepreneurs, investors and exporters. A very similar strategy was later adopted in the 1980s. Policymakers remained convinced of the ability of free markets and minimal state intervention to bring equilibrium and stability, with markets adjusting to ensure full employment and optimal growth. The social implications of these adjustments, along with the multiple barriers that prevented equilibrium, were simply ignored.

Critics such as Keynes argued that the real world did not conform to the simplistic theories of the classical school, and that market adjustments alone would not solve the problem of mass joblessness caused by inadequate economic demand, while the cosy pro-orthodoxy club – the Treasury, the

Bank of England and the City – dismissed calls for state interventions as 'socialist'. The outcome of deflation was persistent unemployment and a further weakening of the older industrial regions. Ministers and advisers would have liked to have added two other measures to the policy mix – a reduction in wages and a cut in benefit levels. Such policies would have had significant social consequences and would have met with at least some resistance from an increasingly restive labour force. By adding to deflation, they would also have been largely self-defeating.

Social reform promises were early victims of this strategy. To tackle deteriorating public finances, severe cuts in public spending were imposed in 1922 on the advice of a committee chaired by Sir Eric Geddes, the wartime minister of transport. The 'Geddes axe' took the Treasury line on a balanced budget. Economic revival, it was argued, depended on lower spending by the state. The Treasury believed that state spending was 'unproductive' and would be a burden on 'productive enterprise'.[17] This was an early and questionable example of the theory of 'crowding out' that has remained a canon of free market thinking.

What about the rentiers?

The decade was mixed for the landed classes, who continued to be overtaken in the millionaire stakes by business tycoons. As in the pre-war period, at least part of these new fortunes derived less from innovation and new wealth creation than from extraction through the use of cartels, mergers and other barriers to competition. As the business historian Peter Scott has explained, 'Rather than revealing the sectors most important to national wealth, or competitive advantage, the clustering of millionaires primarily reflects rising barriers to competition in interwar Britain and the abnormal profits they generated.'[18]

With higher rates, tax avoidance became commonplace during the 1920s, with schemes increasingly advertised in newspapers such as the *Times*. Those known by the Inland Revenue as successful tax avoiders included the shipping magnate Sir John Ellerman, the clothing manufacturer Montague Burton and the meat and shipping industrialists, the Vestey Brothers. Some millionaires avoided estate duty altogether simply by moving overseas, mainly to the Channel Islands, the Isle of Man and other British dependencies, the beginnings of the offshore route to tax avoidance.[19] Many of the devices still used today to avoid tax – from wrapping wealth into trusts and hiding assets in offshore companies to turning income into capital gains – date from this time.

While conditionality was being tightened for the jobless, legal tax avoidance, despite its impact on revenue from taxation, carried little social stigma. Even illegal evasion rarely led to criminal prosecution or public censure. With no effective legal or reputational sanctions against avoidance, paying full tax rates became largely voluntary, just as it is today. As the *Times* put it in 1938, outside of the United States, 'England offers the most opportunity of any country for such avoidance.'[20] The sanctity of property rights was given the upper hand over tax laws in a way which undermined the principle of reciprocity and attempts to make the tax system more progressive. The 'Hansard procedure' (announced in parliament on 19 July 1923) allowed tax fraudsters to simply 'own up' and repay the tax, without the matter becoming publicly known.[21] Prosecutions were rare. Although this 'procedure' was terminated in 1942, working-class perpetrators of minor fraud continued to be treated far more harshly than wealthy tax fraudsters. The Inland Revenue Staff Federation informed the 1953 Royal Commission on Taxation that while rationing offences, misuse of petrol and breaches of licensing regulations often ended up in court, 'prosecutions for evasion or fraud by traders are rare'.[22]

In a new fortune-chasing rush, speculative money – mostly financed by a frenzy of borrowing – poured into real estate and the stock market, though most spectacularly in the United States. The 1929 global meltdown was the bubble finally bursting. Keynes likened the 1920s stock market to a casino.[23] F. Scott Fitzgerald, author of *The Great Gatsby* – a story of hedonism and the failure of the 'American Dream' – described 1920s America as the 'most expensive orgy in history'.[24]

Many scholars have identified the maldistribution of income as a significant cause of the 1929 stock market crash. In his book *The Great Crash, 1929*, the influential American economist J.K. Galbraith identified 'the bad distribution of income' as the first of five factors causing the crash. Making the American economy increasingly dependent on a high level of 'luxury consumption' by a small minority made it highly fragile.[25] Marriner S. Eccles, Federal Reserve chair from 1934 to 1948, drew a similar conclusion:

> A giant suction pump had by 1929–30 drawn into a few hands an increasing portion of currently produced wealth ... as in a poker game where the chips are concentrated in fewer and fewer hands, the other fellows could stay in the game only by borrowing. When their credit ran out the game stopped.[26]

A parallel argument had been made two decades earlier by John Hobson, who because of his heterodox attacks on the classical school, was sidelined by the academic economics establishment. Hobson, who had an important influence on Keynes, argued that economic instability, and especially the 'Long Depression' that began in the 1870s, had been caused by a shortfall of demand stemming from 'under-consumption' and 'over-saving'. This he attributed to too great a concentration of income and wealth at the top leading to excessive spending on extreme luxuries and low spending power among the industrial workforce, an argument which strengthened the case for greater equality.[27]

The shock waves from 1929 plunged the world into prolonged economic and political turmoil. In August 1931 the prime minister, Ramsey McDonald, grappling with the consequences, bowed to mainstream demands for austerity measures to bring public spending and revenue into line. With the cabinet split, Labour's second government collapsed. It was replaced by a national government, dominated by Conservatives but led by McDonald. Clement Attlee accused McDonald of making the poorest bear the brunt of retrenchment. 'What about the rentiers', he declared at a meeting of Labour MPs on the crisis.[28] Labour's two periods of minority government had brought limited advance on its social goals while the catastrophic fallout for the party from the rift over enforced austerity – a form of state-imposed deflation – simmered throughout the decade.

McDonald had bowed to the demands for 'sound finance' from the City, the Treasury and the Bank of England. It was a clear victory for economic conservatives, and their contention that government spending was unproductive, over the then radical view that higher public spending would help beat the slump. The expansionary strategy promoted by Keynes was backed to some degree by then Tory mavericks such as Harold Macmillan, a member of the dissident Next Five Years Group. He was sympathetic to the plight of the unemployed and thought that the Conservative Party leadership was too close to the City of London. Nevertheless, state-driven expansion by allowing a budget deficit was an idea that was at odds with mainstream thinking and had never been tried, while at that point, central government was a very small player in an economy dominated by private enterprise. For the biographer of Keynes, Robert Skidelsky, '1929 was the major missed opportunity of the interwar period.'[29]

The turbulence of the time raised further questions about the classical economists' rule book while adding a new argument to the moral case for egalitarianism. Because of capitalism's tendency to disequilibrium and boom and bust, the declared incompatibility between greater equality and economic dynamism was highly questionable.

Keynes' demonstration that full employment was not, as the classical economists claimed, a normal outcome of markets, but rather a special case and a rarity, and that governments would sometimes have to run deficits to ensure employment for all, was not laid out in full until the publication of *The General Theory* in 1936. Although this became the most influential book on economics since *The Wealth of Nations*, Keynes' ideas were easily dismissed in the early 1930s. Despite his connections and high profile, he was an economic outlier. Instead of a programme of public works, the new national government adopted a policy of further economic retrenchment.

The package included a 10 per cent cut in already meagre insurance benefits (not reversed until 1934), the return of tighter rules on seeking work, cuts in wages for teachers and public officials and the reintroduction of the means test for top-up payments. Keynes' prescriptions were eventually recognised. The deflationary strategy, although mitigated by withdrawal from the gold standard in 1931, cut demand and prolonged and deepened the slump while weakening the benefit system at a time when it was most needed. It was a lesson forgotten in the great economic crisis eight decades later.

Icy indifference

Heightened by the deflationary cycle triggered by the national and international response to the crash, the dole queue peaked at over one in four of the workforce at the start of 1933. Unemployment levels were even higher in the coal mining, steel and shipbuilding areas of Wales, Scotland and the North of England. They varied from a high of 67 per cent in Jarrow to 3 per cent in High Wycombe. Mass unemployment tested human resilience as well as the system of social insurance to the limit. A report by the charity the Pilgrim Trust exposed the realities of what they described as 'enforced idleness'. The long-term jobless faced a 'weekly cycle of impoverished living', little more than bare existence. Between weekly payments, families could afford one or two proper meals, but were then to survive on tea and bread and the pawn shop.[30]

Local public libraries became full the minute they opened as the unemployed sought refuge in free newspapers and heating. One man from Sunderland took photographs of victims of the Great Depression. 'There's not a day goes by', he reflected in 1980, 'but what I feel bitterness and shame at what this country did to its working people.' One picture was of a miner. 'After the general strike he never worked again. He cut his throat one afternoon in 1931. I came home from school and found him. He'd left a message written with a cake of soap on the looking-glass saying he was sorry. He was my father.'[31]

The early 1930s saw a stream of protests and rallies, some of them ending up outside Buckingham Palace and the most expensive West End hotels. When the coal mine, steel works and Palmer's shipyard closed, one by one, in the North East town of Jarrow, the victims of foreign competition and perverse economic policy, the local job market collapsed. 'Utterly stagnant', wrote the town's dogged Labour MP 'Red Ellen' Wilkinson. Infant mortality – a sensitive indicator of malnutrition – stood at ninety-seven per 1000 births in the town, two and a half times the national rate.[32] 'Wherever you went, there were men hanging about, not scores of them, but hundreds and thousands of them', witnessed the broadcaster and playwright J.B. Priestly. 'The men wore the drawn masks of prisoners of war.'[33]

In 1936, a small delegation from the town was told by the president of the Board of Trade, Sir David Runciman, a Liberal MP and son of the shipping magnate the First Baron Runciman, that Jarrow must work out its own salvation.[34] Political leaders claimed that they could do little about unemployment. Despite the recession, public attitudes in the early part of the 1930s were often unsympathetic to the plight of the jobless. As one letter to the *Times* put it, the unemployed were 'drugged by the dole'.[35]

Galvanised by what Wilkinson – Jarrow's Joan of Arc – dubbed 'this icy indifference', two hundred workers, stripped of work, mostly gaunt, marched in protest from Jarrow to London. A half were ex-serviceman and wore their British Legion badges. The oldest, George Smith, had served in the Boer War as well as the First World War, in which four of his brothers were killed. They were led by the diminutive, red-haired MP – the only woman on the march – and accompanied throughout by Palmer's band, a black Labrador called Paddy and a single national newspaper journalist, Ritchie Calder. In the same month, there were three other marches, including one by the National League of the Blind. The marchers were not totally ignored by officials. Because they were 'unavailable for work', their unemployment benefits were withdrawn by local officials.

During the march, the cabinet agreed that to discourage the public 'from furnishing assistance to the marchers', selected journalists should be 'given material for exposing the origin, motive and uselessness of the hunger march'.[36] Despite this, with the public now showing greater sympathy, the marchers were warmly received in nearly all towns. Calder, from the Labour-supporting *Daily Herald,* reported how 'Motorists took off their hats or saluted respectably as they passed the Jarrow Crusade.'

On one morning at dawn, Calder was woken by one of the marchers. When the journalist remarked on the hour, the man replied: 'Man, ye don't know what it means to waken up with somewhere to go and something to do. For years, days have been nowt but dates to me.'[37] Nothing came of the march. The petition was presented and ignored, while new arms factories were located outside the most stricken areas. As the Conservative MP and later prime minister Neville Chamberlain explained in a private letter to his sister, 'There must remain a large number of people for whom we can find no work ... and who must either move, or stagnate there for the rest of their lives'.[38]

George Orwell's journey across northern Britain, *The Road to Wigan Pier,* published two years before Rosalind Cubitt's debutante ball, gave a devastating picture of the impoverished communities created by the slump: 'The frightful doom of a decent working man suddenly thrown on the streets after a lifetime of steady work, his agonized struggles against economic laws which he does not understand, the disintegration of families, the corroding sense of shame.'[39] Orwell's descriptions were echoed by others. 'If T.S. Eliot ever wants to write

Figure 4.1: Jarrow march, 1936

Source: Mirrorpix/Reach Licensing

a poem about a real wasteland instead of a metaphysical one, he should come here', commented J.B. Priestly on a visit to Newcastle in 1933.[40] Orwell's book touched nerves, not least among left critics who resented his attack on the state of British socialism in the second half of the book. Victor Gollancz, who published the book in his influential Left Book Club series, wrote a forward challenging Orwell's negative views on the attitudes to the working class of the middle-class liberal elite, many of whom were the club's primary market. Gollancz removed this section in a later edition.

There was no UK equivalent of the recovery New Deal programme initiated by Franklin D. Roosevelt to raise public investment and boost wage levels. As the new president of the United States explained in his 1937 inaugural address, "The test of our progress is not whether we add more to the abundance of those who have much; it is whether we provide enough for those who have too little."[41] In his first term as President, Roosevelt replaced Herbert Hoover's deflationary strategy with 'aggressive, interventionist, expansionist' policies while attacking the excesses of the economic elites he labelled the 'money-changers', and curbing the freedom of Wall Street and American big business.[42] It was the first systemic attempt to forge a mildly regulated capitalism and encourage a language of the common good. Britons had to wait another decade for their own new deal.

Although workhouses were being phased out in favour of direct relief – in kind or in cash – the depression breathed new life into the Poor Law. In the 1920s, some locally elected boards of guardians (many Labour controlled) in areas such as Poplar had sought to humanise the way they administered help. In response their powers were, in 1929, transferred to public assistance committees (PACs) run by county councils. Those seeking help, such as those who had exhausted or lacked insurance entitlement, were subjected to stricter testing and sometimes surveillance by the new committees, often viewed as run by petty tyrants. 'Officials used to camp out in front rooms, poking and prying into all the family's private domestic affairs.'[43]

The means test was also extended from individuals to households to include the incomes (and possessions including furniture and other assets) of all family members. Under the 'household rule', an out-of-work man could be refused help if there was a working son or daughter living at home, if the family had a lodger, or even if a child was found to own a new coat or toy. There were regular protests against the means test, which became one of the most hated institutions in Britain. In 1932, an estimated one million people signed a petition against it.[44] Labour made it a condition of joining the wartime coalition government that the family means test should go.

Helped by recovery among the new industries concentrated in the Midlands and South East England, *average* living standards in 1937 were around a tenth higher than a decade earlier. There had also been a rise in spending on social and public services, including on healthcare and slum clearance.[45] During the decade, the poorest gained better access to free primary medical care, hospital care on a means-tested basis and free elementary education. Despite this, the gains of the time were not evenly spread, and interwar surveys found high levels of poverty due to unemployment, low pay and casualised labour.[46] Half the population was found to lack an adequate diet in 1936, and a fifth of children were chronically malnourished, while class differences in height were barely changed since the 1880s.[47] In the decade to 1935, more than a half of those volunteering for the army were rejected because of their poor physical condition as a result of malnutrition, illness and poor housing.[48] Despite the evidence, ministers continued to claim that the benefit system was adequate while denying any link between unemployment, deprivation and ill health.[49]

In 1936, Seebohm Rowntree repeated his survey of York. He found that, because of smaller families, higher real wages and improved social protection, the living standards of working-class households had improved on average. But with many missing out on rising prosperity, 31 per cent of the working-class population were estimated to be poor. Rowntree stuck to the concept of subsistence, but, while continuing to err on the side of stringency, modified his 1899 minimum living standard as too harsh for 1936. 'Ideas of what constitutes obvious want and squalor have changed profoundly since then.'[50]

The slump years did have implications for wealthy elites. Some bankers and speculators lost badly in the financial chaos of 1929, and there was a continuing loss of stately homes, while smaller landowners, especially among the gentry and minor aristocracy, faced a fall in land values. The new business classes suffered less heavily.[51] By the end of the 1930s, the super-rich's position at the centre of the nation's power structures was prominent rather than towering.

Yet despite the slow erosion of its once unrivalled power and status, Britain's wealthiest managed to hang onto most – if not all – of their wealth and the privileges and lifestyles that came with it. While democracy, war, tax and depression had been gnawing away, the top 1 per cent's share of all privately owned assets still stood at a little over 50 per cent, and the top tenth's at over 85 per cent in 1939. These were falls from 1920, but some of this transfer was the result of the dispersion of wealth holdings within families following the waning of the traditional practice of primogeniture (with family wealth passed down the male line), largely as a way of avoiding the impact of estate duty. Much of the fall involved a transfer from the very top social tier to the next, from the super-rich to the very rich, and to a group Thomas Piketty has called 'the patrimonial middle classes'. Far from representing a process of trickle down *across* society, ordinary people – the poorest half of the population – apart from small levels of savings in insurance schemes and savings banks, still had little or no wealth at all and had seen no gain in their share since 1920.[52]

The primary goal of policy in the 1930s was to refire the private sector of the economy. Despite an eventual boost to public spending, social policy, considered outside the remit of the state even a few decades before, was still marginalised, in part because of the weakness of the opposition. 'Social reform was simply a live grenade the front benches tossed back and forth in the hope that it would explode while in the opponent's possession', as Bentley Gilbert has written.[53] With a continuing emphasis on individual responsibility, the question of the state's responsibility towards its citizens, of what society owes its members or of what is an acceptable minimum, remained a minor diversion. Despite some attempts to alleviate the impact of deepening recession, its bruising fallout was borne most heavily by the poorest and least powerful. Although it had been improved, the benefit system offered the unemployed, on harsh terms, merely enough to survive. The policy response to poverty was largely dictated by expediency, 'to prevent unrest, without giving so generously as to offend the City of London'.[54]

In 1938, despite recovery from the mid-1930s, 14 per cent of men and 13 per cent of women were still unemployed, while on the eve of war, one million people were still supported by outdoor relief.[55] In spite of the slipping of the landed supremacy after centuries of unrivalled power, there was still an entrenched moneyed elite, with all of the trappings of hierarchy which went with it.

PART II

1940–59

5

The future belongs to us

The war years were to have a profound effect on the destiny of the generation that lived through them. The lingering memories of the bruising years of the depression and the personal costs of war were critical factors in the political and social earthquake that was to come. Both put the public's patience with their lot, the hierarchical structures that defined life chances and the sense of entitlement of the rich under severe strain.

A patrician last fling

The top social tier had a strong sense of what was to come. Despite its grandeur, Rosalind Cubitt's party in the summer of 1939 was infused with foreboding. The occasion turned out to be the last of the full-blown debutant parties, a patrician last fling. Henry Channon called it 'a sunset glow before the storm'.[1]

Traditional high society pastimes, from polo to fox hunting, petered out. Restrictions on foreign currency limited overseas excursions, if fuelling a lively and lucrative currency black market. With cooks, butlers, gardeners and maids called up or redeployed to vital civilian tasks, a major preoccupation of the wealthy classes was the loss of servants. Grandee houses still required a small army of servants and a sizeable fortune to run them. In 1939, at the grand Londonderry House at the south end of Park Lane, there was a staff of forty-four. The Duke of Bedford owned two fully staffed townhouses in London's Belgrave Square and kept more than fifty servants at Woburn. 'The whole social edifice came crashing down', described two historians, 'for the abrupt disappearance of servants made the old style of life no longer possible, regardless of the level of affluence.'[2]

Many of the wealthy played their part in the war effort, just as they had in 1914–18. More historic homes that had not already been sold off were requisitioned for use as barracks, hospitals or schools for those displaced from urban centres. The new central controls on trade, prices, investment and profits eroded the incomes of some of the financial elites. Rent levels were pegged, and with no buyers, the prices of property and art and furniture collections fell sharply. Then there was the deepening shadow of the Inland Revenue. There were sharp increases in taxation, especially on the rich. The first emergency war budget, in September 1939, increased the standard rate of income tax from 5s 6d to 7s 6d in the pound (then only a quarter of wage earners paid it) and raised surtax and death duty rates. Henry Channon recorded the effect on the House of Commons in his diary:

> With many a deft blow [the chancellor] practically demolished the edifice of capitalism. One felt like an Aunt Sally under his attacks (the poor old Guinness trustee, Mr Bland, could stand it no more, and I saw him leave the gallery). Blow after blow; increased surtax; raised duties … substantially increased death duties.[3]

These were followed by further tax rises while reduced allowances brought an extra 3.25 million people into the income tax net. With war bringing healthy and often questionable profits for some, an excess profits tax, first used in 1914–18 but repealed in 1921, was revived, though with a number of concessions.[4]

Contemporary writers could not resist the opportunity to parody the plight of the upper classes, a group portrayed in contemporary writing as a class out of step with its time. The poem written in 1827 to celebrate the English stately home was slickly rewritten by the popular comedy playwright Sir Noël Coward:[5]

> The Stately Homes of England,
> How beautiful they stand,
> To prove the upper classes,
> Have still the upper hand.
> Though the fact that they have to be rebuilt,
> And frequently mortgaged to the hilt,
> Is inclined to take the gilt,
> Off the gingerbread,
> And certainly damps the fun,
> Of the eldest son.

In 1944, Marghanita Laski, niece of the economic adviser to the Labour Party Harold Laski, published *Love on the Supertax*, a parody of *Love on the Dole*, a novel set in the depression years. A year later, the satirist Evelyn Waugh published *Brideshead Revisited*, a nostalgic portrayal of the old class order. Waugh lamented the decline of the gentry and their opulent lifestyles. As a young army private puts it in the novel, 'The future belongs to us.' Others were less concerned. 'The defeat of privilege did not appear to destabilise society', wrote the novelist Frederick Raphael: 'Only a posturing reactionary such as Evelyn Waugh could claim that Attlee's England made him feel as if was living in an "occupied country"'.[6]

James Lees-Milne, Eton educated, a progeny of minor gentry and the secretary of the National Trust, used his account of a journey across Britain to paint a bleak picture of a class unable to come to terms with its loss of influence and status. In February 1945 – with the end of the war at last in sight – he visited Ham House in Richmond, London and the owners, the ninety-one-year old Sir Lionel Tollemache and his sixty-year-old son Lionel. 'I walked around the garden with the young Lionel ... oh what an unhappy man. All of them seem hopelessly defeatist, anti-Government, anti-people and anti-world.'[7]

But despite the sweeping changes, the decline of the aristocratic classes can be overstated. Many found ways of clinging onto the privileges that came with wealth. Dukes were allowed slightly more generous petrol rations – twenty gallons a month – than others. Some of those who had lost or closed their London homes moved into luxury hotels. A monument to the rise of new money, Park Lane's Dorchester Hotel, designed for 'pleasure in surroundings of ultimate extravagance', was especially popular. One of the sought-after benefits was access to exclusive shelters. The 'deluxe' shelter at the Dorchester came with waiters, cots, curtained spaces, silk sheets and 'lovely fluffy eiderdowns'.[8] The shelter at the Ritz was known as the Abri du Ritz, while the most elaborate facilities were to be found at the Savoy Hotel shelter, which boasted of having nurses on standby.

With servant quarters emptying, London grandees took to dining more frequently at their private clubs – the Carlton, White's and Brooks – all in the heart of London's Mayfair. Despite patrician complaints about the prices, booking a table at the Dorchester, the Ritz and Claridge's became increasingly difficult. While the clubs were doing roaring business, ordinary restaurants faced severe restrictions on what they could offer.

Some of those recruited into government were wealthy business leaders. Andrew Duncan, a director of the Bank of England and the Imperial Chemical Industry, was brought in as president of the Board of Trade and minister of supply. Some of those offered jobs wavered because of the effect on their businesses. When asked to become minister of food in 1940, the prominent businessman Lord Woolton explained that this would involve immense financial sacrifice in 'giving up my several and very lucrative business appointments'.[9]

The turning of the public mood

While old privileges persisted, the war, despite its privations, rationing and the blitz, proved a remarkably effective engine of greater equality. With industrial mobilisation, real earnings rose above peacetime levels while unemployment fell sharply. Some workers, including miners and farm labourers, received substantial pay rises. Women drafted into the war effort, often taking on 'men-only' jobs in areas from engineering to transport, had an important effect on gender norms. Over 200,000 joined the Auxiliary

Territorial Service, the women's branch of the army, where they worked as supply drivers, ammunition inspectors and mechanics.

Although historians differ about its scale and impact, there was a noticeable turning of the public mood. Attitudes to the rich, a curious mix of intrigue, deference and outrage in the pre-war years, turned cooler. As the *Observer* newspaper noted, there had been 'a deep surge towards progressive ways'.[10] An anti-establishment mood had been brewing during the slump years, but from 1939, the top tier lost one of its trump cards – a broad, if shallow, public tolerance they had long enjoyed. The war indulgences of the rich – well documented by the press – did not play well with popular opinion. Perhaps accepted during peacetime, social divisions, the jumping of queues and ostentatious displays of wealth proved less acceptable when upheaval and loss were the norm. Even the pro-establishment the *Times* was swept up in the changing mood: 'The new order cannot be based on the preservation of privilege, whether the privilege be that of a country, of a class or of an individual.'[11]

During the war, the BBC broadcast a series – *Postscript* – by J.B. Priestly. The most outspoken and controversial of these, on 6 October 1940, raised the issue of the 'idle rich' occupying scarce hotel rooms which could have been used by bombed-out families.[12] 'If you want a Hogarthian contrast go down any time after seven pm into one of the tube stations and follow it up by a visit to the Ritz bar', wrote the Anglo-Irish poet Louis MacNeice in the New York periodical *Common Sense*.[13] As novelist Margaret Kennedy warned, 'England after the war is going to belong to the shelterers.'[14]

For all the talk of 'equal sacrifice', the dominant feeling was that the establishment looked after themselves. Despite the greater mixing of people from different social backgrounds, the class system remained largely intact, with the wealthy able to avoid some of the hardships of war. Women conscripted for the war effort were mostly working class. The better-off were less likely to offer their help. Many were open about how, by 'lying low', they evaded the process. Although the evacuation of one million children from the blitz – often arriving ill-clothed, undernourished and in poor health – raised wider public awareness of deprivation, most of those hosting the voluntary evacuation scheme were also working class.[15]

Newspapers such as the *Mirror* were relentless in their negative portrayals of the old elites. London's *Evening Standard* used its cartoon character, the old befuddled British military officer, Colonel Blimp for a series of attacks on what they portrayed as the persistence of vested interests and the reactionary views of the upper classes. Caroline Blake, a sixty-one-year old nurse and diarist for the independent Mass Observation polling organisation, established in 1937 to monitor ordinary opinion, inveighed against the 'greed, selfishness and snobbery of the "rich" who take unnecessary taxis, can afford to buy extra food or clothing coupons, and avoid the call-up or billeting evacuees'.[16] In a lecture in Glasgow on his eightieth birthday, the distinguished social scientist David Donnison recounted a story of waiting on a train packed with servicemen while on leave in 1945. Two civilians in dark suits and bowler hats were 'looking for a first class carriage. The sailor standing next to me ... shouted "First class? First class? When this war's over there'll be no more bloody classes!"'[17]

In the early days of the London Blitz, when shelter facilities were hopelessly inadequate, there was a spate of protests demanding better protection and the opening of tube stations as shelters. These included the picketing of the shelter at the Mayfair Hotel and the forced opening of several underground stations by large crowds. In September 1940, Phil Piratin, a Communist Party councillor in Stepney – an area especially badly hit by bombing – and later its MP, staged an occupation with seventy people at the Savoy Hotel. Good natured as it was, the placards made their point: 'If it is good enough for the rich it is good enough for the Stepney workers and their families.'[18] After one bombing raid, the King and Queen were booed during a visit to the East End of London, with locals protesting over the lack of deep shelters.[19] 'Everybody is worried about the feeling in the East End of London where there is much bitterness', recorded Harold Nicolson, minister for information, in his diary.[20] Mass Observation asked its panel what changes would emerge from the war. Their predictions of the top four post-war trends were: 'Less class distinction'; 'more state control'; 'education reforms'; 'the levelling of incomes'.[21]

Not for patching

The growing pressure for change played a big role in the outcome of the peace when it finally came. As J.B. Priestly argued in *Out of the People* – a title borrowed from Walt Whitman – change should come not just from above but from below.[22] The momentum from above came from a high-profile public figure, Sir William Beveridge. The sixty-two-year old, the first director of the London School of Economics and R.H. Tawney's brother-in-law, was drafted into the Ministry of Labour at the start of the war to help with manpower planning, a task he was devoted to. In 1941, Ernest Bevin, a member of the war cabinet, asked the somewhat difficult Beveridge to review Britain's inadequate and convoluted system of social insurance. Bevin, general secretary of the Transport and General Workers' Union at the start of the war, a powerful personality in his own right and later foreign secretary, hoped that this would keep the clever but arrogant Beveridge out of his hair.

Beveridge was asked to find ways of 'tidying up' the existing mess of social support, a complex mix of national, local and voluntary provision. Although the Liberal reforms had been extended, the social security system remained a complex and incoherent stew of insurance run by state, voluntary and private providers and managed by seven government departments. Households were better protected than they had been in 1914, but large numbers were still not covered, while the multiplicity of schemes offered different and often contradictory levels of support.

Despite these multiple faults, Beveridge was not being commissioned to recommend fundamental change. Not one to tinker, and angered by being shifted from his central planning role, he ignored his brief. Drawing on the work of earlier social reformers, including Beatrice and Sydney Webb, he tore up the existing hotchpotch of schemes in favour of a new blueprint for the state's role in welfare. As he wrote in the report's introduction, published on 1 December 1942, 'A revolutionary moment in the world's history is a time for revolutions, not for patching.'[23]

The two-hundred-thousand-word Beveridge report, *Social Insurance and Allied Services*, may have lacked a compelling title, but it captured the public imagination. On the day of publication, queues formed outside Her Majesty's Stationary Office headquarters in London's Kingsway. Some six hundred thousand copies were sold in the UK, while a shortened version was distributed to British troops to foster morale in the immediate aftermath of El Alamein, the first Allied victory of the war. Translated copies were dropped by the RAF on Germany and one was found in Hitler's bunker at the end of the war.

Beveridge set out to tackle what he called 'the five giants' – of want, disease, ignorance, squalor and idleness. The words were spelt out in bold capitals in the report. To tackle these social ills, Beveridge argued that a more comprehensive system of national insurance, paid for by contributions from state, employers and employees, had to be accompanied by other path-breaking changes: free healthcare, universal cash allowances for children, a national assistance safety net and full employment. Policy needed to fire on all fronts.

The popular reaction to Beveridge was a sure sign of the cultural, political and intellectual shift that had been seeded in the 1930s and gathered pace during the 1940s. No government – even one engaged in a titanic battle for Britain's survival – could ignore the plan. The weekly 'Home Intelligence Reports' by the Ministry of Information, based at Senate House in Bloomsbury, showed that the Beveridge Report was the most talked about topic in the country in its week of publication. Of the 947 letters examined about Beveridge, almost all were favourable. One wrote that the plan would give 'the boys who are fighting something to look forward to'; another that its recommendations would bring about a 'complete social revolution ... without bloodshed'.[24]

In a national poll, 86 per cent were for the plan, with only 6 per cent against. While most thought Beveridge's plan should happen, however, few

Figure 5.1: Poster: campaign for the Beveridge plan, 1942

Source: LSE Library

thought it would happen. Many thought that big business would kill it, while another letter predicted 'serious trouble in this country after the war' if the report was not adopted.[25]

The proposals received a much chillier reception elsewhere. Winston Churchill had feared that with his attention elsewhere, Labour ministers would encourage socialist ideas to take root. He did not welcome such a costly programme or the distraction from the war effort it would involve. The divided reactions were a sign of the contrasting visions about post-war reconstruction. The report mostly went down badly in business circles, with the opening volleys fired, predictably, by the insurance companies, while the medical profession was overwhelmingly hostile to the idea of a 'national health service'. The *Daily Mail* and *Daily Express* gave grudging support. There was opposition from the *Daily Telegraph*, claiming that the plan would take Britain 'halfway to Moscow', while the City's paper the *Financial Times* dismissed the proposal as 'that of the Trades Union Congress'. The right-wing periodical the *Truth* went much further, calling it 'the very nightmare of paternalism'. The pro–Conservative *Daily Sketch* described the proposal for a free health service as 'a socialist plot'.[26]

6

Britain's 'New Deal'

On VE day, 8 May 1945, euphoria and relief mingled with apprehension. With 750,000 homes destroyed, many of the four million servicemen demobilised came back to bombed homes and the dole queue. The Conservative Party and their supporters thought the election – set for July 5 – was in the bag. In the event, the public demanded and then voted for change. The great hope was that 1945 would offer a clean start – Year Zero – with history reset.

When Labour won a landslide victory in the election of 1945, with a majority of 146, one not to be surpassed until 1997, no one was more surprised than the party's leader Clement Attlee and his wife Vi. 'Vi went round for months telling people the Attlees "expected Churchill to win."'[1]

When the new prime minister went to the Palace, the self-effacing, pipe-smoking Attlee was driven by Vi – dressed in her Sunday best – in their modest family saloon, the same car used to cross the country during the election campaign. It was a striking symbol of the change about to sweep Britain. When he informed King George VI that Labour had won the election, the king is reported to have said, 'I know. I heard it on the Six O'Clock News.'

Figure 6.1: 'Industry Must Serve the People – Not Enslave Them', Labour Party election poster, 1945[2]

Source: People's History Museum

Treachery

The result was a jolt to the old elites. They expected Churchill to win, their fortunes to be restored and the old order to bounce back along with the servants, the lifestyles and the deference. On the day the results were announced, London's most prestigious hotels had laid on special lunches for their clients. "But this is terrible – *they've* elected a Labour Government, and *the country* will never stand for that!" declared one horrified diner at the Savoy.[3] 'I am stunned and shocked by the country's treachery', wrote 'Chips' Channon a day after the result.[4] Some years later, Peregrine Worsthorne, a man with an impeccable patrician background and later editor of the *Sunday Telegraph*, wrote that he would 'never forget the panic that hit some of my rich fellow officers when the news of Labour's victory reached our mess in Holland. They ... blocked the 21st Army Group's headquarters' communications system telephoning anguished instructions to sell to their stockbrokers.'[5]

On social reform, Churchill was out of step with the public. The experience of war meant that the collectivist ideas that had failed to capture enough of the public's imagination in the 1930s had finally found some resonance. The Tory Party 'is rejected because it has no message for the times', declared the *Manchester Guardian*.[6] Public opinion had turned sufficiently for the old elites to become easy targets for ambitious politicians on the up. A young activist, Denis Healey – dressed in his officer's uniform – summed up the mood of the times in a speech to the Labour Party Conference in Blackpool in May 1945: 'The upper classes in every country are selfish, depraved, dissolute and decadent.'[7] It was not the last time that Healey, Labour's chancellor of the exchequer in the 1970s, was to express strong views about the wealthy classes.

A sense of gloom descended over the city – where a third of the Square Mile had been reduced to rubble. 'A new era has started which may be less comfortable than that to which we have been accustomed in the past', wrote the wealthy banker Evelyn Baring.[8] Harold Macmillan, who lost his seat at Stockton-on-Tees, took a less sombre view. 'It may well be that by a sound instinct, the British people felt that it would wiser for a government of the Left to be in control.'[9] A sign of what might be in store came on 1 August, the first sitting of the new parliament. The depleted Conservative benches gave Churchill a rousing ovation while the packed Labour benches responded spontaneously with the 'Red Flag'.

Despite post-war fatigue, intense economic pressures and continuing austerity – some continued to sleep in the London Underground to keep warm – what followed was an unprecedented programme of change, the construction of Britain's own New Deal. A few months after becoming prime minister, Attlee visited the United States, where, in an address to Congress, he emphasised the moral base to Labour's vision, with its pursuit of social justice and the common good: "Man's material discoveries have outpaced his moral progress."[10]

Labour faced a near-bankrupt economy and the almost immediate withdrawal of American aid through the cancellation of the Lend-Lease agreement, a decision described by Keynes as a 'financial Dunkirk'.[11] But the new government had a number of detailed plans for action prepared during the war years, many of them coming with a long-standing history of debate, inside and outside of Whitehall. Family allowances had originally been proposed in the 1920s by Eleanor Rathbone, a long time campaigner for women's suffrage and an independent Member of Parliament from 1929.[12] The Ministry of Health had been evaluating the state takeover of health services for a decade.[13] Public interest had been stirred by the bestselling 1937 novel *The Citadel* by Dr A.J. Cronin, with its portrayal of the contrast between healthcare for ordinary people and the easy, and often unethical, money to be made in private clinics.

Some significant bipartisan social reforms had already been enacted during the war years. By 1945, a third of children enjoyed school meals, a tenfold rise over 1940, while free childcare was extended to support working women. These and other policies improved the nation's health while boosting the popular case for universal over the targeted provision of the past. In 1944, an historic education act (drawn up by the Conservative education secretary Rab Butler) raised the school leaving age to fifteen – to be implemented in 1947 – and instituted free school education for all, albeit ignoring the role of the public schools. In the same year, an official *White Paper on Full Employment* was published, somewhat upstaging the publication of Beveridge's own report – *Full Employment in a Free Society*. In June 1945, the caretaker government enacted the introduction of family allowances for all children after the first in each family. Ministers had been persuaded that the payments would boost work incentives and defuse demands for a minimum wage. Initially this was to be paid to fathers, but Rathbone persuaded the government to pay them to mothers, who were more likely to use them for the needs of children.

The introduction of family allowances paid to mothers was a highly significant move in the history of social policy, and was the source of numerous political skirmishes in the decades to come. Up to this point, income assistance had been confined almost entirely to those with very low incomes, and was financed in a largely regressive way. The introduction of non-means-tested family allowances – paid for from general taxation – was a significant shift in philosophy and a clear break with the past. A policy mindset that singled out only the poorest had given way to an enhanced principle of entitlement through a belief in common citizenship, with all children entitled as of right to support on an equal basis.

The post-war reforms established the principle that the best way to relieve poverty and build a more robust society was not through targeting but through a new emphasis on universalism and collectivism. As Attlee declared, Labour's aim was to move beyond past struggles to secure 'for the underprivileged some crumbs from the rich-man's table', and towards a new universalism, 'providing for all the things which all should enjoy in a modern community'.[14]

Most strands of the new deal came into force on the 'appointed day' in July 1948, while economic problems slowed the pace of change in the following years. Along with the payment of family allowances and free national healthcare, there was a comprehensive, compulsory and universal system of national insurance. This covered sickness, unemployment, industrial injuries, retirement and widowhood, and was to be paid for by employers, employees and state contributions. 'Little short of remarkable' is how the reforms were described by the academic Richard Titmuss, one of the principal architects of the development of the post-war welfare state. 'No longer did concern rest on the belief that, in respect of many social needs, it was proper to intervene only to assist the poor.'[15] The civil and political rights granted earlier had now been extended to what the sociologist T.H. Marshall called 'social rights'. These rights were embraced through universal access to decent education, healthcare and housing as well as improved income support.[16]

As a 'safety net', households could apply for a new, means-tested system of discretionary national assistance to top up incomes that fell below a national minimum, in essence a replacement for the Poor Law. In 1948 a centralised National Assistance Board replaced the pre-war system of administration, but was only intended to have to deal with a small residual of cases. From report to implementation, the plan took six years. Three elements of the new deal – family allowances, the NHS and National Assistance – were paid for through general taxation. The obligations that had long been imposed in a skewed approach to reciprocity were now balanced with a commitment to the right of all citizens to 'a minimum income for subsistence'.[17] The plan aimed to deliver a form of 'social minimum' via a mix of cash support through national insurance, family allowances, National Assistance (as a last resort), free healthcare, full employment, decent wages and affordable rents. The Webb's earlier call for a national minimum and greater universalism was finally being given some flesh.

The agenda of change overturned much of the thinking of the interwar years, including a new emphasis on government responsibility for economic management and full employment. Such ideas had earlier been dismissed as 'humbug' by Neville Chamberlain, prime minister from 1937 to 1940.[18] This somersault owed much to Keynes, who believed that full employment would challenge the power of rentiers. Although he clashed with the Treasury in the 1930s, he worked there from 1940 developing plans for post-war reconstruction. Once hostile to outside influence, the Treasury converted to Keynesianism. The remarkable shift in direction included state-guided investment, progressive taxes, a nationalised Bank of England to run monetary policy, strict capital controls and regulations to prevent casino-style financial markets.

Keynes did not live to see the implementation of his vision for a managed economy. He died in April 1946, after the arch negotiator had helped shape the post-war global monetary system. Brokered at the Mount Washington Hotel in Bretton Woods, New Hampshire, the new system helped ensure a more stable global financial future. The reform of welfare, state-led reconstruction and a new interventionist economic strategy involved a decisive shift from the market-dominated, weakly regulated and pro-inequality model of capitalism in place before the war. The hands-off state had been replaced by a new proactive economic order. The great divisions over policy during the convulsions of the 1930s had given way to a new broader-based agreement about the responsibility of government and of business. The plan was able to draw on the legacy of a state-directed war economy and its vast array of economic powers – from planning machinery to a high tax and budgetary base – greater than any peacetime government had possessed.

There was also a shift in mood within business. In 1942, the newly appointed archbishop of Canterbury, the Labour-supporting William Temple, had called for the workforce to share 'in some form ... at least equally with capital in the control of industry'.[19] Eventually, corporate leaders found themselves bending – some willingly, others reluctantly, some fully, others less so – to the calls for a wider view of their responsibilities. By helping to build a more stable and vibrant economy, industry was to gain from the new direction.

The state – with a cabinet which contained seven ex-miners – was now to be a much more prominent player in preventing poverty. The heightened rates of tax on top incomes were kept. In place of the 'everyone for themselves' guiding philosophy, Britain constructed a new social contract between state and citizen, and if weaker and less formalised, between workers and boardrooms. The hand-wringing response to the unemployment of the interwar years had gone, and the market had been largely despatched from the provision of healthcare.

The 1940s was a decisive decade in the history of poverty and inequality. Perhaps for the first time in modern history, the distribution question – a concern not just with the creation of wealth, vital as it may be, but also with the way it was shared – was now central to the political agenda. In 1950, Tawney argued that capitalism had 'acquired a slightly less unsocial nature'.[20] For the MP, leading Labour Party thinker and later foreign secretary Anthony Crosland, 'the most characteristic features of capitalism have disappeared – the absolute rule of private property, the subjection of all life to market influences, the domination of the profit motive, the neutrality of government, typical laissez-faire division of income and the ideology of individual rights'.[21]

But what about the fundamental roots of the seismic shift taking place? Was it inspired by a new moral revolution, as some have suggested?[22] Or was it the culmination of a long struggle between business owners and workers, and between rich and poor, with elites finally forced to give way? 'It is not through the benevolence of the right that capitalism was transformed, but because the upper classes, chastised by past experience, decided to follow their own enlightened self-interest: give up some in order to preserve more.'[23]

Both factors were at work. But it was the shock of war, five long years that followed the hardships of the 1930s, and decades of protest, argument and marches that were the most powerful levers. 'There was no gradual, consensual, conflict-free evolution towards greater equality', wrote Thomas Piketty. 'In the twentieth century it was war, and not harmonious democratic or economic rationality that erased the past.'[24] The American historian Walter Scheidel argues that, despite counter-examples (the social reforms of the late nineteenth century for example were not triggered by war, pandemic or social revolution but by a process of institutional change responding to popular demands), periods of equalisation have depended on one of 'Four Horsemen' – warfare, revolution, state collapse and pandemics. He claims that the two world wars stand as the central cause of levelling in the mid-twentieth century.[25] Both wars led to a speeding up of social reform, higher top tax rates – which rose to 98 per cent on investment income in the 1940s and 94 per cent in the US – and active state interventions. They also boosted political demands, led to the destruction of some existing wealth and boosted the returns for labour while lowering them for capital and landholding.

Shortly after the new government took office, fifty-five-year-old housewife Nella Last from Barrow-in-Furness wrote in her Mass Observation diary, 'I used to think how happy people would be when the war was over. But beyond thankfulness that it's over, I see few signs of the brave new world.'[26] Two years later, most of the new 'cradle to grave' system of social support was in place. But how much impact would the Labour reforms have? Had the British system of capitalism been permanently changed?

7

Brave new world

In October 1951, the *Daily Herald* carried the headline: 'Poverty is Almost Down and Out.' *The Herald* was reporting the results of the third survey of poverty by the now eighty-year-old Seebohm Rowntree. This was the first analysis of the anti-poverty effectiveness of the post-war reforms. The survey results, published just ten days before a general election, found that the proportion of York's working-class households in poverty stood at 4.6 per cent in 1950, a dramatic fall compared with the 1936 survey.[1] 'To a great extent', wrote Rowntree's co-researcher George Russell Lavers, 'poverty has been overcome by the welfare state'.[2]

Although the survey was less rigorous than Rowntree's earlier work, the findings had an important influence on the politics of social policy. They showed 'a remarkable improvement, no less than the virtual abolition of the sheerest want', according to a leader in the *Times*.[3] Labour had hung onto power in 1950 with a slender majority of five. They lost the 1951 election, despite trying to make capital out of Rowntree's findings and enjoying 48.8 per cent of the vote to the Conservative's 48 per cent. With a majority of seventeen, the seventy-seven-year old Winston Churchill, shaken by his 1945 defeat, returned to Number 10.

A Plimsoll Line for incomes

That poverty had finally been tamed was the central social story of the time. Apart from a few residual problems that could be solved by policy tweaks, Britain, it was widely believed, had turned its back on the squalor, deprivation and insecurity of the past. Part of Anthony Crosland's argument in his important and influential 1956 social democratic tract *The Future of Socialism*, and its claim that capitalism 'had been almost transformed out of existence' was that 'primary poverty had been largely eliminated'.[4] It was a view widely shared across the Labour party. As Barbara Castle, a leading figure on the party's left, put it, 'The poverty and unemployment which we came into existence to fight have been largely conquered.'[5]

With economic recovery initially slow in coming, heightened national debt and a new set of social priorities, the immediate post-war years were ones of continuing austerity and rationing. Nevertheless, aided by reconstruction, a world economic boom and the new international monetary system, the 1950s was the first decade in recent history to see a largely uninterrupted rise in living standards, with growth rates reaching new peaks.[6]

Britain now had a firmer – if modest and far from complete – income base, one described by the research and policy institute Political and Economic Planning as a 'Plimsoll Line for incomes'.[7] Unemployment rates – for men – stayed well below Beveridge's 3 per cent benchmark for full employment, while for many families there was a new hope of a secure job and a decent home. There was also a steady rise in the proportion of women in work, if often low paid, with the rising number of 'professional' jobs – from engineers to teachers – going mainly to men.[8] These trends brought important boosts to average household incomes. With 'more room at the top' from the growth in the number of middle-to-higher-income jobs, ministers were able to claim they had delivered rising social mobility.

High levels of employment and the rising number of trade unionists – from 4.8 million in 1939 to 10.3 million in 1965 – brought a gradual improvement in wage levels and in working conditions. This boost to labour's bargaining power, making it a more equal partner with capital, as called for by Archbishop William Temple, was a key driver of one of the most significant economic shifts of the time, the boost in the share of output accruing to wages. In the United States, where the post-war years also saw a boost to labour's share, some unions were able to make such progress a contractual commitment. In 1950, the United Auto Workers and General Motors signed a contract – the so-called Treaty of Detroit – under which GM, in return for labour peace, agreed to link wages to productivity, a deal which spread to other unionised industries.

In Britain, the Labour Party could take credit for laying the foundations for the new 'welfare capitalism', but it was the Conservatives who were the political winners from rising prosperity. Labour struggled to develop a compelling new programme, in part because 'the widespread perception that poverty was a thing of the past implied that a central part of Labour's mission had been completed'.[9] In some ways exhausted, politically and ideologically, from the reforming zeal of 1945 – and offering 'cold porridge' as the architect of the NHS Nye Bevan remarked[10] – the party was riven by internal and very public schisms on issues such as nationalisation, state control and planning.

The mood of optimism was better news for the Conservatives. In 1957 then prime minister Harold Macmillan – Churchill retired in 1955 – famously told the nation, 'Most of our people have never had it so good', and there was little dissent. The consumer revolution that helped define the decade slowly changed the way people lived. Twenty million Britons watched the 1953 coronation on three million tiny black-and-white television sets, most courtesy of their neighbours. By the end of the decade, more than three-quarters of households had their own set. Homes filled with new refrigerators and twin-tub washing machines, while the number of families still living with an outside toilet or lacking their own bathroom gradually declined. For the middle classes, these improvements spread to car ownership and foreign travel. The health of the population improved markedly, with infant mortality rates continuing to fall.[11]

When the Conservatives won the election in 1959, Macmillan announced that 'class war is now obsolete'. The influential American political scientist Daniel Bell declared 'an end to ideology', the product of political realignment free of extreme positions of left and right and broad cross-party support for a pro-welfare, interventionist state.[12] Both declarations were wide of the mark. The role of welfarism and the questions of poverty and inequality would soon return as issues of political controversy and stay there for the next sixty years. Even through the 1950s, there were questions about the 'crisis in the welfare state'.[13] While 'class politics' was declared to be over, Conservative cabinets continued to be heavily drawn from the landed classes and those privately educated. In 1963, when Macmillan stood down and Sir Alec Douglas-Home became prime minister, Iain Macleod, then editor of the *Spectator* magazine and a future cabinet minister, alleged that the succession had been stitched up by a 'magic circle' of Old Etonians.

Looking back fifty years later, respondents to a BBC Online request for memories of the time mostly describe a spirit of contentment. 'Britain was truly an innocent land of hope and glory, where the welfare state and national health were improving the post-war quality of living no end', wrote one respondent from Harrogate. 'Having survived a war, everything seemed full of great promise', reported another. For others, the post-war promise proved more elusive. 'No cosy memories of the fifties for me. My childhood memories are of deprivation', wrote a man from Hatfield in the North East. 'No hot and cold running water in our houses, toilet and a cold tap at the end of the back yard. ... Rabbits kept in hutches – for food not as pets. The 1950s were no Golden Age in the North East.'[14] There was no shortage of challenge to the wider mood of optimism, from the foreboding of pop idol Tommy Steele's *Doomsday Rock*, released in 1956, to the work of a string of 'angry young' playwrights and novelists.

The cracks appear

While the gains from economic progress were being more evenly spread, deep-seated social divisions remained. At the end of the 1950s, unemployment rates, living standards and infant mortality rates still varied sharply across regions and classes.[15] The grand claim that society had been largely insulated from poverty also proved difficult to sustain. In 1954 an official report found a number of old people 'living on or near the borderline of poverty'.[16] Three years later, a survey of the elderly in London's East End found that a third had incomes below the National Assistance minimum. "I manage on what I've got. I don't smoke and don't drink, and I've never been used to eating much. I'm not a cadger. I've never been that way brought up", a female pensioner told the enquiry. "I don't want to tell people all my affairs. They ask too many questions. I'm proud I suppose", said another.[17]

Reports of hardship, not just among the elderly but among other voiceless groups – from widows to deserted wives – kept coming. Evidence grew of widespread aversion to applying for National Assistance. Claiming involved the surrender of personal privacy, with detailed scrutiny by local officials visiting homes and talking to relatives, bringing back unhappy memories of the 1930s. As one widow with five young children described the experience: "I hate the thought of the place. I feel really degraded. They give the impression that you're begging."[18]

In 1960, a Fabian Society pamphlet, *Casualties of the Welfare State*, had to be reprinted twice within nine months of publication. Its conclusion: 'We have been deluded into thinking that not only do we already have a Welfare State, but that it is second to none.'[19] In 1963, a BBC documentary, *Waiting for Work*, highlighted the impact of high unemployment among both manual and white-collar workers in Hartlepool. Vividly exposing the persistence of poverty despite the rise of affluence, the programme caused quite a storm, with presents and clothing sent by viewers to the families.[20] The cracks were beginning to show in the new multilayered and complex welfare state.

There was a distinct fall in poverty between the 1930s and 1950s, but subsequent reanalysis concluded that Rowntree and Lavers understated the level of poverty in York, and overstated the actual fall. The actual proportion of working-class households in poverty in 1950 was found to be 11.8 not 4.6 per cent, while the impact of the post-war social reforms was weaker than had been suggested.[21] Although Britain's new system of social support was strongly superior to the one it replaced, it had been implemented during a period of economic constraint. The inevitability of compromise left many holes in the 'Plimsoll Line'. In the post-war years, Britain was a low spender on social services by European standards, while the biggest expansion in state expenditure was not on welfare but, in response to growing concerns about the Cold War, on armaments. The historian David Edgerton called Britain as much a warfare as a welfare state.[22]

The extension of social rights was also limited. 'As-of-right' social insurance did not cover all risks, and could not help those with inadequate contributions or who had exhausted entitlement. National insurance benefits only went to those who paid contributions when in work, and this excluded those permanently unable to work, the self-employed and small employers. Most women were excluded except as dependants of their husbands, for example, through widow's benefits. The Women's Freedom League called it a 'man's plan for man'.[23] The system was geared to a world in which men were the breadwinners, women were expected to rely on their husband's contributions and the needs of married women – including for a pension of their own – were largely neglected.

One of the most important cracks in the system was the low level of benefits. Central to the Beveridge plan was that insurance benefits and family allowance would guarantee basic subsistence living and that insurance recipients would not therefore have to resort to National Assistance. But there was a crucial flaw with this plan. The social insurance system (excluding the cost of family allowances) was designed to be largely self-funding, with the cost of payments met by contributions: the higher the benefits, the higher the contributions. Because contributions were flat rate, they would have to be fixed at a level the lowest paid workers could afford.

Together with other concerns – the need to constrain costs, and that generous levels would stifle independence and reduce work incentives – the subsistence principle was watered down. First, most National Insurance benefits were set around 15–20 per cent below the National Assistance scale, after adding in rent.[24] In 1948 the National Insurance rate for a married couple of £2 2s compared with the National Assistance rate of £2 plus housing costs. This meant households with no other income and average rent would have to turn to National Assistance.[25] In part to encourage parental responsibility, family allowances were set at five shillings compared with the Beveridge-recommended eight shillings per child. In addition, while Beveridge recognised that subsistence was not a scientific and immutable concept, his own austere estimates of a subsistence minimum – on which National Assistance rates were based – were set below Rowntree's 1936 standard.[26] With the 1948 National Assistance rates strikingly meaner than Rowntree's minimum standard, there were big questions about the adequacy of the post-war safety net from the outset.

The arrangements for pensioners were also a compromise. Although the pre-1948 pension level was raised, it still fell below the National Assistance rate, with large numbers of pensioners with no or only limited income from an occupational scheme, dependent on means testing. In the mid-1960s, the system of social security still remained patchy for groups such as the long-term unemployed, the chronically sick and disabled, lone parents and the low paid.

The principle of universalism was perhaps the most important strength of the Beveridge plan. 'The insistence on universality can be seen as one of the few aspects of Labour policy that do show a genuine social revolutionary intention', wrote the historian Arthur Marwick, 'in the sense of aiming at a substantial modification of the class basis of British society'.[27] Beveridge intended that National Assistance would play no more than a small and transitory role: 'The scope of assistance will be narrowed from the beginning and will diminish throughout the transition period.'[28] Yet the means test came to take more and more of the strain of income support. The number of households in receipt of assistance rose from one million in 1948 to over 2.6 million twenty years later, mostly because of the inadequacy of insurance benefits. In 1965, an estimated half a million pensioners were found to be failing to claim the National Assistance to which they were entitled.[29]

Because the income floor was delivered not through insurance but through National Assistance, the relief expressed by the public at an end to means testing was premature. A key principle of the old Poor Law was effectively transferred to the new system, if in a much less coercive form, while the old distinction between the 'deserving' (those on National Insurance) and the 'underserving' (those on Assistance) was essentially preserved.

Although managed more gently than pre-war poor relief, National Assistance required policing and a huge administration. It was still operated with a high degree of discretion, sometimes in a controlling and intrusive way in the case of those deemed 'work-shy'. The system ended up perpetuating some of the weaknesses of the pre-war system, including its judgmentalism. As one commentator put it, 'Viewed in the long run, we are forced to conclude that the nineteenth century poor law has made a deeper impact on British social policy than the Beveridge Report ever did.'[30]

For those who had lived through the Great Depression, the memories of the 1930s, the means test and the workhouse never really left. One official who worked in the welfare department at Lewisham Council in south London in the 1960s recalled some refusing the offer of residential care in local care homes such as Ladywell Lodge because it had been a workhouse.[31] In Aberdeen, elderly residents still talked about the slump years decades later. Despite its dissolution in the late 1920s, they still worried that they might 'end up in Auldmill' – the local 'poorhouse' – or its equivalent.[32] The legacy of those times stayed with many who had to survive on the barest of incomes. From the 1970s, as unemployment returned, the fear of a return to joblessness began to mount, while it was not uncommon for the elderly to worry about whether they could afford a funeral.

What is poverty?

One of the first to raise doubts about the effectiveness of the post-war social reforms was a young Peter Townsend. When Rowntree and Lavers published their findings in 1951, the twenty-three-year old researcher was working at the think tank Political and Economic Planning (PEP). In a PEP broadsheet questioning Rowntree's methodology and findings, Townsend fired a number of broadsides against the orthodoxy that poverty had largely disappeared.[33] The article did not go down well with Rowntree and Lavers, and before it was published, the PEP Board 'required a debate – or confrontation – with Commander Lavers … who had protested at a draft rejecting their optimistic conclusions on poverty'.[34]

In subsequent papers, Townsend questioned the use of poverty measures based on past standards and norms. He targeted the very concept of a subsistence standard, however carefully constructed, and called for a fundamental rethink of the nature of poverty in an affluent society. A minimum standard, he argued, should not be based on the views of external, middle-class experts (from Booth through to Beveridge and himself), with moralistic judgments about how families should manage their lives.[35]

Townsend's work eventually transformed thinking about poverty in rich countries. It further developed the idea that poverty is an essentially relative and dynamic, not absolute and static, concept. Measuring poverty by some minimum subsistence level of consumption necessary for physical health, he argued, ignored the realities of social norms. It should not be based on the standards of the distant past. 'Society itself is continuously changing and thrusting new obligations on its members', he wrote.[36]

The first person to give substance to the idea of relativity in defining the 'necessaries of daily life' was Adam Smith:

> By necessaries I understand not only the commodities which are indispensably necessary for the support of life, but whatever the customs of the country renders it indecent for creditable people, even the lowest order, to be without. A linen shirt, for example, is, strictly speaking, not a necessary of life … in the present times … a creditable day-labourer would be ashamed to appear in public without a linen shirt.[37]

The idea of relativity was also implicit in Rowntree's approach, as the standard he used in his second and third surveys was adjusted upwards to reflect changes in living patterns in the intervening years. Even if his standards were harsh, his 1936 and 1951 studies were an explicit acknowledgment that poverty measures would have to reflect improvements in economic and social conditions, revealing just how difficult it is to apply an absolute standard in the real world.[38]

This did not mean that it was straightforward to pin the idea of poverty down to a single, simple idea. As the social scientist Howard Glennerster warned:

> People carry around with them two very different but equally valid notions of poverty. One is absolute. People in 1950 remembered life in the 1930s and recognized that it *was* better in 1950. Another view is that poverty is a measure of relative disadvantage. Young families might be better off than in the 1930s, but be less well off relative to others.[39]

Townsend's work provided a way of reconciling these contrasting perceptions:

Individuals, families and groups in the population can be said to be in poverty when they lack the resources to obtain the types of diet, participate in the activities and have the living conditions and amenities which are customary, or at least widely encouraged or approved in the societies in which they belong.[40]

'Understanding poverty as relative to time and place', wrote the York-based social scientist Jonathan Bradshaw, 'was the only way in which we could reconcile talking about poverty in the 19th and 20th centuries, and the only way to reconcile poverty in Ethiopia and Luxembourg.'[41]

While he acknowledged that poverty 'was more than inequality', and that inequality does not always lead to poverty, Townsend, along with the early social critics, made an explicit link between the two: 'The poor undoubtedly receive an unequal share of resources and any explanation of this fact must be related to the larger explanation of social inequality in general.'[42] Social reforms to this point had been mainly concerned with relieving hardship and squalor in a largely market economy. The development of a relative approach linked poverty to exclusion from typical living standards and thus the way resources were distributed *across* society. The numbers falling below a relative poverty line would therefore have a clear, if partial, link with wider inequality. Poverty was about exclusion, not just survival. As the distinguished economist, philosopher and Nobel laureate Amartya Sen put it, poverty was not just about low income and an inadequate living standard but about the denial of 'the capability to realise one's full potential as a human being'.[43]

The idea of poverty as 'relative' was an important step forward, but hardly put the issue to bed. How to draw up an acceptable minimum was to remain an issue of continuing controversy, while it was another decade before the issue was to shift out of the shadows of academia into the wider political agenda. By the early 1960s, although there was no official monitoring of poverty levels, the argument that poverty had been largely abolished was looking increasingly thin. Nevertheless the new evidence on the persistence of poverty generated little public or parliamentary interest. The Conservatives had no wish to puncture the image of prosperity they had so carefully nurtured. For Labour, there was no political capital in proclaiming that their reforms were less effective than they had claimed.

It was inevitable that compromises had to be made in the circumstances of the post-war years. For all its flaws, the new social security system abolished many of the indignities of the pre-1948 system. It embraced important new principles of the sharing of risks and of collective responsibility while lowering the risks to livelihoods from the evolution of industrial capitalism. However, although it built a more robust income floor, that floor was neither especially generous, nor free of holes. A guaranteed 'social minimum' had yet to be constructed. Many of those dependent on the new benefits system found that it did not live up to the promise of 1945. The fall in poverty that did take place, when compared with the interwar years, was as much to do with wider improvements in the economy including improved wages and employment levels, as the improved system of benefits.

Even Beveridge had his doubts. 'The picture of yesterday's hopeful collaboration in curing the evils of want and disease, ignorance and squalor ... looks like a dream today', he concluded in 1953.[44] Richard Titmuss used to put 'welfare state' – which he viewed as 'unfinished business' – between inverted commas. Looking back from 1970, the academics Vernon Bogdanor and Robert Skidelsky described the 1950s as 'an age of illusion'.[45]

8

A shallow consensus

Part of the reason for these flaws was that although the much-heralded post-war consensus was real, it was also shallow. The official committee established by the wartime cabinet to examine the Beveridge report argued that the proposals would, by abandoning the principle of deterrence on which social relief had always been based, encourage fecklessness. The committee also expressed doubts about the need for family allowances and argued that, if needed, they should be paid in kind not cash.[1] Similar issues have continued to dog the progress of social reform.

The 'people' versus the 'old gang'

David Cannadine has described the 1945 election as 'a contest between "the people" and the "old gang"'. This was especially stark among the armed forces. As the American critic Edmund Wilson noted when mingling among British troops in Greece, there was an almost 'complete class line-up' between troops and officers. He could find 'no English soldier who had not voted for Labour and only one officer who had'.[2]

The old gang -- the traditional upper classes, City grandees and the new industrial rich, along with some members of the professional classes – did not sign up to the new welfare priorities. While the post-war reforms enjoyed widespread public support, they were, added Cannadine, widely viewed by the wealthy classes as an attack on 'aristocrats, the rich, bankers, doctors, newspaper owners and shareholders'.[3] In her 1948 political satire *Tory Heaven*, Marghanita Laski portrayed a totalitarian Tory government enforcing the unwritten rules of the British class system, and its hierarchy of privileges, through a strict system of social classification – A, B, C, D and E. Breaches of the rules meant being downgraded by the 'Degrading Court' to a lower class. In Frederick Raphael's novel of a group graduating from Cambridge in the 1950s, *The Glittering Prizes,* one of the key aristocratic characters, Lady Frances, describes the Attlee government as 'the greatest tragedy in our history since Henry the Eighth'.[4] Some leading academics also opposed the levels of redistribution accompanying the reforms. Lionel Robbins, a leading anti-collectivist economist at the London School of Economics described them as 'quite indefensible', arguing they involved a 'discrimination against enterprise and ability such as has never before existed … in any large scale civilized community'.[5]

The Conservative Party bought into parts of the post-war plans but not all of them. They were opposed to the hikes in taxation and remained lukewarm about family allowances. When they did support the government, it was invariably through gritted teeth. As the Conservative MP Harold Nicolson noted in 1945, 'Class feeling and class resentment' were very strong.[6] Henry Channon dismissed Stafford Cripps' 1948 'penal' budget as a 'monstrous and quite unnecessary piece of class legislation'.[7] Throughout the 1950s there were profound differences between the parties over key issues from the scale of public spending to the public-versus-private provision of welfare. The decade saw several, if mostly failed, attempts by ministers to reappraise the level of funding for the NHS, to rein in social spending and to cut the level of family allowances.

When they lost in 1945, the Conservatives believed that to win back power they needed to build an alliance of 'the haves': the wealthy, the professional middle classes and the growing number of highly paid skilled workers. Throughout the war years, these groups, in the words of the historian David Kynaston, 'grumbled for Britain' over rationing, taxes and for the wealthiest, their loss of status and power, and what they saw as a 'Santa Claus' state created at their expense. In the summer of 1948, a Conservative Party memo on how to win the next election described how an aggrieved group of floating voters – some of whom voted Labour – 'was now finding it impossible to live. The chief fear of the middle-class voter is being submerged by a more prosperous working class'.[8]

Britain's experiment in humanising capitalism fell short of a wholescale root-and-branch makeover of society. Much of the status quo was preserved. There was no resolution as to whether social justice required 'equality of opportunity' or 'equality of outcome' – or both. Through the 1950s and 1960s, there was little change in the class gaps in health, school leaving ages and university entrance compared with the pre-war years. The 1944 Education Act's new tripartite system of secondary schools did much less to deliver greater equality of opportunity than had been hoped.[9] Outside of the newly nationalised industries, there was little attempt to promote alternative business models such as co-operatives and mutuals that could act as a counter to the force of the large private corporations.

The nation's long-standing and self-perpetuating 'cycle of privilege' – and one of the sources of the broader inequality-poverty cycle – was only lightly touched. Although the voluntary hospitals were abolished, private schools were unreformed, a missed opportunity that had a profound impact on the future shape of society as well as its past. As the historian Hugh Thomas wrote in 1959, 'The fusty establishment with its Victorian views' had been left largely in place.[10] We have 'to fight against privilege', the Eton-educated Orwell had exhorted during the Blitz:

Although there are gifted and honest *individuals* among them, we have got to break the grip of the moneyed class ... The England that is only just beneath the surface, in the factories and the newspaper offices, in the aeroplanes and the submarines, has got to take charge of its own destiny.[11]

For all the panic from some sections of 'the fusty establishment', the pre-war hierarchy of economic power – embedded in the City and large company boardrooms, and muted for a while – remained remarkably durable, in part because Conservative governments from 1951 were committed to preserving large chunks of the past. The only part of the 'old guard' that had been seriously dented was the landed gentry, though their decline was less precipitous than they liked to claim. In the preface to the revised 1959 edition of *Brideshead*, Evelyn Waugh admitted that he might have overstated the sense of impending doom facing the aristocracy, or as he put it, the book was 'a panegyric preached over an empty coffin'.[12]

The fragility of consensus was also reflected in rifts on the left. For the 'New Left', welfarism was a way of propping up rather than transforming capitalism. One of the sternest critics was the Marxist academic Ralph Miliband, a lecturer at the London School of Economics and the father of David and Ed Miliband, rivals for Labour leader in 2010. For Miliband the father, post-war welfarism was ameliorative. It failed the key test: the need for a much more comprehensive reordering of capitalism, and that was why poverty and inequality remained in place. As Ed – the younger son – recalled in a lecture in 2006 on the anniversary of Crosland's *The Future of Socialism*, 'In the household in which [they were] brought up, Crosland and his ideas were not popular.'[13] What did engage the younger Milibands was a board game called Class Struggle, a kind of anti-capitalist version of the Monopoly game with the forces of 'socialism' pitted against those of 'barbarism'. Not exactly a bestseller, and only available in the United States, the American creator of the game, a politics professor – Bertell Ollman – knew Ralph and had sent him a copy. The game, according to some who'd played it, was, like the wider class struggle, somewhat long and tortuous.

Ralph Miliband liked to dismiss Crosland's book – with its claim that power had been shifted from the business class to the state and to labour – as 'the bible of Labour revisionism'. Despite being a periodic member, Miliband saw the Labour Party's 'dogmatic' commitment to parliamentary politics as a fatal flaw.[14] His position was a fringe view within the wider labour movement at the time and has mostly remained so. Influenced in its early years by the ethical socialism promoted by Tawney and others, Labour's leaders and its intellectual wings have rejected the revolutionary road in favour of parliamentary democracy and a pragmatic programme of incremental improvement largely by working within the system. For them, the diseased tree had to be pruned and shaped not replaced. Attlee, with his programme of Keynesian and Beveridge reform, has been the most radical of Labour prime ministers, while the first post-Attlee Labour government, under Harold Wilson from 1964, never came close to accepting Miliband's critique. Both Attlee's and Wilson's goals were to soften the impact of capitalism, through a mix of public ownership, regulation and 'tax and spend', not to eliminate it. Labour has flirted with greater radicalism in opposition, but in power, anxious not to stray too far from perceived political realities, has taken, outside of 1945, a cautious and gradualist approach to change.

There has been no shortage of clashes on the left over how transformative Labour's programme should be. On several occasions, mostly in opposition, the party has flirted with policies that went well beyond ameliorative change. In 2015, for example, in a bombshell moment in Labour history, the veteran MP and parliamentary outsider Jeremy Corbyn, and with him various strands of the British left, unexpectedly won control of the party. These leftward shifts failed to deliver power but brought internal ruptures and years of fractious manoeuvring. Labour, through its 120-year history, has remained a mainstream social democratic party, with its leaders accepting the inevitability of a mixed, pluralist economy, embracing private, public and social enterprise, though with varying degrees of radicalism and internal struggle about how capitalism should be tamed, and a fudging of the distinctions between the reformist and transformative goals.

A commitment to lowering Britain's deep-seated wealth and income divide, built into Labour's DNA from its birth, has been a goal shared across the wings of the party.[15] Roy Hattersley, who later became deputy leader, recalls being recommended Tawney's *Equality* in 1951 at the age of eighteen. After reading the tract, one which had a huge influence on the shaping of post-war society, his commitment to the Labour Party 'had been transformed from tribal to ideological. From then on, I had no doubt that the good society was the equal society.'[16]

Yet, like socialism, the search for equality has remained 'elusive and somewhat intractable', with much less clarity about what the commitment means in practice and the equality goal mostly subordinate to the less comprehensive target of poverty.[17] Such ambiguity has dogged Labour's social policy agenda. Along with Attlee, Wilson made commitments to reducing inequality. Labour opposes today's "closed society, in which birth and wealth have priority, in which master-and-servant, landlord and tenant mentality is predominant", declared Wilson in 1963 in a speech in Birmingham.[18] Blair, in contrast, peddled backwards. Corbyn's 2019 manifesto – although in some ways a reinstatement of mainstream social democratic values – was long on policies, but less radical than that of 1945 on the question of welfare and the benefits system. Compared with earlier Labour programmes, according to David Edgerton, it was 'decidedly non-welfarist'.[19] It certainly failed to capture the electorate.

Egalitarian optimism

The dominant theory in the immediate post-war years was that capitalism had reached an inequality turning point. The Belarusian-born Harvard economist Simon Kuznets theorised that growing prosperity would be associated first with rising and then with falling inequality, a pattern corresponding to an 'inverted U-curve'.[20] As an economy industrialises, Kuznets argued, new investment opportunities would increase the returns to those with capital, while the need for a 'reserve army' of the unemployed would keep wages down. As higher average incomes brought democratisation and a more developed welfare state, however, this process would reverse. Alfred Marshall had made a similar argument that poverty 'was a passing evil in the progress of man upwards'.[21]

The theory fitted the trends of the previous 150 years. In the 1950s, it seemed to be borne out by the combination of planning to boost growth and employment, social policy to distribute the gains from growth more equitably and new restraints on the rate of return on capital. In more developed nations, inequality had initially risen with industrialisation and then stayed high until the end of the 1930s, albeit it with some modest reduction. Then, during and after the war, the politics of sacrifice – of who should bear the burden of disruptive change – worked, arguably for the first time, in favour of the poorest members of society in most Western industrial nations.

Others had their doubts about Kuznets' 'egalitarian optimism'. One of the effects of rising affluence and the new welfarism was a lessening of political concern with the distribution question. 'Few things are more evident in modern social history than the decline of interest in inequality as an economic issue', wrote J.K. Galbraith. The reason, he argued, was that economic growth had displaced the need to shuffle incomes around.[22] 'A limited version of the Keynesian alternative to strict central planning, the greater buoyancy of the international economy after the war and the near achievement of full employment by 1950, suggested Pat Thane, 'had made more drastic controls and more thorough-going redistribution of wealth and power seem less essential than some had previously thought'.[23]

But there was another explanation to doubt the optimistic scenario. Tackling the coexistence of privilege and poverty was, as David Donnison noted, 'rarely an objective in its own right for the founders of the welfare state'. The long list of the pioneers of social reform through and beyond the nineteenth century, from Octavia Hill, Joseph Chamberlain and Beatrice and Sidney Webb to Rowntree and Beveridge, were motivated mainly by 'a sense of shock at the squalor, pain and poverty they saw around them, and a rejection of their predecessors' inadequate responses to these problems.'[24] Those, such as Titmuss and Tawney, who put greater emphasis on equality were in a minority. Tawney saw the struggle against poverty as essentially one against privilege, and never believed that it was possible to abolish what Matthew Arnold called the 'religion of inequality' simply by statute.[25]

The post-war reforms were primarily about raising the income base and providing more equal access to vital services like schools and healthcare. Inequality was not one of Beveridge's 'five giants' that had to be conquered. He favoured using the power of the state to create a basic safety net, but his report said little about using that power to dismantle the structural sources of inequality.

The welfare state was, as T.H. Marshall put it, of 'mixed parentage'. As well as tackling poverty, the stormtroopers of welfare reform wanted to protect private enterprise from too much interference. Seebohm Rowntree was a Liberal, and the Liberal Party had been founded on a commitment to free markets and free trade. [26] When elevated to the House of Lords, Beveridge sat on the Liberal benches. He was described by Noel Annan, later provost of King's College, Cambridge, as 'far removed from socialism'.[27] As with Rowntree, who had a big influence on the post-1906 reforms, Beveridge's aim was to mould a social security system within the framework of a liberal market economy, albeit one with a stronger degree of state regulation, but which also emphasised the importance of personal responsibility, incentives and reciprocity.

In the 1930s, Keynes and Beveridge both made a point of refusing to join the Labour Party, despite the decline of the Liberals as an electoral force. Although Keynes believed strongly in social justice, and favoured some redistribution, the standard view is that his main contribution was on how to smooth capitalist instability.[28] As one of his disciples, Roy Harrod, argued, his proposals were not about resolving 'the fundamental conflict of interests between rich and poor', the main reason why Keynes was not popular with the Labour left in the 1930s.[29] 'Keynes analyzed the reasons why the capitalist system did not but could function properly', wrote the economist Lawrence Klein, an early champion of Keynesian economics. 'Keynes wanted to apologize and preserve, while Marx wanted to criticize and destroy.'[30]

By raising the income floor, giving free access to healthcare and persisting with higher tax rates at the top, the post-war reforms added to the process of equalisation stemming from other sources such as a fully employed economy and buoyant wages.[31] But the impact of the tax and benefit changes, important as they were, was limited by two key factors. First, from the further growth of tax avoidance and evasion. Second, from the funding of social insurance largely by a flat-rate system of contributions that bore most heavily on the low paid. This new system, as in 1911, involved a process of 'horizontal redistribution' covering the risks of unemployment and illness as well as retirement, in which income was redistributed between different stages of the life cycle.

By ensuring nearly everyone would benefit at some stage, dipping in between cradle and grave as necessary, this has been one of the system's great strengths, at odds with the idea of 'them' and 'us', between those who claim and those who pay in. That the system works for the entire community has been a key source of its sustained public support and middle-class buy-in.[32] But this construction has also meant, from the outset, a lower degree of 'vertical redistribution' from rich to poor.

Under Attlee's legacy, post-war business leaders faced new constraints for a while, but for all his achievements, these lacked durability. While the rich did take a hit, including from a lowering of the returns to capital from rent, profits and dividends, the economic system continued to be loaded, if a good deal less strongly than in the past, in favour of 'the haves'. Many of the gains from the advent of social democracy, including the creation of a better power balance between capital and labour, were also to prove fragile and temporary. The 1945 reform process, it turned out, was aided by 'historical contingencies that could not last'.[33]

With hindsight, Tony Crosland underplayed the extent to which the inequality question had been settled, and overstated the reformist power of 'organic utopia' – the mix of Keynesian contra-cyclical demand management, the managerial revolution in industry and incremental social change.[34] Despite the extent of reform, key elements of continuity remained. As the post-war boom faltered and ideological differences became more explicit, the new economic and social model proved much less robust than in the earlier, more stable 'contingencies'.

PART III

1960–79

The rediscovery of poverty

The question marks being raised about the persistence of poverty had, initially, little impact. But this was about to change. In 1957, Peter Townsend moved to the London School of Economics (LSE) in the department run by Richard Titmuss. At his modest three-bedroom house in Ealing, where he lived with his wife Kay and daughter Ann, frequent guests included an elderly Richard Tawney, colleagues like Townsend and Labour politicians such as Richard Crossman. Titmuss had an unparalleled influence over the course of British social policy. He is one of few social scientists to have an English Heritage blue plaque marking his former home. A few months before he died in April 1973 at the age of 65, he was still able to fill lecture halls to overflowing.[1]

Those working with Titmuss became part of a group of LSE academics known as the 'Titmice'. Applied sociologists and close friends, their work soon began to get under the skin of politicians and administrators. At the LSE, Townsend started work on a novel approach to the measurement of poverty with another of the 'Titmice', Brian Abel-Smith. Reputedly twenty-seventh in line to the throne, Abel-Smith was an unlikely champion of the poor. While the studies by Charles Booth and Seebohm Rowntree were based on their own local surveys, the Abel-Smith and Townsend study used the government's Family Expenditure Survey, with its host of information about incomes and other aspects of household lifestyles. The Central Statistical Office had already used this source for some groundbreaking analysis of the distributional impact of public spending on household income.[2]

The poor and the poorest

Townsend and Abel-Smith set out to compare poverty rates in 1953 and 1960. The authors had, fleetingly, considered calling their report *Poor, Poorer, Poorest*, but decided that would be too flippant. The study, finally titled *The Poor and the Poorest*, found that in 1960, 14 per cent of the population – 7.5 million Britons – were living in poverty.[3] Their measure of where the poverty line should be drawn was not based on a minimal subsistence standard, nor was it linked to prevailing living standards, and was essentially expedient. The study's novelty was to reject the subsistence principle and redefine the level of National Assistance as the 'official', government-determined operational poverty line –

a 'floor' below which nobody was supposed to fall – while making it clear that this did not imply any judgement about its adequacy.[4]

Although the National Assistance rate had never been explicitly defined as the state's poverty line, and there had been no attempt at an official assessment of its adequacy, this approach revealed how many people fell short of the de facto safety net. Since its introduction in 1948, the National Assistance scales – at least for some family types – had been revised upwards at a slightly faster rate than average earnings.[5] This was an implicit acceptance of the principle of relativity, that the floor should rise to reflect wider improvements in living standards. In this sense, the National Assistance level was a quasi-relative poverty line.[6]

While around a third of those in poverty in 1960 were pensioners, 30 per cent (2.25 million) were children, and 41 per cent lived in households where at least one person was in work. The revelations about poverty among children and those in work finally exposed as false the widespread political assumption that what poverty still existed was confined largely to a small group of the elderly.

As well as rediscovering poverty, the researchers were redefining it. According to one analysis of their impact fifty years later, they 'cast a shadow of doubt over the contemporary perception of post-war prosperity … and undermined the complacency surrounding the success of the post-war social democratic project'.[7] The post-war expectation was that as prosperity spread, poverty would gradually disappear, or as the historian Jeremy Seabrook put it, 'Poverty would in due course become a distant memory, a curiosity like slavery, child labour, penal servitude, abolished by the inevitable march of progress.'[8] It had not turned out like that. The persistence of poverty amid affluence meant that a significant minority had become bystanders in the wider march of prosperity.

While British social scientists were rocking the boat over poverty, it had already been 'rediscovered' in the United States. While there was still a concerted opposition to greater equality among conservative thinkers, several hard-hitting studies exposed how rising prosperity disguised a sizeable group of 'the invisible poor'. J.K. Galbraith's *The Affluent Society,* published in 1958, contrasted the coexistence of 'private affluence and public squalor' and became an international bestseller.[9]

Four years later, Michael Harrington's exposé of two Americas, one of deprivation and one of affluence, in his book *The Other America* found 40–50 million Americans to be poor, 'existing at levels beneath those necessary for human decency'. They included unskilled workers, migrant farm workers, the aged, minorities and those who lived in the 'economic underworld of American life'. 'The fate of the poor', Harrington concluded, 'hangs upon the decision of the better-off. If this anger and shame are not forthcoming, someone can write a book about the other America a generation from now and it will be the same or worse'.[10]

The Other America, and its revelation of a national blindness to poverty, was later listed as one of the twentieth century's ten most influential books by *Time* magazine. It helped to force the hand of President Kennedy, who demanded answers on why so many were being cut adrift. Following Kennedy's assassination in November 1963, his successor, Lyndon Baines Johnson, launched a 'war on poverty' as part of his 'Great Society' programme. Influenced by the civil rights and feminist movements, this programme, albeit leaving many, including African Americans out in the cold, included Medicaid, subsidised housing, new legal services, the raising of the minimum wage and, later, food stamps. It was an ambitious programme, with a mixed record that was to prove highly controversial, and not just on the right. Indeed, far from going away, poverty in America kept on rising, even on the starkest of measures.[11]

Similar concerns that prosperity went hand in hand with poverty were also being raised in Western Europe.[12] Martin Ravallion, a World Bank economist, called this awakening 'the second poverty enlightenment'. The first poverty enlightenment had come in Western Europe in the late eighteenth century, with the first stirrings of the idea that poverty could be tackled by appropriate state intervention, though the idea met with considerable elite resistance during the nineteenth century. The second enlightenment coincided with the growing emphasis on relativity and with what Ravallion called 'an explosion of interest in the measurement of poverty'.[13]

Up to this point, the question of distribution had been largely confined to the question of 'factor distribution', of how the cake was divided between wages and profits. It now began to shift to how it was distributed between individuals.[14] Although the former is a central determinant of the latter, this new approach took the issue out of the fringes of economics, and became, for several decades, the dominant theme in the inequality debate.

The rise of the poverty lobby

An important sign of the second poverty enlightenment was the formation of the first anti-poverty pressure groups. When Labour won the general election in October 1964, the hope among campaigners was that the new government would finish the job started in 1945. But, when Labour's first Queen's Speech failed to mention family poverty, a small group of academics and social workers gathered, in March 1965, at Toynbee Hall, an East End settlement where Beveridge and Attlee had been volunteers sixty years earlier. Six months later, the Child Poverty Action Group (CPAG) had been born.

To launch the new organisation, CPAG sent a letter, signed by thirty-seven public figures, to the prime minister, Harold Wilson, calling for new initiatives to boost family incomes. The following day, the prime minister met representatives of the group in Downing Street, leading to a wave of carefully crafted press publicity. In the *Times,* the headline read, 'Many British children living in hardship and poverty.' In the *Daily Express*, it was 'Poverty plea to Wilson'. Two days before Christmas, CPAG helped launch the seventy-eight-page monograph *The Poor and the Poorest*. Brian Abel-Smith appeared on several news programmes, and the BBC screened a documentary about children in poor working families. The producers were so moved that they returned with toys and food for the families.[15] The issue of poverty – and especially child poverty – had finally been placed firmly on the political agenda.

Other pressure groups followed. In 1968, the Claimants' Union movement was launched in Birmingham to become a vigorous grassroots campaign on welfare rights issues. The most high-profile of the new groups was Shelter. Despite record levels of housebuilding, severe housing shortages and widespread overcrowding persisted, while housing conditions, especially in the private rented sector, were often little better than squalid. In 1966, Ken Loach's gritty docudrama *Cathy Come Home*, about a young family sliding into poverty and homelessness, was watched by twelve million viewers.

Evidence of the real social state of Britain mushroomed. A study of mothers alone – a group of widows, separated wives, divorcees and unmarried women – painted a picture of intense overcrowding and deprivation. Two out of five families lacked sufficient beds – with some mothers forced to share with their children. Holidays were rare, school activities were unaffordable and Christmas was mostly a burden. "I hate Christmas coming, I dread it", as one mother put it. "I've had to tell the children that Father Christmas hasn't got any toys for our house this year. I've had to wait 'til Marks and Spencer have their sale, and then I've had to buy a doll for them and say that Father Christmas has remembered after all." Many mothers missed meals, or were regularly eating very little, mostly to ensure their children didn't go without. As one separated wife described it, "In the school holidays, I sometimes stand there and cook a full dinner for them, and tell them to go in the kitchen and get it, and when they say 'where's yours?', I say I'm on a diet." 'Only the word "poverty" adequately conveyed the kinds of deprivation which the mothers were experiencing', wrote Dennis Marsden, the author of the study.[16]

Such evidence, it was believed, would force a political response. According to Frank Field, director of CPAG from 1969, 'None of the founder members thought in terms of a long campaign; they assumed that after a year, or the most, two, they would have achieved their original purpose.'[17] The group was so convinced of this that a year elapsed before it opened a bank account. Poverty, however, was now a highly sensitive political issue. In the mid-1960s, John Veit-Wilson, one of the founding members of the group, obtained access to a National Assistance Board's unpublished study which revealed the inadequacy of its benefit levels. This brought an early morning home visit by senior civil servants demanding, without success, access to his files.[18] When it became apparent that it was going to take a bit more than a brief meeting with the prime minister to get action on poverty, CPAG established itself as a national organisation, with paying members, and appointed its first full-time secretary, Tony Lynes, another of the 'Titmice'.

Based from 1967 in cramped, shabby rooms off Drury Lane in Central London, the group raised the pressure on the Labour government. The office consisted of Lynes, a typewriter and a part-time secretary. Lynes, who had strong links with key civil servants, initially worked behind the scenes to prod Westminster's and Whitehall's social conscience. 'His mode of operation was to cycle to the House of Commons in the morning, listen to what was being said, cycle back to the office, bash out a press release in the afternoon, and then cycle round Fleet Street distributing it.'[19]

Leading Labour ministers, including Barbara Castle and Richard Crossman, were certainly wedded to the goal of ending poverty, but they were also practical politicians and felt that the job had largely been done. Labour also had other priorities. Like the previous Conservative government, ministers were preoccupied with economic problems, from poor industrial management and dated production methods to a lack of skilled workers. Another problem – deteriorating labour relations – was parodied in the popular 1959 film *I'm All Right Jack*. Despite significant improvements in employment levels and health and education, as well as rising living standards on average, Britain's economy was lagging behind its leading competitors.

Believing that great strides had already been made towards greater equality, Labour's leadership presented the party as one of modernisation and industrial dynamism, thus giving emphasis to the economic over the social. The solution to the evidence of persistent poverty was now seen to be found in stimulating growth. Without an uplift in the growth rate, it was argued, tackling deprivation would lead to tensions across society. As the Labour cabinet minister Patrick Gordon Walker put it:

> In a democracy, it is very difficult to reduce private affluence. ... All one can reasonably do is to take a larger share of any increase from them. ... Those who advocate that we should simply take more and more money, whatever is happening to the economy, aren't on the whole people who have to win votes and stay in office and try to get things done. Large increases in expenditure on the social services are just not possible unless economic growth is going happily forward.[20]

The question of the relative priority of wealth creation and wealth redistribution, and how far these were compatible or in conflict, was to be the source of much contention in the coming decades.

With the government proving a hard nut to crack, CPAG began to suspect that the labour movement might be an uncertain ally of the poor, and soon became a public thorn in the flesh for ministers. In these early years, there were internal splits within the group about tactics, including how far to work with Labour and how far to remain independent and openly criticise it. At one point there was even some talk about merging with Shelter. The path taken was to turn the group into a campaigning organisation, just as Shelter had become.

The champions of universalism, the group launched a campaign to raise family allowances, which had seen only modest rises since 1948. It was a universal benefit and one of the most innovative of the post-war measures. Labour, however, believed that family allowances were not popular with the public, being widely seen as a handout to large families. Their first priority had been to raise the state pension. It was a much-needed and popular, if expensive, measure.

Aware of the economic difficulties facing the government, and tipped off by civil servants that the idea might get support in the cabinet, the group proposed a compromise plan: to increase family allowances, funded by reducing child tax allowances. This was a form of 'clawback' which would withdraw the increase from standard-rate taxpayers, thus concentrating the gains on lower-income families. The proposal was strongly opposed by the Treasury, which favoured a new, and much cheaper means-tested benefit for working families. Although the cabinet was divided over the options – 'one of the bitterest Cabinets I have attended', wrote Richard Crossman[21] – the government eventually settled for the CPAG proposal.

Family allowances were raised – the first rise for a decade – with the increase clawed back from standard-rate taxpayers. Although the clawback concentrated the gains on the working poor, it caused confusion, as opponents had warned, among families, with husbands' take-home pay falling while wives' family allowance went up. George Brown, Labour's deputy leader, described clawback as 'the most unpopular thing that Labour did'.[22] Nevertheless, the move paved the way for an even more radical and progressive reform a decade later.

There were other changes. In response to the low level of some benefits, the government introduced earnings-related supplements to unemployment and sickness benefits and contributions, a significant departure from Beveridge's flat-rate system. New means-tested rent rebates were introduced along with free school meals for fourth and subsequent children. In 1966, National Assistance was renamed Supplementary Benefit, a somewhat cosmetic change, but one aimed at giving the system a more humane face and encouraging take-up. It was the first of many subsequent attempts at reforming a poorly functioning system by changing its name. With the Treasury insisting on compensating spending cuts, prescription charges – which had been abolished in 1964 – were reintroduced, charges for dental treatment and school meals raised and free milk withdrawn from secondary schools. Supplementary Benefit claimants were exempted.

Despite a lack of significant social strides, the Wilson government was a reforming government in many ways. Wilson was surely right that technological progress needed to be harnessed by an active state in partnership with business to ensure it met the public good. Labour, during the 1960s, also targeted various forms of discrimination, including banning discrimination by race. Until then, many companies – often supported by local trade unions – refused to employ black or Asian workers. Labour set Britain on a more liberal path by also legalising divorce and homosexuality and abolishing the death penalty. It ended school selection outside of the private schools and set up the Open University.

Barbara Castle's 1970 Equal Pay Act was the culmination of a long struggle for equal pay for women, including a strike by women machinists at Dagenham's Ford factory, a story later made into a film, *Made in Dagenham*. Castle, first elected to parliament in 1945, had fought a long campaign for equal pay, often against the old, almost entirely male, guard of the labour movement and a largely hostile Labour cabinet. The Act opened the door to challenging the way gender inequality was baked into the system. Despite these measures, race and gender inequality remained a deep scar on society, while the union movement, fearful of the impact on men's pay, were slow, and reluctant, to take up women's employment issues. The 1975 documentary *Nightcleaners* exposed the struggle by low-paid women cleaners, working because of their husbands' low earnings, to become unionised in the face of a largely disinterested Transport and General Workers' Union. "No woman does nightwork unless she's got to", said Elsie, one of the cleaners. It was not until decades later that mandatory gender-pay-gap reporting exposed the limited progress had been made on pay since the 1970 Act.

10

Poorer under Labour

When Harold Wilson unexpectedly called a general election for June 1970, CPAG seized the moment to raise the stakes. They prepared a private memorandum, *A War on Poverty: Poor Families and the Election*, highly critical of Labour's record. Before it was released, Richard Crossman, secretary of state for social services, agreed to meet Frank Field and Peter Townsend, now the group's chair. Crossman brought Brian Abel-Smith. He had joined Crossman as an adviser in 1968, forcing him to resign from CPAG's executive committee. The two friends – Abel-Smith and Townsend – were now on opposing sides.

The meeting was stormy. In Field's account: 'Crossman banged the table, he shouted, he mocked. ... The only action he didn't try was to swing from the chandelier.'[1] After the meeting, Field released the document to the press with the provocative headline 'Poor get poorer under Labour', thus launching a highly publicised turf war between the new lobbyists and the government.[2] Field later explained that this attack was partly about exposing the myth that Labour 'was on the side of the poor'.[3] Not only did the row stoke considerable press interest, it was eagerly taken up by Edward Heath, the Conservative Party leader.[4]

A few months earlier, Field had secured a meeting with the shadow Tory chancellor Iain Macleod. With none of the grandstanding displayed by Crossman, Macleod committed the next Conservative government to raising family allowances as the 'most effective way of dealing with the growing problem of family poverty'.[5] Field had not been expecting such a pledge, as the Conservatives had long been cool towards universal benefits. He used it to exert pressure during his meeting with Crossman. In response, Crossman asserted that Macleod's pledge would be reneged on if they were in government.

While CPAG's tactics established its independence from Labour, its more aggressive approach was controversial among supporters and added to a rift that had already been opening among the Titmice. Both Titmuss and Abel-Smith, for example, sided against Townsend over the high-level campaign against Labour's record on poverty and the accuracy of its report. Part of the explanation for the splits lay in the approach of these social policy pioneers. While Townsend and Lynes were campaigners as well as researchers, Titmuss was very much the hands-off academic, if one with strong views on social policy. 'Both Lynes and Townsend had', as Titmuss' daughter Ann Oakley describes it, 'entered into the uncertain land between public policy and activism. This wasn't a place with which Richard Titmuss felt at home.'[6]

About-turn

In June 1970, with Labour unexpectedly losing the general election, Edward Heath became prime minister. Although the state-schooled Heath was known as a 'one nation' Tory, a phrase first coined by Disraeli, he campaigned on building a smaller state. This high-profile shift away from the broad pro-welfare consensus emerged from a shadow cabinet brainstorming at the Selsdon Park Hotel in South London a few months before the election. In the event, Heath's pro-market conversion, an attempt to capitalise on what was perceived as waning public support for welfare, was short lived. Rising unemployment and a spurt in inflation forced Heath into a rapid U-turn. As one historian described it, 'The government now went from the extreme of non-intervention to new heights of corporatism.'[7]

For a quarter of a century after the War, a tiny cluster of thinkers on the right, influenced by the libertarian and free market evangelist Ayn Rand, had argued that the egalitarian drive had gone too far, that earnings differentials were excessively squeezed and that the tax system had become too progressive.[8] They had been mobilised by Friedrich von Hayek, the leading post-war prophet of small government, who had joined the LSE in 1931. When he published his anti-state tract *The Road to Serfdom* in 1944, he was swimming against the tide of mainstream opinion.[9]

In the same year Karl Polanyi had published *The Great Transformation*, his critique of a 'market society'. Taking the polar opposite view to Hayek, Polanyi attacked what he saw as the destructive nature of the dogmatic market fundamentalism of the pre-war era, condemning it for its 'stark Utopia'.[10] Neither work made much impact at the time, even in the United States. *The Road to Serfdom* had been rejected by several publishers before being taken by the University of Chicago Press.

Hayek dedicated his book to 'The Socialists of All Parties.' While his anti-welfare views did not sit comfortably with the mood of the times, he set about laying the groundwork for the counter-attack that was eventually to come. In 1947 he helped establish the Mont Pèlerin Society, an international network of ideologues. It was named after a Swiss spa where the founders met that year at the Hotel du Parc. Other attendees included the philosopher Karl Popper and the libertarian economist Ludwig von Mises. The society's strategy was to influence 'makers of opinions' through the establishment of think tanks such as the American Enterprise Association in the United States.

In the UK, the Westminster-based Institute of Economic Affairs (IEA) was founded in 1955. Led by 'full frontal market economists', the IEA's goal was to spread the teachings of Hayek, and later, the outspoken Chicago-based Milton Friedman.[11] The architect of monetarism, Friedman was another exponent of free market capitalism, and had also attended the Mont Pèlerin meeting. 'Our basic function', wrote Friedman, 'is to develop alternatives to existing policies, to keep them alive and available until the politically impossible becomes the politically inevitable'.[12]

In the 1970s, Hayek and Friedman were both awarded the Nobel Memorial Prize for Economics. It was a prize that had been created, controversially, by the Swedish central bank in 1969, seventy years after the original five awards were founded. The prize helped lift the reputations of both men and contributed to the rise of their market philosophies. Eight members of the Mont Pèlerin Society received the Nobel, while between 1990 and 1995, five out of six prizes were awarded to academics at the University of Chicago, the spiritual home of market fundamentalism. Although those with more sceptical views on the power of markets were chosen at times, a number of high-profile scholars such as Barbara Wootton (one of six remarkable women chosen for the 1984 BBC series *Women of Our Century*) and John Kenneth Galbraith were ignored.

Another to be ignored was the highly influential Cambridge theorist, Joan Robinson. Robinson helped to develop Keynes' theories, upended Alfred Marshall's standard text-book theory of competition among firms, and shattered the myth of a world of competition and of free markets. She was one of the first economists to show how corporate concentration and a tendency to monopoly was not just undermining competition but, by concentrating bargaining power, was also able to suppress wages over long periods.[13] Rewarding pro-market theorists above all others was contentious and might well have encouraged the subsequent shift in the ideological tectonic plates away from social democratic thinking. Alfred Nobel's descendants have repeatedly asked for their family name to be removed from the Economics prize, and repeatedly been ignored. Peter Nobel, the great-grandson of Alfred Nobel's brother Ludwig, calls it 'a cuckoo's egg in the Nobel nest'.[14]

One of the New Right's targets was John Maynard Keynes. Keynes had been the power economic thinker of the age, while post-war economies, domestic and global, very much his construction, enjoyed much greater success compared with the interwar years. During the 1960s, welfarism and Keynesianism retained their hold over global policymakers, with radical voices on the right confined to the political wilderness. But gradually, the debate about the way forward became more polarised. With New Right theorists demanding a smaller state, and left critics calling for more comprehensive reforms, the battle lines of the next fifty years were being drawn. At first, the pro-welfare lobby got the better of these clashing views, but began to lose the argument in the crisis years of the 1970s.

Burying Beveridge

Poverty was given some prominence in the main political parties' 1970 manifestos. Labour's mentioned it nine times, though with a cautionary note: 'We never thought, or promised, that the job of ending poverty ... would be an easy one.' The question of inequality got much less attention. Despite the Conservative's flirtation with rolling back welfare, Heath exploited Labour's discomfort over CPAG's allegations, and gave poverty seven manifesto mentions.[15]

The election left a number of social policy issues hanging. The Treasury had been opposed to Labour's partial reform of family allowances and child tax allowances, and favoured a new means-tested benefit for poorer working families. CPAG, along with a number of social policy academics, supported a 'Back-to-Beveridge' approach to social security reform by raising benefit levels and maintaining universalism. Strongly opposed to an extension of means testing, the group continued to push for the conversion of child tax allowances and family allowances into a single cash payment. David Donnison, later chair of the Supplementary Benefits Commission, used to quip, in an entirely friendly way: 'Whatever question you ask the Child Poverty Action Group, universalism would be the answer.' In the event, Macleod, who had promised to raise family allowances, died a month after the election, and was replaced as chancellor by Anthony Barber.

The next step fell into the lap of Keith Joseph, the new secretary of state for social services. Joseph was a wealthy baronet, and had gained a reputation, according to his biographer, as a man 'who wanted to pull down all of society's safety nets'.[16] But Joseph was a more complex figure. By his own admission, he carried a sense of guilt about being rich. The cerebral Joseph studied the options in detail, and in the end lined up with the Treasury and their long-favoured, ready-made plan for a new means-tested benefit – Family Income Supplement (FIS). As Crossman had warned, the Conservative's pre-election promise was discarded.

FIS, developed by civil servants, topped low wages up to a fixed ceiling, with the benefit withdrawn at a rate of 50 per cent as wages rose. The move was highly controversial. The new means-tested benefit was reminiscent of the pre-1834 Speenhamland system of wage supplementation, with the new supplement filling the gap between earnings and a set minimum income. While CPAG launched attack after attack on the new scheme, its introduction was a signal of the future direction of social policy. The issue of take-up, which failed to rise much above 60 per cent over the next five years, was only part of the problem.[17] The social security system had already begun to drift away from Beveridge's original plan for universalism with its emphasis on the rights of citizenship. Governments, Conservative and Labour, showed a growing preference for selectivity, despite the past memories and attendant problems of stigma, complexity and confusion. Means-tested benefits singled out those applying, while qualification became the proof of poverty. They carried a very different message from universalism, not of entitlement but of 'them' and 'us', of dependency, of being second class.

The case for means testing was that a given level of cash support would go further if it was concentrated on the poorest. All social security systems involve a tension between meeting need and containing costs, and it was the cost pressure that had been winning the argument. In 1958, the director of the Conservative Political Centre had criticised 'squandering public money on providing indiscriminate benefits for citizens, many of whom do not need them'.[18] The principle of selectivity also came to be applied in other policy areas such as health prescriptions and council housing. The Wilson governments had already turned to selectivity to cover gaps in social security. In 1967, the former Labour cabinet minister Douglas Houghton argued that universalism was 'on the defensive'.[19] The growth of means testing was never part of a grand plan. It evolved gradually. Each new benefit – from the introduction of free school meals to rent and rate rebates – had its own rationale.

By the mid-1970s Britain's social security system had become heavily targeted, with means-testing accounting for a growing share of all benefit spending. Beveridge was being quietly buried. In addition to FIS, rent and rate rebates, rent allowances for private tenants and free school meals, there was means testing for prescriptions, dental treatment, welfare foods and a great variety of local services. Although the new benefits could deliver significant help to those on low income, selectivity brought a further erosion of the principle of national insurance. It also meant advertising campaigns, the use of euphemisms by officials, from 'income-testing' to 'targeting', a maze of complexity and form-filling and complicated qualifying conditions that left increasing numbers 'lost in the welfare jungle'.[20]

One consequence of piling means test on means test was for incentives. As people moved into work or secured higher earnings, they would pay additional tax and national insurance contributions while benefits would be proportionately withdrawn. Low-income families were caught in a 'poverty trap', facing a high marginal withdrawal rate, a significant cap on their ability to rise much above poverty-level incomes. What was being built was a tight income ceiling for the poorest, a cap on progress that was increasingly difficult to breach in an economy with widespread low pay, a falling tax threshold and weakening opportunities.

Despite buoyant wage growth on average, low pay among the unskilled and semi-skilled remained widespread, especially among women. Abel-Smith and Townsend found low pay to be a significant cause of poverty in the 1960s, just as Booth and Rowntree had found six decades earlier. While the stronger union movement helped to boost aggregate wages, that strength was also used to maintain differentials for skilled workers, and between men and women. Women were also much less likely to be unionised. Beveridge had ducked the issue of low pay and a minimum wage. Instead, this was dealt with through the 1945 Wages Councils Act. This built on the existing patchy system of wages councils to fix wage minimums in other low-pay sectors such as hairdressing and certain forms of manufacturing. This fell well short of establishing a legal right to a minimum wage, a gap that was not finally filled until 2000. As a result, being in work was still not a guarantee of avoiding poverty.

Because of the flaws of multiple means testing, there was growing interest about whether targeted help could be delivered more effectively through a greater integration of the tax and benefit system, without reliance on, as the *Times* put it, 'any overt or invidious income test'.[21] The possibility of a single unified tax/benefit system was also being debated in the United States at the end of the 1960s in the form of a negative income tax. Advocated by Milton Friedman, such a scheme would top up low incomes through the personal tax system. Friedman's plan, however, offered only minimal support. It was designed merely to relieve destitution and as a route to cutting other social spending. The Heath government flirted with a proposal for a 'tax credit scheme' along similar, if more generous lines, but the idea was quietly dropped.

There had also been a long-standing parallel, if somewhat marginalised, debate about the idea of a 'universal basic income for all', in which all citizens would receive a guaranteed, no-questions-asked weekly income, one delivered directly and not through the tax system. Its aim was to boost universality, cut reliance on means testing and promote greater social resilience.[22] Such an idea had been advocated by a long line of thinkers over several centuries. During the 1940s, the Liberal Party political activist Lady Juliet Rhys-Williams had argued for a universal basic income or 'social dividend' to cover subsistence need. The introduction of family allowances could be seen as the first example of such a social dividend for children. Rhys-Williams' plan was in many ways more radical than Beveridge's. It would, for the first time, have guaranteed an income floor and shifted the emphasis of the benefit system away from its conception by some as state charity to one based more fully on citizen's rights. Her scheme was also less gendered than Beveridge's assumptions of the ideal family.[23]

The idea of a guaranteed basic income for all continued to be pushed by small groups of academics and campaigners, as well as internationally, but was widely dismissed as utopian and failed to find favour with most reformers and politicians. It was not until after 2010 that the idea began to move from the fringes of debate, with a number of detailed proposals offering a progressive reform of what was about to become a greatly weakened social security system.[24]

The social record of the Heath government was mixed. Despite the economic pressures, some social security gaps were filled. An improved Attendance Allowance was introduced for those needing care at home, the scope of widow's benefit was extended and there were new pensions for the over-eighties. In a further break with the regressive flat-rate principle, contributions became a percentage of earnings from 1975, though with an upper earnings limit.

In contrast to these advances, different rates between long- and short-term benefits were set. These brought a more generous rate for pensioners and those on invalidity benefit, compared with a lower rate for the unemployed and the sick. This distinction was highly controversial among officials and campaigners. It introduced an explicit two-tier benefit system, resurrecting the pre-1948 distinction between the 'deserving' and 'undeserving' poor and taking the British social security system a step back into the past. One expert described the move as 'the start of harsher treatment for the unemployed compared to other claimants and particularly for the long-term unemployed'.[25]

What eventually sank the Heath government was the emergence of the first full-blown economic crisis since the 1930s. Heath's regime coincided with the early signs of 'stagflation', with the inflation rate rising from 5 per cent in 1969 to 25 per cent in 1975. As inflation rose, so did unemployment. When unemployment first hit a million in January 1972, angry outbursts in the House of Commons from the Labour benches forced the speaker to suspend the sitting. The number of days lost through strikes rose sharply, while there was similar unrest in Italy, Germany and in the United States.[26] One simple measure of public well-being, 'the misery index', calculated by adding the inflation and unemployment rate, rose sharply to peak at 30 per cent during the 1970s.

The crisis had multiple roots, many of them external: a dramatic hike in oil prices, intensified global competition and the waning of productivity rates (output per worker) in a number of developed economies. The stable post-war global monetary system built on exchange rate stability was dismantled unilaterally by the American president Richard Nixon in 1971, precipitating global currency speculation with no effort to develop a replacement. The end of the successful Bretton Woods system set the world on the path to a new era of unfettered globalisation, with its opening up of capital flows and the international outsourcing of jobs.

To tackle rising unemployment and falling industrial output, the chancellor, in what turned out to be a reckless move, initiated a substantial monetary boost – the 'Barber boom' – which added to inflationary pressures and the bust that followed. Industrial unrest spread in the face of unemployment, successive attempts at wage curbs and wage-earners' determination to retain the greater share they had secured in the post-war years. The confrontation with the National Union of Mineworkers over the counter-inflation incomes policy, bringing power cuts and a three-day-week, led to Heath calling a general election on 'who governs Britain'. In March 1974, Wilson returned to Downing Street – for the third time – in charge of a minority government facing deepening crisis.

11

Consolidation or advance?

Labour had several items of unfinished business from the 1960s. One of them was inequality. Its 1974 manifesto called for 'a fundamental and irreversible shift in the balance of power and wealth in favour of working people and their families and to eliminate poverty wherever it exists in Britain'.[1] It was some promise. There were echoes here of the 1945 manifesto, which had challenged the way business elites acted like 'totalitarian oligarchies within our democratic state' without 'any responsibility to the nation'.[2]

For three decades, social democracy – and its European counterpart, Christian democracy – had been a powerful progressive political force. Living standards had risen and welfare states been built, if of varying strengths.[3] In the UK, tax revenue had risen to nearly 40 per cent of national income by the mid-1970s compared with 8–10 per cent in the pre-1914 years. Labour was now proposing a further step along the social democratic path with a new and highly ambitious goal, to make further strides towards greater equality.

A doomed species?

Progress towards this goal had already been made. The post-war years had seen a further, if gentle, dilution of top fortunes that had begun as a trickle in earlier decades.[4] Changing social values had also brought a check on expectations among the 'old gang'. The earlier era, when huge fortunes could be made in commerce and business, were yet to be replaced by the voracious financial dealmaking that was to come not that much later. There were fewer examples of the pre-war displays of extravagance and the open flaunting of wealth. 'Ostentation was becoming vulgar', wrote Crosland in 1956.[5] In 1963, at the Royal Variety Show, John Lennon asked people in the cheaper seats to clap and the rest to 'rattle your jewellery'. The landed gentry continued to bemoan their plight. 'The wealthy, especially those who had inherited their wealth, appeared to be a doomed species, scheduled for extinction', declared the wealth historian William Rubinstein, a signed-up member of the laissez-faire fan club.[6]

While in the nineteenth century the wealth boom at the top came with impoverishment at the bottom, many of the mechanisms that had been driving greater equality also brought lower rates of poverty, if a long way from its elimination. These included a more comprehensive benefit system, full employment, private sector rent controls, subsidised social housing, higher tax rates on top incomes and growth in the proportion of women in work.

These mechanisms raised lower incomes while taming some of the forces favouring the richest members of society. A critical pro-equality factor was the improvement in the bargaining power of labour. The share of national output going to wages settled at a consistently higher rate compared with the pre-war era. Business had to live with lower profits and a better-paid and more demanding workforce. Far from being damaging to capitalism, the boost to aggregate wages raised living standards and helped to sustain the demand that was central to higher levels of growth.

None of this meant that the inequality issue had finally been settled. Data on trends in income inequality at the time, even across the broad range of incomes – there were few figures on what was happening at the extremes – was severely limited and 'characterized by almost unmatched control of the state over the numbers'.[7] The best, mostly independent, if somewhat contradictory evidence at the time – stronger evidence became available later – was that the egalitarian trend was at its sharpest between the late 1930s and early 1950s but then moved at a slower pace.[8] While the richest continued to lose income share, this process did not percolate much beyond the middle point of the income chain. The main gainers were the affluent middle classes, while the bottom half gained only 0.8 percentage points in share between 1949 and 1976.[9]

This was equally true of wealth, with the trend towards greater equality of asset ownership largely confined to the top half of the distribution and the 'patrimonial middle classes'. The key drivers of this process – the growth of pension entitlement and home ownership – had barely touched those below the middle. For all the political and social changes at work, the poorest half's share of property, company shares and savings peaked in the mid-1980s at around a tenth, but then started slipping back, while the top one and ten per cent's share started to rise again.[10] There is also evidence that the rate of wealth equalisation in the fifty years from 1920 has been overstated because of the growing use of mechanisms to disguise real levels of wealth.[11] As long as capital assets were overwhelmingly owned by a small slice of society, even if rates of returns had been falling, there was a built-in limit to the degree of equality that could be achieved.

Another constraint on the equalisation process was the growth of a parallel 'welfare system' – a system of subsidies, tax reliefs and fringe occupational benefits – that overwhelmingly benefitted the rich and affluent. Examples included employer contributions to private healthcare and tax relief on mortgage interest payments for homebuyers. In the mid-1970s, the system of housing support was not just expensive but highly regressive, with the greatest subsidies going to those with the highest incomes.[12] There was no lack of pressure on governments through the 1970s to implement a phased reduction in pro-inequality tax relief on mortgage payments. Such relief was not fully abolished until 2001, while the value of other reliefs continued to mount over time. As Titmuss had warned, 'There are other forces, deeply rooted in the social structures and fed by many institutional factors inherent in large-scale economies, operating in reverse directions [against equality].'[13]

Although the political climate was more lukewarm to the scale of personal wealth-making of the past, a small group of business tycoons turned to controversial ways of making big money in the boom conditions of the 1950s and 1960s. Property developers such as Joe Levy and Harry Hyams made fortunes from exploiting loopholes in planning laws and surging rents for offices. The financier Charles Clore pioneered the hostile takeover bid, becoming reviled as a destructive corporate raider. Workers lost their jobs while Clore made a killing. Clement Attlee once referred darkly to 'nature red in tooth and claw – particularly Clore'.[14] Clore was part of a small group of ruthless financiers that included Jim Slater, James Hanson, Gordon White and James Goldsmith. Together they set out to challenge the post-war politics of consensus.

Goldsmith was educated at Eton where he gained his ruthless streak. The day he left, he offered the headmaster a recording of *The Marriage of Figaro*. As the delighted headmaster moved to take the present, Goldsmith dropped it – deliberately. The group became known as the 'Mayfair set' because of their regular attendance at John Aspinall's Clermont gambling club in London's Berkeley Square. None of them were conventional entrepreneurs. They rarely added to the size of the cake by making anything new, building a company from scratch or introducing more productive methods. They built giant fortunes through dismantling and engineering the balance sheets of existing companies, a new instrument of wealth extraction that was to accelerate in later years as business controls were weakened and the political climate towards personal wealth accumulation relaxed. Such activities helped lead to a revival in the number and size of top fortunes during the 1970s, checking the decline seen in the immediate post-war years and renewing interest in the lives of the rich.[15] In 1969, the *Daily Express* published the first example of a British rich list, one dominated by dynastic families, if based on a strong element of guesswork.

Spreading wealth

In opposition in the 1950s, Labour's revisionist wing had flirted with radical ideas on wealth. Despite the claim from some critics that Labour was more interested in 'consolidation' than 'advance', some leading figures in the party had come to accept that the post-war reforms were indispensable but not sufficient to build a permanently more equal society. The main instrument used in 1945 to tackle the question of property ownership and the power that came with it was the state ownership of key industries, but this did little to empower ordinary workers. It was now felt that further nationalisation was not the route to greater equality.

The question of property ownership, its distribution and how much should be socially owned had been a preoccupation of the early social reformers. As Leonard Hobhouse had put it, they had to find 'some way of securing for the State the ultimate ownership of the natural sources of wealth and of the accumulation of past generations'.[16] The Webbs made a similar point: the central wrong of the capitalist system is 'the power which the mere ownership of the instruments of production gives to a relatively small section of the community over the actions of their fellow citizens and over the mental and physical environment of successive generations'.[17] For Tawney, there wasn't a problem with private ownership as such, as long as it had a function, and for him and others, spreading its ownership was about giving people more security and autonomy.[18]

In 1955, Labour's leader Hugh Gaitskell convened a working party on the way forward on egalitarianism, while there were wider attempts to develop policies to spread wealth across society. Ideas examined included progressive taxes on wealth, ways to spread capital gains, the diffusion of private property ownership and new forms of social ownership other than state nationalisation, measures that moved beyond the 'top down' to ones with a potential to diffuse wealth.[19]

One of the first to advocate a 'property-owning democracy' for all was a young economist, James Meade, who had headed the economic section of the Cabinet Office from 1946–47. 'If private property were much more equally divided we should achieve the "mixed" citizen – both worker and property owner at the same time', he wrote in a paper for the Labour Party in 1948, a potentially transformative idea he was to expand on in later years.[20] Meade had worked with Keynes and was an adviser to the Wilson governments of the 1960s and later the SDP/Liberal alliance. His ideas also drew on the work of earlier progressive thinkers. These included Thomas Paine in the late eighteenth century, Hobhouse, Tawny, J.II. Hobson's distinction between 'property' and 'improperty' and a group of contemporary 'left Keynesians' including Roy Harrod, Keynes' first biographer, and Joan Robinson.

Pro-equality thinkers had long argued that wealth inequality, and the growth of 'unearned' income, was a central source of injustice. It was accepted that property rights are necessary to encourage security and reward merit, and that rent, interest and profits along with the savings of the rich play an important functional role in economic development, including as a reward for risk. But these returns, they claimed, were often excessive, while legitimate gains could be much more widely shared through the diffusion of private property and their returns.

Apart from the introduction of a capital gains tax in 1965 – which generated less revenue than predicted – none of these ideas were taken further by Labour in the 1960s, though they continued to be developed by others, including Meade. Contrary to Kuznets, he believed that inequality was set to become a growing problem, driven by the way accelerated automation would increase the return to capital, lower the wage share and unleash greater workforce insecurity. In this he anticipated a number of future trends, including the fall in the wage share from the early 1980s, the new robotic revolution and the rise in work insecurity.

Following other Liberal and Labour figures, Meade – later a Nobel laureate – argued for the spreading of capital ownership, not by the state buying up and managing private firms but by society establishing a growing stake in national assets through the creation of a publically owned social fund. Returns on the fund could then be used to pay 'an equal social dividend to each citizen'. This was a variation on earlier ideas for a basic income for all, including the Webbs' call for a guaranteed national minimum paid as of right to all citizens. Meade, who argued that tax and benefits alone, however progressive, would not be sufficient to achieve 'a really substantial equalisation', was pressing the case for rethinking the dominance of individual property rights in favour of a greater emphasis on collective property ownership.[21] This was a very different vision from the model of a private property-owning democracy later advocated by Mrs Thatcher.

In 1973, an opposition green paper – *Capital and Equality* – set out a new framework for socialising a proportion of private wealth.[22] The study group behind the green paper included Barbara Castle and Labour's leading economic adviser Sir Nicholas Kaldor. Labour's ideas for tackling rentiers had moved on from the top-down political economy and nationalised corporations of 1945, and were edging closer to the pleas of the libertarian socialist and Fabian G.D.H. Cole for greater workplace democracy and power-sharing.

Among the range of measures proposed was, drawing on Meade, a national capital fund owned by all citizens. If implemented, even in part, it would have moved the debate on from the public ownership of industry and put some real meat on clause 4 of Labour's constitution. This had been drafted in 1917 and called on the party to 'secure for the workers by hand or by brain the full fruits of their industry and the most equitable distribution thereof that may be possible upon the basis of the common ownership of the means of production, distribution and exchange'. The fund, which would have taken clause 4 to a level beyond tokenism, would have been financed by the compulsory annual issue of new shares – of the order of 1 per cent of the total equity – by all companies over a given size. One aim of the scheme was the goal of 'extending opportunities for economic democracy, by giving fund members – through their ownership of shares – direct powers over key financial decisions such as mergers, capital movements or investment in overseas subsidiaries'.[23] A similar idea for a state investment fund, with estate tax paid in assets so that society would participate in the gains from rising asset values, had also been considered, but rejected, by Labour in the 1950s.[24]

If adopted, such a strategy would have challenged perhaps the key institutional driver of an unequal society – the concentrated ownership of capital. By locking in part of the gain from economic activity to be shared evenly across society, it would have taken the social reforms of 1945 a significant step further.

One variant of the idea was implemented by the Swedish Social Democratic government in 1982. They introduced local 'wage-earner funds'. These were created by the gradual transfer of a small portion of corporate wealth and gave local trade unions considerable power over the assets transferred. Unpopular with business, and lacking much public support, in part because of the dominant role played by unions, the funds were axed by the incoming Conservatives in 1991, by which time they had grown to be worth some 7 per cent of the economy. In one sense the great ambitions of the 1970s that had given birth to this experiment in socialisation ended in defeat. While a sign of the political limits to the Swedish experiment in social democracy, the plan was implemented at a time when the right was seizing the intellectual ascendancy.[25]

That half the British population still held only a minuscule share of private wealth, and the wealth gap greatly exceeded the income gap, was a significant hole in the social democratic legacy. Although Labour dropped the idea for a capital fund, they maintained a commitment to higher taxes on wealth. As the shadow chancellor Denis Healey told Labour's 1973 conference at Blackpool: 'There are going to be howls of anguish from the rich.' In 1974, the new government published a green paper on taxing wealth, though one that was vague on how this might be achieved.[26] The party 'apparently had very little idea of what they wanted or what the implications might be', according to one tax expert, while a Commons Select Committee report split four ways on its merits.[27]

The government did implement one important reform on wealth. In 1975, despite widespread hostility from the business lobby, they introduced a more comprehensive capital transfer tax (covering lifetime transfers) to replace estate duty – introduced in 1894 – which, according to Healey, had become 'a laughing stock'.[28] But because of a range of widely exploited concessions, its yield was low. The take from all wealth taxes as a proportion of tax revenue halved between 1964–65 and 1976–77.[29]

The traditional route for governments trying for consensus solutions to tricky political problems is to appoint a royal commission. Although Wilson himself once quipped that such commissions 'take minutes and waste years', he appointed one on the distribution of income and wealth. The commission was chaired by Lord Diamond, a widely respected former Labour treasury minister, and described by the *Sunday Telegraph* as 'an amiable socialist'.[30]

Following a second general election in October, 1974 – in which the party gained a narrow majority of three seats – Healey announced that a wealth tax would not be introduced. This was not the first time that Labour would get political cold feet over its manifesto promises or rethink their position on wealth inequality and the issue of inheritance. In his memoirs, Healey explained: 'I found it impossible to draft [a wealth tax] that would yield enough revenue to be worth the administrative cost and political hassle.'[31] This was a signal that, at that time, British social democracy, and Labour's 'crisis of philosophical belief', was unable to find a politically acceptable way of delivering the greater equalisation of the rising pool of privately owned wealth.[32] From then, the debate on the issue of wealth concentration stayed largely on the sidelines until some revival of interest following the 2008 financial crisis.

Peak equality

Despite being a minority government, Labour made several improvements to the benefits system. The most important was a controversial innovation that was to have a significant positive impact on the living standards of families, even if it had to be wrestled out of a reluctant leadership. In both 1974 manifestos, Labour committed to the measure campaigned for by CPAG, a new tax-free child benefit for all children to replace child tax allowances and family allowances.

This commitment was incorporated in the 1975 Child Benefit Act, passed with cross-party support. By then the living standards of families had been eroded by the falling value of benefits for children and a shift in the burden of taxation towards families.[1] In the event, Harold Wilson resigned in March 1976. Faced with mounting economic problems, the new prime minister, Jim Callaghan, a former trade union official and a wily operator, was eventually forced into accepting a loan from the Washington-based International Monetary Fund (IMF). The loan – the largest the fund had ever given – came with a tough condition: significant public spending cuts. This was a painful political requirement that meant a cut in the 'social wage' – the gains to individuals from the provision of public services such as free education and healthcare. The social wage was a key part of the goal to provide all with a decent social minimum.

The battle for child benefit

Callaghan was concerned that transferring tax allowances, mainly benefitting fathers, to child benefit paid to mothers would further boost inflation-fuelled pay demands. As chancellor in 1967 he had backed the Treasury's pet scheme for a new means-tested benefit over raising the value of family allowances. As with the issue of equal pay, the male-dominated trade unions were far from cheerleaders for the move. Mostly representing well-paid workers, the union movement had a mixed record on campaigning for the low-paid and reducing pay differentials. They had supported free public services but were more lukewarm about in-work cash benefits, which some union leaders saw as undermining the negotiating rights of workers. As Jack Jones put it in 1972, over-reliance on benefits to fight poverty would make 'virtual State pensioners of hundreds of thousands of ordinary healthy men and women'.[2]

In May 1976 it was announced that the child benefit plan had been scrapped and that instead, family allowance would be extended to the first child. Frank Field, still director of CPAG, was leaked the minutes of the cabinet meetings at which the decision to ditch this double manifesto commitment was taken. In an anonymous article in the weekly journal *New Society*, he published details of the cabinet's bitter wrangling over the issue.[3] Echoing the US Watergate scandal, he called his source 'Deep Throat'.

The minutes revealed the duplicity and misinformation used by Callaghan and the chancellor, Denis Healey. They included a report to cabinet from the chief whip, Michael Cocks, warning that the withdrawal of fathers' tax breaks could not be sold to the electorate. Although Cocks claimed his report was based on a survey of backbenchers, they had never been consulted. The episode revealed, Field wrote, 'the ease with which a majority of the Cabinet can be stampeded against a long-term commitment of the party'.[4] The furore over the way the cabinet had been misled dominated the news agenda, while the internal wrangling was a portent of just how hard fought the struggle for further progressive change would be.

With the negative publicity and growing external pressure from the Church of England synod and women's organisations, Callaghan caved in. Child benefit was to be phased in to reach £4 a week per child by April 1979. The battle had been won, but only in part: the relative value of family support remained lower than in the 1950s and 1960s.[5]

Field went to great lengths to protect his source from the subsequent leak enquiry, which involved the fingerprinting of civil servants and the tapping of Field's phones. He burned the papers he had received. The source of the leak, kept a secret by Field for twenty-eight years, was Malcolm Wicks, a senior official in the Home Office at the time, with access to a range of Whitehall papers. Wicks, who died in 2012 aged sixty-five, became a Labour MP from 1992, and later a minister. He revealed his role in his posthumous autobiography *My Life,* published in 2014, in which he wrote of his outrage about 'the manoeuvring, the downright lies and the attempt to play off Labour MPs against trade union bigwigs.'[6]

Child benefit was a significant anti-poverty instrument: it extended cash help to the first child, paid benefits to mothers, raised the level of universalism, reduced dependency on means testing and improved the incentive to work. Crucially, it was a benefit that helped all families, not just the poorest, thereby gaining the support of the 'sharp elbows of the middle classes'. Without Wicks' intervention, the new benefit might never have happened. It was, however, far from the end of its story.

Statistical darkness

Although Labour fell well short of the radicalism of its manifesto, there were other improvements in social protection. As in 1965, one of the earliest acts of the first 1974 government was to honour a commitment to raise pension rates well above the increase in prices and earnings. There was also the introduction of statutory maternity leave and new benefits for those with disabilities. Labour also tried to remedy the inadequacy of the flat-rate state pension by introducing the State Earnings Related Pension Scheme (SERPS), an update of a 1960s' Labour scheme that had fallen because of the general election. SERPS, which replaced an inferior scheme introduced by the Heath government, would eventually top up pensions, lifting more out of poverty. However, large numbers with occupational pensions opted out and the plan did little in the short term to lower the high dependence of pensioners on Supplementary Benefit. Poverty rates at the time were especially high among pensioners, despite the 1974 rises.

While the social security system was strengthened for pensioners and children, the differential between long- and short-term benefit rates widened further. As one study concluded, 'The government was able to temper the effects of the recession for some. ... It was not able to prevent the greater intensification of difficulty for many families of working age.'[7] There was still no strategy for low pay. In January 1979, the London *Evening Standard* carried case studies of low-paid workers: a gardener, a domestic, a gravedigger, a nurse, a caretaker and a porter.[8]

The Diamond Commission sat for nearly five years, but economic turbulence helped to neutralise its impact. To illustrate the day-to-day realities of low incomes, several people were invited to give evidence. A disabled mother of three, a former state-registered nurse, separated from her husband, explained that her weekly income was almost 30 per cent short of what was necessary for the barest of living standards. Her children "were aware that they were deprived in comparison with their friends: they had little, if any, pocket money; they could not join in school activities that entailed payment; they did not have holidays". A second witness, married with two children and suffering from a congenital heart condition, had been unemployed for two years, despite applying for over one hundred jobs in that time. He had exhausted his entitlement to unemployment benefit but could not obtain Supplementary Benefit because of his wife's earnings.[9] In their evidence, the Campaign for the Homeless and Rootless estimated there were at least 100,000 single people on low incomes with no permanent or secure home, many of whom had been homeless for years.

While it published eight comprehensive reports which greatly improved the documentation of inequality, the commission's overall impact was limited. Ministers and officials attempted to exercise some control over its work, while some of its reports were embarrassing to Labour. The party, for example, unsuccessfully attempted to suppress the seventh report, which concluded that the purchasing power of the poorest had fallen under Labour.[10] Britain's powerful business lobby submitted evidence calling for a rise in the incomes of top executives and a lowering of their tax burden.[11] In response, the commission made a detailed examination of trends in managerial pay, in part to examine the claim by business of a 'brain drain' because of an alleged fall in top relative pay. The analysis showed that while British managers were sometimes paid less than their counterparts in some rich countries, comparative pay among the lower paid was also less than their peers elsewhere.

The media loved to cherry pick the evidence, and the submission by the Confederation of British Industry received more publicity than any of the other findings. While there had been no rise in the migration of managers, the *Daily Mail* attacked the government for 'deliberately trying to drive Britain's managerial class into inertia or emigration'.[12] According to one study, the commission's findings 'were rarely used to justify greater moves towards income and wealth equality, but rather to … make the case that Britain was too equal'.[13]

Governments had long kept a firm grip over official statistics. The important Central Statistical Office study of the distributional impact of public spending, for example, was initially circulated only within parts of Whitehall. During the 1970s there was resistance from several countries, including the UK, to attempts by the United Nations to provide internationally comparable data on inequality. As a result, cross-country inequality comparisons were not produced until the 1990s, when the deadlock was broken by an independent research institute, the Luxembourg Income Study. Britain also lobbied against the anti-poverty programmes of the European Community. As one Treasury official explained, 'One of our concerns has been to try to put off the day when international social reporting would result in league tables, providing possible fuel to UK social expenditure lobbies.'[14] In the late 1970s, the Central Statistical Office killed off calls for a new wealth survey which the Diamond Commission 'regarded as one of the most pressing concerns'.[15] This 'statistical darkness' meant continuing uncertainty about important social trends including changes in poverty and inequality.

A harsh lesson on the politics of distribution

During the 1970s, there had been progress in upgrading Beveridge. A statutory commitment to regular inflation uprating and the end of the flat-rate National Insurance stamp along with the introduction of the new SERPS and universal child benefit were significant reforms. Wage inequality was lower than in the pre-war period and the tax system was broadly redistributive. The social security system, for all its limitations, remained a powerful tool for relieving hardship and poverty.[16]

Nevertheless, there was a limit to the role that the tax and benefit system alone could play in tackling poverty, while Labour's periods in office in the 1960s and 1970s – beset by fragile majorities and day-to-day firefighting – failed to deliver the kind of social policy leap forward their supporters had hoped for. Labour made few attempts to build a more multifaceted anti-poverty strategy aimed at narrowing the income and wealth gap before the benefit system came into play by, for example, introducing a minimum wage, creating the pro-equality capital fund developed in opposition or reforming the 'shadow welfare state' of pro-rich tax breaks. The total sum spent on tax allowances was estimated at £26 billion in 1978 compared with total public spending of £65 billion.[17]

Labour received a good deal of flak for its social policy record, not least from often-bleak television dramas – such as Tony Garnet's and Jim Allen's *The Spongers* in 1978, about a struggling single parent. But the record needs to be judged against the economic convulsions of the time. The Wilson and Callaghan governments were battling to arrest Britain's relative economic decline, while facing a growing ideological critique both from a resurgent left's attack on the limitations of reformism and from the new right's calls to roll back post-war welfare.

Despite these hurdles, and though there are no data sets on annual poverty rates on a consistent basis for the whole period from the end of the war, the line on poverty was just about held.[18] Moreover, in the long history of the poverty and inequality debate, the 1970s retains a special significance. While the full evidence did not become available until a good deal later, the mid-to-late 1970s was a period of peak *income* equality – an egalitarian high water mark.[19] The peak in the process of *wealth* equalisation came a little later, in the early-1980s. Peak equality was some achievement, even if it had multiple roots, and proved somewhat short lived. Indeed, the income gap began to widen shortly before the royal commissioners were forced to shut up shop. The record of the time, patchy as it might have been, was to prove distinctly superior to that of the decades that followed. For all its turbulence, the 1970s was as good as it was going to get in terms of the scale of poverty and inequality. David Edgerton called the decade 'the highest point' for social democracy in the UK.[20]

The seeds for reversal were already being sown. Thomas Piketty has called the progress under post-war social democracy 'an incomplete equality'. Even at its 1970s high point, the income share of the whole of the poorest half failed to get close to that of the richest 10 per cent.[21] In some ways, incomplete progress was written into mainstream Labour thinking. Crosland had argued that 'further redistribution [of income] would make little difference to the standard of living of the masses', and that the equality agenda should target 'social equality' through, for example, the reform of schooling.[22]

Between 1951 and 1976, two thirds of the proceeds of growth had been spent on boosting the social wage through better public services and building a stronger welfare state (even if spending on defence still took a significant share of all public spending).[23] Later in Labour's second term, buffeted by deteriorating public finances, a lower priority was given to social spending in the hope that this would boost the productive side of the economy. By the end of the 1970s, the wider debate had already begun to shift to issues such as the size of the state and the acceptable level of taxation.

There were also signs of a turning of opinion on welfare. The late 1960s brought the first wave of newspaper attacks on benefit claimants, a trend that accelerated over the next decade. Popular music lyrics – from the Kinks' 'Sunny Afternoon' to the Beatles' 'Taxman' – parodied the high top rates of tax of the 1960s. Pop stars joined entrepreneurs, businessmen, City dealers, footballers and television presenters exploiting tax avoidance schemes dreamt up by the big accountancy firms.

When Bianca Jagger divorced Mick Jagger in 1979, she revealed how the wealthy pop star was obsessed with avoiding paying taxes, not just in Britain. 'Throughout our married life, he and I literally lived out of a suitcase in a nomadic journey from one place to another in his quest to avoid income taxes.'[24] History was moving against social democracy. 'The intellectual mood of post-war Britain, still relatively homogeneous down to 1970, was changing fast', argued the historian Kenneth Morgan. 'In its wake was a growing disillusion with the Keynesian economists, the Fabian planners, the post-Beveridge social engineers, the consensual liberal positivists who had governed the realm like so many conquistadors for a quarter of a century.'[25]

Labour's leaders did not take the New Right seriously. Crosland dismissed them as 'froth'.[26] Yet even on the left there was a palpable sense that the welfare state was reaching its limits, as – without a commitment to more systemic change – was the capacity to do much more about poverty. Others warned of a 'fiscal crisis of the state' caused by a growing gap between public spending and tax revenue.[27]

Part of the explanation for the apparent tiring of the social democratic experiment lay in the state of the economy. The tools of economic management, so successful for the previous twenty-five years, proved less able to cope with inflation than stagnation, let alone both, while the 'disorganised capitalism' that was emerging, along with the brittle pro-welfare consensus of the 1950s, were ill-equipped to cope with the external shocks of the time.[28]

There was also a growing tension between the greater regulation of the economy and of the public provision of goods and services on the one hand, and as the social theorist, Ramesh Mishra suggested, the new 'context of individualism and the pursuit of self-interest' on the other.[29] Or as the economist Fred Hirsch explained, pessimistically and presciently, in his important 1978 book *The Social Limits to Growth*, we 'may be near the limit of explicit social organisation possible without a supporting social morality. Additional correctives in its absence simply do not take.'[30]

Others warned that the welfare state had come to be too heavily captured by those who worked in it. Officials, often pressurised and poorly paid themselves, came to play the role of gatekeepers – to homes, discretionary benefits and social help – and had an important impact on the 'outcome' of state policy. With the self-interest of state officials not always aligned with those of their clients, parts of the welfare state apparatus – from local housing departments to job centres – came to be seen by some of those in need as restrictive and unresponsive, helping to contribute to a growing sense of frustration and the political shift that was to follow.

Another emerging argument was that high state spending was starving the wealth-creating private sector. The idea of the public sector 'crowding out' the private was an old Treasury view, promoted in the 1920s and 1930s but disputed by Keynes. It was now resuscitated by two Oxford economists, Roger Bacon and Walter Eltis. In *Britain's Economic Problem: Too Few Producers*, their thesis seemed to offer an apparently simple explanation and solution for Britain's growing economic plight: there were too many social workers, teachers and civil servants and not enough workers in industry and commerce.[31]

This thesis was too simplistic. The economic problems of the 1970s had many roots, but according to later academic studies of the period, excessive state spending played only a minor role. Even simulations of the Treasury's own model at the time could find no crowding-out effect. Although there were some difficulties with financing the deficit, these seem to have derived 'from the much enhanced role played by the financial markets once Britain abandoned a fixed exchange rate in 1972, and the new circumstances occasioned by much higher levels of unemployment'.[32] The central economic issue of the time was not the public sector crowding out the private but waning international competitiveness and the mostly externally driven inflation. This particular interpretation also conveniently ignored other forms of 'crowding out', from the negative impact of private wealth-extraction mechanisms on the strength of the real economy, to the corporate process of swallowing up competitors that was to accelerate in future years.

The 1970s delivered a harsh lesson on the politics of distribution. Crosland's theory, conceived in the 'egalitarian optimism' of the boom years, was that the mild taming of capitalism combined with Keynesian fine-tuning would deliver the sustained economic growth necessary to secure redistribution without resistance from higher-income groups. The theory worked in the 1950s and 1960s. Finding the resources for the next steps proved a much harder call with faltering growth, rising unemployment and weakening public support. There were already signs in the second half of the 1970s of what was to come. Unemployment was up and the long-run decline in Britain's manufacturing base was gathering pace, while following the political heart-searching over the IMF demands, "the [public spending] party was over", as Tony Crosland put it in a speech in Manchester.[33]

Although she had yet to build a coherent political philosophy, Mrs Thatcher, who defeated Heath to become Conservative Party leader in 1975, was swift to exploit the fading fortunes of the social democratic model. New Right thinkers had been battling against Keynesianism for decades, but it took a Labour prime minister to write the first obituary. In response to the financial crisis and the IMF loan, Jim Callaghan told a shocked 1976 Labour conference that the days when 'you could spend your way out of recession' were gone. It would not be long before a new set of ideologues – sensing that 'the politically impossible' was about to become 'possible' – would take control of the political agenda.[34] Rocked by the 'Winter of Discontent' – the industrial disorder launched against the government's pay policy – and brought down by a parliamentary vote of no confidence – albeit by a majority of one – Labour lost the 1979 election. The ideological baton was passing on.

PART IV

1980–96

13

Don't mention the 'p' word

Despite their political differences, post-war governments of all colours had taken the question of poverty seriously. Living standards for most moved broadly in line with wider improvements in prosperity. That was about to change. The politics of sharing was to be slowly replaced by the priorities of the market. Judging that rising poverty could be tolerated with little political price, Mrs Thatcher set very different priorities. Under her watch, officials were banned from using the word 'poverty'.

This is what we believe

When Mrs Thatcher became Conservative Party leader, she was far from a fully signed-up member of her own fan club. On winning the leadership, the right-of-centre columnist Peregrine Worsthorne had advised her to get a better understanding of the Labour Party by reading Tawney. Thatcher was disillusioned with a politics of consensus, but it was not until she fell under the spell of pro-market thinkers, none more so than Friedrich von Hayek, that she began to develop a distinctive ideology. Hayek was the philosopher king of the right and a name she loved to drop. During speeches she would sometimes wave well-worn copies of his works, declaring: 'This is what we believe.'

Another key source of influence was Keith Joseph. After the 1974 election defeats, he renounced his high-spending ministerial days. 'I am steeping myself in Hayek', he wrote to Ralph Harris, director of the Institute of Economic Affairs. He established his own think tank to promote the guru's ideas and the case for laissez-faire. He considered calling it the Erhard Foundation, after Germany's former chancellor Ludwig Erhard, but ended up with the somewhat bland Centre for Policy Studies.[1] In April 1975, he presented a paper to the shadow cabinet, which firmly rejected 'the path of consensus'.[2]

Mrs Thatcher moved towards an individualist philosophy of market liberalism in steps. Only free markets, low taxes and personal wealth accumulation, she began to argue, would deliver a more entrepreneurial and prosperous society. Among those sending congratulations on her becoming prime minister were Milton Friedman – 'Britain can lead us to a rebirth of freedom – as it led us all down the road to socialism' – and Hayek – 'Thank you for the best present on my 80th birthday anyone could have given me.'[3] Mrs Thatcher was not alone in her crusade. Four years earlier, the leader of the Australian Liberal Party, Malcolm Fraser, had been elected prime minister with a similar agenda. A year after coming to power she was joined by an even more powerful soulmate, Ronald Reagan, heavily influenced by the American 'welfare backlash' of the 1970s and the neo-conservative thinkers who exploited it. The Reagan administration soon declared that 'the war on poverty has been won except for a few mopping up operations'.[4]

Over the next decade, the British prime minister and the American president subjected their economies to an all-embracing experiment. At the heart of this quantum leap-in-the-dark was a shift from the post-war model of 'managed' towards one of 'market capitalism'. It was built on a belief in efficient and self-regulating markets, and rooted in earlier ideas of natural equilibrium and economic balance. The switch involved dismantling parts of the policy apparatus constructed to ensure more equal societies and minimise poverty and preparing the conditions for the forward march of the super-rich. Keynes and Titmuss were out. Hayek and Friedman were in.

In one episode of the satirical BBC series on Whitehall, *Yes, Minister*, the permanent secretary Sir Humphrey asks the minister, Sir Desmond Glazebrook, if he's read the morning's *Financial Times*:

Sir Desmond: Never do.
Sir Humphrey: Well, you're a banker. Surely you read the *Financial Times?*
Sir Desmond: Can't understand it. Full of economic theory.
Sir Humphrey: Why do you buy it?
Sir Desmond: Oh, you know, it's part of the uniform.
Sir Desmond: It took me thirty years to understand Keynes' economics. And when I just caught on, everyone started getting hooked on these monetarist ideas. You know, *I Want to Be Free* by Milton Shulman.
Sir Humphrey: Milton Friedman?
Sir Desmond: Why are they all called Milton? Anyway, I only got as far as Milton Keynes.
Sir Humphrey: Maynard Keynes.
Sir Desmond: I'm sure there's a Milton Keynes.[5]

One of Mrs Thatcher's most important achievements was to win the war of ideas. Shortly before the 1979 election, Callaghan had speculated whether there was about to be 'sea-change in politics' that would benefit Mrs Thatcher.[6]

The twentieth century had already seen one about-turn in political economy, from the pre-war classical market model to post-war social democracy. History had been turned in 1945 and was now being turned again. Although there were elements of continuity in both, these two paradigm shifts had their roots in common factors: a severe external shock, inspired and determined leadership, the collapse of the existing model's intellectual backing and a public losing faith with the system. Egalitarianism, born with much hope, had ultimately run out of steam. As Milton Friedman once observed, 'Only a crisis, actual or perceived, produces real change. When that crisis occurs, the actions that are taken depend on the ideas that are lying around.'[7] The one-generation truce between labour and capital, one mediated by Britain's first social democratic state, was breaking down. Among the big questions of political economy that would preoccupy the following decades were how far would the new anti-egalitarian model of capitalism be taken, would it deliver on its claims and how long would it prevail?

Even though state investment had played a significant role in employing underused resources, encouraging new industries and supporting innovation, the idea of 'crowding out' became a central justification for Mrs Thatcher's plans.[8] As the new chancellor, Geoffrey Howe, told the House of Commons, '[we need to] roll back the boundaries of the public sector' in order 'to leave room for commerce and industry to prosper'.[9]

Although there had been attempts to trim budgets, and some ministers had seen the health service as a drain on the public purse, post-war Conservative governments had accommodated the welfare state in order to adapt to the broad, if soft, pro-welfare orthodoxy of the time. Mrs Thatcher – the only member of the cabinet, bar one, not educated privately – came to believe that conservatism had made too many compromises with welfarism.[10] At least initially, some cabinet members tried to oppose the new anti-welfare goals. Although he joined Mrs Thatcher's first cabinet as Lord Privy Seal, Ian Gilmour, along with other senior figures from the 'wet' wing of the party in the mould of Macmillan and Macleod, stood up to Thatcher. As he put it in a lecture in February 1980: 'In the Conservative view, economic liberalism à la Professor Hayek, because of its starkness and its failure to create a sense of community, is not a safeguard of political freedom but a threat to it.'[11] Similar warnings against a confrontational economic strategy were made by Harold Macmillan.[12] Such warnings were ignored. Gilmour, along with other wets, was finally sacked from the cabinet.

Mrs Thatcher paved the way for a very different agenda on both poverty and inequality. While in the nineteenth century poverty was widely attributed to the failings of the individual, it was the 'societal view' that underpinned the post-war welfare state. Tackling poverty, it was believed, required strong collective intervention and the granting of new statutory entitlements, though with some emphasis on individual responsibility. Under Margaret Thatcher's premiership, it was the 'individualist' school of thought that returned to dominance. She embraced the Victorian view that poverty was a matter of weak values, and that the best solution was self-help. This explanation rejected a relative approach to poverty, dismissed the link with inequality, and allowed harsher social attitudes towards benefit claimants. 'The rich admire the poor less and less', wrote Ferdinand Mount, adviser to Mrs Thatcher, 'partly because the poor are not as poor as they used to be – but also because the poor fritter their money on such trash, video cassettes and cars with fluffy dice'.[13]

An early sign of the marginalisation of social policy came with the issue of health inequality. In 1977, Labour had appointed a working group headed by Sir Douglas Black, president of the Royal College of Physicians, to examine the ongoing health gap between classes and its link to the wider socioeconomic divide. In April 1980, *The Black Report* was submitted to Patrick Jenkin, the new secretary of state for health and social security. It found that the health gap had widened over the previous twenty years. It attributed this to a mix of factors like income, employment patterns, education and housing and their impact on the structure of opportunities, as well as 'lifestyle' and cultural factors. Closing the gap depended heavily on a radical improvement in the material conditions of life of poorer groups.[14]

The then head of the Department of Health and Social Security's (DHSS) private office, Alan Healey, remembers asking Sir Douglas what he thought would happen to his report. 'He said it would probably gather dust on a shelf because the necessary actions were too difficult and costly for politicians to contemplate.'[15] As Black had predicted, Jenkin tried to bury the report. With no DHSS press release or conference, Sir Douglas decided to hold one at the Royal College of Physicians. The 'bury it' strategy badly backfired, with the report gaining high-profile coverage. While the report was thin on how effective its recommendations might be in practice, the question of health inequality continued to resonate, while the health divide has never been closed.[16] In 1986, a leader in the *British Medical Journal* summed up the report's impact: 'Much quoted, occasionally read, and largely ignored when it comes to action.'[17] The legacy of this failure was all too apparent when later reports, including the 1992 Acheson Report and the 2010 Marmot Review, confirmed the persistence of health inequality.[18] The link between social background and deep-seated health was strikingly confirmed in 2020 when those dying from COVID-19 were disproportionately from disadvantaged backgrounds and poorer regions.

Let our children grow tall

Six months after the 1979 election, Peter Townsend published *Poverty in the United Kingdom*, the delayed report of his pioneering survey of poverty conducted in 1968–69.[19] Although its impact was muted by coming out so long after the survey, the 1200-page book had an important influence, outside of liberal market thinking, on our understanding of poverty, even if it was not without critics, including among the social policy community. The social scientist Dorothy Wedderburn, who had long claimed that poverty and inequality were related, argued that Townsend had not done enough to draw a clearer distinction between the two: 'He uses these terms almost synonymously.'[20]

There was also controversy over Townsend's claim that poverty could be measured in an objective and scientific way, and that his study had contributed to finding such a measure. Others took the view that defining poverty would always be subjective and moral, and that there is no single cut-off point that separates 'the poor' from the 'non-poor'.[21]

Amartya Sen maintained that it was a mistake to focus entirely on relative poverty and to dismiss absolute poverty quite so resolutely. 'There is an irreducible core, of absolute deprivation in our idea of poverty which translates reports of starvation, malnutrition and visible hardship. ... The approach of relative deprivation supplements rather than competes with this concern with absolute dispossession.'[22] Absolute poverty is also the overriding issue in poor countries, while relative poverty becomes a more important concept at later stages of development. Townsend's response was that poverty was far more than just hunger and starvation, and that concentrating on basic subsistence raised the risk of the newly installed Conservatives cutting benefits to a level just sufficient to keep body and soul together. It was a prescient warning. One way of resolving these differences would have been to see absolute poverty as destitution, as an extreme version of poverty.

Market theorists rejected the idea of a relative poverty measure that reflected actual ways of living. For them, state action should be confined to 'hardcore' poverty. Within a few weeks of Townsend's book being published, a much shorter book was issued. Co-authored by Keith Joseph, *Equality* added fuel to the absolute-versus-relative debate and contested the idea that needs should be defined in contemporary terms. 'An absolute standard means one defined by reference to the actual needs of the poor and not by reference to the expenditure of those who are not poor. A family is poor if it does not have enough to eat. ... By any absolute standard there is very little poverty in Britain today.'[23]

A similar view was advanced by the American liberal philosopher Harry Frankfurt. In his 'doctrine of sufficiency', he argued that what matters is not having as much as others but having enough. 'The egalitarian condemnation of inequality as inherently bad loses much of its force', he wrote, 'when we recognize that those who are doing worse than others may nevertheless be doing rather well ... what is of genuine moral concern is whether people have good lives, and not how their lives compare with the lives of others.'[24] By implication, once all have passed above an 'absolute' poverty line, it does not matter if the rich then colonise the gains from growth. Defining poverty in this way is highly politically convenient: it means that those on low incomes not experiencing destitution or extreme poverty could be dismissed as non-poor, and society could abandon any commitment that all should benefit from rising prosperity.

Also back was a central thesis of the pro-inequality school, that the way to tackle poverty was not through greater equality but through boosting growth, and too much equality would hinder that goal. A stiff dose of inequality, a rise in rewards at the top and higher profits, it was claimed, were necessary conditions for economic success. On this view, allowing the rich to get richer would lift Britain out of its tepid entrepreneurial culture and expand the size of the economic cake so that even if the wealth gap grew, all citizens would still be better off through a 'trickle-down' effect. As the Austrian-born but New York–based economist Ludwig von Mises, a founding member of the Mont Pèlerin Society, wrote in 1955: 'Inequality of wealth and incomes is the cause of the masses' well being, not the cause of anybody's distress. ... Where there is a lower degree of inequality, there is necessarily a lower standard of living of the masses.'[25] The pro-inequality school accepted the need for a safety net, but a minimal one. Their view of the state was as little more than 'night-watchman' while unlimited inequality was fine.

In 1975, this theory got a considerable boost from the mainstream American economist Arthur Okun. In an influential book, *Equality and Efficiency: the Big Trade Off*, he argued that, whatever the morality of a widening gap, you could have more equality or a bigger cake but not both.[26] This was because the costs of redistribution would lead to reduced efficiency. This 'equity-efficiency trade-off' theory meshed with thinking on the right and became part of economic orthodoxy and integral to the economics curriculum in universities. As Keith Joseph wrote in 1976: 'Making the rich poorer does not make the poor richer, but it does make the state stronger ... The pursuit of income equality will turn this country into a totalitarian slum.'[27]

These arguments clashed not just with the social goals of the immediate post-war decades, but with the economic case for reducing inequality to tackle the problem of 'under-consumption' caused, as in the pre-war era, by a concentration of purchasing power at the top. Attlee had used this argument in 1946 to make the case for social insurance.[28]

They were at odds too with the theories of the Harvard philosopher John Rawls, who advanced a new and powerful case against unjustifiable inequality in his 1971 *A Theory of Justice*. Rawls argued that far from being in conflict, the principles of freedom (enshrined in the rule of law and individual rights) and equality (the granting of social rights including inclusion and social justice) were indivisible. Inequality, he argued, could be justified only when it benefits everyone in society, particularly those who are most poor and vulnerable. An ideal society would be one where 'social and economic inequalities ... [are] to the greatest benefit of the least-advantaged members of society'.[29] A similar argument – that inequalities can only be justified if they serve the common good – had been advanced by others, including Hobhouse sixty years earlier.

Using a new tool he called the 'veil of ignorance', Rawls argued that if we had no idea what our own place in society would be, we should hedge our bets by advocating a society in which everyone was as equal as possible. In this way, all could be assured of a comfortable if not luxurious existence. Reasserting the importance of limiting economic distance, Rawls – whose book coincided with the stirrings of the New Right – argued that it was not only important to consider the position of the most disadvantaged but also how incomes are spread above the poverty line. He accepted the inevitability of some degree of inequality, but only if its effect was to help the poor. Teachers or doctors, for example, could earn more than others if that financial incentive increased their supply and therefore ensured that the poorest were not deprived of adequate education or medical care. So inequality could be allowed, but only on egalitarian grounds, not because people have the right to acquire extreme wealth.

The anti- and pro-inequality schools promoted very different visions of an ideal society, especially of how big a gap is acceptable; of how tall is too tall. The goal of greater equality has often been misrepresented by its critics. In L.P. Hartley's 1960 novel *Facial Justice*, for example, beautiful people are given cosmetic surgery to make them uglier while ugly people are made less ugly. 'If a brain surgeon and a taxi driver earn the same amount, we won't have enough brain surgeons. Why bother?' wrote the high-profile American economist and voluminous author Deirdre McCloskey.[30] Egalitarians have never denied that some inequalities are natural and desirable and that people are born with different gifts and skills and make different contributions. Tawney, Titmuss and Crosland never advocated full equality and uniformity. They welcomed diversity, and accepted that differentials are necessary for incentives and to reward merit and effort and that too much redistribution can be counterproductive. In his 1931 book *Equality*, Tawney argued that egalitarians were not arguing for 'equality of capacity or attainment, but of circumstances, institutions and manner of life. The inequality which they deplore is not inequality of personal gifts, but of the social and economic environment'.[31] Attlee agreed. His strategy was to work 'steadily towards a greater equality. Not a dead level, but fewer great differences, more opportunities, and more social justice.'[32]

By the late 1970s, it was the critics of egalitarianism that were making the running. In the US, conservative thinkers exploited the growing cost of the Vietnam War and deepening economic problems to argue against pro-welfare policies. In the UK, this school gained support from unexpected quarters. In 1977, during the Queen's Silver Jubilee celebrations, the Duke of Edinburgh wrote an article for the magazine *Director*, suggesting that contemporary Britain should 'not concentrate so heavily on the unfortunate, the underprivileged'. A few weeks later he laid into what he called 'the nanny state'.[33]

In part because of the rediscovery of poverty, others called for a clear separation of the issues of poverty and inequality, which some felt had become too muddled. In his 1978 presidential address to the economics section of the British Association held in Bath, the British economist Wilfred Beckerman, an expert on poverty, told his audience that "the objective of equality is given too much weight relative to the objective of reducing poverty". It was time, he added, that the "fashionable and intellectually intriguing concern with equality took a back seat and priority be given to the relief of poverty and to efforts to eradicate it in advanced countries".[34]

It was the market liberal view that came to prevail: that the pursuit of greater equality didn't just distract from tackling poverty but *greater* inequality was less the cause of than the *solution* to poverty. And for Hayek, 'nothing has done so much as to destroy the juridical safeguards of individual freedom as the striving after this mirage of social justice'.[35] Such views were embraced by Mrs Thatcher, though she was always careful to couch them in terms of the virtues of meritocracy – achievement, reward and mobility – and the need to boost wealth creation. 'Let our children grow tall, and some taller than others', she told the BBC in 1980.[36]

Steps were taken to restrict the availability of up-to-date information on the government's record. One of the early moves of the new government was to abolish the Royal Commission on the Distribution of Income and Wealth. There was 'no continuing need for a standing commission', explained the secretary of state for employment Jim Prior, 'and the Queen has approved that the Royal Commission be dissolved'.[37] Internal work on improving measures of inequality was pared back and data published less frequently. An interdepartmental group on poverty was renamed the Working group on Work Incentives and its policy remit altered.

Serious consideration was given to what the social policy journalist David Walker called 'the assassination' of the Social Science Research Council, the state-funded body which financed social research.[38] According to Walker, a former head of policy at the Academy of Social Science, ministers at the time regarded social science as 'inherently dangerous'.[39] In 1981, Oliver Letwin, special adviser to the education secretary Sir Keith Joseph, was despatched to find evidence of socialist 'bias' in sociology. Three years later, Joseph demanded that an offending section in the Open University's social science foundation coursework be rewritten. One section on 'the great feudal families' had in fact come from an article in the left-of-centre *New Statesman* magazine in April 1975. The author was one Keith Joseph. He was paid £40 for writing it.[40]

The pro-inequality philosophy had little empirical foundation. Okun's trade-off principle had effectively been applied in the 150 years up to the late

1930s, yet allowing the richest groups in society to capture large chunks of national income came with very mixed economic results and mostly negative social consequences. This turned out to be equally true of other predictions of market theorists, despite their claims of developing a watertight theory of how the economy worked.

The tenets of neoliberal thinking were far from eternal truths written on tablets of stone. The real-life experiment launched in the 1980s revealed just how shaky such ideas would prove to be, with many examples of what the seventeenth-century philosopher Francis Bacon called 'wishful science'. The evidence from that experiment showed that heightened inequality did little to boost entrepreneurialism, while the subsequent moves to lower taxes on top incomes greatly benefitted the rich but failed to yield faster growth.[41] Public provision is sometimes more efficient and appropriate than private provision, while it is not the case that the common good is best served by placing economic goals above those of the social.

These doctrines have, conveniently, promoted an ideology that has been of greatest benefit to a super-rich class many of whom have helped pay for its dissemination. By buying into these ideas, political leaders became bag carriers for the powerful. Yet while there was scant evidence that the theories worked in the real world, and lacked any moral compass, they were presented, as in the nineteenth century, as fundamental laws of the way society worked. Later studies – as well as history – showed just how shallow such theories were. Far from raising productive efficiency, banking deregulation brought financial meltdown, while corporate tax cuts failed to boost productive investment because the tax savings were used to reward executives and shareholders.[42] The American economist and Nobel laureate Paul Krugman later dismissed them as 'zombie economics'.[43]

Zapping labour

By 1980, Britain was facing a further surge in inflation and in unemployment. If the flagging capitalist patient was to be revived, Mrs Thatcher believed, the medicine had to be taken, and in multiple doses. As they were unimportant, the side-effects on inequality and poverty could be ignored. There was a new emphasis on the 'micro' over the 'macro', while a new 'supply-side economics' promised to raise economic efficiency. Faster deindustrialisation aimed to push Britain more quickly down the road of a finance- and service-driven economy, a new war on unions and business regulation set out to empower boardrooms, while spending on the welfare state was to be reined back.

Inflation – at 17 per cent by the end of 1979 – had to be dealt with, but became the overriding goal, while the post-war commitment to full employment was dropped. The UK and US governments greatly tightened the mild fiscal and monetary restraint introduced by the Callaghan and Carter administrations. Monetarism – the belief that controlling the supply of money was the key to economic stability – was seen as a way of imposing economic discipline, but was applied with what one commentator called 'a wilful application of fuel on fire'.[1] The medicine worked eventually. Inflation took until 1986 to fall below 5 per cent, but not without subjecting the patient to a series of deeply unpleasant, prolonged and predictable side-effects. Moreover, although there was eventual control over the price of goods and services, this was not the case with an equally damaging asset price inflation.

The unforgiving cocktail of change plunged the UK (and US) economies into their second recession in a decade. It also brought bad news for companies, at least initially. At its trough in 1981, the aggregate valuation of the top 100 UK companies was lower than it had been, adjusted for inflation, at the time of Dunkirk. The radical economist Andrew Glyn used to joke to his Oxford students that British capitalists had been more optimistic about the future of UK companies on the eve of the expected invasion of Britain by Hitler than they were during the early years of Margaret Thatcher's government.

The most visible effect of full-blooded monetarism was on the length of the dole queue. In 1981, unemployment broke through the three million barrier for the first time since the 1930s. The government had bought into Friedman's claim of a 'natural rate of unemployment' that was consistent with low inflation. Attempts to influence unemployment were seen, as in the 1930s, as self-defeating. Official unemployment levels remained stubbornly high for years. In 1986, the number unemployed for over a year stood at 1.3 million.[2]

The fallout from the new economic direction was unevenly borne, with industrial workers at the front of the firing line. Once again, large parts of the labour force had to pay the price for ideologically driven change. The government believed that Britain's comparative advantage lay in finance not manufacturing. Britain's industrial base had been in slow decline for decades – the product of intensified competition from industrialising countries with cheaper labour. Despite this erosion, and the deteriorating state of part of Britain's industrial infrastructure, manufacturing in 1979 remained at the heart of the economy. Ford Motors in Dagenham employed more than 40,000 workers, while a significant proportion of the workforce in the West Midlands worked in local car and motorcycle factories or steel mills. Stoke-on-Trent was still the pottery capital of the world, and Royal Doulton had eighteen local factories. GEC was one of the world's leading electronics companies, and Raleigh's Nottingham factory was still producing 100,000 bicycles a year.

A few years later, large parts of the industrial landscape had been turned into a wasteland. The plight of jobless communities was captured in pop songs such as 'Ghost Town' by the Specials. The band UB40 named themselves after the title of the unemployment benefit form. One of their hits – 'One In Ten' – was an attack on the dehumanising impact of joblessness. Alan Bleasdale's *Boys from the Black Stuff*, a drama of five unemployed tarmac gang workers from Liverpool struggling to find work – and first shown on BBC Two – had such an impact it was swiftly repeated on BBC One. Across Britain, factories lay rusting, home dispossessions soared and bailiffs were in growing demand. An adviser at a money advice centre in Birmingham spoke of the 'new poverty', of how 'the old idea that debt happens to feckless irresponsible people who don't deserve help or sympathy has gone. Some of our clients are in their forties and fifties, skilled men who'd thought "it's only temporary"'.[3]

A further decline in steel, textiles and coal mining was inevitable, while the process of deindustrialisation and the expansion of the service sector is in many ways a hallmark of economic maturity. Nevertheless, the fall in manufacturing employment was especially steep in the UK.[4] With large sections of domestic industry – from food to machine manufacturing – wiped out in favour of overseas suppliers, Britain became a net importer of manufactured goods.[5] For big capital, market-driven globalisation meant an ever-larger and cheaper labour force. As starkly revealed during the COVID-19 crisis, the ongoing decline in manufacturing left Britain with great gaps in economic capacity, making the nation increasingly dependent on uncertain overseas production. Globalisation and lax regulation meant that many national strategic companies – among them Scottish Power,

Asda, Pilkington, British Energy, BAA and Cadbury – were bought in the following decades by overseas buyers. Despite upfront promises by the new owners to protect jobs, pay and pension commitments, such takeovers have typically led to further rounds of job losses and wealth extraction.

A wave of panic

Central to the new strategy was a shift of bargaining power to boardrooms. Here, as in other policies, Britain took its cue from the United States. In 1974, Arnold Weber, the head of President Nixon's Wages and Prices Board set up to try and cap wage demands, boasted that the business goal was "to zap labor". It was a telling phrase that echoed the advice given by Andrew Mellon, America's treasury secretary – 'to liquidate labor' – in response to the 1929 Wall Street Crash.[6] From the mid-1970s, US employers launched a campaign of virulent anti-unionism, later described by *Business Week* as 'one of the most successful anti-union wars ever'.[7]

In the UK, industrial unrest in the 1970s had sent a wave of panic across the governing elite. A few months after Heath lost the election in 1974, Lord Chalfont, a former Labour defence minister, wrote – in an article headlined 'Could Britain be heading for a military takeover' – of 'the massive power and often ruthless action of the great industrial trades unions'.[8] One poll in 1977 named Jack Jones as the most powerful person in Britain, with more influence than the prime minister. A few years later, the Labour MP Chris Mullin wrote his bestselling novel *A Very British Coup* – twice adapted for television – in which leading figures in the intelligence services, the media and business plot to unseat a radical Labour prime minister, the fictional Harry Perkins.

While industrial relations were poor across some sections of British industry, and the union movement sometimes pushed its power too far, it was widely accepted by economists that the main pro-inflation forces were the oil price hike and the Barber boom. 'In part, but mostly not' is how Adam Posen, a member of the Bank of England's Monetary Policy Committee, replied when asked if unions caused inflation at the time, adding that the primary role of unions had been 'to ensure that wages kept up with gains in productivity, that is, that labour got its share.'[9] Despite this, the new government removed employment rights and weakened wages councils. Union membership fell from a post-war peak of 13.5 million in 1979, more than half the workforce, to 6.7 million by 2010.

Skilled and semi-skilled jobs in manufacturing were replaced, with a lag, by often lower-paying jobs in retail, call centres and warehousing. In 1988, nearly nine million workers were found to be paid less than the Council of Europe's 'decency threshold' of two-thirds of median earnings. Low pay was concentrated among women workers, still used as a primary source of cheap and flexible labour. The average hourly rate for women workers was almost a third lower than for men, while the European Court of Justice warned the UK government of the inadequacies of its equal pay legislation.[10]

The government again swallowed Milton Friedman's advice: 'Few trends could so thoroughly undermine the very foundations of our free society as the acceptance by corporate officials of a social responsibility other than to make as much money for their stockholders as possible.'[11] One of the most important implications of the power switch to boardrooms and City institutions was a steady reduction in the share of economic output distributed to wages as pay rises fell behind productivity gains. Yet, far from undermining capitalism, the boost to the wage share had been a key ingredient in post-war economic success, contributing to a virtuous circle of better pay, rising prosperity and decent profits.

In the early 1970s, global competition, international financial uncertainty and slipping productivity had brought a 'profits squeeze' across developed economies, a squeeze that was intensified, if not caused, by the rocketing wage settlements that followed the surge in inflation. In the middle of that decade, the wage share in the UK jumped to an historic high, reducing profitability to an unsustainable level. Either labour would have had to accept a decline in wages and a return to the post-war norm or the capitalist model would have faced a growing risk of collapse. 'The consequence of a strategy which attempts to obtain wage increases or to resist wage cuts in a period when capital faces increasing competition, is that capitalists find it harder and harder to meet those demands and to remain profitable at the same time', argued the political economists Andrew Glyn and Bob Sutcliffe. 'Sometimes, therefore, capital and labour are bargaining not only about wages, but about the survival of the capitalist system.'[12] What the squeeze on profits required was a modest correction in the wage share and the restoration of profit levels to the post-war norm, thereby restoring balance between the maintenance of demand and the necessary rate of return on capital. In the event, such a modest correction is exactly what happened *before* the market revolution implanted from 1980.[13]

The profits squeeze of the mid-1970s was a blip caused by an exceptional set of circumstances – the oil shock, the collapse of the international monetary system and the near-peak power of trade unionism. By the time the Conservative government launched its anti-union crusade, the imbalance between wages and profits had already been corrected. If the wage share had been allowed to settle at its 1979–80 level – roughly the average of the 1950s and 1960s – the future course of the economy would have been very different. But the move towards a rawer model of capitalism ensured that the share of national output accruing to wage earners continued to fall. The strategy met the immediate interests of big corporations, helping to steer the gains from economic activity disproportionately towards profits. But while it would not have been in the interests of labour or capital to return to the stand-offs of the militant 1970s, making the labour force pay disproportionately for the international crisis, just as they had during the industrial revolution, had significant economic and social consequences.

It was later admitted by Sir Alan Budd, chief economist at the Treasury in the 1980s, that the multilayered assault was quite deliberate:

> The nightmare I sometimes have about this whole experience runs as follows ... there may have been people making the actual policy decisions ... who never believed for a moment that this was the correct way to bring down inflation. They did, however, see that it would be a very, very good way to raise unemployment. ... Raising unemployment was an extremely desirable way of reducing the strength of the working classes.[14]

What had been engineered, he continued, was the creation of 'a reserve army of labour [which] has allowed the capitalists to make high profits ever since.'

Financialisation

In the UK, and the US, finance became an increasingly dominant force. The policy of 'financialisation' pursued by Thatcher and Reagan was highly favourable to the City and Wall Street. The abolition of international controls over exchange rates, along with the end of exchange controls (the rules that had restricted movement of money between nations from the Second World War), high real interest rates and the appreciating pound from 1979, produced what one observer described as 'dream conditions for London's financial apparatus'.[15] Hot money flowed into London and bankers enjoyed, for the first time since 1939, much greater freedom over where to invest it. A similar issue had occurred in the 1920s with the subordination of 'the interests of industry to those of international finance' – through, for example, the return to the gold standard at its pre-war parity.[16]

The Conservatives knew that these policies would be damaging to manufacturing. A less aggressive approach, one that cultivated new developments and initiated a more determined investment in skills and retraining, could have softened the impact and preserved more manufacturing jobs. There were no attempts to tackle the overvaluation of the pound, upgrade manufacturing or follow the examples of other countries such as Germany – with its explicit goal of reducing regional inequalities – to nurture and modernise cities with clusters of specialist skills, such as cutlery in Sheffield and pottery in Stoke-on-Trent. The party's electoral strength lay outside the industrial heartlands, while its pro-service economic policies helped to shift the centre of gravity of the economy further towards the South.

Not for the first time, or the last, the party fell out with its business base, becoming less a party of Britain's productive base than of finance. As Milton Friedman said in 1980, Britain's manufacturing should be allowed to fall to bits.[17] In 1981 the Confederation of British Industry director general Sir Terence Beckett promised Mrs Thatcher a 'bare-knuckle fight' over the impact of her policies on manufacturing.[18] A parallel process was at work in the US. 'Wall Street had once been the handmaiden of industry', wrote Robert Reich, US secretary of labour under President Clinton. 'After 1980, industry became the handmaiden of finance'.[19]

The new economic strategy had a grand aim: to trigger a new entrepreneurial renaissance in which the new rich would make society generally wealthier, dragging up the rest of us along with them. This is not how it turned out. With manufacturing crowded out by political choice, the runaway winners of the 1980s were finance and a small corporate class. Far from stimulating economic dynamism, the empowerment of the City helped sow the seeds of future economic weakness and instability. The fall in the wage share produced a growing deficit of demand that made the economy increasingly reliant on rising levels of debt to keep it afloat. These debt levels were to become unsustainable. Freer markets, the rising profit share and escalating rewards at the top simply made the economy more prone to crisis. In acknowledgement of these failures, two of the central features of the new strategy, that the economy did not need to be managed and that the money supply needed to be tightly controlled, were finally abandoned from the mid-1980s. 'Monetarists ran up the white flag', as the economic journalist Will Hutton put it.[20]

On only one count – curbing inflation – can the post-1980 era be judged a clear success. On all other counts, 'the economic record of market capitalism has been inferior to that of managed capitalism', according to one study. 'Growth and productivity rates have been slower, unemployment levels higher. As the proceeds of growth have been very unequally divided, the wealth gap has soared, without the promised pay-off of wider economic progress. Financial crises have become more frequent and more damaging in their consequences.'[21]

The human cost of industrial and social dislocation was immense. The new strategy led to a transfer of risk from government and companies leaving workers to bear most of the cost of restructuring in 'reduced job security, lower wages and job intensification'.[22] Once again, a large part of the industrial labour force was sacrificed in the name of progress, heightening the risk of working-age poverty.

It would be wrong to romanticise factory work and the trappings of industrial society. Opportunities for many communities were still limited in the 1950s and 1960s, with jobs confined to what local industry could offer, while there remained deep racial and gender divides. But stripping the heart out of industrial towns at speed reduced the resilience of communities. Accelerated deindustrialisation, a form of state asset-stripping, brought lasting damage and opened up new gaps between already divided regions. It exiled many older skilled workers into workless lives, and a descent into prolonged poverty. Growing numbers of young people left school with weakened job prospects. Communities which had once enjoyed sustained economic security found that they – and their children – had lost control over their futures. As Kenneth Clark, a senior cabinet minister under Thatcher, admitted many years later, 'We neglected that bulk of the population left behind and living in post-industrial towns where their living standards were static or falling.'[23]

Poverty: a no-go area

The impact on poverty was initially poorly charted. Poverty remained a largely no-go area for government. There was no official definition or measure and no official series showing poverty levels or trends. The DHSS produced annual (later reduced to biennial) reports – the *Low Income Statistics* – on the number of families below, at or near thresholds defined in relation to Supplementary Benefit rates. These reports had initially been produced because of pressure from social scientists for more reliable and frequent information on low incomes.[24] Widely used by pressure groups and academics to chart the government's record, they showed a steady rise from the mid-1970s to the mid-1980s in the numbers on low incomes according to these definitions.[25]

The DHSS reports avoided the use of the word 'poverty'. As Mrs Thatcher reminded the House of Commons, 'There is no Government definition of poverty.'[26] Although Supplementary Benefit rates were widely used outside of government as a proxy for poverty, there were significant issues with this measure. They bore no systematic relationship to trends in wider living standards, and were essentially arbitrary. From 1979, the rates lagged behind rises in average earnings. They fell somewhere below a relative measure.[27] The level of Supplementary Benefit was in essence an historical accident. As one expert put it:

> There is no good reason why official definitions of financial poverty should be accepted as having any special validity. Government policy is based on what it thinks can be afforded at any particular time rather than on judgements about the income people need to maintain any kind of decent existence.[28]

In the thirty-five years from the end of the War, there had been no official public evaluation of the adequacy of National Assistance or Supplementary

Benefit. Independent studies suggested they were much too stringent. As one concluded, families dependent on the benefit were unable to meet 'normal everyday living requirements', while the interviewers found 'themselves shaken by the grind and stress of the poverty the scale rates impose'.[29] The government's Social Security Advisory Committee – whose members were appointed by ministers – reported in 1983 that the Supplementary Benefit rates 'are too near the subsistence level to provide an adequate standard of living for the poorest people in our society'.[30]

While conservative thinkers claimed that poverty was a matter of subsistence, social scientists continued to debate the question of definition and adequacy. Townsend's research gave substance to the idea that poverty is about the ability of people to participate in the societies in which they belong. For his 1968 survey, he drew up a 'deprivation index' of twelve items – ranging from diet to recreation – and used this to identify a poverty line at the point at which people were most likely to lack these items.

Townsend's work was a highly significant advance on earlier work, but had some limitations. First, the items chosen were essentially arbitrary. Why these twelve and not others? Critics argued that the chosen indicators failed to take account of any generally accepted view of 'need'. For David Piachaud at the LSE, this weakness left the term 'poverty' devoid of any 'moral imperative that something should be done about it'. Another flaw was that there was no allowance for choice. Lack of some of the items on the list – such as a 'Sunday joint' and a 'cooked breakfast' – were likely to be determined by taste as well as poverty.[31]

In 1983, a survey conducted for an ITV television series – *Breadline Britain* – set out to develop Townsend's work through a new 'consensual approach'. First, it attempted to measure the public's perception of contemporary necessities. Secondly, it allowed for choice in lifestyles. The list of items receiving majority support – the modern day equivalents of Adam Smith's 'linen shirt' – covered a cross section of social and personal life, from food and clothing to household goods, leisure and social activities. The public accepted that minimum living standards needed to reflect contemporary and not past standards. Surveys have shown a plurality of public views on what poverty means, from austere to generous.[32] The *Breadline Britain* survey indicated that participants did not see needs as standing outside of society. They gave high scores not just to basic levels of food and shelter but also to items that enable people to play a wider social role.

The consensual surveys – repeated over time and across countries – have shown that the public identify items as necessities that would not have been present in a subsistence or absolute standard of the distant past. They endorse the idea that in a wealthy country such as Britain, no child should have to manage without essential clothing or be prevented from going on school trips because their parents cannot afford to pay. Relativism turns out to be a core principle, across time and across developed and developing economies alike, that gels with public perceptions of what it means to be poor.[33]

Households interviewed for the 1983 *Breadline Britain* series confirmed what living on low income was like. "I can't cope on the money" and "It's very difficult to manage from day to day" were typical responses. As in earlier decades, many parents, especially mothers, made personal sacrifices, even to the detriment of their own health, so that their children did not miss out. Pamela and her nine-month-old baby Emma lived in a tiny, one-roomed attic flat in Inner London: "The rain starts falling in from the window; and the beasties start coming up through the floorboard; slugs, beetles, the lot. They go all over the bed, the cot and all over the floor". And an unemployed father of three from Birmingham: "You don't worry about things like unemployment until it happens to you – and then it hits you like a bomb. Your standard goes down and it just keeps going down".[34]

The wider response to the survey results reflected the diversity of views about poverty at the time. There were hundreds of letters of support together with offers of financial and other help for those featured in the series. *The Sunday Times* ran a report on some of the main findings, and offered this message for the government in an accompanying editorial: 'Too often, it is precisely this [sympathetic understanding] that the cabinet collectively has seemed to lack, its rhetoric and increasingly its policies based on all the old, populist prejudices against the poor.'[35]

Others were less sympathetic. *The Sunday Times* also carried several critical letters.[36] Dr Rhodes Boyson, minister for social security, dismissed the idea that poverty had anything to do with lacking items such as refrigerators on the basis that, '50 years ago, or even 25 years ago, people merely aspired to have such things'.[37] This was equally true of items such as access to hot water and an inside toilet. In recognition of progress, the census stopped asking if households had hot running water in 1971. The minister seemed to be saying that if previous generations of the poorest managed without such goods – some of which had yet to be invented – so should today's poor, even though such views were a long way out of line with public opinion. The implication was that it was acceptable for social progress to be thinly shared.

Critics of relative poverty continued to duck the issue of where to draw the line.[38] What about birthday presents and the occasional evening out? How far back would we need to go? Would the basic physical survival standard provided in workhouses at the turn of the nineteenth century, or Rowntree's 1900 or 1936 standard, be sufficient in the 1980s?

The dark shadow of the Poor Law

When Mrs Thatcher arrived in Downing Street, she inherited a middling social security system, one ungenerous by the standards of Northern Europe.[1] Yet she was determined not to be seen as 'soft' on welfare. An early target was public spending. One of the government's first moves, overcoming some tepid opposition within the cabinet, was to freeze child benefit at the £4 rate.

With inflation high, this meant a serious cut in real terms. Geoffrey Howe also wanted to cut the state pension, but this time met stiffer cabinet resistance.[2] Instead, he won approval for linking future pension increases to prices rather than average earnings, a move which had a significant negative impact on the future living standards of pensioners. During the 1970s, pension levels had broadly kept pace with wider income rises. Abolishing the earnings link was a big money saver, but meant that the state pension would fall in relative terms over time. Patrick Jenkin claimed that pensioners would continue to share in the 'increased standards of living of the country as a whole'.[3] It was an empty promise. Between 1980 and 1995, the basic pension fell from 26 to 17 per cent of average earnings, one of the lowest ratios in Europe. There were also cuts in the value of other benefits, including invalidity benefit, while the earnings-related additions to unemployment and sickness benefit were abolished.[4]

A war of attrition

The war on benefits was a decisive moment in the politics of social security. This was the first time since the early 1930s that a government had launched an explicit policy to cut the real value of benefits, and deliberately removed the promise of social advance for all citizens so carefully built over the previous twenty-five years. While there was little vocal public opposition, there were loud protests in the House of Commons, with the parliamentary committee handling the 1980 Social Security Bill suspended twice. 'The ease with which the government got away with such a harmful piece of legislation made this one of the most profoundly depressing moments in all my time with the Child Poverty Action Group', wrote Ruth Lister, who became the director of the group in 1979. What had been launched was 'a steady war of attrition' which made it 'hard to mobilise effective defence'.[5]

The strategy was driven by wider goals than the new imperative to shrink the state. Ministers held that benefits were sapping the working-class work ethic. Cutting them would 'remoralise' the class and end the corrupting influence of 'the Father Christmas state' on the middle class, who, ministers maintained, were starting to rely less on their own hard work and thrift and more on state handouts. Thatcher, according to one historian, wanted to revive 'what she saw as the "Victorian" or "bourgeois" values of thrift, self-reliance and charity among all classes'.[6] This was to be achieved by chipping away at the social security system, turning it into a last resort for the poorest minority, as in the Victorian Poor Law, and shifting the emphasis from poverty alleviation to moral correction.

The early abolition of the earnings-related supplement for unemployment and sickness benefit, for example, would cut the middle classes' ties to benefits while encouraging them to opt for private provision. Tackling poverty was not on the government's radar. Rather, the incremental reductions clashed with any idea that poverty is rooted in social norms and relationships. Allowing benefit recipients to fall behind rising prosperity had become an explicit goal of policy.

There were further waves of change. One of the most radical was a reduction in the generosity of SERPS, a scheme dismissed by Nigel Lawson, chancellor from 1983, as a 'doomsday machine'.[7] Before the 1987 general election, the prime minister's office had drawn up plans to abolish SERPS altogether. So sensitive was the proposal that Mrs Thatcher had 'personally ordered the collection and burning of every single copy'.[8] Just as there had been political limits to the goal of expanding the welfare state during the 1960s and 1970s, the 1980s brought its own set of limits on how far to shrink it.

Under the new plans, individuals were encouraged to take out personal private pensions. For the next thirty years, millions of workers opted out of the state top-up scheme and into the personal pension schemes being promoted by the private insurance companies which, standing to gain hugely from the shift, had put huge pressure on ministers for the change. As Titmuss had warned, insurance interests will 'increasingly become the arbiters of welfare and amenity for larger sections of the community'.[9]

The boost to private pensions quickly turned into a charter of mass financial abuse. Private pensions became the subject of one of the earliest of a string of miss-selling scandals by Britain's financial sector following the 1985 'big-bang' bonfire of financial controls. The new schemes came with excessively high and often covert charges, delivered often very poor returns and with the generous commission and enhanced executive pay involved, were promoted by predatory and high-pressure selling.[10] This turned into a form of mass 'extraction', if largely hidden initially, from those paying into private pensions. An investigation into pension miss-selling in the 1990s by the City watchdog the Financial Services Authority led to a multi-billion-pound payout to the 1.7 million people who had wrongly switched into private schemes.[11]

The 'burden' of the welfare state became a dominating theme of the 1980s. On 14 February 1982, the *Sunday Times* carried an analysis of 'Why the welfare state is starting to crack.' Two years later, the BBC chose the Oxford sociologist A.H. Halsey to make a four-part Radio 3 series entitled *A Crisis in the Welfare State?* Halsey began by asking if we were witnessing a rerun of the debate a century and a half earlier that led to the 1834 Poor Law. Did the Iron Lady's promise to 'roll back the frontiers of the state', he asked, mean a return to the much more anti-poor political agenda of the past? Halsey's conclusions were nuanced. What was at work, he told his listeners, was a shift towards 'class inequality and away from the social wage of citizenship'. But, he also claimed: 'The fiscal facts do not add up to a crisis. ... It is much more the end of economic growth and full employment which gives rise to alarm than anything that has actually happened to the budget for social security, health and welfare.'[12]

Shirkers and scroungers

Despite the rights-based benefits system, the 1980s was not a good time to be a claimant. Mrs Thatcher's strategy, supported by the popular press, was to shape public opinion on welfare while encouraging a meritocratic view of the rich. A war on claimants carried political risks, but the prime minister, well aware of the limits of her experiment and the no-go areas of welfare, was confident that there would be limited public opposition. Indeed, she captured the public mood sufficiently, notably among parts of the affluent working class, to win three consecutive elections.

The Beveridge system of benefits had sustained its broad popularity during the immediate post-war years.[13] Influenced by press claims about benefit 'scroungers', a 'four-week rule' was introduced in 1968. This was a new form of work-test limiting Supplementary Benefit for single, unskilled men under forty-five to four weeks if work was deemed to be available. As in its earlier guises, this rule was based on the presumption that, without state discipline, the unemployed would avoid work if they could get away with it.[14]

Following the 1970 Conservative manifesto promise to tackle 'the shirkers and the scroungers', Keith Joseph appointed the Fisher Committee to investigate benefit abuse. The committee saw its role as one of deterrence through encouraging 'an attitude among the public of disapproval'.[15] In 1971, an anonymous official made claims of widespread abuse.[16] In 1976, a Conservative MP, Iain Sproat, alleged that only half those receiving unemployment benefit were really looking for work, and submitted a list of 441 cases to the DHSS.[17]

During his visits to social security offices and groups of claimants in the late 1970s, the chair of the Supplementary Benefits Commission, David Donnison, detected a 'deeply rooted prejudice' towards the unemployed among some staff. 'Many of them saw the Commission as a bunch of social workers and trendies, lacking the moral fibre to stand up for hard work, thrift and moral rectitude. ... Younger staff attacked me with complaints about fraud, workshy claimants, feather-bedded claimants.' In the summer of 1979, he attended a lunch by the British Institute of Management where the discussion had turned to the need to cut public spending. Put on the spot, Donnison was asked, 'We have the biggest spender of them all amongst us. Professor Donnison, I constantly hear about how our social security system is abused. What do you think?'[18] A little over a year later the commission was dissolved.

The question of abuse has long dogged the issue of benefits. The evidence on the scale of abuse, however, was flimsy. 'Knowledge of the full extent of abuse is incomplete and fragmentary', concluded the Fisher Committee.[19] The Supplementary Benefits Commission's regular investigations found the number of 'work-shy' claimants unwilling to work and the number working unlawfully on the side to be a small minority.[20] Other studies found that the estimated level of fraud was a small fraction of all benefit spending.[21] When the DHSS examined the cases of alleged fraud submitted by Iain Sproat, they found evidence of fraud in only twenty-two of the 441 cases.[22]

There was much confusion over definition. Some cases of fraud were clear cut. In 1976, Derek Deevy, dubbed 'King Fiddler' by the press, was convicted of drawing £36,000 in benefits using forty-one aliases. Public concern, however, was directed at small infringements, such as those claiming while enjoying small outside earnings, or mothers claiming they were living apart from the father when they were cohabiting. Yet the cohabitation rule attached to benefits was questionable and contradictory. While enjoying the economies from families living together, the rule discouraged family formation.

Although infringements undoubtedly existed, those working with claimants argued that they needed to be put into context. As a charity supporting families told the Fisher Committee:

> All the cases of abuse described by [our] workers occurred in families living for long periods on extremely low incomes. The vast majority were ... not 'rogues' but ordinary claimants either unknowingly or in desperation making wrongful claims in order to ease unbearable situations, created in the main by the vicious circle of long-term poverty, and in some instances by personal problems including psychiatric ill health.[23]

The work-shy question was complex. Although it existed, there was little evidence of the mass opting out of work by choice, or of a significant loss of work ethic. There just weren't enough jobs. During the 1970s, a rising dole queue signalled an overall labour surplus, especially in unemployment hotspots and among the poorly qualified. While the great majority of households on benefits would still be better off in work, a small minority – those with large families where the only realistic jobs were low paid – would sometimes have been better off staying on benefit. One 1974 estimate suggested that, because of downward pressure on wages in areas of high unemployment and a falling tax threshold, 70,000 people in work would have been 'better off on benefit' in this way.[24] Workers were aware of how jobs sometimes paid little more, or sometimes even less, than benefit, and the Fisher Committee recommended that they should not be penalised for failing to take such jobs.[25]

Yet the stream of anti-claimant press stories and a return to the 'blame-the-poor' attitudes of the past were highly damaging to a considered public debate on the issues. A mix of myth and scapegoating led to the indiscriminate shaming of those most vulnerable to the unemployment created by forces outside their control. As one survey of social attitudes in the late 1970s found:

> The mass media organise popular anxieties around a series of insistent themes, both strenuously denying the existence of real poverty (a figment of the misguided imagination of academics and dogooders) while replaying the motif of 'scroungerphobia'. Hostility to social security claimants rose to a hysterical crescendo in the mid-1970s.[26]

In a signal of the erosion of the social solidarity that helped drive the post-war reforms, the survey showed that many blamed poverty on claimants themselves. Only a minority attributed poverty to an unfair distribution of income and wealth. 'Professional people have been squeezed to help the poor', as expressed by a teacher's wife, was a typical view. Six out of ten thought social security benefits were too generous and too easy to get.[27] Such stereotyping was not confined to the UK. In Australia the prevalence of 'dole bludgers' was a key feature of the 1975 election campaign, while newspapers ran endless stories of 'dole dollies' exploiting the welfare system. In Canada in 1978, with unemployment soaring, the government launched an advertising campaign to expose dole cheats.

The hardening public mood served the politics of retrenchment. Outside of the occasional 'march for jobs', the failed 1984 miners' strike and later the protests against the poll tax, public resistance to government policies was mostly muted. In many ways the unemployed as a group had been not just marginalised and dispirited but depoliticised. During the 1980s, the long-term unemployed were among those least likely to vote.[28]

This was an early sign of what the political scientist Colin Crouch has called 'post-democracy', with 'the poor gradually ceasing to take any interest in the process, to not even vote, returning voluntarily to the position they were forced to occupy in pre-democracy'. For Crouch, opting out was driven by the 'residualisation of the welfare state as something for the deserving poor and no longer a universal right of citizenship, the return of the role of the state as policeman, the growing wealth gap, and the way politicians responded principally to the concerns of a handful of business leaders'.[29] Political alienation continued to grow. The 2010 general election saw a 23 percentage-point gap between the turnout of the richest and poorest income groups.[30] It was a trend that served the interests of those wedded to the status quo.

The failure to create a clear politics of inclusion also carried wider economic risks. In their book *Why Nations Fail*, Daron Acemoglu and James Robinson argue that, compared with the negative impact of 'extractive' regimes that only serve the interests of the ruling elite, 'inclusive political institutions' that ensure all interests are met are a crucial precondition for sustained progress.[31]

Heavy-handed tactics

While the Victorian Poor Law in its purist form had been formally abolished in the post-war reforms, it continued to cast a deep shadow over policy. The response to mass unemployment bore strong echoes of the social politics of the past, if taking a less primitive, twentieth-century form. 'The same Social Darwinist rhetoric [of the nineteenth century] today firmly and irreversibly stamps the poor as stigmatised, permanent outcasts, undeserving of citizen status', wrote the sociologist Zygmunt Bauman in 1987. 'Thus the poor are not just growing poorer. They are being made into a deviant category, a separate entity by the withdrawal, or at least suspension, of political and personal rights which were thought to be the lasting and universal achievement of modernity.'[32]

Successive cuts to benefit levels were aimed not just at lowering the welfare budget but at 'pricing the unemployed into jobs' through a weakening of the statutory right and entitlement to help first introduced in partial form in 1909. As unemployment rose, ministers liked to argue that rising joblessness was the fault of over-powerful trade unions and excessive wages. Despite the limited evidence, this theory was aired on television programmes, including an October 1984 edition of ITV's influential current affairs programme *Weekend World*, presented by former Labour MP Brian Walden. Some monetarist economists, such as Patrick Minford of the University of Liverpool, claimed that high unemployment was the product not of recession but of the generosity of unemployment benefits. Repeating an earlier claim, Minford argued that too many low-paid workers would be better off on the dole than in work. The Institute for Fiscal Studies, a leading independent observer on spending and tax issues, showed that Minford had greatly

Figure 15.1: Poll tax riot, London, 1990

Source: Andrew Moore

overstated the scale of the problem. In 1983, only 2.6 per cent of those in work would end up with a higher income on the dole.[33]

The pressure on the jobless to find work was extended to areas that had been considered off limits in the post-war welfare model. The values and statutory rights to help underpinning the post-war reforms, ones that had buried the harsher principles of the Victorian Poor Law, were eroded in the 1980s by a mix of withdrawal (in the case of housing), the further extension of means testing and a tougher approach to entitlement. The early social pioneers, including Hobhouse and the Webbs, along with key Labour figures, including Attlee, had recognised the importance of mutual obligations between society and individuals. Tawney had warned of the danger of 'encouraging social malingering' and of the need for 'the preservation of personal initiative'.[34]

Conditionality rules had been tightened in the 1920s, relaxed in the post-war years and then progressively tightened again from the 1970s. The post-war benefit system was built around the idea of limited state coercion, with its architects acknowledging that 'the wartime contribution of the working class had already established the entitlement of the workers to social security'.[35] This view was not to last. In 1986, the maximum length of benefit disqualification for not seeking work was extended from six to twenty-six weeks, with even tougher job requirements imposed over the next three decades. Over the course of the 1980s there were nineteen changes to the way the unemployment statistics were compiled, mostly aimed at massaging the headline figures down, and twenty-seven separate cuts in support for the jobless.[36]

From 1979, official estimates of the extent of 'fraud' were revised upwards and much tougher control procedures introduced.[37] The drive against 'social security abuse' was given high levels of publicity, with some operations by the DHSS deliberately manipulated to ensure a much greater publicity splash.[38] A senior official in the DHSS later reported complaints of 'oppressive methods and unjustified harassment' by new specialist abuse investigation teams.[39] Local staff were often highly critical of the notorious hit teams for their heavy-handed tactics, and sometimes refused to co-operate. In 1986, staff at the Hove unemployment benefit office struck on three separate occasions over the methods used. One woman recovering from illness was interviewed by three investigators. Despite offering to show her medical certificates, she was told, "It's scum like you that ruin this society. ... We think your Doctor was lying about your operation." Other allegations against the Special Claims Control teams included locking people in interviewing rooms, tearing up benefit books in front of claimants and stopping batches of claim forms being sent out.[40]

At the heart of the overall strategy was a paradox. 'Thatcherism' wanted a 'weak state' when it came to social protection, but a 'strong state' to underpin capitalism and enforce labour market discipline. While the regulatory and protective role of government was downgraded, justified as necessary to save money, reduce dependency and improve work incentives, the state's coercion was strengthened. In this and other ways, the state, as in the nineteenth century, became an agent of inequality.

The policing of the tax and benefit system was – and still is – full of examples of Halsey's 'class inequality'. While the number of benefit inspectors kept rising, the number of wage inspectors enforcing minimum wage rates in industries covered by wages councils was cut. From 1985, the government began a highly controversial process of abolishing such councils altogether. There were minimal attempts to cut tax abuse despite the headache it presented for tax-raising capacity. While estimates of the scale of benefit fraud and tax avoidance need to be treated with caution, there is no question that the latter greatly exceeded the former.[41] DHSS fraud officers were each estimated to save an average of £50,000 a year, while the equivalent for tax officials was £138,000. Yet, while the number of social security fraud busters soared, there was stiff ministerial resistance to measures to control tax evasion or raise the size of the tax fraud inspectorate.[42]

During the 1980s, the top rate of income tax was cut in two steps from 83 per cent to 40 per cent, while the standard rate of tax paid by most taxpayers was lowered from 33 per cent to 25 per cent. The cost of these reductions was met by a hike in the VAT rate and by higher National Insurance contributions. These and other changes led to a shift in the overall tax burden away from those with the highest incomes. In the immediate post-war decades, the tax system had been an equalising force. By the late

1980s, it had become regressive, taking a bigger slice of low than of high incomes.[43] The combined effect of the squeeze on benefits and the lowering of the tax burden on the rich was to lower the anti-inequality power of the overall system.[44] This weakened power has, with the partial exception of the New Labour years, stayed that way ever since.

This shift clashed with the principle that tax should be progressively related to 'ability to pay', one first advanced by Adam Smith and then endorsed by the 1906 Select Committee on Tax and enshrined in Lloyd George's budget of 1909. The 1993 Ontario Fair Tax Commission concluded 'that a fair tax system is one primarily based on the ability-to-pay principle, and that in turn requires the overall tax system to be progressive'.[45] Far from boosting revenue, cutting tax rates for the rich and failing to tackle growing tax avoidance has shrunk the tax base while transferring more of the cost of public welfare onto middle- and lower-income groups and strengthening the link between inequality and poverty.[46] The post-war tax take peaked in the early 1980s at 40 per cent of GDP. Since then it has hovered around 36–7 per cent, well below levels of public spending. A cross-national study has shown that higher-rate tax cuts over time have merely benefitted the rich and had minimal impact on boosting business investment.[47]

With unemployment displacing inflation as the most important problem facing the country, attitudes towards those on benefits gradually softened, with a sharp rise in the number saying poverty was a serious problem. The annual poll of British social attitudes that began in 1983 found trends that suggested, from the middle of the decade, a 'pretty definitive contradiction of the notion that people bought wholesale into the doctrines pursued by Mrs Thatcher in the 1980s'.[48]

The shift in lobbying power

Despite their former influence and the softening of the public mood, the small group of once-influential social policy academics and the anti-poverty lobby found themselves out in the cold. In response, CPAG attempted to broaden its campaign. With its forty-five local branches and six thousand members, it helped to form the Save Child Benefit campaign with seventy other charities, unions, churches, women's institutes and Mothers' Union branches. A group of female stage, screen and TV stars presented Margaret Thatcher with a Mother's Day card, designed by a six-year-old, with the message: 'Give all Mothers a Happy Mother's Day – Save Child Benefit.' But it was tough going for a small, slenderly funded organisation. In 1983, it tried to establish a working group of journalists to present a more positive image of the benefit system, but only two turned up.

The authority once exercised by progressive pressure groups acting as the conscience of government shifted in favour of pro-market think tanks which were generously funded by wealthy benefactors and large corporate donors, from IBM to Shell.[49] As Frank Field reflected, CPAG had been outstripped by the pro-market Institute of Economic Affairs (IEA). 'When they started out, everybody thought they [the IEA] were a crowd of cranks. ... The IEA's brilliance was that it went out and captured a party.'[50]

By the mid-1980s, the Institute of Directors, once little more than a sleepy Pall Mall Club, had become a lobbyist for the marketisation of the economy and even sniped at Mrs Thatcher for not being radical enough. Its director Sir John Hoskyns, the former head of the prime minister's policy unit, wrote in the *Times* on 12 February 1985 that collective bargaining should be replaced by individually negotiated contracts and unions reduced to 'a sort of 21st century friendly society concerned with training, advice and unemployment insurance'.[51]

Yet, even on the Conservative's own terms, the social strategy of the 1980s was of limited success. The government did succeed in slimming the state overall. Public spending as a percentage of GDP fell from 48 per cent in 1983 – a figure inflated by the impact of the recession – to 39 per cent by the end of the 1980s.[52] In contrast, the social security budget as a percentage of GDP ended up staying roughly the same over the decade.[53] The loss of so many jobs imposed enormous pressure on the income support system, by now one of the weakest and most targeted in the rich world. The numbers receiving Supplementary Benefit, later renamed Income Support, and Family Income Supplement, renamed Family Credit, surged.[54] High unemployment, low pay and the weakening of universalism turned the means test into one of the growth stories of the time.[55] This reinforced welfare dependency while undermining 'incentives to work and to save and made it harder for individuals to stand on their own two feet', concluded one study.[56]

There were other pressures on the social security budget, including the cost of the way the jobless were encouraged to move from Unemployment to Invalidity Benefit (later Incapacity Benefit), a policy aimed at disguising the real level of unemployment. Although Incapacity Benefit was more generous, the shift was a largely one-way trip, consigning hundreds of thousands to permanent unemployment and, in many cases, poverty, isolation and depression.[57] There were other long-term trends, including the steady rise in the number of pensioners and the changing nature of the family. The increase in lone parenthood (predominantly female-headed households) from the 1970s was in part down to the greater choices open to women, with a growth in the number of divorces as married women enjoyed greater economic independence, but also the declining employment prospects for men. One study found that the latter 'explains between 38% and 59% of the 1.16 million increase in lone parent families over the period 1971–2001'.[58]

The 1980s was a defining decade in the history of social policy and trends in poverty. In tearing up chunks of the post-war social contract, Mrs Thatcher had a profound impact on the effectiveness of the social security system, on the gap between top and bottom and on wealth and power at the top. Many of the policy shifts of the 1980s weakened the principles of National Insurance. 'For those of working-age, the reward for paying what used to be known as "the stamp" – i.e. NICs – has shrunk over the years as the social security system has become more means-tested and more conditional', concluded one study.[59]

The combative approach to trade unions, claimants and what Thatcher saw as the socialist entrails of the post-war settlement had sweeping social implications. New forms of poverty emerged, concentrated among the long-term unemployed and the lowly paid, a return to the pattern 100 years earlier.

The mechanisms that had driven lower levels of inequality and poverty – a more generous social security system, full employment and a rising wage share, a narrower earnings gap, and the weakening of corporate extractive power – were set in reverse. After the war, the distributional impact of economic expansion had been neutral or pro-poor. The big post-1980 policy shifts, from financialisation to welfare austerity, ensured that the gains from growth were increasingly colonised by the mega-rich, the rich and the professional middle classes. The distribution question was again being settled, without public debate or awareness, in favour of the highest income groups.

The great widening

In 1986, the main official series on low-income trends, the biennial *Low Income Statistics*, was scrapped, and for the government, the uncomfortable head-count figures with it. They were replaced two years later by a new annual series, *Households Below Average Incomes* (HBAI). The hope was that this new series would defuse some of the pressure on the government's record. As one of the civil servants working on the changes explained in an internal memo, 'The government shifted the basis of the "poverty" debate onto grounds of their choosing' and 'took away the poverty lobby's favourite propaganda instrument.'[1]

Poverty in paradise

This was optimistic. The new HBAI series introduced a new concept of low income – those falling below various fixed proportions – from 50 to 90 per cent – of *mean* household income (the mean is the average income calculated by dividing the sum of all incomes by the number of people in the distribution). The first issue gave trends for both an absolute measure – based on a 1981 income threshold held constant in real terms – and several relative thresholds. Only too aware of the views of their political masters, officials were careful to tread carefully in what was a political minefield. The new series offered no judgement on which if any of the thresholds was favoured, and like its predecessor, avoided the word poverty. Ministers judged that it was better to continue to fudge the issue by sheltering behind the 'low-income' label. By the end of the 1980s, after a century and more of heated debate, there was still no official resolution of the thorny issue of what constituted poverty, or how to count it.

Despite the hostility to the use of contemporary standards, the new series was the first time that officialdom had used *explicit* 'relative' measures. Outside of Whitehall, among the small group of academics and activists watching these issues closely, this was a significant moment. The first set of published findings seemed to support the government in its claims. They suggested that the living standards of the poorest tenth had risen at twice the rate of the average household. Doubting these figures, which contradicted the wider evidence, the House of Commons Select Committee on Social Services commissioned the Institute of Fiscal Studies to check the findings. This recalculation showed that there had been errors in the first set of HBAI statistics and that low incomes had in fact risen by half as much as the average.[2]

The intervention of the Institute for Fiscal Studies (IFS) ended the government's monopoly on statistical evidence, and from that point government and IFS statisticians worked together on the data. The adjusted series showed that in the decade to 1989 the proportion of the population living on low incomes more than doubled, from 9 to 22 per cent, and from five to twelve million individuals. The rise for children was even steeper.[3]

The Secretary of State for Health and Social Services at the time of the first HBAI release was John Moore. One of Margaret Thatcher's favourite ministers, he had warned that the "sacred cows" of the welfare state needed to be "swept away".[4] Once again, the first target was child benefit. Moore's proposals to freeze its value and then allow it to be either taxed or tapered away as incomes rose was in conflict with the 1987 manifesto and a commitment made by John Major, the new chief secretary to the Treasury, that child benefit would remain universal, non-means-tested and tax free.[5] Moore, not for the first time, had to back down.

In May 1989 he made his most high profile speech. Entitled, somewhat unwisely, 'The end of the line for poverty', he dismissed the growing body of evidence, including that from his own department, on what had been happening to poverty. The speech included a public broadside against the poverty lobby's promotion of a relative measure of poverty. "It means that however rich a society gets it will drag the incubus of relative poverty with it up the income scale. The poverty lobby would on their definition find poverty in Paradise".[6]

Moore was, if robustly, restating the view earlier expressed by Keith Joseph and other conservative thinkers: what mattered was not whether those on low incomes were keeping pace with rising living standards but whether they were getting better off absolutely, even if slipping further behind those above them. There would have been a big political dividend if the idea of relativity, reflecting the standards of the day, could be dumped in favour of a measure rooted at some point in the past. Such an approach would over time define poverty out of existence, bringing 'an end to the line'. Though the living standards of low-income households were rising more slowly than those higher up the income ladder, most (though far from all) were getting absolutely better off (the John Moore criterion for success). In the event, Moore's speech was badly received, even by some MPs on his own side.

The government liked to think that poverty was invisible and could easily be ignored. Yet, far from being inconspicuous, the evidence of poverty, including destitution, had become more visible. In 1984, Shelter reported that half of the 14,000 teenagers leaving council care ended up on the streets.[7] Begging was commonplace, and with the rise of youth unemployment and the ending of Income Support for sixteen- and seventeen-year-olds in 1988, it jumped among teenagers. To illustrate the growing problem, the charity published *Down and Out: Orwell's Paris and London Revisited*, an updated version of George Orwell's 1930s chronicle.

Across Britain's major conurbations, rough sleeping had been on the rise for years. A widely filmed small community of the homeless in the underpass near London's Waterloo Station – 'Cardboard City' – (later the site for BFI's new IMAX cinema) had become a potent symbol of the social state of Britain. One of those in 'the City' was Arthur, a sixty-six-year-old Glaswegian ex-labourer. Every morning at 4 am he would go for a clean-up to a local all-night toilet. "You feel that you are not wanted, eh? I always try to keep myself respectable, but it's not very easy when you've got no home to go to". One of the volunteers providing a daily soup wagon worked for a marketing company. When asked by a reporter what her colleagues at work thought, she said, "They don't know!"[8]

The government's housing policies, a shift towards private renting, the discounted sale of council housing and a cut in new social housebuilding, represented a decisive break with the earlier commitment to housing as a core social entitlement. The plight of the homeless was portrayed in a number of television documentaries such as ITV's 1987 *What a Way to Grow*, about the rising number of children in B&B accommodation. Westminster Council developed plans to 'remove the borough's homeless – with or without their compliance – from the B&B hotels of Bayswater and Pimlico to accommodation as far away as Barking or Heathrow'. One town on the list of possible relocations was Reading, in the South East of England, even though the local council was close to the limit of its capacity to cope with the rise in the number of local homeless families.[9]

Moore's attack on relative poverty was also challenged by the IFS. 'Mr Moore is right to say that compared with 100 years ago, all those on benefit are not in the sort of grinding poverty seen then', wrote Andrew Dilnot, the Institute's future director.

> But within that there is a subset of benefit recipients, including the homeless, who are poor to the point where it's affecting their health, and another group who are better off, but nonetheless, seriously excluded from things they should not be excluded from. Whether you want to call that poverty, most people would call that unacceptable.[10]

Three months later, Moore – whose department had already been split in two, with health hived off – was replaced by Tony Newton, judged to be a safer pair of hands.

An economic megashift

The sharp rise in inequality and relative poverty during the decade was largely the product of the uprooting of the post-war model of political economy.

Until then, governments had accepted the need for a more restrained capitalism through a mix of regulation and moral pressure.

In 1971, the Conservative chancellor Anthony Barber told a group of five thousand businessmen at London's Albert Hall that "left to its own devices, the capitalist system is inherently unstable".[11] Two years later, Edward Heath, in an echo of the 'hard-faced men' jibe in 1919, denounced Tiny Rowland, chair of the global mining company Lonrho, as the 'unpleasant and unacceptable face of capitalism'. Rowland, who later bought the *Observer* newspaper, stood accused of unethical and exploitative corporate behaviour. He was another of the growing number of tycoons who, holding the accepted rules of corporate governance in contempt, built huge personal fortunes by the use of extractive corporate practices. Any hope Heath might have harboured that political leaders could bring out-of-control magnates to heel were already being dashed. The business methods of the corporate buccaneers of the time, from Rowland to James Goldsmith, were soon to be widely copied, and the cry of 'the unacceptable face of capitalism' increasingly voiced.

The history of big business after the war comes in two halves. In the first half, it had become broadly accepted within business circles on both sides of the Atlantic that companies, which were working in largely closed economies with controls over capital flows, had obligations to employees and the local and national community as well as shareholders. Monopoly power was limited, while for the most part executives accepted that the entitlements of corporate leadership also came with wider responsibilities. New norms emerged about acceptable corporate behaviour, and executive and worker pay rose broadly in line with each other.

'Well into the 1960s', wrote the *Washington Post* columnist Steven Pearlstein, 'corporations were broadly viewed as owing something in return to the community that provided them with special legal protections and the economic ecosystem in which they could grow and thrive'.[12] J.K. Galbraith – who held office under both John F. Kennedy and Lyndon B. Johnson – described typical executive behaviour at the time: 'A sound management is one expected to exercise restraint.' He continued: 'With the power of decision goes opportunity for making money. ... Were everyone to seek to do so ... the corporation would be a chaos of competitive avarice'.[13]

Up to the 1980s, executive salaries in the UK were moderated by a kind of hidden 'shame gene', an unwritten social code which acted as a check on greed, and one largely abided by partly through fear of public outrage of overt excess. 'The system', argued Andrew Bailey, who later became governor of the Bank of England, 'relied on ... an unstated code in society that the remuneration of senior executives should not rise beyond a quite limited multiple of average pay'.[14] In 1982, the distinguished poet T.S. Eliot – a director of the publishing house Faber & Faber (which also published his

Figure 16.1: 'The Unacceptable Face of Capitalism', Les Gibbard cartoon, *The Guardian*, 24 May 1973 (depicting Edward Heath, William Whitelaw, Anthony Barber and Robert Carr)

I was just hanging up my 'unacceptable face of capitalism' suit . .

Source: Susannah Gibbard and the British Cartoon Archive, University of Kent

work) for forty years – wrote to the publisher's chairman, Geoffrey Faber, 'I have been thinking for some time that I am probably being overpaid. I think I might feel happier if my salary were reduced ... as something nearer my true value.'[15] High top rates of marginal taxation also worked to cap the scale of pay at the top. The staggering increase in rewards that came from the mid-1980s would not have been acceptable to public and political opinion even a few years earlier.

In the second half, this culture of restraint was dismantled, replaced at some speed by a much more ruthless model of capitalism and a great surge in the rate of personal enrichment. In the United States, a parallel explosion in business rewards in the 1980s was likened to an 'economic megashift'.[16] It took a while for these exploding rewards to be translated into fortunes large enough for the new corporate barons to top the rich lists. When the *Sunday Times* published its first rich list in 1989, it was dominated by family dynasties such as the Duke of Westminster and Lord Vesty.[17] Far from a lost class, the 'old gang' had never really gone away. The paper's editor, Andrew Neil, not known for his sympathies for the old establishment, was said to have been shocked by the continuing dominance of the landed and old business class. Despite this, subsequent lists revealed the way the old rich were being joined and then outpaced in the wealth stakes, as in the nineteenth century, by a new breed of business mogul, property tycoon and tech entrepreneur, and in the next tier, corporate lawyers, accountants, financiers and portfolio managers.

In the UK, the newly granted political licence to make big money was reinforced by the wider process of liberalisation that followed the breakdown of the post-war international finance system. In the discussions in the 1940s which constructed that system, the lessons of 1929 had been learned and bankers were excluded from the debates. In the post-war era, the domestic and international finance industry was highly regulated with restrictions on capital flows and on bank lending behaviour. The opening up of global capital markets in the 1970s, followed in the 1980s by the sweeping away of domestic credit controls, including over mortgage lending, enabled UK finance – and its bosses – to return to their pre-war supremacy, thus undoing the lessons of the 1920s and 1930s.

The 1985 'big-bang' financial reforms brought the giant American investment banks – from Goldman Sachs to Merrill Lynch – into London, and Wall Street's much more aggressive culture with them. This helped to transform the role of the City and the practices of big business, while reconcentrating power in the hands of the leaders of finance. One of the ways this power was used was to boost personal remuneration. While the benefit floor and wage share were managed down, the income ceiling across business and finance rose to new highs. By 1987, eleven UK company directors were earning in excess of £1 million. One of them, Christopher Heath, at merchant bank Baring Brothers, was paid £2.5 million.[18] In the mid-1970s, the pay ratio of chief executives of FTSE 100 companies to their average employee stood at a modest 9:1. By 2002, it had soared to 54:1 and carried on rising.[19] More than a hundred years earlier, the business financier J.P. Morgan – then one of the most powerful men in America – argued that executives should earn no more than twenty times the pay of the lowest-paid company workers.

During the 1960s and 1970s, a typical City bonus would be a turkey or a hamper from Harrods. In 1993, more than one hundred partners at the London offices of Goldman Sachs – or 'Goldmine Sachs' as it was known – were paid year-end bonuses of more than $1 million each. 'The guaranteed bonus', a curious oxymoron, became commonplace. In 1997, the City bonus pool hit the £1 billion mark. A decade later it had soared to £9 billion – equivalent to half the UK's transport budget. The lion's share of this sum went to a tiny proportion of the City's 350,000 staff. The City and Wall Street were so marked by frenzied rivalry that bonus day became known as the 'Valentine's Day Massacre'. As one insider put it, 'Most salesmen and traders are so infused with greedy, revolutionary fervour that no matter what amount the firm actually pays them, they automatically think they have been screwed.'[20]

Central to this remarkable bonanza was a new business goal – 'shareholder value'. Gradually, companies came to be run primarily or solely for the interests of their owners and executives, subordinating all other goals, with a weakened social state left to pick up the consequences. The chase for shareholder value – which too often collided with the national interest – meant maximising the short-term rise in the share price, while linking executive rewards to shareholder interests. As the American economist William Lazonick described the process:

> At that point, some people looked around and said: Wait! There's a huge pot of gold there, and it belongs to shareholders. They didn't want the profits going to workers or taxpayers. They didn't think that society, which had supported these companies in all kinds of ways, should benefit. They wanted the profits going to public shareholders – the group of people who really matter least to the firm's success.[21]

The concept was pioneered in the United States by companies like the giant General Electric (GE), run by one of the most ruthless company bosses of the decade, Jack Welch. In Britain, the first company to embrace the new idea was Lloyds Bank. At a board meeting in 1985, the bank set itself a single, overriding new goal 'of doubling our shareholder value every three years'.[22] One by one, even companies long wedded to the social 'stakeholder model' – with its greater emphasis on collective success, consensus and the long term – fell under the spell. By the mid-1990s, this 'almost unassailable mantra' had become near universal in British boardrooms.[23]

Gradually, corporate financiers gained an increasing stranglehold over company executives as to how to maximise share prices and swell their personal bank accounts in the process. Pay came to be more heavily linked to share prices, enabling industry bosses to build personal fortunes on a scale previously enjoyed only by aristocratic landowners and risk-taking entrepreneurs. The most effective way of upping the short-term share price was to shed labour, and the 1990s saw huge lay-offs. Jack Welch at GE led the way, shutting down factories, ruthlessly eliminating jobs and cutting wages. In return, GE's profits boomed, and its market valuation soared. Welch – 'Neutron Jack' as he was known – later dismissed shareholder value as 'the dumbest idea in the world. ... Your main constituencies are your employees, your customers and your products'.[24]

Under the new mantra, company owners and executives were granted the primary right to the fruits of economic activity. Fuelling the search for much higher returns on investment, this rule came to have a sustained and profound impact on the way economies were run, with significant effects on the level of poverty, inequality and economic performance.

Far from boosting growth, the evidence was that, over the half century to 2015, economies with large domestic financial systems had a tendency to low growth and high inequality.[25] Instead of being seen as an invaluable asset, company workforces became, as during the industrial revolution, an expendable commodity, a mere cost of production, to be hired and fired as required. Business dropped any intrinsic social dimension, with the biggest corporations treating their workforces as little more than 'cost centres', a return to buying and selling as the norm for human relations. Executives engaged in a constant process of restructuring, with the transfer of the risk of change to staff, adding an additional layer to the conflicting interests of labour and capital.

By the end of the 1980s, finance had become the centre of gravity of the new capitalist model.[26] A rejuvenated global finance industry became increasingly concentrated in London, spreading its wings from the old financial centre of the Square Mile to Canary Wharf and to chic office space in Mayfair. With bankers off the leash, a new 'shadow banking system' emerged, largely hidden and little understood by regulators. 'Here is an elite of the elites', according to the *Financial Times*, 'whose power has grown to a dimension that is truly imperial in the modern world'.[27]

International rules on capital requirements were bypassed, while the credit risks were passed elsewhere. If the bets went wrong, as they did, it was others who picked up the bill. Soon, international capitalism – 'financial liberalization on steroids', as one journalist described it[28] – was being driven by the demands of a tsunami of global footloose capital that amplified the risk of financial crisis. The assets held by the ten largest UK banks rose between 1960 and 2010 from 40 per cent to five times the size of the economy, light years away from the economy's needs, and a ratio higher than nearly all other rich countries.[29]

The pull of big money transformed boardroom ethics and corporate values. Increasingly, the emphasis was on 'fast buck' deals that were at odds with the patient organisation-building on which enduring companies and long-term wealth creation depends. The predatory and extractive corporate behaviour pioneered in the nineteenth century and then developed afresh by Clore, Hansen and Goldsmith became increasingly commonplace, if in mutant forms. Big money came to be made in fees and bonuses through a landslide of audacious corporate raiding, hostile takeovers and large-scale financial speculation.

Money worship

The deal that most came to symbolise the extractive processes at work was the dramatic buy-out of RJR Nabisco, the giant US tobacco and food conglomerate. The $25 billion 1988 bidding war, a nail-biting and high-stakes game of corporate poker, involved a river of money so great that it greatly distorted the American money supply figures. The fees enjoyed by the two top executives – $53 million and $46 million respectively – were stratospheric even by Wall Street standards.[1]

In the UK, the takeover deals of the time were often hatched in private clubs and restaurants. The Savoy Grill in the Strand, a favoured haunt of the rich and the famous, became known in business circles as the 'Deal Makers' Arms'. While some deals improved overall corporate performance, they too often extracted, and sometimes destroyed, rather than built value. A lucrative game of corporate pass the parcel became the source of personal enrichment for a generation of financiers whose route to wealth bypassed the entrepreneurialism that is the backbone of a wealth-creating economy. Companies were cracked open like piggy banks to extract the spoils. As the author of *Barbarians at the Gate* – the story of RJR Nabisco – put it, 'This was wealth created by tearing apart companies rather than building them up, by firing or downsizing companies rather than by hiring them.'[2] 'There is no historical precedent for such regressive redistribution within one generation without either legal title or economic disaster', concluded one study.[3]

Tomorrow's money today

The actions of the new tycoons and their accomplices brought another wave of upheaval to staff, small businesses and communities. The journalist Paul Johnson, former editor of the *New Statesman*, on the left in his early career and never a man to mince his words, described the rampaging dealmakers of the time as 'typical of the rottenness that is poisoning British society'.[4] What drove the deals was not a crusade to re-energise industry. The future viability of the companies targeted, the welfare of their employees and the 'national' or 'social interest' had no place in the calculations. Lord White used to boast that he had never set foot on the shop floor of any of the companies that he bought. The name of the game, as James Hanson acknowledged, was to get hold of 'tomorrow's money today'.[5]

Although the productive side of the economy has always depended on available finance, the interests of these two economic tracks became increasingly at odds. The City's primary role should have been as an intermediary, providing the capital for innovation and long-term wealth creation. Gradually, it stopped being the servant of the 'real economy', the world of work or the productive base, and became its master. By the end of the 1980s, largely abandoning its entrepreneurial role, it had become a cash cow servicing the demands of a domestic and global super-rich elite.

The new financiers had found a way of climbing the rich tables without building a business, creating new wealth or taking much of a risk. They also benefitted from rising returns on investment, the result of higher real interest rates, and eventually booming stock markets and rising property values. 'The rich simply got richer by being rich.'[6] Even when new wealth was being created, the gains were often shared by narrow groups – shareholders, executives and high-skilled professionals – with large sections of the middle- and less-skilled missing out.

The sybaritic lifestyles of the rich soon returned to the front pages. 'The signs of money worship multiplied', wrote Anthony Sampson, a leading chronicler of British society.[7] To find out about the typical lifestyle of a financier, you needed to look no further than the adverts carried by SE-DOL, the *Stock Exchange Official List* of all officially-quoted securities. The *List*'s most common adverts in the 1980s were for shooting holidays, private schools, safe deposit boxes, rare wines and exclusive Thames-side flats. Twenty years later, trophy assets had extended to the private jet, the privately-owned island, even a small submarine.

'Britain is on the money-go-round', reported the *Daily Express* in 1987. 'Rich man, poor man', headlined *Today*.[8] Following its purchase by Rupert Murdoch, the *Sunday Times* became a champion of the rich. 'Very little space is any longer available for the discussion of poverty, inequality, injustice or anything that might be recognisable as a moral issue', wrote Hugo Young, deputy editor of the newspaper until 1984.[9] The new unrestrained spirit of the times, and the political devaluation of the distribution question, was captured in films, novels and plays – from Caryl Churchill's *Serious Money* to Martin Amis' *Money*. Geordie Greig, the editor of *Tatler*, applauded the 'rise of the flashocracy'. 'Stealth wealth', he added, 'is so yesterday.'[10] Despite falling rates of taxation on the very rich, the tax avoidance industry boomed. The money-moving and money-making professions became the most sought after for top graduates.

Adam Smith had warned 220 years earlier of how the allure of extreme wealth distorts the pattern of human empathy, with the public admiring the wealthy but shunning the poor. He had a low opinion of the disproportionate power of 'the superior stations of society' and the way they prevented impartial government. According to the Conservative MP Jesse Norman, he would have been appalled by today's 'crony capitalism' and its neglect of the public interest.[11] In *The Theory of Moral Sentiments*, Smith spelled

Figure 17.1: Poster for Caryl Churchill's play, 'Serious Money', on its West End transfer, 1987. Poster designed by Iain Lanyon and play directed by Max Stafford Clark.

Source: V&A Museum

out the moral impact of the public's dazzlement with the wealthy. The 'disposition to admire, and almost to worship, the rich and the powerful, and to despise, or, at least, to neglect persons of poor and mean condition', he concluded, is 'the great and most universal cause of the corruption of our moral sentiments.'[12]

A parallel process was at work from the 1980s. The 'get-rich-quick, something-for-nothing mood of the late-eighties' helped to erode the limits of acceptable business behaviour, with high-level corporate scandals, from Blue Arrow, Robert Maxwell and British Airways to Barings, Equitable Life and later the Royal Bank of Scotland and the rigging of the LIBOR, EURIBOR and foreign exchange markets, hit the headlines with monotonous regularity.[13] According to one account:

> The moral order of British society has altered. [It] lays stress on individual success as a priority greater than that of collective obligations. The privileged values of individual success lend further credence to the idea that social inequality is not only inevitable, but that it is also desirable in a society which seeks prosperity.[14]

The rich were of course a heterogeneous group, and there were different routes to wealth. Some of those ascending the wealth league in the 1980s did so through traditional and inspired entrepreneurial activity, taking risks with their own money to build new businesses, add to productive capacity and create jobs in a way that, in most people's eyes, justified the resulting rewards. The single-minded, determined and innovative qualities that are required to build big fortunes are often the same qualities that provide work and promote wider progress. Many of the pioneering and innovative business leaders of the past – from Jesse Boot, who expanded this father's herbalist store to bring chemist shops to poorer areas in the mid-nineteenth century, and the early retail moguls such as Simon Marks and Marcus Sieff who launched Marks & Spencer, to Arnold Weinstock, the man who turned GEC into a world leader – also contributed to the national and social interest by reducing costs, expanding markets and spreading opportunity. In 1920, the thirty-four-year-old John Spedan Lewis, despite his father's opposition, pioneered the first employee-owned partnership and profit-sharing scheme – an 'experiment in industrial democracy', as he described it – at the Peter Jones department store in central London.

Contemporary examples of the 'deserving rich' might include founding entrepreneurs such as Sir Clive Sinclair, who produced the UK's first mass-produced and affordable home computer, the ZX80, and Tim Waterstone, who modernised bookselling in the UK by setting up his national book chain using a £1000 redundancy cheque from WH Smiths. The author J.K. Rowling toiled away in an Edinburgh café to write her first *Harry Potter* novel and has since given generously to child charities. The influential founder of the Body Shop, Anita Roddick, was one of the pioneers of the drive for a more ethical capitalism.

Thousands of today's flourishing small companies, started by local entrepreneurs and lacking the kind of state support and infrastructure for smaller firms provided by other nations, have, by boosting local economies, made significant economic and social contributions. Examples include London's Brompton Bikes, Stoke's Emma Bridgewater pottery, Stroud's green energy firm Ecotricity and John and Irene Hays' successful travel company that, in 2019, stepped in to buy the shops of the failed, badly managed and over-indebted Thomas Cook. The nationwide shoe-repair and key-cutting specialist (and family-run) Timpson, with 5500 employees known as 'the family', is among the largest employers of ex-offenders. The British scientist

Tim Berners-Lee – the inventor of the World Wide Web – could have become supremely rich, but is content with the way the wealth he created came to be shared more widely.

A multi-speed society

It took time for the impact of these multilayered changes in inequality to be fully charted, with details sometimes forced out of government only by parliamentary questions. The scale of transformation first became clear in the early 1990s. The new HBAI series showed that the gap between top and bottom had widened sharply. The 1980s was the first decade since the War in which growth not only bypassed some but in which a minority of the poorest had become worse off, thus confirming the link between changes in inequality and trends in poverty.

Drawing on official data, a detailed study funded by the social research body the Joseph Rowntree Foundation painted a devastating picture of the fallout at work. Led by Sir Peter Barclay, former chair of the official Social Security Advisory Committee, it found that while average net incomes among the poorest tenth fell between 1979 and 1992, they rose by 62 per cent among the richest tenth.[15] Comparisons with seventeen other developed countries found that 'the pace at which inequality increased in the UK was faster than in any other with the exception of New Zealand'. The long-term unemployed, and others dependent solely on state benefits, concluded the report, 'no longer had a stake in rising prosperity', while ethnic minority groups were especially vulnerable to falling living standards.[16]

In less than a decade, as incomes fanned out from the middle, Britain had become a multi-speed economy, with a super-fast lane for a privileged few, a fast lane for the affluent, and a series of progressively slower lanes for almost everyone else, with minimal switching between them. For those in the slowest lane, the rate of social progress had been capped and for some set in reverse. In the thirty years from 1978, real wages for those who were already at the bottom of the pay league barely increased, while there were significant surges for professionals, especially those working in finance, law and medicine.[17] One of the principal sources of the unravelling of the single-track society nourished in the post-war years was the way business and financial leaders took advantage of the new pro-rich culture to colonise an increasing share of the existing cake.

There were other factors at work. These included the greater mobility of capital and labour generated by the opening up of global markets, the impact of new technology in factories and the shifting pattern of skill requirements that it involved, and the pace of deindustrialisation. The same processes helped to steer Britain, with its poor record on technical education and training, innovation and social and private investment, down the 'low road' of a weak-wage, low-skilled, low value-added economy, with the rising levels of low pay concentrated among women and Black and other ethnic minority workers. Britain's poor productivity record was intimately linked to wage stagnation, with abundant cheap labour dulling the incentive for large firms to invest.[18]

While no government could have done much in the short term to resist some of these external forces, the state-initiated new economic ideology, with its belief in higher rewards at the top and a weaker social safety net, was a potent pro-inequality and pro-poverty force. Many other countries of comparable wealth and subject to the same global and technological pressures, including the Scandinavian nations, France and Germany and the Netherlands, were able to counter these forces.[19]

Despite its bipartisan membership, the Barclay Inquiry proved highly controversial. As it warned, 'the pattern [of inequality] had not yet been fully grasped by policy makers'. Instead of acknowledging the report's central message, ministers launched a number of attacks on its findings. In the House of Commons, the secretary of state for social security Peter Lilly dismissed the report's findings as too ideological. 'Unfortunately the politics of envy, though never clearly stated, lies behind (and weakens) much of the analysis in the Report.'[20] In the House of Lords, Lord Jenkins, the former secretary of state for health and social security, described the report as 'not only flawed but tainted'.[21] Yet, as pointed out in the debate, the findings were drawn from official statistics, and had been submitted to the Department of Social Security for checking well in advance of publication.

The press response was also divided. The social policy journalist Nicholas Timmins declared that its findings 'should make the blood run cold. It is not a [picture] of a nation at ease with itself'.[22] In contrast, a leader in the *Times* disputed the report's findings that Britain had become more unequal than other rich nations.[23] *The Sunday Telegraph*, on the other hand, reported that Whitehall's most senior civil servants had been brought together by Sir Robin Butler, the cabinet secretary, to discuss the report and 'to raise Whitehall's awareness of the problems caused by Britain's growing social divide'.[24]

A two-thirds, one-third society

The decade left exposed the strategies of both major political parties. The market experiment largely failed to deliver the promised entrepreneurial renaissance that might have raised the speed of those caught in the 'slow lane'. The period spawned some important new companies, such as the global giant Vodafone, but there were few British high-tech successes. One, the specialist chip designer ARM Holdings, did not manufacturer their product and employed only some 3000 people. According to the historian David Edgerton, few of the high-profile entrepreneurs of recent times – from

Richard Branson to James Dyson – have been in the same league as the pioneering industrialists of the past, from the car manufacturer Lord Nuffield to Sir Freddy Laker, founder of the first 'no frills' airline operator.[25]

The lessons for Labour's long wilderness years were also uncomfortable. The continuing rise in *average* levels of affluence – typical real incomes rose comfortably during the 1980s – along with the erosion of working-class politics and voting patterns had weakened the party's traditional support base. While less well-off voters began to abandon their former political affiliations, those doing OK switched off from cries of rising inequality. As Ron Todd, the leader of the Transport and General Workers' Union, expressed the dilemma: 'What do you say to a docker who earns £400 a week, owns his own house, a new car, microwave and video as well as a small place near Marbella? You do not say: "let me take you out of your misery, brother".'[26]

The deep-seated changes driving the more fractured society were a challenge to Labour's egalitarian philosophy. Progressive thinkers struggled to come to terms with the revolution in ideas unleashed by Mrs Thatcher. The main exception came from *Marxism Today*, the journal of the Communist Party, with some of its contributors later becoming part of Tony Blair's inner team. With its call to embrace the new affluence, and in one sense Thatcherism, the monthly journal challenged the traditional left's critique of an increasingly commodified society. For some of its writers, the new consumerism was emancipatory, offering an end to the grey uniformity of the past and an opportunity for greater self-expression and new ways of living. 'Ideologies of affluence have had very real effects. ... Some of these have been potentially liberating, consuming as a source of power and pleasure.'[27] It was a theme that embraced the new throwaway culture of the times, but one that failed to understand the shallowness of the quick fixes being offered by the consumer revolution and their impact on the global environmental crisis that was soon to emerge.

If the limits to markets had been exposed, so too had the limits of Labour's social strategy. As the academic and former Labour MP David Marquand had warned, Labour had failed to develop a coherent new model of social democracy sufficient to build a progressive anti-Conservative majority in favour of sustained social reform.[28] Labour found this to its cost when they lost the 1992 general election, fought on a pro-redistribution platform to be financed by higher taxation on the better-off middle classes. When the architect of Labour's tax strategy, the shadow chancellor John Smith, replaced Neil Kinnock as leader, he was only too aware of the message from the electorate. Smith had attempted to build an alliance of the better-off and low-income Britain largely by an appeal to altruism, a plan apparently rejected by much of middle Britain.

One year after Smith became leader, the dilemma facing egalitarianism was highlighted in a new book by J.K. Galbraith, *The Culture of Contentment*.[29]

Galbraith argued that affluent societies had spawned 'contented majorities', a comfortable, complacent and self-interested group with a weak commitment to the interests of the insecure minority, raising doubts about the redistributive strategy of traditional social democracy. A similar argument was made in the 1980s by Peter Glotz, the general secretary of the German Social Democratic Party. He described Germany as a 'two-thirds, one-third society', with the 'contented' happy to detach themselves from the poorest third.[30]

Well aware of this dilemma, one of Smith's early acts as leader was to appoint a Commission on Social Justice chaired by Sir Gordon Borrie, former director general of Fair Trade, and like Peter Barclay, another member of the 'great and the good'. The commission became part of the wider process of modernisation that Labour had begun under Neil Kinnock and now continued by Smith. Smith hoped it would help bring Labour more in tune with changes since it was last in power, and show to the electorate that the party understood the need to combine economic competency with social improvement.

For some observers, the commission was merely a way of parking some difficult political issues, 'to disembarrass it of social policies which seemed an electoral burden: in other words, to get the Labour Party out of a hole'.[31] But established on the fiftieth anniversary of the Beveridge Report, its timing was also highly symbolic, raising hopes amongst some insiders that it might be the source of a 'new Beveridge plan' for the modern age. Some commission members had hoped to open the door to new ideas on how the welfare state might be reconciled with the demands of a changing social and economic order, but in the end it fell short of such ambition.[32]

For all the force of some of its proposals for change, the commission's report ducked the question of how a powerful economic elite was able once again to accumulate runaway fortunes too often unrelated to the productive economy, and via their impact on jobs, wages and opportunities, often at significant cost to those on lower incomes. The report was published six months after the untimely death, through a heart attack, of John Smith. He was fifty-five. Smith's replacement, Tony Blair, came with a very different vision of the way forward. And that turned out to include a pretty relaxed view of the new plutocracy, if not of poverty.

PART V

1997–2010

18

The elephant in the room

In early January 1998, a large group of traders, fund managers and financiers braved the pouring winter rain to gather at the Mansion House, the grand official residence of the mayor of the City of London. They were to debate the motion 'This house believes that City salaries are totally fair and justified.'

Supporting the motion was George Cox, a director of the London International Financial Futures Exchange, established to trade in 'futures', essentially bets about the future course of share prices, currencies and commodities. "If you cut City remuneration tomorrow", he argued, "there will be less available for society at large and we would all be poorer as a result". Andrew Winckler, former chief executive of the Securities and Investment Board – set up to supervise the financial markets – spoke against the motion. The Square Mile had become "smug and complacent" about salaries and bonuses, he told the audience. "The current bonus system encourages a degree of speculation that is not warranted and is rewarding failure." To the surprise of the audience, the motion was lost – with 52 per cent against, 45 per cent in favour.

For the previous decade, Britain's financial services industry had been on a roll. Profits, bonuses and share prices had soared. But eight months before the Mansion House debate, Labour ousted the Major government with a record post-war majority of 179. Labour's landslide victory came with a huge weight of expectation. In the morning after the election, commuters at Brixton tube station in South London were greeted by the electronic boards showing not the usual train destination but the election results: 'Labour, 419, Tories, 163.' As the numbers were spotted, waiting passengers broke into spontaneous applause. With its massive majority, supporters hoped and opponents feared that the new government would deliver a radical programme of change that would unravel at least part of the Thatcherite legacy.

Many in the City expected the worst, that Labour would rein in the more self-serving practices of finance and launch a concerted attack on the way high rates of poverty and inequality were built into the economic system. The surge in the income and wealth divide might once have been natural territory for Labour. But Thatcherism had shifted the political ground rules and Blair had been engaged in a profound rethink of the Party's priorities. 'The Blair project', wrote Eric Hobsbawm in 1998, 'is still essentially framed by and moving on terrain defined by Thatcherism.'[1]

Pragmatic realism

Far from a programme for transformative change, Blair believed that Labour had to adapt to the world of free markets, globalisation and privatisation. Buying into the 'end of history' and the 'victory-for-capitalism' thesis, this meant embracing a new 'third way' politics, locating the party – according to its manifesto – between 'the old left and the Conservative right'.[2] Determined to distance the party from 'Old Labour', Blair rechristened the party 'New Labour' and set out to reassure voters, big business and the City that Labour had changed its spots. He was heavily influenced by Bill Clinton, who had become president of the United States four years earlier. Clinton changed his party's name to the 'New Democrats', wooed Wall Street and adopted an intermediate ideology between pro-equality social democracy and pro-market, pro-inequality Reaganism.

In September 1998, Clinton and Blair held a conference in New York to officially launch the new ideology. Guests included the Swedish prime minister Göran Persson and Italy's Romano Prodi. The following year, Blair joined with the German chancellor Gerhard Schröder to launch *The Third Way – Die Neue Mitte* – a manual for a new ideology of 'pragmatic realism'. There was even speculation that Clinton and Blair were keen to replace the Socialist International, the global alliance of social-democratic parties, with a new, fully fledged 'Third Way International.'

For critics, the new mantra was dismissed as the 'latest buzz phrase being used to give some intellectual ballast to New Labour's rightwards drift'.[3] As the Labour peer David Sainsbury commented, New Labour 'suffered from not having a credible, alternative political economy to neo-liberalism'.[4] The veteran *Financial Times* columnist Samuel Brittan agreed: 'Labour could have won the election on a much more anti-capitalist platform', he wrote on the day after the election.[5]

In their search for a 'big new idea', Labour's leaders had flirted, briefly, with other ideas. These included 'stakeholding', in which firms' goals would be extended to include the interests of their workforce and the wider community, promoted by, among others, Will Hutton, later editor of the *Observer*, in his bestselling *The State We're In*. Another idea – 'communitarianism' – would have involved the strengthening of the moral, social and political foundations of society, in part through the decentralisation of power and resources to local communities.

That Blair settled on a quite different route owes a good deal to the sociologist Anthony Giddens, director of the LSE, who had long been calling for a new politics 'beyond left and right'. A between left and right political strategy, aimed at a society between market capitalism and radical social democracy, still begged the question of where the 'between line' should be drawn. In the event the 'third way' ended up as a somewhat fuzzy umbrella term for a number of strands of Labour thinking, including areas that were to have a profound effect on the course of inequality. Among these strands were the need to embrace a tougher philosophy on welfare and an acceptance of the trade-off between equality and efficiency.

Giddens argued that the old egalitarianism was no longer tenable. Social democracy had failed to deliver sustained equality even in more benign conditions, and it was even more difficult to deliver in the more competitive markets ushered in by globalisation. The egalitarian project, he argued, is 'part of a now lapsed historical endeavour'.[6] Instead he called for 'a new egalitarianism', one that still embraced a degree of redistribution but which would focus on a narrower goal of 'equalizing life chances across the generations'.[7] After fudging the issue for decades, Labour had come down in favour of 'equality of opportunity' over 'equality of outcome' and 'meritocracy' over 'egalitarianism', with new weight given to creating a culture of aspiration.

For the third way's architects, there was no need to tackle the question of property ownership and its growing concentration. In some ways this rethinking was less of a departure from the past than it might have seemed. While creating greater equality had been Labour's central purpose since its foundation, and for its members a key litmus test of its success, the party had been much less precise about what it meant or how to achieve it. 'The commitment of the Labour Party to equality is rather like the singing of the *Red Flag* at its gatherings', wrote the economist Tony Atkinson. 'All regard it as part of a cherished heritage, but those on the platform often seem to have forgotten the words.'[8]

Labour inherited a high inequality, high poverty wave, with both at unprecedented post-war levels. Despite this, they bought into some of the new orthodoxies of the time. Openly relaxed about the growing concentration of income and wealth, Labour's primary social goals were to tackle poverty and a lack of social mobility. Targeting poverty, desirable as it was, was less politically challenging than reducing inequality, which required confronting vested interests, corporate power-brokers and, to some extent, the public. It involved tackling one end of the distribution, while leaving those sitting at the top largely undisturbed. As Titmuss had warned in 1965, 'To recognise inequality as the problem involves recognising the need for structural change, for sacrifices by the majority.'[9]

The idea that cutting poverty depended on a direct attack on institutionalised inequality was now being explicitly rejected. Instead, resurrecting earlier theories, poverty was seen as a stand-alone, one-dimensional condition that could be tackled by raising the floor while leaving the concentration of wealth at the top untouched. Any link between inequality and poverty was implicitly denied. There were only two passing references to inequality in the 1997 manifesto, while in its introduction,

Tony Blair wrote that he had 'no time for the politics of envy'.[10] This was more than a symbolic gesture or vote-seeking rhetoric. It was a watershed moment in Labour's central philosophy, a defining characteristic of the shift away from the social-democratic values that once dominated post-war politics and opinion. For some it was a cardinal sin. 'At some point during the revisions of Labour ideology and policy in the 1990s, economic inequality became a taboo subject ... to be dismissed simply as an Old Labour shibboleth', wrote two critics of Labour's new stance.[11]

While Gordon Brown, the new chancellor, called the level of child poverty a 'scar on the nation's soul', there was little evidence from Labour's early days in power that they meant business on poverty.[12] Unlike the early moves by previous Labour governments, such as in 1964 and 1974, to raise some benefit levels, there was no early action to improve the level of benefits, most of which had sunk in relative terms over the previous two decades.

Rather, the new government's intentions on benefits got off to a bumpy start. Determined to convince the electorate of a responsible approach to economic management, Gordon Brown committed Labour to maintaining the previous administration's planned budget for the next two years. This included pressing on with a projected cut in benefits for lone parents, a measure which caused a good deal of heart-searching within Labour ranks, not least for Harriet Harman, the new secretary of state for Social Security. It was Harman who had to force the cut through the Commons, with Labour facing a backbench rebellion of forty-seven MPs over the measure, denting Brown's public reputation for being on the side of the poor in the process.[13]

In 1998, Blair gave nine lectures across the nation on the need for 'welfare reform'. Before the lectures, he hinted in a BBC interview at a number of possible radical changes, including 'affluence-testing' the basic state pension. With 'Affluence exam for benefits' the headline in the *Telegraph*, the ideas were quietly dropped.[14]

An early move was to appoint Frank Field as deputy to Harriet Harman, with a brief to devise a bold plan for benefit reform. Field – MP for Birkenhead from 1979 – had become something of a maverick, and had been placed there to shake things up. It was not a successful move. Harman was part of Labour's modernising project and her role included getting people on benefits into work, 'making work pay' and ensuring responsibilities went hand in hand with rights, if necessary through a more coercive welfare-to-work programme. As Harman put it in her autobiography: 'Our mantras were "The best form of welfare is work", "a hand-up not a hand-out".' She implemented the voluntary 'new deal for lone parents', a largely successful initiative in encouraging more single parents into work.[15]

Field clashed with both Harman and Brown. He submitted a number of ideas, some wilder than others, but all deemed unworkable. Thinking the unthinkable and putting Harman and Field together proved, as Blair later conceded, 'the dating agency from hell'.[16] Fifteen months later, the internal power struggle came to an abrupt end. Harman was sacked, but returned to the front bench as solicitor general in 2001. Field became a backbencher, where he continued to offer a constant stream of advice, some a good deal more workable, and welcome, than others.

Blair's war on poverty

Labour was off to an uncertain start on one of its primary social goals, but in March 1999, Blair was invited to give the 'Beveridge revisited' lecture at Toynbee Hall. No one outside a small inner circle knew what he was planning to say. Although expectations were muted, Blair used the occasion to announce a dramatic and unexpected new commitment: to halve child poverty within a decade and 'eradicate' it within twenty years.[17]

There has been much speculation as to why Blair made such a commitment, which was never going to be achievable and seems to have been plucked out of the air. It's possible that Blair was concerned about the UK's unenviable global ranking. The country was third from the bottom for child poverty among comparable nations, just above the US and Italy, and second from the bottom on inequality, behind the US. Its level of public spending as a percentage of GDP was the lowest in the European Union.[18] More likely is that the commitment to abolition was a somewhat hyped political move pressed on Blair by his key adviser, Alistair Campbell, to get 'a good headline'. There was no evidence of much pre-planning, and as one social policy academic recalled, 'nothing underlying it. There was never any strategy for how you get to that point.'[19]

The groundbreaking promise came out of the blue and, while widely welcomed, raised the eyebrows of the experts assembled in the lecture hall. The move – which ensured that poverty would never be far from the headlines – was as ambitious as it was unprecedented. The targets and the timetable were daunting – even the Scandinavians with their higher social spending had failed to come close to ending poverty.

Little serious thought seems to have gone into the declaration. Blair was unspecific on what he meant by 'poverty'. There was still no official definition or measure, and it is likely that the prime minister had no clear view himself.[20] As it turned out, government statisticians had been working for some months on ways to respond to an earlier European Union initiative to adopt a new primary threshold. This threshold was a clearly defined relative income measure based on an income level set at 60 per cent of the midpoint of the income range (the *median* income), and was designed for making comparisons across member nations.[21] Eventually it was the 60 per cent, median-based threshold that emerged as the central target.[22]

According to one government statistician, 'The median rather than the mean average [which had mostly been used before that point] was ultimately preferred given the skew/non-normality inherent in most national income distributions.'[23] The choice of 60 per cent, according to the minutes of an internal departmental seminar, was an essentially pragmatic decision to opt for a single measure.[24] Whatever the real reasons, the adoption of the 60 per cent point was arbitrary – why 60 and not 50 or 70 per cent? It was not based on evidence about household needs or an acceptable minimum level of material well-being, and estimates suggested it was unlikely to provide for an adequate level of social participation and inclusion.[25]

Nevertheless, the new measure, emerging after much internal heart-searching, was a pivotal moment. It was the first time any government had committed to a precise and relative measure of poverty. Linking the poverty target to the standard that was typical also brought a direct link with inequality, if only in the bottom half of the distribution. It was a recognition that those falling more than a certain distance below the norms in society were unlikely to be able to participate fully in it. As UNICEF argued, 'Median income is a strong indicator of what is considered normal in contemporary society.'[26]

To move towards its new goal, Labour launched a raft of measures. The first of these was the introduction of the National Minimum Wage in April 1999, a move that followed decades of division and campaigning, and which was bitterly fought by the Conservatives and business with warnings of heavy job losses. The move put a much firmer floor under wages – a key strand of the earlier calls for a 'national social minimum' – and helped to mitigate the broader drift towards a low-paid economy.[27] Another important step came in the introduction of a revamped, means-tested tax credit scheme. This replaced Family Credit and was a key part of the 'make work pay' strategy. The new system introduced further reliance on means testing, and acted, in effect, as a further subsidy for low-wage employers, especially in the service sector where profitability can depend on a ready supply of cheap and flexible labour.[28] But for those claiming it, it also led to a significant improvement in the take-home pay of those on low wages.

Other measures included free nursery places for all three- and four-year-olds, new and well-used Sure Start Centres, giving more integrated support for families, and improved maternity and paternity rights. It is no coincidence that this string of 'family-friendly' work measures – with an emphasis on empowerment – followed the election of 158 women as Labour MPs in 1997. Gone were the days when women MPs raising issues like childcare in the Commons were booed. Labour's principal focus was on child poverty, but there were also new measures to help pensioners, including a new means-tested benefit to replace income support for pensioners – the Minimum Income Guarantee, which became the Pension Credit. There was also the

Winter Fuel Payment, free TV licences for the over-seventy-fives and free bus travel.

While Labour fell short of its target, and poverty rose slightly among single people, the proportion of children in relative poverty between 1997 and 2010 fell by just over a third to 17.5 per cent, while pensioner poverty fell by a quarter, also to 17.5 per cent. This was significant progress and widely acknowledged. The UK also improved its ranking on poverty levels among EU members.[29] Yet, despite the new measures, the initial success could not be sustained. Child poverty levels fell initially and then levelled off before rising slightly by 2010.[30] Nick Pearce, a former adviser to Tony Blair, later admitted that Labour's anti-poverty strategy 'had been running out of road even before 2008'.[31]

This was largely because of mounting pressure on public spending levels, but also in part due to the way the boom years raised the median income target. The falls in poverty were dependent on a significant hike in annual spending on benefits, amounting to £18 billion in the case of families with children and £11 billion for pensioners in 2010.[32] It was estimated that to meet Blair's abolition target by 2020 would have required an additional £28 billion in public spending.[33] The strategy mitigated but hardly solved the intractable rise in poverty since the 1970s. The falls in poverty – and the redistribution that they required – were also much more difficult to sustain under successor governments much less wedded to an anti-poverty agenda.[34]

Despite the high-profile attempt to cut poverty, Labour dropped its traditional commitment to greater equality. In the run-up to the general election of 2001, Tony Blair was grilled on the BBC's *Newsnight* by Jeremy Paxman. "Prime Minister, is it acceptable for the gap between rich and poor to widen?"[35] Blair wriggled and Paxman repeated the question many times before Blair explained that he wanted a society that encouraged "levelling up" not "levelling down". It was a view echoed by senior ministers. 'Rather than questioning whether huge salaries are morally justified', argued business and enterprise minister John Hutton, 'we should celebrate the fact that people can be enormously successful in this country'. Child poverty, Hutton added, 'can be abolished while people at the top are very wealthy. It is not only statistically possible – it is positively a good thing'.[36] Labour, it seemed, had succumbed to a version of Stockholm syndrome. They had first been captured by wealthy financiers and then become their defenders.

Inequality was the elephant in the room for Labour's anti-poverty targets. Determined to 'play safe', Labour did 'social democracy on the quiet'.[37] The term 'redistribution' was largely avoided, and the cash transfers that were taking place were implemented 'by stealth'.[38] Its leaders did not want to appear soft to a public perceived to be cool on benefits, while what progress had been achieved involved redistribution as much from middle class as from rich Britain. To cut poverty on a sustained basis while allowing the process of top enrichment to continue apace was always going to be a tough call. The richest 1 per cent continued to boost their share of the nation's income and wealth under Labour's watch.[39] Three-fifths of this rise in the top income share – the product of record bonuses, pay and City fees, some of it accruing from debt repayments from ordinary households – went to a relatively small number of already well-paid City traders and executives.[40]

Despite Labour's focus on relative poverty, there were few attempts to root relativity in the idea of creating a more equal society. 'Both the Conservatives and New Labour tend to frame poverty as a discrete problem, or set of problems, rather than as part of the grossly unequal overall distribution of income and wealth that marks the UK', wrote Ruth Lister in 2007.[41] In his eightieth birthday lecture, David Donnison reinforced his earlier warning that tackling poverty requires a strategy that focuses on 'the rich as well as the poor' and 'recognises that if we are not working to include our fellow citizens in society's mainstream we are probably helping to exclude them. The policy implications of a concern about inequality and the cast of mind they spring from are quite different from those associated with poverty'.[42]

In 1997, the economist John Kay coined the phrase 'redistributive market liberalism' (RML) to describe the approach to social protection that followed the post-war reforms. By this he meant it had been driven by a mix of largely unregulated markets and limited state transfers.[43] For free marketeers, this approach had the merit of justifying – outside of limited transfers – minimal interference in markets through, for example, wage regulation or improved collective provision of services. In this way, poverty could be dealt with through essentially technocratic solutions such as through Friedman's negative income tax, Norman Fowler's Family Credit, Gordon Brown's tax credit system or later, Iain Duncan Smith's Universal Credit.

Cash transfers are a vital and primary mechanism for cutting poverty, but they are not enough on their own to overcome the embedded institutional structures that drive large-scale impoverishment. Conservative governments from 1979 to 1997 applied essentially minimalist models of RML. They reduced the generosity of benefits, tightened conditionality and extended means testing. They also outsourced the provision of public services, a process that had begun in parts of the Civil Service in the 1970s.

Progressive systems of redistribution help to offset wider rises in inequality, if only partially. The weakening of the redistributive impact of the tax and benefit system during the 1980s through the adoption of a minimal RML lowered its poverty- and inequality-reducing power. More were made dependent on a less effective social support system.[44] In 1984, cash benefits and taxes reduced the level of market inequality – before the operation of the tax-benefit system – by nineteen percentage points. Six years later, the redistributive impact had fallen to twelve points.[45]

New Labour greatly softened the RML model, but remained dewy-eyed about the merits of markets. We might call New Labour's approach 'RML plus'. They introduced more generous working-age benefits and the National Minimum Wage, and gave a significant boost to social spending and public investment. Nevertheless, the progress made was reversed in the harsher political and social climate that was to follow. Labour's social strategy showed that it is possible to make short-run cuts in poverty while the rich continue to grow their share of the national wealth, but that such success will be limited and unlikely to be sustainable. Such short-term shifts failed to challenge a deeply embedded inequality-poverty relationship. This is why, compared with Attlee's managed welfare capitalism, which helped, for a while, to at least partially break the inequality, poverty wave, New Labour lacked a lasting footprint.

Still born to rule

Labour's second key social goal was to create a modern, meritocratic society. The term 'meritocracy' had been popularised in 1958 by the sociologist Michael Young in his anti-utopian fictional essay *The Rise of the Meritocracy*. The book was a satire that looked at what a futuristic Britain would be like if economic success was based not on social origin but on talent and effort.

Far from advocating such a system, Young was issuing a stern warning that a winner-takes-all world would become ruthlessly competitive, hierarchical and unstable, with an even more tiered system of polarisation with those unable to make it ranked as failures. Others have dismissed a politics of aspiration, whereby success is measured by how far you rise and how much you are paid, as creating a society that justified inequality, where, 'by definition, certain people must be left behind'.[1] The contributions that people make to society, often outside of the market system through unpaid caring and volunteering, have long been out of step with pay levels and traditional hierarchies of status, as society found during the opening months of the COVID-19 pandemic when views on who were the most valuable members of society were turned upside down.

Morally naked

Despite these concerns, creating a more meritocratic – and competitive – society came to be a widely shared goal across the political divide. Margaret Thatcher, the daughter of a Grantham grocer, wanted a society based on merit not birth. Even though earlier Labour thinkers, such as Crosland, had warned that a meritocracy would not be a 'just society',[2] Blair, minor public school and Oxford, picked up the baton. In 2001, Young reiterated his earlier prophetic warning with a lament of meritocracy's dominant position in the ideology of New Labour and the way it would further undermine the class who don't make it: 'It is hard indeed in a society that makes so much of merit to be judged as having none. No underclass has ever been left as morally naked as that.'[3]

Some free-market commentators have argued that modern societies are already highly meritocratic, with income differences more closely linked to the genetic inheritance of intelligence and aptitude than to background. The most powerful advocate of this view has been the influential American welfare critic Charles Murray, co-author of the controversial *The Bell Curve*, published in 1994. Murray claimed that American society was already close to an IQ meritocracy. Peter Saunders, a pro-market British academic, argued in *Unequal But Fair?* that Britain was 'much closer to achieving a meritocracy than pundits and public alike seem to suppose'.[4]

The title of Saunders' tract was significant. Inequality, he was claiming, is acceptable if it is based on merit. It was seized on by other conservative thinkers to claim that the rising inequalities of the time 'do not in fact reflect any serious social injustice but simply the varying capacities of individuals, whatever their social origins, to take up the opportunities that are available to them'.[5] This 'because I'm worth it' claim also became a handy justification for the newly enriched corporate bosses who liked to see themselves as part of a deserving elite who had earned their place at the income summit. As Jean-Pierre Garnier, head of the pharmaceutical giant GlaxoSmithKline, put it, 'If you pay peanuts, you get monkeys.'

Creating a society with more equal life chances had already proved an elusive goal. A hundred years on from the days when such chances were almost totally determined by birth, the post-war years had brought a more even, if still heavily limited, spread of opportunities. Nevertheless, despite the claims of Saunders and others, the evidence pointed to a still relatively fixed society where the opportunities for upward advancement continued to be highly skewed. Researchers distinguish between two types of mobility, absolute (where all groups, from the poorest to the richest, enjoy progress, with no one switching their relative position) and relative (where some of those born into a disadvantaged background improve their relative position, outpacing some born into more advantaged groups). Improving relative mobility without an improvement in absolute mobility is a zero-sum game – one person's gain in the income and social rankings is someone else's loss.[6]

From the 1950s, the persistent power of privilege was disguised by the growth of white-collar service jobs leading to an apparent upward shift in the class structure. In the four decades up to 2007, the proportion of the population classified (by sociologists) as working class fell from 70 to 44 per cent, while the middle class rose from 31 to 55 per cent.[7] But this 'elevator society', in which workers upgraded their status and expectations, was something of an illusion. The social shape of Britain barely changed. As the cultural critic and historian Richard Hoggart wrote in an introduction to George Orwell's *The Road to Wigan Pier*, 'Class distinctions do not die: they merely find new ways of expressing themselves. ... Each decade, we shiftily declare we have buried class; each decade the coffin stays empty.'[8]

By the 1990s, the scale of absolute upward mobility had slowed significantly, while rates of relative ascent up the social ladder remained low, especially for women. 'The prevailing situation', concluded two of Britain's leading experts, 'is one in which children of less advantaged origins need to show substantially more "merit" than do children from more advantaged origins in order to enter similarly desirable class positions in the course of their adult lives'.[9] An influential academic study published in 2005 found that the UK stood at second from the bottom among developed nations, just ahead of the United States, on income mobility. Mobility rates had also been worsening. Children born in 1970 were less likely to move from the bottom to the top quarter than those born in 1958.[10] Little progress had been made in fifty years of policy innovation, while today, with the spread of low pay and job insecurity, we may be witnessing a deterioration in rates of absolute mobility.

Of course, there have always been individual examples of breaking the class barrier. Leading business figures who lacked a head start have included the managing director of GEC, Lord Weinstock, the son of a tailor. Tesco's former chief executive, Terry Leahy was brought up on a Liverpool council estate while the Body Shop's Anita Roddick went to a secondary modern school. Harry Evans, who became editor of the *Sunday Times*, was the son of an engine driver. Tim Campbell, the first candidate to win a job with the self-made Alan Sugar through the television reality show *The Apprentice*, came from a humble background. In 2018, the actor Kwame Kwei-Armah, whose father worked in a local factory and mother as a nurse, became one of British theatre's leading figures as artistic director of the influential Young Vic. Elite football players have mostly come from humble backgrounds.

These are the exception. The breeding grounds for the business elite up to the millennium had barely changed in a hundred years. One study showed that top business executives in the 1990s continued to be drawn from an economic and educational elite. 'There has been no democratisation of British business over the last century and a half.'[11] The proportion of the wealthiest section of society after the Second World War who were self-made rarely exceeded a fifth. Because of the impact of inheritance – a significant proportion of the wealth at the very top continued to derive from a shrewd choice of parentage – there was still a substantial overlap between the rich of one generation and the next, a persistence of the pattern before the war.[12]

The top fee-paying public schools and leading universities have long been the nursery of each generation of the power elite. In 2012, three out of four senior judges, three out of five cabinet members, 57 per cent of permanent secretaries, 44 per cent of public body chairs and 33 per cent of the shadow cabinet attended Oxbridge, compared to less than 1 per cent of the public as a whole. New recruits to the top stream of the Civil Service from a working-class background that year were greatly under-represented.[13] Although elite recruiters, including universities, had begun to take steps to widen the background of their intake, the 'new egalitarianism' remained anything but egalitarian.

The Great Gatsby curve

On improving life chances, the third way philosophy had a poor record, in large part because of its central belief that significant progress could be achieved through tinkering alone. This strategy – encouraging personal aspiration without willing the means – left untouched the gilded cages of the public school system, the recruitment practices of the top universities and professions and the skewed structure of power and wealth which protected children from privileged backgrounds from downward mobility. Politically demanding as it would have been, Labour never set out to challenge the institutional structures that give the rich and the affluent middle classes a pass to the best schools, colleges and jobs. The forces that had for decades driven low levels of social mobility remained largely in place.

Breaking Britain's embedded 'cycle of privilege' was always going to be a daunting task. When an exhausted Labour Party finally lost power in 2010, the distance between the rungs of the mobility ladder had proved resilient to change. Despite a long list of progressive social and educational initiatives, the historic divide between a small group 'born to rule' and a much larger group 'born to fail' had barely been dented. The relationship between parental background and children's future remained much as it was in 1997. Life expectancy still varied sharply between social class, region and neighbourhood.[14] The number of sixteen-to-eighteen-year-olds not in education, employment or training (the so-called NEETS) stayed roughly the same between 1997 and 2010, at around one million.[15]

During the Labour years, the question of how to share the national cake remained 'rather peripheral in economics'.[16] This was equally true of politics. 'Divided Britain' played a marginal role at best in the machinery of government under Labour. Despite repeated warnings from leading academics that official data was not up to the job of charting the real level of inequality, steps to correct for these flaws were mostly left to independent scholars, while big gaps still remain in official sources.[17] Although there were internal seminars and debates about tackling social mobility and poverty, the wider distribution question, of how different groups were managing, was not on the agenda of key departments, from the Treasury to the Cabinet Office.[18] 'The truth is that no department in Whitehall really sees it as their job to worry about big trends in living standards facing the working population of this country', declared Gavin Kelly, former adviser to Tony Blair and Gordon Brown.[19] Partly as a result, ministers were unaware of the way living standards had begun to stall for a section of the workforce from the middle of the 2000s, well before the financial crisis of 2007–09.[20]

One of the important lessons of the previous half-century was that the balance between wages and profits needed to play a much bigger role in strategic economic and social planning. While this was a vital determinant of the course of living standards, of wider inequality and of the stability and durability of the economy, it slipped and still slips through the net of the UK's policymaking machinery. Leading social scientists had long warned that the income divide could not be ignored. Boosting opportunities for all depended 'not only on an open road, but upon an equal start', wrote R.H. Tawney in 1931.[21] Or as the economist Tony Atkinson put it: 'If we are concerned about equality of opportunity tomorrow, we need to be concerned about inequality of outcome today.'[22] The limited success of Labour's main social goals after such comprehensive, if limited, new proposals, and at least initially benign economic conditions, exposed the deep-seated and intractable nature of the social divide. Achieving a permanent dent in the level of poverty and social immobility depended on much more than adjustments to family policy and the tax and benefit system, important though these undoubtedly were.

While Labour's 2010 legacy included the Belfast agreement, devolution, better paternity and maternity rights, advances on equality on a wider front, improved youth facilities, freedom of information, the Human Rights Act, a huge investment in public services and the national minimum wage, it had a big blind spot on inequality.

In 2012, firm evidence emerged that Tawney and Atkinson were right: the great wealth and income divide mattered. In that year, Alan Krueger, President Obama's chief economist, threw significant new light on the debate about inequality and life chances. He reproduced a graph of the relationship between income inequality and the average chance of someone from a poor background rising up the income league over a generation for the world's most developed nations. This showed that high inequality was strongly associated with low mobility.[23] This was delicate political territory for Americans. The much-vaunted 'American dream' – that all had the possibility of rising from rags to riches – was one of the nation's most enduring beliefs, the ideological glue that united rich and poor alike behind the country's free-market philosophy. Yet it had long been short of reality, and had gradually been replaced for many by a new 'fear of falling'.

Krueger's status ensured that his findings – that the opportunity dice is much more heavily loaded in favour of the rich in unequal than in equal countries – were noticed. He called the graph the 'Great Gatsby curve'. The name – taken from F. Scott Fitzgerald's bestselling novel of the excess of the 'roaring twenties' – had been chosen by his researchers, who were offered a bottle of New Jersey wine if they could come up with a memorable title.

The curve has immense significance for policy. The long political debate over whether to aim for 'equality of opportunity' or 'greater equality of outcome' offered a false choice. The former depended on the latter. Labour was firing on half an engine. Its strategy – to focus on opportunity – was set to fail without a simultaneous assault on outcome.

20

I'm not Mother Teresa

In May 2003, shareholders gathered at the Queen Elizabeth II Conference Centre in Central London for the annual general meeting of one of Britain's largest companies, the pharmaceutical giant GlaxoSmithKline (GSK). While company AGMs are usually formal and self-congratulatory events with anodyne speeches and luxury biscuits, this one was full of acrimony. For hours, shareholders and directors were locked in a bitter row over the pay of the company's chief executive, Jean-Pierre Garnier. A fraction over half of shareholders voted against the deal. In response to the revolt, a riled Garnier, who lived in Philadelphia rather than the UK, declared, "I'm not Mother Teresa".

An orgy of self-enrichment

The explosion in corporate rewards that began in the 1980s continued from the millennium. This was despite the evidence that rewards were largely unrelated to corporate performance, and the way other countries such as Sweden, France and especially Japan (where group cohesion is more highly valued than individual reward) operated successful economies with lower levels of top pay.[1] In July 2005, Richard Desmond, the proprietor of the *Express* newspaper titles, paid himself a 'chairman's remuneration' of £52 million. Just nine months earlier the global steel magnate Lakshmi Mittal, Indian born but resident in the UK, chief executive of the world's largest steel-making company, ArcelorMittal, paid himself a £1.1 billion dividend. It was then the highest private dividend ever received.

The record did not last for long. A year later, the swashbuckling and controversial high-street dealmaker Philip Green topped it with a dividend of £1.2 billion from his Arcadia group of shops from Miss Selfridge to Top Shop. This was the equivalent of the annual pay of 54,000 people on average earnings. The company was used as a kind of private fiefdom by Green. Set up in his wife Tina's name, the payment went to her. Living in the tax haven of Monaco, she paid no tax on the giant payout.

'The past decade of Labour government has proved a golden age for the rich', concluded the *Sunday Times*.[2] In the opening years of the millennium, the average earnings of the chief executives of FTSE 100 companies rose eight times as fast as those for all full-time employees.[3] The fortune needed to join the ranks of Britain's wealthiest two hundred swelled from £50 million in 1990 to £430 million in 2007. There was talk of a new 'Gilded Age', echoing the heavily atomised societies of the late nineteenth century.

Labour turned a blind eye to these runaway fortunes. They believed that political options were constrained by globalisation. 'A successful market economy generates far greater prosperity than any rival system', argued Anthony Giddens. 'In effect, there is no rival system in place any longer.'[4] Labour's overall strategy was now one of market-driven prosperity, with the state's role being to ensure no one was left behind. Blair rejected Labour's traditional goal, that at least part of the national wealth pool should be socially owned. For him, the adoption of clause 4 in 1918 was the 'wrong turn'.[5]

Giving freedom to market forces, Blair contended, would promote growth and bring the rewards in improved public services. Brown struck a Faustian pact with the City, continuing the political love affair launched by the Conservatives. Allowing the City to play the vanguard role in the economy as the engine of prosperity, Labour ignored the seedier activities of the business elite and the way the wider gains from globalisation and higher levels of trade were so narrowly shared. In some ways this strategy could be likened to that advocated by Crosland, that the way to tackle poverty was by using the proceeds of growth to build a firmer social floor. It was a strategy that was largely successful in the post-war years under a softer model of capitalism, but it failed to work under the more full-blooded model initiated by Thatcher and left in place by Blair.

The rise of the modern extractive business class has had profound national and global implications. It has created a new layer, a mega-rich super-elite, parallel to but different from the old landed class and the new nineteenth-century industrial plutocrats. As Leo Hindery, the multimillionaire head of HL Capital, warned in 2004, "You're setting up a class system the likes of which we've never seen in the world."[6] Many members of this club have set out to build fortunes not by getting their hands dirty, or through the sweat and risk of creating new products or growing existing firms, but by skimming off existing wealth, a process often paid for by staff, small shareholders, suppliers, taxpayers and weaker nations.

In some ways, this new extractive generation, if still in search of the highest speculative returns, is distinct from its predecessors, from those identified by John Stuart Mill and others, who waited somewhat passively for the rents and interest accruing from their property. It is less monolithic than those of the past, while its wealth is often based on extraordinary earnings as well as income from capital. But while its members are more diverse, and sometimes dependent on short-term contracts and immediate success and thus more insecure, they share common goals and values with their forerunners. They are still mostly driven by 'ruthless self-interest'. They oppose business regulation and interference in labour markets, lobby successfully for the minimisation of corporate and personal taxes and remain unrestrained by the social impact of their activities.[7]

Those rising to the top of contemporary wealth tables, becoming income *and* asset rich on a scale that has often surpassed the wealth piles of earlier generations, have been City financiers, takeover, technology and property barons, hedge fund and private equity partners and investment bankers, as well as some traditional entrepreneurs. They include the high-profile retailers Philip Green and Mike Ashley and the insurance financier Arron Banks, one of the largest donors to the UK Independence Party and pro-Brexit campaigns. Others include media magnates like the Barclay Brothers and Richard Desmond as well as those inheriting landed fortunes like the Duke of Westminster and Viscount Portman. There is another striking difference between the two gilded periods. The post-1980s saw much weaker pressure for social reform than was the case in the late nineteenth and early twentieth centuries. At least until 2008, the immense wealth being accumulated was widely seen as normal and beneficial, with popular and political opposition largely muted.

Western hubris

From the mid-1990s, Britain and most of the world had been riding a wave of economic success, if one driven by unsustainable asset bubbles and easy credit, themselves key sources of soaring financial gain. Punctured briefly by the bursting of the dot.com bubble in 2000, the period brought rising prosperity (on average), falling unemployment and in the three years to 2007, an extended bull run for the London Stock Exchange. With life easing, the public seemed broadly content with their lot.[8] Labour embraced an optimistic view about the future of capitalism built around information and knowledge industries as new sources of wealth and high-skilled jobs. Western leaders were easily beguiled by the promise of perpetual growth. Gordon Brown, the longest serving post-war chancellor of the exchequer, advised by independent and Treasury economists that the boom was sustainable,[9] rarely missed an opportunity to pronounce on what he liked to call 'an end to boom and bust'.

Across the globe there was talk of an 'economic miracle', while in the United States, company chief executives, viewed as key players in the resurgent American economy, started to be treated as superheroes. Few turned an eye as executives started to translate the new public reverence into staggering personal reward, an 'orgy of self-enrichment', as one critic called it.[10] The 'miracle' also conveniently followed the fall of the Soviet Union, a dramatic moment that triggered a new, if short-lived, era of Western hubris. The 'end of history' claim from Francis Fukuyama – that with the end of the Cold War, liberal capitalism had finally proved its superiority – was an update on the earlier 'end to ideology' thesis.[11]

In this heady atmosphere, progressive thinking was easily dismissed. There were few attempts at international co-operation to tackle tax avoidance and corporate power or to build a new egalitarian movement that would respond to the new age of hyper-capitalism. There was much boasting of how the medicine of the markets had overturned the failings of post-war welfarism. In February 2004, Ben Bernanke, soon to be appointed chair of the Federal Reserve, coined the term 'the Great Moderation' to describe what he saw as the way modern macroeconomics had conquered the business cycle. With such grandstanding, surging inequality seemed a small price to pay. The prophets of the market revolution – American theorists such as the Chicago-based Milton Friedman, Gary Becker and Robert E. Lucas, all holders of the Nobel Prize for Economics – were quick to claim credit for their teachings. "The central problem of depression-prevention has been solved, for all practical purposes", declared Lucas.[12]

Using the tools of advanced mathematics, these free-market thinkers – who wanted to turn working economies into textbook models – had constructed highly sophisticated economic models that claimed to demonstrate that government failure was much more likely than market failure. It was such thinking that fuelled the way key areas of the economy, including parts of healthcare, most of social care and a large chunk of housing provision, were handed over to markets.

While market mechanisms are the most efficient way of meeting many everyday material demands, and profits are a vital source of innovation, market values became normalised, infecting areas much less suitable to the 'discipline of the market'. In recent years, the injection of markets into universities has reduced the number offering important but niche subjects from classics to pure mathematics. Giving excessive power to the market always favours those with money over those without. A long list of goals that serve the common good – from the development of drugs for diseases of the poorest to the guarantee of public transport in rural areas and decent affordable housing – will not be met by markets.

Yet capitalism was allowed to spread to areas formerly immune to monetisation, despite the fact that vital needs could be equally well and often better delivered – by non-market, non-profit and collective mechanisms. Leisure and sporting activities, as well as the provision of a range of public services, were commercialised and given a price, a form of market monopolisation that ignored the distributional impact of the mixing of profitability and the provision of vital public services. The 'marketisation of everyday life' was to have a profound effect on the level of civic engagement and social capital.[13]

'Value' was again being equated with price, with market transactions given priority over personal well-being and planetary sustainability through a system 'that sees no value in any human or natural resource unless it is exploited'.[14] In 2003, a headmistress of a top girls' private school complained about the 'values vacuum' being created in a society dominated by money and self-interest. She described how one father used to drop his daughters to school by helicopter, and how his relationship with the school was purely transactional.[15] Premier football clubs now charge families up to £600 for a 'VIP mascot package' that includes the now familiar sight of children walking onto the pitch with players. 'Today commerce has invaded pleasure with a vengeance.'[16]

In the service of power

J.K. Galbraith had warned of the danger of economics becoming the servant of the establishment.[17] From the 1980s, the mainstream economics profession, previously rarely at one, had become increasingly monolithic in its uncritical pro-market thinking that, as the economist Jayati Ghosh concluded, 'operated in the service of power'.[18] By ignoring real behaviour, the mathematical models that underpinned the new hubris failed to predict a number of critical economic trends, including the wider risks of growing inequality and the build-up of unsustainable levels of debt from the mid-1990s.

Over time, the course of political economy has been heavily determined by, along with popular pressure, the extent of harmony between the 'moneyed' and the 'ideas' elites. Thomas Piketty has called these rival groups the 'merchant right' (a pro-deregulation, small-state financial elite) and the 'Brahmin left' (the well-educated, secure and socially progressive liberal elite). It was the latter that gradually came to form the voting base of mainstream centre-left parties which had previously depended heavily on working-class support.[19] Change came about in the post-war years in part because the 'Brahmin left' won the battle of both ideas and politics, with the 'moneyed elite' outplayed by a new pro-equality political class. From the late 1970s, the two power elites began to converge, both favouring the market revolution. It largely stayed that way until and beyond the 2008 crash.

Neoliberal economics – and the way it ignored the social impact of economic decisions – rose to orthodoxy not because of its superior explanatory power but because it fitted well with the biases and preferences of the 'merchant right'. As two critics argued, the economics profession 'has been captured by the powerful and they are not in the mood for fairness ... you will not find articles about fairness in the top economic journals'.[20] Modern developed economies have increasingly been constructed with an emphasis on the private over the public realm, on the virtues of unrestrained private property ownership and on the acceptance of inequality as the outcome of fair rewards. Yet, there is nothing natural or superior about such a model. It would be equally possible to build an economy around wholly different principles, including a greater role for non-market activity, greater equality and the greater sharing of the pool of national assets.

Singing from a new political song sheet, Labour's leaders applauded the rise of a new wealthy class, with many invited to parties at Number 10. They were also made a special case for taxation. Labour introduced some progressive tax changes, including the abolition of two major income tax allowances – for mortgage interest and for married couples – and in 2010 a new temporary top rate of income tax of 50 per cent. Against this, there was a cut in corporation tax (from 35 to 28 per cent) and in the rate of capital gains tax, and a doubling of the threshold before inheritance tax was payable. As a result, the incidence of tax continued to fall more heavily on lower- than higher-income groups.[21]

The City and big corporations, as well as their lobbying organisations, were able to exercise disproportionate leverage over the political process. As part of a new, ever-revolving door between government, Whitehall, the City and multinational companies, a succession of former top Treasury officials moved to take senior and lucrative posts in banking. 'Whitehall grandees do not join the boards of Shelter, Action on Poverty or the RSPB', wrote a former editor of the *Times*.[22]

The embedded pro-inequality institutional structures, including the more egregious financial practices at work and the gaping tax loopholes for the rich, were left largely untouched. The counterweight exercised through civil society, organised labour and community pressure, persistent as it was, was no match against this network of corporate power. Capital and effective democracy had become badly out of line, with the state machine increasingly open to business pressure. As the distinguished American economist Avinash Persaud described it, 'The regulators have been captured by those whom they should be regulating.'[23]

The 'three-comma club', as the ever-growing global billionaire class came to be dubbed, took full advantage of the supportive political climate to intensify their grip on the way economies worked. The frontline engineers of the market system found new ways of first building and then protecting their own wealth against economic failure, taxation and state regulation. The American political scientist, Mancur Olson, had earlier warned of a rigged system that allowed 'distributional coalitions` to secure an excess share of the cake in ways that undermined the wider economy.[24] The anthropologist Peter Turchin warned of the dangers of 'elite overproduction', whereby an excess number of the very rich make governments 'much more attuned to the wishes of the rich than to the aspirations of the poor'.[25] An excessively skewed pattern of power contributed to what the political scientist David Runciman called 'a growing sense of impunity amongst small networks of elites who think that the normal rules don't apply to them'.[26]

Recent studies have shown just how wide of the mark the central hypothesis of political science – that the direction of change in democracies is ultimately powered by public opinion – has been. For most of the last two hundred years, the exception being the post-war years, it has been power elites that have played the dominant role.[27] One study found that in the case of the United States, 'the preferences of the top 10%, and the views of a handful of interest groups suffice to explain policy changes with impressive accuracy. Resorting to the preferences of less affluent groups actually degrades predictive accuracy.'[28]

While the term 'neoliberalism', first coined by Thorstein Veblen, has come to be used as a generic description of the new model of capitalism that emerged from the 1980s, it fails to capture the shock waves from the return of extractive capitalism.[29] Corporate society constructed a 'wealth defence industry' – a small army of highly paid accountants, financiers, pro-business lobbyists, public relations advisers and trade associations – to oppose regulation, resist restrictions and capture parts of the public sector.[30] Globally the new centi-billionaires funded political parties, poured money into pro-market pressure groups and acquired newspapers and television stations. In the UK, 85 per cent of the media in 2012 was owned by a handful of billionaires, with all of their companies registered abroad, thus paying little or no UK tax.

Free-market principles became deeply embedded in key UK institutions, from the City and the Treasury to business schools. Appointed to the Treasury, the former Labour minister Angela Eagle found senior officials 'wedded to free-market fundamentalism'.[31] 'Britain is governed by a self-involved clique that rewards group membership above competence and self-confidence above expertise', declared the pro-market weekly the *Economist*.[32] Hence the ratcheting up, from the millennium, of the share of economic output taken by profits compared with pay, as shown by the Bank of England.[33]

Gap thinking

Warnings of the fallout from concentrated wealth were dismissed. 'There is not a shred of evidence that wealth in itself harms those without it', wrote one British academic philosopher. 'To resent their good fortune would be to succumb to the nasty, small-minded vice of envy. … Egalitarianism has been the most corrosive, illiberal and murderous of modern beliefs.'[34] 'Why do we care so much?' asked the columnist David Aaronovitch about runaway pay.[35] Harvard's Martin Feldstein described those who are against increases in incomes at the top even if nobody at the bottom end is worse off as 'spiteful egalitarians'.[36]

Playing the politics of envy is a common charge against those questioning the merits of runaway wealth. Yet the evidence on envy is that it is largely a 'vice' of the rich. 'My experience', wrote one well-to-do columnist, 'is that the rich themselves are extremely interested (and competitive) about wealth totals'.[37] Investment bank traders are obsessed with their relative pay and bonuses. According to one insider at Morgan Stanley, each wants 'to be paid more than his peers ... because it would signal that he had beaten the others'.[38] Some traders, unhappy with their bonuses, have been known to try and 'get even' by hiring limousines at odd times, making drivers wait and billing the fees to their clients. Top executives have come to expect a tycoon lifestyle. One of those featured in the annual *Forbes* list of the global rich for 2012 was Prince Al Waleed bin Talal, the Saudi owner of London's Savoy Hotel. With a recorded wealth of $20 billion, he complained that his wealth had been understated.[39] In 2000, Larry Ellison, the owner of Oracle and the second-richest person in the world, was in the middle of a global conference call in his San Francisco office. Before the call, Ellison gave instructions that he was to be interrupted for only one thing, the moment he dethroned Bill Gates as the richest man in the world.

The 'stealth wealth' culture and 'conspicuous abstention' of the post-war decades was replaced by voracious excess. In 2001, six bond traders ran up a bill of £44,000 at Gordon Ramsay's Michelin-starred restaurant Pétrus in London's Mayfair, most of it going on vintage wine. Unprecedented demand for 'super-prime' properties, private jets and the world's rarest paintings led to soaring prices and growing waiting lists. Big money was to be made in the market for private islands. Musha Cay in the Bahamas would have set you back £31 million. A Bugatti Veyron, introduced at the 2005 Frankfurt Motor Show, the most powerful and expensive production car in history, cost £810,000.

New Labour sympathisers lined up to argue that the wealth gap did not hurt the poor. As explained by David Goodhart, editor of *Prospect* magazine:

> Gap thinking is based on a defunct zero-sum idea of wealth creation. In a 19th-century mining village it was clear that the mine owner's wealth in a sense caused the poverty of the miners. Other than the odd sweatshop, that is not the case today. The poverty of the poor does not create the richness of the rich and vice versa. The point is that the rich and what, if anything, to do about them ... is a separate issue from improving the conditions of the worst off.[40]

While Gordon Brown's account of his political career, *My Life*, discusses Labour's anti-poverty programme in depth, it only mentions inequality twice, and very briefly. 'The facts about the scale of inequality in Britain', wrote Will Hutton, 'still fail to ignite a popular outcry.'[41]

Gradually, eyebrows began to be raised, including among industry insiders. One former banker called the finance industry 'bloated and parasitic'.[42]

Lord Adair Turner, then chair of the Financial Services Authority, described some City activity as 'socially useless'.[43] 'At no previous time in British history have the financial and business elites been as dominant as they are today', wrote a former adviser to the Conservative Party, Hywel Williams, in 2006.[44] In the same year, the American megabank Citigroup circulated a confidential note on how American society resembled a 'plutonomy' where wealth, economic decision-making and consumption were heavily concentrated in the hands of a tiny minority. According to the note, America had allowed 'the economic disenfranchisement of the masses for the benefit of the few'.[45]

Immune to inequality

Despite these doubts, the question of how the cake should be divided continued to be sidelined. Hayek, Friedman and Lucas stayed in. Pro-equality theorists stayed out. The 2003 report of the annual *Survey of Social Attitudes* asked if Britain had become 'immune to inequality'. It found declared public opposition to Britain's wealth and income gap to be shallow and contradictory.[46] 'People's overall quiescence [in a deepening divide] appeared remarkable', recorded another study of public attitudes.[47] 'I get more letters from constituents about Spanish donkeys and circus elephants than on child poverty', explained Jim Murphy, minister for welfare reform, in 2007.[48] In contrast with 1945, the nation's collective blood pressure had evidently failed to rise over the yawning divide.

Part of the explanation lay in a lack of awareness of the full extent of inequality. One study found that most greatly understated the scale of the gap in earnings between a shop assistant and a chief executive of a large company.[49] Another showed that most had a very poor idea of where they ranked in the income hierarchy. High earners knew next to nothing about other people's incomes, and would compare themselves not with those below them but with those even richer than themselves. It was the rich who were most at odds with reality, while the poorest had the best grasp of their relative position.[50] The Conservative MP Alan Duncan gave the game away when he described an MP's salary of £64,000 as 'rations'. Another, Boris Johnson, described his annual fee of £250,000 for his weekly column in the *Daily Telegraph* as 'chicken-feed'.[51]

Although it would be possible in theory, if in a highly rare set of conditions, to secure low relative poverty levels in high-inequality countries – if, for example, a higher income gap was the product of genuine wealth creation that boosted the relative position of the poorest – there are few historical examples of this happening.[52] Poverty fell in the UK in the post-war era when divisions were narrowing, largely because the forces that lowered the income gap also raised the income floor. When inequality started to rise after the 1980s, poverty rose along with it, largely because of the negative impact on wider society of the methods wealthy elites used to build their personal fortunes. Poverty did fall under New Labour, even while the rich secured a bigger share of national income, but this success was temporary and quickly reversed.

Those few studies critical of excessive wealth concentration published before the 2008 crash generated little interest outside of a small group of academics and activists.[53] While there were few attempts to research the links between poverty and wealth, poverty figures came to be given microscopic scrutiny.[54] Some social scientists began to question the plethora of research charting trends in poverty, mostly using identical methodology and data sources. 'They are very unlikely to bring about any significant change in the government's policy', wrote the social policy expert Peter Beresford. Governments and their allied media merely 'dismiss such findings as the chattering of the "metropolitan classes."'[55] Reviewing two new books on the scale of poverty, the former director of the Webb Memorial Trust, Barry Knight, argued that, unfortunately, 'the fact is that facts don't change things'.[56]

A century earlier, Tawney had issued a similar warning: 'Too much time is spent today on outworks, by writers who pile up statistics and facts, but never get to the heart of the problem.'[57] In 1974, Frank Field suggested it would have been better to divert some of the energy of the anti-poverty lobby to produce an annual report on the rich. 'Wouldn't this approach be a more effective way of communicating Titmuss' belief that poverty and inequality are inextricably intertwined than in an endless succession of poverty reports?'[58] It was a view echoed by Kate Green, Labour MP and a former director of CPAG. The academic monitoring of changes in child poverty, she wrote, generates 'an enormous range of sometimes contradictory research findings, the subtleties of which often get lost in translation, and the range of which facilitate a good deal of political cherry picking'.[59]

Academic sociologists showed limited research interest in the rise of a new pro-market plutocracy. This was despite their longstanding interest, compared with economists, in class and elites. Indeed, 'elite studies' had become 'deeply unfashionable'.[60] The Guardian's leader writer on economics, Aditya Chakrabortty, asked why research was concentrating on 'esoteric minutiae' and failed to get to grips with the big issues of the day.[61] There had been few attempts to 'take a critical look at property rights and above all to revive the classical distinction between earned and unearned income', wrote the social theorist Andrew Sayer in 2012.[62]

'System justification' – that the present system worked pretty well – was dominant. The orthodoxy that dismissed inequality as unimportant also made it difficult to obtain research grants to study it. Some key issues – that, for example, the distribution of national income between capital and labour was held to be largely stable over time – were widely felt to have been settled.[63]

The Economic and Social Research Council, which invests £150m a year in academic research, largely flew 'under the radar'.[64]

There had been important improvements in the quality of data on poverty and inequality, largely due to the efforts of independent scholars and think tanks which helped to put government under the spotlight in the process. It was the IFS that had compiled comparable data on low-income and inequality trends going back to 1961.[65] During the 1990s and 2000s, there were several applications to the Joseph Rowntree Foundation to support research on the link between wealth and poverty. Examples of the applications included one to study the impact of trends in the wage and profit share on the way incomes were distributed. Another sought to see if there was a consensus on what might constitute a 'rich line', a line above which privilege begins to impact disproportionately and people should be asked to make a bigger contribution to society. There had been an ongoing debate on how to define a poverty line, but no attempts to put some flesh on the idea of a 'wealth' or 'rich' line.[66] In rejecting these applications, the Foundation explained that they didn't commission research into the rich or inequality. Although this position changed in later years, what was happening at the top was then explicitly not part of the Foundation's brief.

Partly as a result, 'gap thinking' – that impoverishment, along with the life chances of the poorest, had little to do with the wealth accumulation strategies of the rich – remained the conventional wisdom. The corporate lobbying machine continued to maintain that most of the rich were there by merit and hard work and that a society in which a small elite was able to pull away from the rest was in the interests of all. As Lloyd Blankfein, chief executive of the giant and powerful investment bank Goldman Sachs, put it, 'The people of Goldman Sachs are among the most productive in the world.'[67]

The house of cards

Eventually the distribution question was to return to the political agenda. "Inequality is emerging after a half-century in the wilderness", declared Andrew Haldane, the Bank of England's chief economist, in 2014.[1] The groundwork for this renewal of interest had been laid earlier. Official statistics suggested that the rise of inequality that began in the 1980s had levelled off during the 1990s, evidence that was in conflict with the persistence of runaway rewards at the top.[2] This data, drawn from government surveys, was good at showing the gap across the broad range of incomes, between, for example, the income of a bus driver and a surgeon, but poor at capturing the tails of the distribution where the starkest changes had been occurring.[3]

From the late 1990s, three leading scholars of inequality – the Oxford-based economist Sir Tony Atkinson and his younger colleagues, Thomas Piketty of the Paris School of Economics and Emmanuel Saez of the University of California, Berkeley – embarked on detailed research into the long-run trend in top income shares. Painstakingly extracted from a new source – national tax archives – these studies were to have profound consequences for the inequality debate.

This pioneering work revealed that from the end of the First World War, the share of total income taken by the top 1 per cent in the UK had fallen continuously until the late 1970s, from a high of 19 per cent in 1918 to a low of 5.7 per cent in 1978. From then, the trend went into reverse, with the share reaching 15.4 per cent in 2009, leaving the rest of society, collectively, to manage on a much smaller share.[4] These new data sets – for a range of countries – tracked the concentration of income at the top deep into the past. They confirmed that the big story of inequality had been the stark nature of the changes at the upper extreme of the income ladder. 'The result has been a revolution in our understanding of long-term trends in inequality', wrote Paul Krugman. 'Before this revolution, most discussions of economic disparity more or less ignored the very rich.'[5]

That a rich elite was able to acquire a share of national income approaching that enjoyed by their counterparts a century earlier was all the more striking for the way these rising shares were occurring in much more mature democracies and regulated economies. In the period from the end of the nineteenth century to the end of the 1930s, the constraints on fortune-making were much weaker, tax rates much lower and business regulations minimal.

Figure 21.1: Occupy London poster, 2011

Source: Occupy London

Although there had been a widening of the gap across the broad range of incomes through the 1980s and into the 1990s, it was the discovery of the sharply rising gap between the very top and the rest that raised the political temperature. The studies showed that most, though not all, rich nations had displayed a clear U-curve pattern, though with the date of the turning point and the extent of the reverse varying across countries. The most pronounced rises were in countries, such as the UK and the US, that had most embraced the market revolution.[6]

The discovery of the U-curve challenged Simon Kuznets' widely accepted theory that growing prosperity would be associated first with rising and then with falling inequality. Once they filtered into the public arena, the new findings provided the robust statistical ammunition used by global campaigners against rising inequality. In September 2011, activists occupied parts of Wall Street, protesting against what the *New York Times* described as 'greed, corporate influence, gross social inequality and other nasty byproducts of wayward capitalism'.[7] As the 'Occupy movement' quickly went global, so did their rallying cry: 'We are the 99%', a phrase which contrasted the '1%' with everyone else. The cry had been drawn directly from the path-breaking research into income shares. The findings were also, eventually, to turn one of the group, Thomas Piketty, into a global economic superstar.

The 2008 crash

While the new data provided the ammunition, the event that helped to turn inequality into one of the hottest political issues of the age was the crash of 2008 and the slump that followed. It was 'the worst financial crisis in global history, including the Great Depression', declared Ben Bernanke, now in the hot seat as the chair of the Federal Reserve.[8]

It was a telling verdict on the hubris of the previous decade. One by one the post-1980 economic orthodoxies unravelled. 'Boom and bust' was back with a vengeance, while the period of sustained growth was revealed to have been greatly exaggerated by an oversized finance sector. The 2008 crash confirmed that the new 'economic miracle' had been built on the sands of an unsustainable boost to asset prices, a spike in household debt and the creation of a bubble economy driven by the creation of fake money, weak wage growth and an over-buoyant housing market. The former chair of the Federal Reserve Alan Greenspan – a follower of Ayn Rand's minimalist state philosophy and a cheerleader for the new market orthodoxy – later acknowledged its flaws.[9] The inability of the economics profession to foresee the self-destructive nature of extractive financial capitalism, its reliance on shadow banking and its creation of unsustainable levels of financial assets was of immense reputational damage for the discipline.

Deregulation had licensed the financial system to engage in reckless behaviour. Two decades earlier, long before the tsunami of new financial instruments, the American economist Hyman Minsky had warned that deregulated financial markets would intensify the tendency of market economies to speculation and instability. Minsky was a post-Keynesian economist and critic of the free-market school who developed what he called the 'financial instability hypothesis' that integrated the role of finance into a Keynesian framework. Because success would breed excess, financiers would develop techniques to generate even higher returns, irrespective of the risks being taken with the economy. Such excess would make economies ever more vulnerable to even the slightest shock. Minsky's analysis was remarkably prescient. He was one of few economists to have so early predicted the credit crunch and the resulting near collapse of the global financial system.[10] In 2015, Terry Jones, one of the stars of the satirical television series, Monty Python, made a documentary – *Boom, Bust, Boom* – to try and popularise Minsky's work. In the film, various talking heads engage with a puppet of Minsky.

Throughout history, banks had lent more than their capital base, meeting the difference by borrowing. During the 1950s and 1960s, this ratio was relatively modest, typically around four or five to one. From the 1980s, to deliver the chase for inflated returns, the banks turned their deposits into lending parcels worth twenty, thirty or even forty times as much. Such leveraging allowed the banks to turn money into more money. 'The essence of the contemporary monetary system is the creation of money, out of nothing, by private banks' often foolish lending', wrote *Financial Times* columnist Martin Wolf.[11]

This process was driven by the creation of exotic, obscure and highly risky financial instruments such as derivatives. In the summer of 2008, the value of these derivatives stood at close to $600 trillion – almost ten times the world's output on real goods and services.[12] The Royal Bank of Scotland (RBS), a small regional bank in the 1990s, was lending up to forty times its deposit base in 2007. RBS had grown to become the largest bank in the world, with its assets larger than the UK economy. With banks free to manipulate their expanding cash bases more or less at will, national and global liquidity and credit exploded. Little of this surge in credit was used to build economic strength. Between 1999 and 2007, the share of all loans going to manufacturing more than halved, settling at a mere 2.4 per cent, while the lion's share of loans went on property, from new office building to the expansion of 'buy-to-let' mortgages.[13] The inevitable result: surging property prices and changes in the pattern of ownership.

The beneficiaries of this financial largess included the new breed of financial extractors, from the shadowy barons of private equity to global players like the Russian oligarchs who borrowed huge sums from British banks to build mammoth international business empires, mostly in 'unsavoury' ways.[14] The satirical magazine *Private Eye* has an online map of properties in England and Wales owned by offshore companies. Those using such companies include property dealers, landed gentry, oligarchs and money launderers.[15]

Philip Green's purchase of Arcadia was financed largely by HBOS, the Anglo-Scottish bank formed from a merger between Halifax and the Bank of Scotland. In 2004, Paul Moore, head of group regulatory risk at HBOS, warned the bank that its excessive bonuses and levels of lending were not just unethical but threatened the bank's viability. Instead of taking heed of Moore's warning, he was called in by the chief executive and sacked. After the 2008 crash, the bank, along with many others, had to be bailed out by the Treasury. Moore later described the financial crisis as symptomatic of a wider malaise, a culture of 'me, more, now'.[16]

What had been initiated was an explosive and giant pyramid scheme. Those who bought in at the beginning made a killing, leaving the rest of society to pick up the bill when it finally collapsed. Leading figures in the industry had known that the financial boom was unsustainable and would end in tears. As one insider explained a year before the debacle, 'Let's hope we are all wealthy and retired by the time this house of cards falters.'[17] That excessive rewards would encourage reckless business strategies was eventually acknowledged by the IMF.[18] Simon Johnson, its former chief economist, declared finance chiefs to be 'more knaves than fools'.[19]

To prevent an even deeper crisis, the immediate response of governments, despite their commitment to weak regulation, was to pump cash into the failing, over-indebted banks. "If the years before the crisis were years of too much market and too little government, what we have seen in 2008 and 2009 has been a spectacular comeback of government."[20] As the crash came to be blamed on a lethal cocktail of excessive profiteering, reckless gambling by global finance and tepid regulation, the once-heralded architects of the economic boom – a mix of Central Bank governors, American and British political leaders, top Wall Street financiers and British bankers and credit agency bosses – were finally exposed.

Economists who had once dismissed the importance of the division of the cake between profits and wages changed their tune. 'I think our eyes have been averted from the capital/labor dimension of inequality, for several reasons', wrote Paul Krugman. 'It didn't seem crucial back in the 1990s, and not enough people (me included!) have looked up to notice that things have changed.'[21] Others from a less progressive corner shared this view. 'Going forward ... labour will fight back to take its proper (normal) share of the national cake', wrote the leading European financier Albert Edwards of the investment bank Société Générale, in a note to his clients.[22] The issue of pay continued to resonate. As the editor of the pro-market finance magazine, *MoneyWeek,* put it, 'The world's biggest companies have had a happy few decades. Their labour costs have been falling fast ... multinationals can surely afford to pay higher wages'.[23]

The decade up to 2008 had many striking parallels with the 1920s. Both periods saw a substantial rise in income concentration at the top. In both, the dominant economic doctrine heralded the self-stabilising nature of markets. Both decades were marked by debt-induced booms, with leading commentators believing the holy grail of permanent prosperity had finally been discovered. There was also another significant parallel: 'an inordinate desire to get rich quickly', the description of the 1920s by J.K. Galbraith.[24]

From the 1980s, there was mostly only minimal oversight of the new activities, from proprietary trading to derivative activity, and a significant fall in lending occurring in regulated sectors.[25] The authorities on both sides of the Atlantic trusted the banks to manage their own risks. Yet instead of self-discipline, there was a mass free-for-all. On those few occasions when the regulators started to get nervous about what was being created, the Wall Street lobbying machine went into overdrive. In 1994, no less than four anti-derivatives bills in Congress were shelved.[26]

For decades, economists who challenged mainstream thinking had been marginalised. J.K. Galbraith had once suggested splitting the Harvard economics department into orthodox and heterodox.[27] One effect of the new crisis was that heterodox thinkers who had earlier warned of the financial risks of excessive inequality stopped being ignored, with an increasingly commercialised publishing industry launching a flurry of new books on inequality.[28] At the 2012 gathering of world economic and political leaders at Davos, the Swiss ski resort that had become the annual talking shop for the world's most powerful political, financial and corporate leaders, 'severe income disparity' was judged to be the most likely global risk.[29] 'Income inequality comes out of the igloo at Davos', as the *Financial Times* columnist Gillian Tett described it.[30] In 2013, President Obama declared inequality the 'defining issue of our time', a phrase he repeated time and again.[31]

Despite these rising concerns, the global mega-rich – who initially took something of a hit from the crisis they had largely created – ignored the calls for restraint and soon returned to their gilded lives. The combined wealth of the richest 1000, according to the *Sunday Times* rich list, rose by more than a half between 2009 and 2011.[32]

Ed Miliband, Labour's new leader from 2010, attempted to steer his party gently away from New Labour's acceptance of inequality and attachment to markets. He argued that more needed to be done to make society more equal before tax and benefits – which would always hit political limits. He called for a greater emphasis on 'predistribution'. This aimed to tackle some of the structural causes of inequality, by encouraging a more responsible capitalism and by drawing a line between what he called 'predatory' and 'producer' capitalism. It was a plan that that received short shrift from leading Blairites, including Ed Balls, the shadow chancellor, who dismissed this approach as too anti-business.[33]

Helped by the tremors from Miliband's defeat in the 2015 general election, Jeremy Corbyn was elected Labour's leader. This brought a new vigour to internal debates and ideas, along with a new challenge to austerity and established economic thinking, with the party adopting a more radical, if a largely state-centred and top-down agenda. This included a commitment to abandon social mobility as a primary policy goal and replace it with the more egalitarian one of 'social justice'. Labour's programme, however, was short on a strategy for the poorest, with the proposals on social security offering little more than tinkering, and a lack of measures to deal with an untapped mountain of private wealth. Although there were attempts to develop new anti-inequality instruments, these were, according to the historian and former editor of the *New Left Review*, Robin Blackburn, 'modest, to put it kindly, but by no means negligible'.[34] Labour's packed 2019 manifesto was seen by some, including Andrew Harrop, general secretary of the Fabian Society, as long on statism and short on egalitarianism. 'The party offered a huge expansion in state collectivism and universalism. But it offered too little in the fight against inequality.'[35]

There was a raft of measures to benefit Labour's now primary support base, white-collar public sector workers and graduates, but less for poorer blue-collar voters, who had become increasingly disillusioned with both Labour and politics. Corbyn certainly stirred financiers into action. In an echo of 1924, the run-up to the 2019 general election was marked by a series of prominent newspaper articles on how, as the *Financial Times* put it, 'the UK's uber-wealthy fear a Corbyn-led government', while wealth management companies reported a surge in interest on how to shift money offshore.[36]

It took 2008 to expose the claim that inequality was necessary for economic progress. 'Excessive inequality is corrosive to growth', argued Christine Lagarde, head of the New York–based International Monetary Fund (IMF). 'The economics profession and the policy community have downplayed inequality for too long.'[37] From 2012, influential studies – from the IMF to the Geneva-based International Labour Organisation (ILO) – showed that high levels of inequality had created brittle economies that were especially prone to crisis and weak growth.[38] They also confirmed other evidence that societies that served the interests of small elites held back wider progress.[39]

The 'trade-off theory', according to the Paris-based Organisation for Economic Co-operation and Development (OECD), had proved a great oversimplification; it presents 'decision makers with a binary choice: either we should promote growth or we should prioritise redistribution; either we should make labour markets more flexible or we should make them fairer; either we should promote welfare spending or we should keep taxes low to promote economic activity.'[40] Over time, structural poverty, irregular employment and a low wage share created consumer societies without the capacity to consume. To tackle the problem of shrinking consumer demand, the UK and US economies were pumped full of private debt. In the UK, personal debt levels rose from 45 per cent of incomes in 1981 to an unsustainable 157 per cent in 2008, a trend that fed the process of growing inequality, with interest charges on the debt benefitting financial asset holders.[41]

Both the IMF and the OECD had earlier championed market theories and put pressure on nations to implement what were effectively pro-inequality economic strategies. Now, in a remarkable about turn, they recognised that it was not possible to have sustained prosperity without sharing the proceeds more equally. At the top level, an economic case had again been added to the social justice arguments for greater equality.

Me, more, now

With multi-billion-pound financial and corporate deals coming too often at the expense of the workforce, taxpayers and small businesses, the positive-sum game theory of distribution, that boosting incomes at the top had no negative consequences for anyone else, was fatally flawed.[42] Growth was not the answer to relative poverty if a disproportionate share of the gains were captured by the already rich and affluent.

Rising inequality also meant that the use of 'statistical averages' to measure living standards was increasingly meaningless. The inadequacies of aggregate measures had been recognised by Adam Smith. The true measure of a nation's wealth, he wrote, is not the size of its king's treasury or the holdings of an affluent few but rather the wages of 'the laboring poor'.[43] US senator Robert F. Kennedy pointed out 150 years later that gross domestic product (GDP) measures everything except those things that make life worthwhile.[44] This most widely used cash measure of the size of the economy has long been a poor indicator of progress. 'It excludes the way nature is affected by production and consumption', argues the economist Diane Coyle. It ignores the distribution of gains, and fails to show 'how far we have run down the country's natural capital to sustain lifestyles by destroying biodiversity and altering the climate'.[45] A measure of progress which incorporates social gains and losses, including levels of poverty and homelessness, for example, would show a very different picture than the traditional measure of GDP growth.

Intense concentrations of wealth also create a form of 'luxury capitalism', with resources diverted to meeting the 'conspicuous consumption' of the super-rich, domestic and overseas. In his influential book *Riches and Poverty*, the Italian-born radical journalist and future MP Leo Chiozza Money had warned in 1905 that 'ill-distribution' of property ownership encourages 'non-productive occupations and trades of luxury, with a marked effect upon national productive powers'.[46] The rise from the 1980s of a new, highly competitive, super-wealthy elite led to a second, super-charged version of this effect with a dramatic increase in demand for what Fred Hirsch called 'positional goods', those such as rare paintings, country houses and remote holiday destinations, which are bought for status and position but which are fixed in supply. Luxury capitalism has spawned a 'leap-frogging culture' through second level positioning - ever-larger homes, fortress developments, secure villages, private airports, and bigger cars. One in three new cars bought in inner London in 2020 were SUVs. These trends have brought a new competitive treadmill, adding to inflated expectations, ecological imbalance and a growing clash with social and personal well-being. They also help to explain the paradox that as societies get richer on average, there appears to be less capacity to meet essential needs from health care to decent housing and work. As Hirsch explained the effect: 'If everyone stands on tiptoe, no one sees better.'[47]

The growth of luxury capitalism is evident in multiple ways. 'The British have found a new vocation', said William Cash, the founder of *Spear's Wealth Management Survey*, 'and that is being financial bag-carriers of the world'.[48] Therapy centres such as the 'ultra-exclusive and discreet' Swiss Paracelsus Recovery, which charges upwards of £60,000 a week, are used almost entirely by the gilded elite. A new London bank run by International Bank Vaults deals 'only with billionaires'. Alongside the growth of multiple property ownership, a rising share of the new homes built in recent times have been luxury flats, town houses and mansions for the rich and affluent, rather than for those on middle and lower incomes. In cities like Manchester, Birmingham and Leeds, the giant cranes delivering luxury new sky-high residential blocks, often bought up by speculative overseas buyers and left empty, have meant booming profits for developers and landowners while casting a deep shadow over those excluded by soaring rents and insecure work.

An important feature of 'luxury capitalism' has been the way it steers economic activity into often highly lucrative 'guard labour' that protects and secures the assets of the mega-rich. Examples include the hiring of 'reputation professionals' paid to protect the errant rich and famous, the use of over-restrictive copyright laws and ways of overseeing and micromanaging workers and neighbourhoods, as well as a massive corporate lobbying machine.[49] The greater the gap between rich and poor, the greater the proportion of guard workers. In the US, there are almost as many security guards as teachers, while one in four of the workforce is estimated to be employed as a guard labourer in security, policing, surveillance or forms of IT that impose work discipline. In the UK, around one in five work in guard labour, compared with one in ten in low-inequality countries such as Sweden and Denmark. The problem, according to one study, is that too much guard labour creates a drag on the economy. 'All of the people in guard labour jobs could be doing something more productive with their time.'[50]

In 2014, Thomas Piketty's 600-page *Capital in the Twenty-First Century* raced to number-one place in the US Amazon charts, turning its author from an obscure French academic into a 'rock star economist'.[51] Piketty's central thesis was that free-market capitalism has a natural, inbuilt tendency to generate ever-growing levels of inequality, 'a fundamental force for divergence', as he termed it. When the return on capital (from dividends, interest, rents and capital gains) exceeds the overall growth rate, asset holders accumulate wealth at a faster rate than the economy expands, thereby securing an ever-greater slice of the pie, and leaving less and less for everyone else.[52]

Piketty has his detractors. He has acknowledged that the return on capital has varied over time, while there has also been criticism of his lack of a distinction between 'productive capital' and 'household wealth', even though inequality in the latter is ultimately linked to inequality in the former.[53] Other critics suggest that the focus on the top 1 per cent misses other important trends, including the rise of significant asset holdings and income gains among the next tier, the affluent or patrimonial middle classes, such as medics, small business owners, middle-ranking bankers, media and sports stars.[54] In the three decades to 2008, for example, the real earnings of accountants, medics and architects rose much more quickly than those of bus drivers and factory workers.[55]

This raises the important question of where the line should be drawn for the purpose of policy, such as where wealth taxes should fall. While the 'affluent' classes may have joined a faster – if not the fastest – lane, and sometimes engage in rentier activity, for example as buy-to-let landlords, they do not hold corporate and financial power on the scale of those at or near the very top who have been the key architects and beneficiaries of extraction on a much larger scale. This is not to understate the significance of this second tier of asset holders.[56] In 2018, while the top tenth held around 45 per cent of the UK's total private wealth, the next tenth held 19 per cent. Where there has been a spread of patrimonial wealth, it has mostly been in the form of property, especially the growth of second or buy-to-let homes. In contrast, while the top tenth held two-thirds of financial wealth, including the ownership of shares, the next tenth held only 14 per cent of the total.[57]

Despite these questions – and they have some force – Piketty's heavyweight reassertion of the importance of the distribution question was a loud wake-up call to an insular economics profession, and helped to revive interest in political economy. For a while, even London taxi drivers began to ask their fares if they had read the book.

22

The good, the bad and the ugly

The pioneers of the discipline of economics had warned of the dangers of a rush to enrichment. Adam Smith spoke of the consequences of the love of quick money by 'the prodigals'.[1] In a modern-day equivalent, the former World Bank economist Branko Milanović has distinguished between 'good' and 'bad' inequality.[2]

Some of the personal wealth boom of recent decades has been associated with 'good inequality', the product of wealth and job-creating entrepreneurial activity and innovation which harms no one and adds to the common good. 'Bad inequality' arises from the exercise of disproportionate and unmerited power that brings negative consequences for wider society, such as through Wilfredo Pareto's 'appropriation of existing wealth'. Such inequality has always been a feature of capitalism, but became less prevalent in the post-war years before making a spectacular comeback. The wealth 'megashift' of the last thirty years is less a justified reward for promoting an innovative leap forward than a large windfall gain stemming from the new licence to get rich. The methods used for modern-day enrichment – the engineering of corporate balance sheets, growing monopolisation, the monetisation of social need, the selling off of socially-owned wealth and the overpricing of financial products, along with tax avoidance and wealth concealment – are a far cry from the culture of productive entrepreneurialism central to classical economic theory and advocated by Mrs Thatcher and Tony Blair.

From the millennium, the corporate buyout juggernaut gathered pace, with the total value of UK deals at twenty times that of the early 1980s. The multi-billion-pound deals of the time include the 1999 acquisition of Amoco by British Petroleum and the bitterly fought and titanic Vodafone takeover of Mannesmann in 2000. In 2004, Royal Dutch acquired Shell, and in 2007, a consortium led by RBS landed the $100 billion takeover of the Dutch bank ABN Amro, a deal which helped sink RBS just a year later. Such deals delivered breathtaking fees and bonuses for those involved. 'Where are the customers' yachts?', runs the Wall Street adage. The investment banks masterminding the Vodafone-Mannesmann takeover earned advisory fees in excess of £400 million. The boom in buyouts helped to create giant conglomerates with the monopoly power to exert new pressure on small suppliers, and was a key driver of worsening pay and staff conditions.[3]

This takeover boom, driven by the hike in leveraged credit, mostly hostile and usually involving excessive valuations, merely flipped the ownership of existing companies and has had a mixed record on building corporate strength. Because such activity delivers much higher cash returns for lower risk than from borrowing for new plants, business development or designing new products, money spent on corporate acquisitions has overtaken that spent on R&D, thus sucking lifeblood out of the wider economy. Britain's 'investment deficit' – its low level of investment compared with other countries – has, according to the economist Andrew Smithers, been the result of a perverse system of incentives that makes it more attractive for executives to line their pockets than build for the future.[4]

Wealth begetting wealth

The new corporate tactics from the 1980s introduced a new pro-inequality bias into the economic system. New Labour's remedial anti-poverty strategy was no match for the institutional forces that minimised the share of economic rewards going to those on the lowest incomes. Allowing a growing proportion of business activity to become associated – through opaque mechanisms – with the carefully manipulated upward transfer (or sometimes the destruction) of existing corporate wealth, has also reduced economic resilience, raised vulnerability to external and internal shocks and made growth a weaker mechanism for tackling poverty.

In a powerful illustration of wealth begetting wealth, FTSE 100 companies generated net profits of £551 billion and returned £442 billion of this to shareholders in the four years from 2014, payments which greatly outstripped the rise in aggregate wages and private investment.[5] Companies listed on global stock markets paid out record dividends of $1.43 trillion in 2018.[6] 'One could expect that companies would have prioritized corporate resilience following the significant injection of public money to prevent the near collapse of the financial system and to rescue many industries during the global financial crisis', declared Thales Panza de Paula of the World Economic Forum. Instead we have seen 'an acceleration of a multi-decade trend, a continued increase in shareholder returns and buybacks, corporate indebtedness and a significant reduction in productive investment'.[7]

Nowhere is the institutionalisation of inequality better illustrated than in the roots of the 2008 financial crash, where the losers were rarely those responsible for economic catastrophe but redundant staff, bankrupt small business owners and taxpayers forced to bail out the architects of the crisis. What was at work, wrote Robert Reich, was 'no-lose socialism for the rich and cutthroat hyper-capitalism for everyone else'.[8] One estimate suggests Britain's oversized financial sector inflicted a cumulative £4.5 trillion hit on the British economy from 1995–2015, slightly less than half from the 2008 crash, and over half from two decades of the process of siphoning off cash from the wider economy.[9]

It is no coincidence that the modern plutocracy is increasingly drawn from industries operating high degrees of wealth transfer. An important study by the economist Brett Christophers has found that all of Britain's thirty largest companies – concentrated in mining, metals, oil and gas production, tobacco manufacturing and munitions – have been engaged in such extraction. Another study found a significant fall over time in the extent to which large firms share economic gains with workers, while US research estimated that between a third and a half of Wall Street's pay was unjustified, deriving from 'rents' rather than wider economic gain.[10]

The race for faster and ever larger returns on capital has been one of the key sources of the modern tycoon lifestyle and the degrading of traditional entrepreneurialism. Two of Britain's once most successful and high profile companies – ICI and Marconi (previously GEC) – were early victims of the rampant market culture and the chase for short-term value. Before they failed, their directors and City advisers had earned colossal fees from finance-led acquisition strategies which ultimately brought the companies down.[11]

The rise of private equity – in which individuals and financial consortiums buy asset-rich businesses in need of cash on the cheap – has been the modern equivalent of the gold rush, delivering outsized returns to the investors, a mix of banks, insurance companies and wealthy individuals. To generate these returns, the new owners have employed a series of devices, from financial engineering and asset stripping to dumping liabilities on third parties. Such tactics have meant lay-offs, the milking of company assets and much tougher deals for suppliers. Drawing on the methods developed during the American leveraged buy-out spree of the 1980s, scores of high-street names – from BHS to Debenhams and Boots – were transferred from the late 1990s from public to private ownership, sometimes by high-profile individuals like Philip Green, but mostly by shadowy consortiums of financiers, such as Apax, Candover and Permira. The partners who ran the firms, such as Damon Buffini of Permira and Martin Halusa of Apax – desperate to keep out of the limelight – were paid at 'gravity-defying' rates.[12]

Companies like Halfords and the formerly mutual Automobile Association all shed jobs when taken private in the 2000s, with remaining employees forced to accept poorer work conditions. When Gate Gourmet, the private catering company supplying British Airways' in-flight meals, was bought by new private equity owners, the US company Texas Pacific, its somewhat crude attempts to cut labour costs triggered a bitter dispute with its workforce, mainly low-paid Asian women. Although some firms have showed improved performance under new management, with Millets and Burger King often quoted as examples, a string of high-street names – from BHS to Bernard Matthews – stripped of their future by new owners, were fatally weakened by the mix of refinancing, cost cutting, reduced capital spending and property sales which made them less resilient to fast-changing shopping habits.

When the 230-year-old Debenhams was taken over in 2003, the consortium partners paid themselves £1.2 billion in dividends over their three years of ownership, a near 100 per cent return on their investment. They loaded the company with debt to pay for the purchase and cut corporation tax liability, while the debt millstone left the company struggling to invest, innovate or compete, thereby weakening its long-run viability, a key explanation for the chain's collapse fifteen years later.[13]

Between 1991 and 2019, privatised water companies in England paid out £57 billion in dividends to shareholders while amassing £48 billion in additional debts, thus making it increasingly difficult for the companies to meet their investment obligations.[14] As the city editor of the *Evening Standard* Anthony Hilton put it, 'The damage done by over-indebted companies has been visible for years in slashed budgets for R&D, inadequate investment in plant and equipment and the premature closure of businesses that could have been turned round.'[15] The value of the international private equity sector has risen more than sevenfold since the millennium. In 2020, the industry claimed to hold a formidable $1.5 trillion in 'dry powder' (around 70 per cent of the combined value of the UK's top 100 companies), while in the UK, the year saw a frenzy of deals that swept up dozens of companies.[16]

An increasingly common means of extraction has been for cash-rich companies to buy back their own shares. This returns money to shareholders using funds that could have been used for investment. It was an activity that was illegal in the US until Ronald Reagan decided it limited market freedom. From 2004, the world's biggest companies, including the giant tech companies, launched a share buy-back binge, essentially a raid on corporate assets. In 2018, for example, Apple spent $73 billion on buying back its stock. By reducing the number available, the share price rises in the short term; an easy way to juice executive pay. 'The pendulum of Silicon Valley swings between recklessly spending massive amounts of money on shareholders, and recklessly spending massive amounts of money on founders', wrote Aaron Freedman, economics editor at the global Institute for New Economic Thinking. 'In both cases, the losers are the workers, who get laid off by corporate raiders or manic founders; and the public, which has potentially life-changing innovations squandered on big egos and deep pockets.'[17]

Governing for all

Through much of its history, Britain has fallen short of a key test of a successful democracy – that all citizens should be treated by common standards. Instead, it has created a system based on tiered membership, with some citizens granted fewer rights and more responsibilities than others. As George Orwell noted in 1941, Britain is like a family, with 'rich relations who have to be kow-towed to, and poor relations who are horribly sat upon'.[18] The heavily tiered system was reformed during and after the War as more national wealth was socialised and the poorest were granted new entitlements as a right of citizenship. From the 1980s, those new social rights were weakened as part of a new political message: that the rich and affluent are at the top because they display the aspiration and responsibility lacking in others. Today it is the rich who get the honours, are feted by ministers and treated gently on tax, while those on benefits are harried, penalised and demonised.

Despite the questionable nature of some of the routes to personal wealth,[19] rich and poor have, for much of the last two centuries, been viewed through very different lenses. The portrayal of 'them' and 'us' – that the welfare state gives handouts to a minority on benefits paid for by a long-suffering and affluent middle class – has always been a convenient myth. Such distinctions have been shaped by the way political classes and parts of the media like to reverse the situations facing those at different ends of the income spectrum. Those labelled 'poor' tend to be viewed as the ones 'living in big houses, wallowing in luxury and not needing to work, while those previously considered rich are redesignated as the ones who work terribly hard for fair reward or less, forced to support this new category of poor-who-are-considered-rich'.[20]

In May 1989, Grenada Television broadcast *Spongers*, a spoof game show compèred by the popular broadcaster Nicholas Parsons. The show featured two couples and their children, the working-class Ackroyds and the middle-class Osbornes. The show used magic boxes opened by Parson's assistant, Pandora, to see how much each couple had gained from the welfare state (state benefits and some tax reliefs and occupational benefits) across their lifetimes. Using the best academic evidence, the show revealed that it was the longer-living, university-educated, opera-loving Osbornes who had gained the most. Designed as much for 'horizontal' (a form of lifetime 'risk pooling') as for 'vertical' redistribution – and both are important – three-quarters of transfer payments today redistribute income across the life span, and only a quarter are 'Robin Hood' transfers, which take from the rich to give to the poor.[21]

The rich and affluent have managed to avoid the 'deserving' and 'undeserving' labels applied to low-income families by officialdom. New Labour used the deserving/undeserving distinction, at least implicitly, in shaping their anti-poverty policy, but saw no need for a parallel differentiation for the rich.[22] Their social and electoral strategy was built on what Tony Blair's former head of strategy Matthew Taylor called a distinction between the 'aspirational and non-aspirational working class'. The latter were seen as lacking the will or ability to rise through the system, and thus effectively responsible for their own fate. The blame, it was inferred, was not the bias of the economic system but a 'poverty of aspiration'.[23]

New Labour embraced the tightened system of work-search requirements ushered in by the 1995 Jobseeker's Act. The party's stress on rights and responsibilities – between state and claimant – was integrated into their flagship welfare-to-work programmes. Despite its conflict with the idea of a social right to benefits earned by compulsory contributions enshrined fifty years earlier, a toughened version of conditionality with new work tests was extended to out-of-work lone parents and disabled people. David Webster, from the University of Glasgow, described the new emphasis on 'rights and responsibilities' as seriously undermining 'the insurance principle, by promoting the idea that benefits are a gift from taxpayers to claimants, rather than an entitlement which people pay for when they are in work'.[24]

Under the Welfare Reform Bill, new claimants for Incapacity Benefit were, from 2008, moved onto the new Employment and Support Allowance which required a 'work capability assessment'.[25] In the same year, single parents were required to seek work when their children were twelve, rather than of 'leaving school age'. This threshold was lowered to five years in 2012, with lone parents with a youngest child aged five or older treated in broadly similar terms to other jobseekers.[26] As well as stricter work-search requirements, there was also a tightening of sanctions. The 'duties' side of the social contract was being toughened while 'rights' were being further eroded.

While Labour's approach was seen – sometimes through the cherry-picking of surveys – as chiming with public opinion, there was also evidence that politics was 'creating rather than reacting to negative political opinion on benefits', and that public attitudes to welfare were not as uncompromising and homogeneous as politicians – of left and right – liked to assume.[27]

In 2008, James Purnell, the secretary of state for work and pensions, floated a package of reforms which included mandatory work programmes for the unemployed and would make long-term claimants sign on every day. Purnell was plotting a social security system where 'virtually everyone has to do something in return for their benefits'.[28] In response, the *Guardian* columnist Owen Jones described Labour's approach to claimants as based on a series of caricatures: 'The feckless, the non-aspirational, the scrounger, the dysfunctional ... and confirming the stereotypes and prejudices many middle-class people have about working class communities.'[29] Purnell responded: 'There is nothing left-wing about people being trapped on benefits, having miserable lives where their universe consists of a trip from the bedroom to the living room.'[30]

A society built around the common good needs a clear set of rules that apply across society, that expand opportunities and meet the aspirations of all classes, including through the provision of public goods and an adequate system of social protection. Britain has only once come close to achieving such a society.

The idea of reciprocal rights and responsibilities has been an important principle at the heart of the history of social support. Despite Victorian capitalism's indifference to the 'inequality of bargaining power', the idea that contributions and benefits should go hand in hand became central to the development of the 'social justice' case from the end of the nineteenth century.[31] This was in part to contest the 'free-rider' objection made by opponents of greater equality, and in part to challenge 'functionless wealth' and the way privileged members of society, including the 'idle rich', had often become wealthy without significant personal effort or social contribution. 'Rights mean duties', the Labour Party argued in the 1950s. 'No-one who benefits from the welfare state ... can contract out of the social obligations which must support these reforms.'[32] As the social policy academic David Piachaud later argued, 'Increases in opportunities and power of the poor and disadvantaged in society will always be limited if these are solely provided *for* them, handed down from above.'[33]

The principle that individuals, or organisations, in receipt of state financial support should have limits imposed on their behaviour has, however, been mostly very partially applied. 'Responsibility is an important element of citizenship', argued Ruth Lister, 'but I am tired of constantly hearing about the responsibilities of "the poor" and the need to change their behaviour and nothing about the responsibilities of the privileged'.[34] Purnell's call for everyone to contribute for their benefits was to be applied only to the least powerful section of society. Labour framed the issue of 'rights and responsibilities' as being 'about the behaviour of welfare recipients', wrote the Oxford academic Stuart White. 'The issue of responsibility in welfare became a discrete issue, bracketed off from wider questions about the fairness of the economic system.'[35]

What evolved in industrial society and in recent decades has been closer to a politics of division than of inclusion. Greater social mutuality based on communal obligations and benefits is a desirable goal, and a vital ingredient of effective social functioning, but it must be a mutualism that embraces all sections of society. Rights and rewards for the rich and responsibilities and penalties for the poor, effectively setting different groups on different paths, is not a politics of reciprocity.

Today there are few social bonds between poor and rich. Those in receipt of benefits have come to be seen – again –as an inconvenience and a drag on society, and have had to constantly prove that they are 'deserving'. State institutions, including the Department for Work and Pensions and the network of jobcentres, have come to be viewed as alien by large numbers who seek their help. Some turning to jobcentres, especially those from an ethnic minority, report a sense of being policed rather than helped. "You just feel like you're constantly being watched, always being judged", said one claimant.[36] For the rich, institutions such as Her Majesty's Revenue and Customs (HMRC) and the Department for Business, Energy and Industrial Strategy are essentially benign. Rights and duties have only come close to alignment for all in the post-war era. In those years, social, economic and civic rights, through a stronger safety net, the expansion of public goods, education and services and access to decent training, work and wages, were extended across society, while sections of the business elite began to accept their wider responsibilities.

Over the last thirty to forty years, those collective rights have been eroded, leaving those with the weakest bargaining power reduced to what the economist Guy Standing has called 'supplicants', 'having to ask for favours, help, a break, a discretionary judgement by some bureaucrat, agent, relative or friend'.[37] In contrast, the rich today have mostly shed responsibilities they once accepted, if by custom rather than statute. The modern plutocracy holds to a very limited sense of their own duty. They see their self-interest and that of society as one and the same. This view handily ignores the immense contribution made by the small army of the low paid – delivery drivers, shop and hospitality workers, transport workers, cleaners and hospital porters – and the huge body of carers, volunteers and community activists, mostly women, without whom society would grind to a halt. As revealed by the COVID-19 pandemic, this largely invisible and unrecognised part of the labour force – paid and unpaid – provides a vital economic and social function, and more than fulfils the obligations of social membership. Yet these groups are poorly recognised and compensated, and are widely short-changed for their role.

Just as the landed interests once believed in their God-given right to rule, so the rich class from the late twentieth century has developed a new culture of entitlement, along with the right both to freedom from scrutiny and to the fortunes they have inherited or accumulated. Yet business leaders enjoy a huge range of benefits – from an educated workforce and a developed infrastructure to a long list of subsidies – all the product of collective action, but which come with virtually no strings attached. The benefit of the doubt has been handed to the rich. Despite their complicity in the 2008 crash, top-level bankers and financiers were bailed out, 'to save them from the consequences of their own folly and greed', on taxpayer credit with minimal conditions and in contrast to the underlying precepts of the 'great moderation'.[38] This was in stark contrast to the story of those on the lowest incomes under austerity.

In 2018, the taxpayer's bill for corporate welfare stood at £93 billion (close to the total benefit bill excluding pensions).[39] Paid to companies in grants and tax breaks – to retain jobs, improve technology or keep businesses in the market – this financial support comes with few if any obligations on tax dodging, employment practices or social responsibility. The Office for Budget Responsibility has described the bill as 'large in absolute terms – approaching 8 per cent of GDP – and also by international standards. The cost has also risen significantly over the past decade'.[40] Business makes a big contribution to jobs and prosperity, but is supported in that role by significant state support.

According to the National Audit Office (NAO), there were some 1,190 tax reliefs in 2019, about many of which very little is known.[41] The growth of such reliefs has not only contributed to the shrinking of the tax base, it has added to the dual standard in the way tax reliefs and cash benefits are treated by state institutions. In contrast to regular official and independent reporting and scrutiny of public spending, the limited material released on corporate tax reliefs is not easily accessible.[42] Despite some better information in recent years after persistent pressure by NAO, there is still very little publicly available information on who gets what and with what impact. Most income tax reliefs are of more value to those with higher incomes and consequently help to reinforce inequalities. The social scientist, Adrian Sinfield, has called them 'upside-down benefits' that, in contrast with state benefits, are means enhancing rather than means tested.[43]

Despite their good fortune, the most affluent have mostly shown little concern about the social divisions that mar society. 'It seems sometimes to be regarded as quite a providential arrangement that some should be born without the necessity of working for their own living', wrote Leonard Hobhouse in 1912, 'so that they have leisure to impose this fundamental duty on others.'[44] As Anthony Sampson wrote in 2004, on the 100th anniversary of the outbreak of the First World War, 'By the new millennium the more prosperous British were taking on many of the characteristics of the Edwardians a century earlier, with their luxury, complacency – and indifference to inequality.'[45]

PART VI

2011–20

23

Divide and rule: playing politics with poverty

In its dying days, the Labour government moved to make the earlier pledges on poverty legally binding. The 2010 Child Poverty Act set four targets to be met within a decade. The Act was an unambiguous statement of the societal obligation to tackle poverty and a statutory recognition that poverty is relative.

Remarkably, given the history of political division over the question of poverty, the 2010 Act was passed with all-party support. In opposition, the Conservative Party leader David Cameron had declared that tackling relative poverty would be a priority in government. 'The Conservative Party recognises, will measure and will act on relative poverty'.[1] This was serious revisionism. Determined to project a more compassionate image, the Conservative Party, in a striking shift, had signed up to the idea that Britain's record on poverty needed to be greatly improved.

Poverty plus a pound

In the event, the consensus barely lasted a week. Signs of what was to follow came during the 2010 election campaign when the Conservatives launched a poster with the caption: 'Let's cut benefits for those who refuse to work.' Almost from the moment Cameron formed a coalition with the Liberal Democrats, 'compassionate Conservatism' was dumped in a way which collided head on with the commitments of the 2010 Act.

In place of the earlier pledges, and a sign of the coarsening of the poverty debate, a number of quite different themes emerged. More money, it was claimed, was not an effective way of fighting poverty. The work and pensions secretary Iain Duncan Smith constantly dismissed what he called the 'poverty plus a pound' approach aimed merely at 'lifting income over an arbitrary line'.[2] The government also sought to replace official measures of poverty with ones that would, at a stroke, greatly reduce the official count. This involved redefining the causes of poverty away from broadly societal and structural explanations – such as low wages and high rents – to individual ones, such as family breakdown and bad parenting. As Duncan Smith put it, 'The nature of the life you lead and the choices that you make have a significant bearing on whether you live in poverty.'[3]

A highly controversial 2012 consultation document, *Measuring Child Poverty*, set out to measure poverty by people's individual behaviours and characteristics as opposed to their circumstances by highlighting issues such as 'poor parenting skills' and 'drug and alcohol dependency'.[4] The proposal bore no relation to any existing method of measuring poverty operating in the UK or worldwide. Jonathan Bradshaw described the document as failing to recognise the fundamental distinction between '*measures* of poverty, the *characteristics* of poor children and the *associations* and the *consequences* of poverty'.[5]

The government also set out to challenge the 2010 Act's 'sixty per cent of median measure'. 'You get this constant juddering adjustment with poverty figures going up when, for instance, upper incomes rise', was how Duncan Smith, echoing John Moore in 1989, put it shortly after the election.[6] Frank Field, who had earlier been appointed the government's 'poverty czar', argued that a target based on relative income was impossible to achieve. 'Any candidate sitting GCSE maths should be able to explain that raising everybody above a set percentage of the median income is rather like asking a cat to chase its own tail. As families are raised above the target level of income, the median point itself rises. Not surprisingly, therefore, no country in the free world has managed to achieve this objective.'[7]

These criticisms revealed a remarkable misunderstanding of the way the relative income measure worked. If the population is lined up in order of their income, the person half way along would have the median income. So, if 'upper incomes rise', as Duncan Smith put it, and just those on top incomes get richer – with incomes elsewhere unchanged – there is no effect on the median income. Thus a poverty line set at a fixed proportion of the median stays exactly the same. Similarly, raising the incomes of those below the target of 60 per cent of the median to just above the target, for example, does not raise the median point. If all households below 60 per cent of the median were to rise above this threshold but stay below the median income, the median – and therefore the target – would stay the same and poverty would be eliminated.

On the BBC's *Today* programme, the presenter John Humphrys once asked a leading social policy expert: "But surely, if you define poverty as relative, it will never be abolished?"[8] Or take this leader in the *Scotsman* on 14 June 2013: 'Given this is a relative, as opposed to absolute, measure, then we can say with mathematical certainty that the poor will always be with us.' While some people, no doubt, will always be poorer than others, this is not the same as saying they are in relative poverty. A distribution where no one has less than 60 per cent of the median is perfectly possible without complete equality. Despite this, such claims kept coming back. 'For far too long', wrote Duncan Smith and George Osborne, 'a fixation on relative income led the last government to chase an ever elusive poverty target'.[9]

Cutting relative income poverty may not be easy but it is possible. The UK rate in 2010 stood at around double that of the most successful countries, Iceland, Norway and Denmark, and was also significantly higher than in Germany, Belgium and France.[10] None of this means that the '60 per cent of the median' measure does not have limitations, though it is a great improvement on what had come before.[11]

The lofty speeches made in opposition on the importance of tackling poverty had given way to a very different political mindset, one that was more 'anti-poor' than 'anti-poverty'. The highly charged debates of earlier decades, in abeyance for a while, had returned with profound implications for the lives of those on the lowest incomes. While an emphasis on prevention and improving life chances was vital, most of the government's claims about behaviour were at odds with the evidence. Morality, not a lack of money, was back as the explanation for poverty.

While a pound may be loose change for most, it is anything but for those on the lowest incomes. "I can't minimise any more than I have", a low-paid worker in Glasgow explained in 2013. "I very rarely buy clothes because I can't afford them. Food is a bare minimum. I have a roll in the morning and a meal at night", he added. "I like to be quite organised. I have everything written down", a lone parent in Gloucestershire explained. "Obviously there are things that get in the way, like emergency things. I don't have anything to fall back on, I have to move it all around".[12]

Marc left college in Redcar 2009 with two A levels. He suffered bouts of depression and homelessness and, in 2012, ended up living in shared accommodation provided by a local charity. Despite scores of fruitless applications, he had only been able to obtain intermittent work; the longest, a four-month job covering Christmas in a local supermarket depot. Redcar was an unemployment hotspot, with twelve unemployed people chasing every vacancy. He lived on £53 a week with his rent paid on top. "I'm not living I'm surviving … it's like rationing on food, rationing on electric and gas, it's not a life at all". He planned his spending with precision: "I put my money into piles just so I don't overspend. £15 for bus fare. £10 gas and £15 food".[13]

An old libel

In 2011, the government launched its much-promoted 'troubled families' strategy. Such families were, the prime minister claimed, a "source of a large proportion of the problems in society".[14] This and other repeated claims had one message: that the actual problem of poverty was small and confined to dysfunctional families.

In a much-criticised estimate, the number of such families was said to total 120,000, a group redefined by ministers first into families that are 'troubled', and then into families that *are* or *cause* trouble. Yet there was no evidence that the families identified were involved in anti-social behaviour or crime or included bad parents. In a classic example of the way statistics could be misused and myths created, ministers had misrepresented official research to support their political philosophy on poverty. Ruth Levitas, professor of sociology at Bristol University, dismissed the claims as 'a factoid – something that takes the form of a fact, but is not. It is used to support policies that in no way follow from the research'.[15]

Of course, some parents manage on low incomes better than others. But just because some make bad choices, neglect their children and lead chaotic lives does not mean that poverty is predominantly a product of individual shortcomings. The key explanation for Britain's high poverty rate lies in profound economic and social shifts. These include the speed of industrial change, the erosion of high-skilled and well-paid jobs, workplace upheaval, a weakened safety net, the end of tax progressivity, polarised and expensive housing, democratic disempowerment and the way the education and adult training system has left those with low and out-of-date skills and qualifications increasingly stranded.

The succession of shocks over the last four decades – from deindustrialisation and the 2008 crash to greater automation, austerity, Brexit and the COVID-19 pandemic – has undermined livelihoods, diminished opportunities and left increasing numbers losing control over their lives. Unlike the impact of war, these shocks, some of them self-inflicted, have typically left the poorest members of society the greatest losers. Poverty has become more deeply institutionalised, baked into the practices of big business, the uneven divisions of the gains from growth, the erosion of mutual systems of support and the rise of new social and economic risks. The description of the US by the political scientist Joseph Hacker applied equally to the UK: 'All of these mounting risks add up to an ever more harrowing reality: Increasingly, all of us … are riding the economic roller coaster. And yet most of seem to feel that we are riding it alone.'[16]

There was nothing new about the 'troubled families' label. There had been endless attempts to develop theories of a 'culture of poverty'. These included the Victorian 'residuum', 'the unemployables' of the Edwardian era, the 'social problem groups' of the 1930s, 'the problem families' of the 1950s, the 'culture of poverty' and 'cycle of deprivation' theses of the 1960s and 1970s and Charles Murray's 'underclass' of the 1980s.[17] Despite successive attempts to find such a 'culture', none of the multiple studies have found any large group with behaviour patterns that could be ascribed to a culture or genetics of poverty. There is little evidence of an embedded and self-perpetuating subculture that lives by different values from the rest of society.[18] As one critic concludes, 'The underclass theory … cannot properly comprehend how the alleged anti-social behaviour of "underclass" youth might be the product not of individual or subculture pathology, but of the complicated interplay of structural forces.'[19]

In evidence to the government's consultation on poverty, Professor David Gordon at the University of Bristol dismissed the idea of such a 'culture' as an 'old libel'. 'Poverty is not like syphilis or a biblical curse across the generations – poverty is not a disease and it cannot be caught and all creditable evidence shows that it is not "transmitted" to children by their parents' genes or culture.'[20] What was at work was what the writer Yuval Noah Harari has called 'a blurring of the line between fiction and reality'.[21]

In the event, the government's attempt to devise a new, multidimensional measure was dropped.[22] The Treasury, doubtful that the Department for Work and Pension's new approach was 'methodologically sound', vetoed change. The proposals were also going to struggle to pass through the UK's devolved governments in Scotland, Wales and Northern Ireland. Here there remained robust support for the importance of relative poverty and the goals of the Child Poverty Act. Both the Welsh Assembly and the Scottish Parliament were highly critical of the coalition government's stance, and took a much more societal view of poverty. In Scotland, the SNP (Scottish National Party) government developed, within the limits of its devolved powers, a more rights-based social security system aimed in part at mitigating the effects of Westminster's programme of austerity and benefit reform and building 'an investment in the people of Scotland'.[23]

In 2016, the Work and Reform Act scrapped the 2010 child poverty targets and replaced them with a new duty to report on two 'life chances' indicators – the proportion of children living in workless households, and children's educational attainment at age sixteen. In the event, the House of Lords voted against the abolition of the targets. The requirement to report to parliament came to an end, but the government agreed to continue to publish regular data on the number of children in low-income homes.[24]

Don't push me in a statistic

Seeing electoral gains from being tough on benefits, negative portrayals of claimants by ministers became more frequent and more strident. In 2012, the chancellor of the Exchequer George Osborne told the Conservative Party conference, to great cheers, "Where is the fairness, we ask, for the shift-worker, leaving home in the dark hours of the early morning, who looks up at the closed blinds of their next-door neighbour sleeping off a life on benefits."[25] Such repeated shaming, as in earlier decades, added to a wider process of 'othering' in which those on low incomes are treated as inferior to the rest of society. Old distinctions were dressed up in new language: 'workers and strivers' against 'shirkers and skivers', while the new hostility began to be extended to groups previously excluded from the 'othering' process. The unemployed were at fault for lacking a job, and those with disabilities for not trying hard enough.

In some ways 'poverty' had become a loaded term, one deliberately misused to help create a barrier to public support. The number of times the word 'scrounger' was used annually in UK newspapers was four times higher in 2012 than in any year between 1993 and 2003.[26] 'Scroungers on £95,000 a year', headlined the *Daily Express* on 6 September 2010. *The Daily Mail*, on 24 January, 2012, went for '75% of incapacity claimants are fit to work'. Television producers dreamed up programmes – such as Channel 4's controversial 2014 series *Benefits Street* and the BBC's 2011 *The Future of Welfare* – that treated poor families as entertainment. These were a sharp contrast with the trenchant social and politically engaged content of earlier television drama from the BBC's *Play for Today* series in the 1970s and *Boys from the Black Stuff*, which explicitly set out to 'rattle the cages of the establishment'.

'Othering' and 'typecasting' were evident in other areas. New housing developments came with ways of segregating buyers of luxury private flats and social housing tenants. These included separate 'poor floors', 'poor doors' and segregated play areas. One development in London constructed an expansive and well-equipped play section for children of homebuyers, but a cramped and poorly stocked area for the children of social tenants.[27] In another regeneration project – at Nine Elms in south London – where the proportion of 'affordable' housing units had been steadily cut from the standard one-third to below ten per cent, local graffiti read 'stop social cleansing our city'. In Manchester and London, metal spikes began to appear in front of new luxury housing blocks to prevent homeless people sleeping on the ground outside.

The popular portrayals were anathema to those on benefits. As a young unemployed man in Birmingham expressed it: "They just think that because you're not in a job you're not trying, like I'm not! Don't push me in a statistic before you get to know me, learn about my aspirations before you make an assumption on me". And a single parent in Birmingham: "When I became a single parent there was always this oh you're a single parent so you know you're a scrounger and she sits at home doing nothing. That used to really, really get to me. Everybody has a reason why they are in the position they are in".[28]

One participant in the North East Child Poverty Commission – set up along with other fairness and poverty commissions, from Sheffield to Edinburgh, to give ordinary people a voice – described how 'the worst thing about living in poverty is the way it gives others permission to treat you as if you don't matter'.[29] Or as poet and anti-poverty campaigner Moraene Roberts put it:

Poverty takes away ownership of our own lives ... I was born into poverty, came out of it a bit through not very good but regular work, and fell back into poverty as a young mum when I got divorced ... For me, it's what I see, it's what I live, and it's what I fight. I am of value to my community and to society; but I'm invisible to those who do not know me; I'm stigmatised by the headlines they read.[30]

A leaner state

The war on benefits was a key part of the government's wider economic strategy. To tackle the post-2008 recession, Labour had boosted public investment and made a temporary cut in the VAT rate. By the general election in 2010, the economy was in modest recovery, though with a sharp rise in the budget deficit, the gap between public spending and tax revenue.

Folklore economics

Labour's declared plan, if lacking in detail, was to halve the budget gap over the next five years. In contrast to Labour's strategy that recovery and job creation was the best way of meeting rising debt, the new chancellor, George Osborne, slammed on the brakes. Claiming that the economic crisis had been caused by Labour's profligate social spending and excessive state borrowing, he launched, as Robert Chote, then director of the IFS, described it, 'the longest, deepest, sustained period of cuts to public services spending at least since the Second World War'.[1]

The year 2010 was hardly a time for playing politics with a still weak economy, yet, by rejecting Labour's mild Keynesianism, Osborne turned to the balanced budget theory of the 1930s, imposing severe fiscal deflation at a time of a deep deficit of demand. This was a controversial strategy that clashed with majority economic opinion. It made attempts to jumpstart recovery almost entirely dependent on a new form of monetary policy called quantitative easing – to pump liquidity into the economy – alongside attempts to boost property prices. The strategy came with profound distributional consequences, and was described by Robert Skidelsky as 'folklore economics'.[2] One critic, David Blanchflower, a former member of the Bank of England's Monetary Policy Committee, concluded that, by destroying productive capacity and making households worse off, the austerity programme simply 'crushed the fragile recovery'.[3] According to one estimate, austerity reduced the size of the economy by £100 billion pounds by the end of the decade.[4]

Central to the policy of retrenchment – another instalment in the live experiment in market economics – was a 'big-bang' package of benefit reforms. By 2019, close to £40 billion had been shorn from the annual working-age benefit budget.[5] Iain Duncan Smith boasted that the package was 'one of the most aggressive programmes of welfare reform Britain has ever seen'.[6] Austerity, David Cameron explained to the Lord Mayor's banquet in November 2013, is not a temporary response to crisis, but 'something more profound. It means building a leaner, more efficient state. Not just now, but permanently'.[7]

Austerity was applied with steely determination by the government machine. To ensure departmental compliance, officials from a central Implementation Unit – 'the little birds' as they were known by insiders – were installed across Whitehall. By 2019, public spending as a share of the economy had fallen from 45 per cent in 2010 to around 40 per cent. This compared with a European Union average of over 45 per cent.[8]

Taking an axe to benefits triggered much soul-searching behind the scenes, and with the state pension more than fully protected, was targeted almost entirely at those of working age. Benefit upgrading was switched to the consumer price index, a lower measure of inflation. From 2013, nearly all working-age benefits rose by just 1 per cent a year, leading to a fall in the real value of benefits that was unprecedented since the economic crisis of 1931. A cap on individual benefit levels was imposed, while a 'spare room subsidy' – the 'bedroom tax' to its critics – meant that households deemed to

Figure 24.1: 'After three years of cuts, I'm a leaner, more efficient poor person', Grizelda Grizlingham cartoon, *The Independent*, 14 November 2013

Source: Grizelda Grizlingham

have too many bedrooms lost part of their housing benefit. Central funding for council tax benefit was reduced, leading to a sharp rise in arrears. By the autumn of 2013, 157,000 people across the country had been summoned to court.[9]

The Educational Maintenance Allowance – which helped adolescents over eighteen from poorer households to stay on in education – was abolished. The DWP-administered social fund, which provided loans and grants for intermittent needs and crises such as broken boilers and lack of furniture, was abolished from April 2013, and its budget – cut by almost a half – devolved to local councils. The package was further tightened in 2015 with a lowering of the benefit cap, a freeze on working-age benefits and the introduction of a two-child limit for tax credits. By 2019, despite the rising risk of in-work poverty, the values of many benefits were lower in relation to earnings than in the 1960s and 1970s. Between 2010 and 2019, child benefit fell by 21 per cent in real terms.[10]

One of the claims supporting the strategy – that social security spending was 'out of control' – did not stand up to much scrutiny. In the immediate post-war period, full employment and buoyant pay limited the cost of the social security budget. From the 1960s – with a more generous system, a rising number of pensioners and single-parent families and growing economic insecurity, the bill began to rise. Despite these pressures, benefit spending as a share of national income remained broadly flat between 1980 and 2009, at an average of around 11 per cent, a figure that placed the UK one from bottom place among the EU15 (the 15 member states of the European Union prior to 2004).[11] Despite the reality, the popular view – encouraged by government and media – remained that benefit spending was excessive. The public greatly overstated the proportion of taxes going on social security, the level of benefit received by the unemployed and the volume of false claiming.[12]

A disciplinary state

The lowering of the benefit floor was also accompanied by a further tightening in entitlement and, despite their mixed record in helping the unemployed find work, in the sanction regime. Those 'who fail to engage as fully neo-liberal citizens lose their claims to universal/collective welfare support', concluded one social scientist.[13] The tougher sanctions fell into three categories: high (such as for leaving a job voluntarily), intermediate (for being deemed to be not actively seeking work) and low (for example, for missing a job centre interview). Between 2010 and 2018, a total of five million sanctions were issued.[14] At the peak in 2013, the DWP was levying more fines through local jobcentres than the mainstream justice system.[15] After pressure from MPs, ministers confirmed that it employed 3,700 people to investigate benefit claimants, often for modest sums, compared with 700 revenue staff for investigating tax avoidance.[16]

The most common reasons for sanctions were 'failure to attend an interview' (which mostly meant arriving late, a mix-up over dates or non-delivery of an appointment letter), non-participation in a training or employment scheme, even if considered unsuitable by the claimant, and not 'actively seeking work' – such as not applying for as many jobs as specified. The average duration of benefit suspension was eight weeks, with two-thirds of those sanctioned left without an income.[17] An independent review found systematic faults in the way sanctions were imposed.[18] A single, fifty-nine-year-old man with diabetes was sanctioned for missing two interview appointments despite completing two periods of unpaid work experience and a forklift truck training course. The man had worked all his life before stopping to look after his mother who had dementia, and was waiting to hear about a job application. He was later found dead at home. He had £3.44 in his bank account, and with his electricity cut off, the fridge where he kept his insulin was no longer working. He died from diabetic ketoacidosis, caused by a lack of insulin.

The sanction system – with jobcentres under considerable pressure from Whitehall to issue them – was not just punitive but out of control. According to the independent Institute for Government, the central aim of the social security system had become 'one of "work first", it being judged important to get people to any type of paid work as a first step, rather than necessarily waiting for a job that might better match their skills'.[19] Because of the high levels of inaccuracy in the tick-box assessments, there was a surge in the number of appeals. In the three months to September 2013, 87 per cent of sanctioned claimants taking their cases to an independent tribunal were successful.[20]

Among those most affected by the new rules were those claiming the new Employment and Support Allowance introduced for people with disabilities under Labour's earlier 'welfare-to-work' push. This group, the most likely to be on long-term benefit, had to undergo new, computerised work-capability assessments.[21] These tighter conditions were in part about getting more claimants into work, but with a sharp rise in the number receiving disability benefits over time, were also about cost. The We Are Spartacus network of disability campaigners cited example after example of recipients being 'wrongly assessed, humiliated, badly treated', including repeated assessments even of patients with long-term illnesses who were unlikely to improve.[22] Ken Loach's 2016 film *I, Daniel Blake* – dismissed by some supporters of sanctions as fictional, but based on the all too typical experience of claimants – provided a powerful portrayal of an inhuman and inflexible system at work. For many claimants, the system involved a constant battle with the authorities. One of the most damning assessments concluded that the overall sanctions regime was not only ineffective at getting jobless people into work, it pushed more into poverty, ill-health or even, for the particularly vulnerable, 'survival crime'.[23]

The coalition government also set out to redesign the benefit system through the launch of Universal Credit. This flagship scheme merged six existing means-tested benefits – Income Support, Housing Benefit, Jobseeker's Allowance, Income-Related Employment and Support Allowance, Child Tax Credit and Working Tax Credit – into a single benefit. At first the broad principles behind this Whitehall 'megaproject' were broadly welcomed. In the event, the scheme was blighted by heated cabinet disputes, inter-departmental rifts, acute software problems and huge cost overruns. It quickly ran out of friends. The government spending watchdog the National Audit Office concluded that it had suffered from 'weak management, ineffective control and poor governance'.[24] In 2019 – two years on from the target completion date – less than a fifth of claimants had been transferred. Similar, if less severe problems of implementation had marred Labour's tax credit scheme.

While the implementation problems began to recede, the new scheme retained a number of flaws, mostly driven by austerity. By reducing the generosity of the new scheme compared with the one it replaced, an estimated six million low-income working households would be £1,000 a year worse off as a result.[25] Another effect of the avalanche of change was growing complexity. The DWP's guidance to staff on the whole benefit system ran to ten thousand pages.

Communist clerics

One of the effects of rolling austerity was to spark an increasingly vocal chorus of opposition. In December 2013, Church Action on Poverty launched a 'Britain Isn't Eating' poster campaign. When the Save the Children Fund launched an appeal to help poor British families with the most basic of needs – from a hot meal to blankets and beds – it was met by a wave of denunciations. This was the first time in its near one-hundred-year history that the high-profile charity – known for its work in providing aid overseas – had intervened to provide direct help domestically. The *Daily Mail* attacked the move as 'obscene'. Christian Guy, director of the conservative think tank the Centre for Social Justice, proclaimed that the charity 'should be fighting family breakdown and welfare dependency'.[26]

Some of the multiple new campaigns spawned from 2010 brought real change. Students across the globe began rebelling against the dominance of narrow free-market theories on university courses, leading to the formation of the 'Rethinking Economics' movement and once ignored heterodox thinkers starting to rewrite the economics curriculum.[27] New trade unions, such as the tiny Independent Workers of Great Britain, began to mobilise low-paid

Figure 24.2: 'Britain Isn't Eating', Church Action on Poverty poster, 2013

Source: Church Action on Poverty

workers, from outsourced cleaners to Deliveroo couriers. Despite the strides made by women in parts of the labour force, the revelations of a gender pay gap of 19 per cent triggered new pressure for tougher action to close it.[28]

Along with grassroots-based projects and new social enterprises, local councils from Wigan to Preston launched new interventions aimed at making local firms more accountable to local communities. With few friends in the press, in corporate Britain and in government, those on the receiving end of austerity joined forces with credit unions, homelessness charities and local pressure groups, helping to build what Karl Polanyi had called, seventy years earlier, a 'countermovement'.[29] In July 2018, a small group of mostly middle-aged demonstrators – members of the Hope Rising Action Group based in Bradford – boarded a packed train to London, paid for by the local Common Wealth Theatre Company. On the journey, they sang their way through the carriages highlighting the effects of eight years of cuts in public spending. "We want an end to austerity", explained Julie Longden, one of the organisers. "It's being used as a way of keeping poor people poor and rich people rich". In one initiative in Northern Ireland, eight local groups from Belfast to Lurgan, Catholic and Protestant, joined together to document the impact of retrenchment. The films and accounts stemming from this project were presented to Stormont, and even reached the European Parliament in Brussels. "We are sitting with the big people now" is how one participant put it.[30]

New techniques developed by social scientists also put government claims under a much tighter spotlight. There was better evidence, for example,

Figure 24.3: 'We're All In This Together', Conservative Party election poster, 2010

Source: Alamy

of the adverse impact of child poverty for future employment, health and well-being.[31] New measures of the intergenerational impact of austerity exposed the way millennials, aged between eighteen and thirty, were paid less and held much less wealth at each point in life than earlier generations, apparently breaking the earlier progressive contract that each generation would be at least as well off as the previous one. While the distribution question had been ignored for decades, there was a revival of research into inequality and its impact, including trends in the wage share.[32] Having been widely assumed to be separate conditions, a study of the impact of rising inequality on poverty concluded that 'higher income inequality ... is associated with higher relative poverty. We simply do not observe countries with high income inequality and low relative poverty; achieving that seems to have eluded the policy-makers in many countries.' Similar research in the United States found that high income inequality was a primary determinant of high poverty rates.[33]

Until the 1980s, the main method for evaluating the impact of policy was to examine the impact on individual household types. This was an imperfect tool, as the households chosen might be unrepresentative. From the 1980s, microsimulation models were developed by independent researchers which tested the impact of tax and benefit changes using data for several thousand households drawn from representative sample surveys. The new techniques played an important role in holding government to account. George Osborne liked to claim that the 'broadest shoulders are bearing the greatest burden' of his tax and spend policies.[34] The 2010 election poster bearing the slogan 'All in this together' sold well at Conservative Party headquarters.

The new microsimulation studies revealed a very different picture. Because such studies were rarely flattering of government claims, ministers continued to sell their policies using the old single-household-profile method. In 2015, David Cameron cited the highly unrepresentative example of a single family to claim that the government's policy of a higher minimum wage and reduced tax credits would make the family better off. Contesting ministerial spin, the new modelling techniques showed that the net effect of the tax and benefit changes would be that low-income households, some experiencing life-changing levels of income, would lose a combined £12 billion from benefit cuts and only gain £4 billion from the rise in the announced minimum wage.[35] It was the poorest – and especially 'disabled people, certain ethnic minorities and women' – who bore the brunt of austerity, a finding supported by new Treasury analysis.[36]

Despite some, if limited, success for the new pressure groups, the government's social strategy was another turning point in post-war social history. It lowered the income floor for those of working age and eroded the social safety net, leaving a small minority of families effectively destitute. The strategy raised the risk of poverty and went a good deal further than Mrs Thatcher believed she was politically able to do.

Burning injustice

For a while, there were signs that the Conservatives were intent on a softer line on social policy. In 2015, cabinet minister Michael Gove called on Conservatives to be 'warriors for the dispossessed'. After winning the 2015 general election with an overall majority, David Cameron, flirting with 'red Toryism', promised 'an all-out assault on poverty'.[1] In support, an informal group of Conservative MPs, the 'compassionate Conservative caucus', was launched.

When, following the 2016 Brexit referendum, Theresa May replaced David Cameron as prime minister, the country had faced the deepest fall in living standards in living memory. Millions in the poorest half of the population were worse off in 2017 than in 2003.[2] While unemployment had been falling from the post-2008 recession, an estimated 4.6 million people were left in 'precarious work'.[3] The ongoing robotic revolution, along with the casualisation of work, including among professionals, had contributed to a steady hollowing out of middle-paid jobs and growing work insecurity, while helping to raise the incomes of those driving the changes and those with the necessary new skills.[4] There remained an extraordinary variation in the quality of work and its capacity to prevent poverty, while some companies adopted a highly controversial 'fire and rehire' strategy with employees losing their job and being rehired on poorer terms. A House of Commons enquiry, for example, found working conditions at the retail chain Sports Direct to be 'Victorian'.[5]

For many, the reality of work was of agency working, of involuntary under- or self-employment and of zero-hours contracts, while insecure work was the most likely destination for those moving off social security and into employment. What was being built was a form of quasi-employment, marked by volatile income in dead-end, low-paid and often intermittent jobs with few prospects.[6]

As wage stagnation became a defining feature of the UK economy, the governor of the Bank of England, Mark Carnie, lamented a 'lost decade' of falling real wages, the worst record since the 1860s when, as the governor put it, "Karl Marx was scribbling in the British Library".[7] Average wages in early 2018 were still below their pre-crisis peak and did not start to exceed inflation until the end of that year.[8]

The net effect of the downward pressure on living standards – from falling wages, employment fragility and benefit cuts – was not just a rise in the risk of poverty but a sea change in the composition of the poor. In the 1980s, those on the lowest incomes were overwhelmingly the unemployed and the elderly. While the risk of poverty among pensioners gradually fell as pensioner incomes improved, it rose for those of working age, less because of unemployment than because of work insecurity and low pay. The problem of jobless poverty had shifted to one of the working poor, returning to the pattern of the late nineteenth century. By 2018, around 60 per cent of those in poverty lived in households where at least one person was in work, up from a third in earlier decades.[9]

One of Mrs May's earliest pledges was to fight what she called the "burning injustices ... of poverty, race, and class".[10] Yet, apart from the occasional policy tweak, including some easing of sanctions, and a slight boost to the national minimum wage, now rebranded the national living wage, another cosmetic name-changing exercise, the promise failed to materialise. Although there was growing pressure for change, ministers – consumed by endless conflict over Brexit – parked their promises once in power. The political forces remained for inertia.

Filling the gaps

As wages continued to stagnate, and for many, real incomes continued to fall, evidence mounted of the rising number of families struggling to meet basic bills, pay for school uniforms, trips and after-school activities and make the payments on mounting levels of debt.[11] With teachers reporting a steady rise in the number of children coming to school hungry, faith groups, charities and schools themselves stepped in to fill some of the gaps left in a shrinking welfare system. In 1916, Beatrice and Sydney Webb had distinguished between two models of social support by charities: the 'parallel bars' model, with the state and the voluntary sector working together, and the 'extension ladder' model, with the state playing a dominant role and voluntary help providing additional support.[12]

While charities played the latter role in the post-war era, that balance now shifted towards the 'parallel bars' model of the pre-war era. While the state continued to play the principal role, charitable groups moved up several gears, taking on the role of what the eighteenth-century British politician and philosopher Edmund Burke once called the 'little platoons'.[13] The largest food aid network, the Trussell Trust – founded in 1997 to help homeless children in Bulgaria – provided nearly 1.6 million emergency food packs in 2019, up from 61,000 eight years earlier.[14] Without public debate, the dual but patchy welfare model of the pre-Beveridge era was being stealthily recreated with food aid, in a huge daily operation involving voluntary and statutory organisations, individuals, communities and businesses, becoming firmly institutionalised. By 2020, the number of food banks exceeded the number of branches of the popular takeaway store Greggs, while support had extended to help with other basic needs from clothing to furniture. Although providing a lifeline, this help also relieved government of responsibility for tackling the root causes of poverty, and raised the crucial question of how food banks could be made redundant, an issue debated within the groups themselves.

While the number of rough sleepers had previously been falling, it rose almost threefold in the decade from 2010.[15] Many of those in local shelters and pop-up tents were in regular work, as Uber or delivery drivers or shift workers for Amazon or McDonalds. In 2019, 778 homeless people died, a 60 per cent rise over 2013.[16] The rising tide of homelessness evoked a mixed reaction. In Manchester, Danny Collins, who had slept rough for years, started an alternative tour, not of the city's traditional highlights, but of its homelessness problem. When a retired firefighter explained, on a radio phone-in, how he and his wife couldn't afford their rent, had sold most of their belongings and ended up sleeping in service stations, listeners donated the couple £25,000. In contrast, there was a steady rise in recorded incidents of violence against the homeless, from dousing them with water to dragging sleepers out of their tents, while many councils across the country forcibly removed tented camps.[17]

For two decades, housing opportunities had become steadily squeezed. Home ownership rates fell from the early 2000s, undermining one of the key cross-party political goals of the post-war era. Caught in a web of high rents, low and irregular pay and unaffordable house prices, 900,000 more twenty-to-thirty-four-year-olds were living with their parents in 2018 compared with twenty years earlier. For young people, buying a home had largely come to depend on who your parents were. Those able to buy in 2018 enjoyed a collective subsidy from their parents of some £5.7 billion.[18] With the stock of council homes halving from its early-1980s peak, a fifth of households depended on private landlords – among the most weakly regulated across Europe. In January 2019, one of Britain's largest landlords issued eviction notices to one street in Folkstone where he owned every property. In this landlords' market, rent levels rose from the millennium at a much faster pace than earnings, adding to the downward pressure on living standards.

Far from the much-promised 'all in this together', the guiding principle of the new social policy was closer to the 'everyone-for-themselves' philosophy of the Victorian era. In 2018 and 2019, a stream of reports delivered what the website Rethinking Poverty called an 'avalanche of bad news'. Paediatricians revealed high levels of respiratory illnesses in children from low-income families, caused or exacerbated by cold, damp and overcrowded homes. Following a fact-finding trip, the United Nations' special rapporteur on poverty, Professor Phillip Alston, claimed that 'British compassion for those who are suffering has been replaced by a punitive, mean-spirited and callous approach.' Studies showed that child poverty rates were rising, and were set to continue to do so. While pensioner living standards had improved on average, a House of Commons committee found that 1.3 million older people were at risk of malnutrition caused by social isolation and cuts to public services such as meals-on-wheels.[19]

The reports, ignored by government policy, were sometimes variously received, with newspapers reporting the same events as if they occurred on different planets. In one example, the *Daily Mirror* wrote a sympathetic article about the desperate circumstances that drove people to food banks. In the same week the *Daily Mail* alleged the debate around food poverty was being 'fuelled by questionable and inflammatory statistics'.[20]

By 2020, the punishing effect on the UK's social infrastructure from rolling austerity and underinvestment was all too apparent. While divided societies create jobs that serve the rich, austerity cut the number that served the community, from youth to family support workers, jobs that were replaced by those making a living out of the effects of poverty. The number working as jobcentre staff, sanction administrators, rent collectors and as debt-chasing bailiffs, for example, rose sharply from 2010.[21]

With town halls losing close to half their core central funding from Whitehall, and several councils declaring insolvency, hundreds of children's centres, libraries and youth clubs had been closed. As the squeeze on school budgets tightened, state-school head teachers were forced to appeal for donations to help fund salaries, buy textbooks and pay for essential repairs.[22] In one primary school, teachers volunteered a pay cut to save the jobs of other teachers. In a continuation of the privatisation of the commons and public goods, councils launched 'jumble sales' of their assets – from former community centres to playgrounds – sites mostly bought, and too often on the cheap, by developers to turn into high-end housing. In some cases the revenue was used to pay staff redundancies.[23]

Inequality denial

From 2010, the slow lane in Britain's multi-speed economy not only moved more slowly, it became ever more crowded. This was echoed geographically, with some towns and regions, hit much harder by the loss of industrial jobs, the financial crisis and austerity, still not recovered from recession by 2018.[24] The failing cities and boarded-up high streets of parts of modern Britain are not so different from those powerfully described in Oliver Goldsmith's 1770 poem 'The Deserted Village':

> Sweet smiling village, loveliest of the lawn,
> Thy sports are fled, and all thy charms withdrawn;
> Amidst thy bowers the tyrant's hand is seen,
> And desolation saddens all thy green.

The impact of the growing divide was not unique to the UK. *Twilight of the Elites* by the French geographer Christophe Guilluy painted a vivid portrayal of a 'higher' and 'lower' France, split between the 'cool capitalism' of prosperous cities and hollowed out, neglected peripheral towns and villages where 60 per cent of the population lived but where prospects were poor, living standards in decline and public infrastructure neglected.[25]

'Inequality denial' – the assertion that inequality was not as great as claimed and in any case was not an important issue – remained a potent force. Influential strands of conservative thinking had never signed up to the calls for greater equality. In 2016, the influential pro-market think tank the Institute of Economic Affairs published *Never Mind the Gap: Why We Shouldn't Worry about Inequality.*[26] In a debate at the British Academy, Fraser Nelson, the editor of the right-of-centre *Spectator* magazine, argued that it was time to end what he called the 'culture of rich-bashing'.[27]

Denial was also alive outside the UK. An editor at the German business weekly *WirtschaftsWoche*, Bert Losse, condemned Germany's school economics curriculum as 'a lot of twaddle about inequality and how the state can address it'.[28] In the United States, the question of inequality was typically ignored in the curriculums of economics departments. 'It is as though the central facts, controversies, and policy proposals that have consumed our public debate about the economy … are of little-to-no importance to the people who are paid and tenured to conduct a lifetime's research into how the economy works.'[29] In 2010, Glenn Beck, a host at the conservative Fox News television channel, devoted an hour to promoting the views of Friedrich Hayek (who had died in 1992), catapulting his *The Road to Serfdom* to number one on Amazon's US bestseller list.[30] Mitt Romney, the Republican's wealthy US presidential candidate in 2012, dismissed President Obama's critique of inequality as 'class warfare'. Romney wanted the inequality debate to be confined to 'quiet rooms'.[31]

Ayn Rand, the 'goddess of the market' according to her biographer, remained a big influence on American conservatism, while her laissez-faire philosophy still enjoyed a significant following among the world's power brokers forty years after her death.[32] Admirers have included Donald Trump and Silicon Valley tycoons. The former Republican speaker of the US House of Representatives Paul Ryan gave his staff copies of her work. In the UK, devotees include the Conservative MP and former chancellor of the Exchequer Sajid Javid, and the former MEP Daniel Hannan, who keeps a photograph of Rand on his desk. In 2016, Javid excitedly presented the 1949 film version of Rand's *The Fountainhead* to the parliamentary film society, and has on occasion read one section, in which one of the key characters rails against the 'collective spirit', aloud to his wife. In 2017, the heavily used UK website *The Students Room* circulated an email from the Ayn Rand

Institute that offered to send all teachers of A level politics copies of Rand's books to circulate to classes.[33]

Though selective use of evidence is hardly new in politics, ministers would regularly cherry-pick from official statistics to defend their record. One claim was that from 2010, their strategy had brought a fall in inequality.[34] In 2020, Boris Johnson, who succeeded Theresa May as prime minister in July 2019, was taken to task by the watchdog the Office for Statistics Regulations. He had used official statistics on poverty levels 'selectively, inaccurately and ultimately, misleadingly', to put a gloss on the government's deteriorating record.[35]

The best evidence of the period from the late 1970s was that inequality across the broad range of incomes jumped sharply in the 1980s, and then stabilised around this higher level, sometimes a little higher, sometimes a little lower, through the 1990s and in the decade after the millennium. In the decade to 2020, the gap between high- and low-income households widened a little, taking the UK back to a near post-1970s high for inequality on this measure.[36]

The central story of inequality remained the way a small financial elite was able to continue to capture such a large chunk of national income. The share secured by the top 1 per cent jumped nearly threefold in the forty years from the mid-1970s. This upward process stalled in 2009, with some of those at the top taking initial losses from the recession, before returning almost to its pre-2009 level. Once allowance is made for the way high incomes are understated, the top income share is estimated to have continued to rise from 2008.[37]

As Ali Smith described the state of the nation in her 2018 novel *Autumn*:

All across the country, the haves and the have nots stayed the same. All across the country, the usual tiny per cent of the people made their money out of the usual huge per cent of the people. All across the country, money money money. All across the country, no money no money no money no money.

So what scale of change would be required to bring about a more equal division of the cake? Over time, various summary measures have been used to describe the extent of inequality. The Gini coefficient, developed in 1912 by the Italian statistician, Corrado Gini, ranges from 0 at full equality to 100 at complete inequality. While it has been the most widely used for measuring trends and cross-country comparisons, it has a number of limitations, especially in picking up changes in the extremes.

An alternative measure – the Palma ratio – compares the ratio of the income share of the richest 10 per cent to that of the poorest 40 per cent. Developed from work by the Chilean economist Gabriel Palma, it has a number of key advantages over the Gini coefficient. It is a better measure of the tails of the distribution, while the Gini coefficient, giving greater weight to the middle, has been poor at picking up the full impact of the shift in income share from the bottom to the top in recent decades. The Palma ratio is also less technocratic and abstract, and offers a more straightforward message about the scale of the task to reduce inequality. It tells us something more direct about the distribution question, and could be used as part of an overall assessment of the social strength of a society. It also has greater potential for guiding anti-inequality policies, while raising the question of what ratio a society concerned about inequality should aim at.[38]

While there is an ongoing debate about the merits of a single target, especially in the case of low- and middle-income countries, some experts have called for countries to aim for a Palma ratio of 1.0, and for such a target to be included in the UN's framework for sustainable development. This is the point at which the top tenth and bottom 40 per cent have an equal share. Others have called for a halving of the gap.[39] Only a handful of nations in the OECD have a ratio of 1.0 or less (they include Norway, Denmark and Belgium). The US has a ratio of 1.85 (the third highest in the OECD, below Mexico and Turkey) while the UK takes fifth place with a ratio of 1.5. That is, the richest tenth have 50 per cent more income as a group than the poorest 40 per cent.[40]

A strength of the Palma ratio is that it could be used as a guide to the scale of the adjustment needed to create a more equal distribution. A reallocation from the top to the lower tail of the distribution, leaving middle-income households untouched, would lower the Palma ratio. Lowering it to 1.0 would require equalising the shares held by the top tenth and bottom four tenths. This would involve raising the share at the bottom from its current 18 per cent to 22.5 per cent and lowering the share of the top tenth from its current 27 to 22.5 per cent.[41] To achieve a more modest goal of a Palma ratio of 1.25 would require a lower level of redistribution from the top. Either target would require a strategy that raised the income floor and lowered the ceiling. Achieving a significant fall in the income Palma ratio would be a big, but not insurmountable, political challenge. It would require considerable economic restructuring, would face elite resistance and would have to be implemented in incremental steps. But lowering today's heightened level of poverty will not be possible without a boost to the lower income share and thus a lowering of the Palma index.

Growing rich in their sleep

Despite ongoing austerity and repeated government promises to check excess, the executive pay gravy train continued to roll. The average pay of a FTSE 100 chief executive rose at four times the pace of employees in the decade from 2009.[1] In the two years to 2021, Denise Coates, the chief executive of the privately owned online gambling firm Bet365, took 'pay' of over £800 million, while fifteen global hedge fund managers pocketed £17 billion between them for betting correctly on the course of the global economy.

While top incomes reached new heights, Britain had also seen a four-decade long surge in the pool of privately owned wealth. Over this period, UK private holding of capital (a mix of property, physical and financial wealth) grew at slightly more than twice the rate of incomes, rising from three to more than six times the size of the economy.[2] As in the nineteenth century, most of this growth has been captured by the already wealthy, reversing the earlier long-term trend towards greater equality, while the share held by the poorest half, a key measure of economic and social progress, fell.[3] Moreover, as Ben Tillett declared a century earlier, little of this surge in wealth has been 'conscripted' for the common good, with the revenue from capital taxes raising a fraction of the total tax take.[4] As with incomes, official statistics have understated the full extent of wealth concentration because of the way a large part of personal wealth is hidden in tax havens such as Panama and Luxembourg.[5]

Giving everyone a stake

Wealth, and how it is generated and shared, matters. A significant increase in private wealth in relation to economic output is not necessarily a sign of a healthy economy and wider economic progress. A boost in private wealth levels that was driven by long-term innovation, for example, would also raise the rate of return on investment and thus the growth rate, so the ratio of wealth to output might not become significantly higher. Rather, the rising wealth–to–income ratio of recent times has been driven by a number of other factors that are more likely to be associated with negative economic and social outcomes. These drivers include the transfer of formerly public assets into private ownership and artificially created inflation in asset prices.[6]

While new wealth creation will boost levels of personal wealth, today's greatly expanded wealth pool contains a significant 'unearned' element, notably that derived from inheritance (which simply reproduces past inequalities, and is often the result of profoundly unethical actions of the past, from the seizure and transfer of land to the slave trade), from privatisation (which transfers assets from common to private ownership), and from a range of extractive financial activity and asset inflation.[7]

Unearned wealth has minimal intrinsic value and comes with little moral or economic justification, while wealth accumulated from rising asset prices is a classic example of, in John Stuart Mill's phrase, 'getting rich while asleep'. Yet, some three-quarters of the growth in UK wealth holdings since 2008 has been the product of asset inflation, or 'passive accumulation'.[8] Far from being associated with an improvement in the productive base, rising asset prices have mostly been triggered by excess financial liquidity. Such inflation, especially in the case of rising land and property values, is one sign of Britain's heavily imbalanced 'luxury economy', and has inflicted significant social damage.

In the seven years from 2009, London house prices doubled, delivering a largely untaxed average windfall of some £240,000 to home owners while 'crowding out' the housing chances of the young. This boom was stoked by Treasury attempts to refire an economy deadened by austerity, not by encouraging investment, but by measures that fuelled another self-defeating property bubble, a process which enriched some sections of society but by-passed the rest. Property developers and housebuilders also continued to make big money from the boost to land prices from planning decisions.[9] One study found that 'the post-tax windfall profit for landowners and other stakeholders as a result of land being granted planning permission was £10.7 billion' for 2017 alone.[10]

Another source of the wealth surge has been rolling privatisation. The socialisation of part of Britain's wealth and asset base through the common ownership of land, some key industries and public spaces through the twentieth century ensured that some of the gains from economic activity were more equally shared. In the 1950s and 1960s, around a third of the national asset base was publically owned. Following the ongoing fire sale of public assets, the commercialisation of public services and the demutualisation of building societies and insurance companies from the 1980s, the share of the national asset base that is publically or socially owned has fallen sharply. It stands at little over a tenth today.[11]

While the selling of the nation's family silver – state-owned enterprises, land, property and infrastructure – was presented as a way of spreading wealth across society, it ultimately proved a bonanza for the already wealthy. Rolling privatisation also weakened public finances, with net public wealth (assets minus debt) becoming negative by 2008, leaving the UK as one of only a handful of rich countries with a deficit on their public finance balance sheet.[12] Prioritising private over public wealth, and the erosion of the common wealth base, have been among the most regressive and socially damaging state-driven trends of the last half century. They have meant that the returns from these once collectively owned assets accrue to a small minority rather than to society as a whole, reducing economic and social resilience and weakening the means for preventing excessive wealth concentration.[13] Over time there have been various attempts to recoup some of the hike in value from land development through levies, including the 1947 Town and Country Planning Act – which nationalised the right to develop land – and the 1967 Land Commission Act, but most of these were largely ineffective and were repealed by subsequent governments.[14]

The windfall from these hikes in land, property and other asset prices could have been the springboard for a national debate about the dominance of individual property rights and the extent to which at least some of these gains should be shared through regulation, socialisation and appropriate taxation. Far from addressing these issues, a series of misjudged state actions have fanned this process. From 2010, the coalition government accelerated the sale of public land, aimed at boosting the rate of housebuilding. Yet just 6 per cent of the houses built on sold land were available for social rent.[15] The government's help-to-buy loan scheme, a subsidy to first-time buyers, poured petrol on a housing boom, boosting development profits and housebuilding executive's bonuses. The Bank of England's post-2009 quantitative easing programme had a limited impact on recovery, but the expanded credit ended up in the banking system, fuelling speculative activity, the takeover boom and property and share prices. Even its own Independent Evaluation Office reported that 'the Bank of England does not understand its own flagship quantitative easing programme'.[16]

As Leonard Hobhouse argued a century earlier, a nation's stock of physical, productive and social infrastructure, from the transport, school and health network to the natural resource base and the legal system, is largely inherited from the efforts of previous generations. Each of us is born into these riches. According to the Nobel prize-winning economist Herbert Simon, this inheritance accounts for around four-fifths of today's pool of social and economic assets.[17] For centuries, leading thinkers – from Thomas Paine in the eighteenth century to Hobhouse and James Meade in the twentieth – have made a powerful case that a greater share of national wealth, natural and created, should be held in common, with the gains from its use equally shared.[18] When the ancient Athenians discovered an unusually rich seam of silver in 483 BC, one proposal was that the revenue stream from the windfall should be distributed annually among all 30,000 citizens. In the event, the Athenian Assembly voted against the transformative idea in favour of expanding the Athenian Navy.

A key consequence of these long-term shifts is that private wealth holdings are much more heavily concentrated at the top than in the case of incomes.

The Palma ratio for wealth stands at around 10, with the top tenth holding a remarkable ten times more wealth in aggregate than the bottom 40 per cent.[19] As with incomes, it is difficult to see how this level of concentration can be justified, economically, ethically or socially, yet over time, even social democratic governments have failed to find politically acceptable ways of making these wealth pools more equal. While Britain needs a more equalising tax and benefit system, this would not be enough on its own to tackle today's entrenched drivers of inequality. While some middle-income groups have been able to gain a stake in corporate capitalism through home ownership, pensions and savings, an effective anti-poverty and pro-equality strategy requires a parallel system of 'asset redistribution'.

Because of this, there has been growing interest in ways of developing the idea of 'people's capital' as a way of narrowing what Roy Harrod called in the 1950s 'the unbridgeable gulf' between 'oligarchic and democratic wealth'.[20] One route would be to build a collectively owned citizen's wealth fund, initially created by government but owned by all on an equal basis. All citizens, including future generations, would have an equal stake in the economy, creating a new 'force for convergence' that would strengthen over time as the fund grew in size. Such a fund does not offer a quick fix but a vision for a much more secure social future, and one that would bring greater fairness between generations. It could be financed from a mix of sources: the issue of long-term government bonds, the transfer of several highly commercial state-owned enterprises, such as the Land Registry and the Ordnance Survey, and by assigning part of the revenue from additional taxation on wealth.

An especially pro-equality approach would be to source the fund in part through a new, modest scrip tax on the top 350 companies. These could pay say, an annual 0.5 per cent share issue into the fund (raising an estimated £12 billion a year) – up to a limit of, say, 10 per cent on the transfer. Such equity stakes would recognise the quasi-social status of companies, and that society is as much a stakeholder as are shareholders. By a gradual dilution of a tiny part of existing share ownership, part of the pool of institutional wealth would become socialised, with the gains that now accrue to a narrow group of private owners shared across society. Such a fund would be highly progressive and would transform the way the fruits of economic activity are shared, while its returns could be distributed through a regular 'citizen's dividend' that could be linked to a new basic income scheme. Even modest wealth transfers could build a fund worth nearly a third of the size of the economy after a decade, and over a half after twenty years.[21] A similar proposal has been made by Emmanuel Saez and Gabriel Zucman at the University of California, Berkeley. They propose all publicly listed companies headquartered in G20 countries should pay an annual 0.2 per cent tax on the value of their shares. With G20 stock market capitalisation at around $90 trillion, the tax would raise approximately $180 billion each year.[22]

One example of such a fund, created in Alaska in the early 1980s from oil revenues, has since paid out a highly popular annual dividend to all. The UK has had ample opportunities to build such a fund from newly discovered resources. When North Sea oil was discovered, two columnists at the *Financial Times* called for the revenue generated to be given 'to the people'.[23] In the 1980s, Shetland Island Council established a charitable trust funded by annual disturbance payments from oil companies in return for operational access to the North Sea. The returns have been used to fund social projects from new leisure centres to support for the elderly. If the UK had followed the path taken by Shetland and a number of other countries to create such a fund, it could have become a national, citizen-owned asset worth in excess of £500 billion today.

Corporate overreach

In recent decades, Britain has succumbed to the 'iron law of oligarchy', a theory developed in 1911 by the German sociologist Robert Michels, that mature democratic institutions would eventually come to be controlled by powerful elites.[24] Many of today's giant personal fortunes are down to the accretion of economic power, monopolisation, elite control over scarce resources, especially land, and misguided national economic policies. Today's rich lists are full of wealth extractors – landowners, financiers, property tycoons, oil barons and monopolists. Merryn Somerset Webb, the editor of the financial magazine *MoneyWeek*, and hardly an enemy of markets, argues that too much personal wealth has accrued from 'mismanaged monetary policy; politically unacceptable rent-seeking; corruption; asset bubbles; a failure of anti-trust laws; or some miserable mixture of the lot'.[25]

While today's most wealthy citizens do not directly hold the reins of power as their forbears did 150 years ago, they exercise a commanding nexus of power over the rules of the business game. The UK's five largest banks hold assets of over £5 trillion, two and a half times the size of the UK economy.[26] The three largest US asset managers – BlackRock, Vanguard and State Street – own a fifth of S&P companies. Blackrock extracts some £5 billion annually in dividends from Britain's largest companies.[27] In 2020, the market value of Apple crossed the $2 trillion line. Apple's cash reserves could launch an investment program to match the post-war Marshall Plan, the huge US aid package to Western Europe after the Second World War. Since the late 1990s, the turnover of the UK's largest 100 companies has risen from a fifth to a third of annual output.[28] 'The founders of the great companies of the 20th and 21st centuries', according to the influential, pro-market American economist Irwin Stelzer, 'have paid scant attention to their impact on small businesses (Amazon), wishes of their customers (Google, Facebook), their responsibility to defer to national security interests (Apple, Google), and avoided sharing in the tax burden borne by middle-class Americans (all of the above)'.[29]

Far from the competitive market models of economic textbooks, the British – and global – economy is dominated by giant, supranational companies. Key markets – from supermarkets, energy supply, food production and housebuilding to banking, soft drinks and pharmaceuticals – are controlled by a handful of 'too big to fail' firms. The oligopolistic economies created in recent decades are a certain route, as Joan Robinson warned 100 years earlier, to weakened competition, extraction and abnormally high profit. In the twenty years from the mid-1990s, the number of large global pharmaceutical companies fell, through merger and acquisition, from around 60 to ten. These companies now account for well over a half of global sales. By pursuing a dominant market position, new digital platform companies – from Deliveroo to Rightmove – have added a new layer to monopoly power. This power, across nations, has been a key determinant of 'the declining labor share; rising profit share; rising income and wealth inequalities; and rising household sector leverage, and associated financial instability'.[30]

Although they helped pioneer popular and important innovations, the new technology giants have entrenched their market power by destroying rivals and hoovering up smaller competitors. They are the equivalents of the American monopolies created by Rockefeller, Andrew Carnegie and Jay Gould through the crushing of competitors at the end of the nineteenth century. Today's largest tech companies are merely the latest to operate a modern equivalent of the 'sabotage' of the Edwardian era, through private-on-private 'crowding out' of small by giant firms, with the original 'makers' turning themselves into 'takers' and 'predators'.[31]

Bill Gates, an undoubted business pioneer, built his personal fortune through the ruthless destruction of rival software. From 2001, Google has bought 234 companies, while Facebook built what founder Mark Zuckerberg called a 'moat around itself' through the acquisition of competitors like Instagram and WhatsApp. It is monopolisation that has given the mostly young, geek tech founders membership of the three-commas club. In August 2020, Jeff Bezos of Amazon saw his wealth surge by $13 billion in a single day. This was not the product of a great jump in productivity or creativity but of immense global monopoly power created by anti-competitive practices.

Although very narrowly owned, large private corporations do not operate in a vacuum. The profits they make, the dividends they pay and the rewards received by their board members stem from interdependence with wider society. Business provides jobs and livelihoods. Society provides the demand, the workforce, education, transport, multiple forms of inherited infrastructure and often substantial state subsidies. Yet big business is weakly accountable to the common good, and most business leaders show little responsibility towards the society on which they depend.

Once linked to clear social goals, housing policy is now determined by the demands of a powerful construction industry and the preferences of the affluent and rich. Following the steady withdrawal of state intervention in housing from the 1980s – with local councils instructed to stop building homes for families by ministers – housebuilders and developers have sat on landbanks, and consistently failed to meet the social housing targets laid down in planning permission.[32] The four giant accountancy firms KPMG, PWC, EY and Deloitte, together responsible for the audit of large corporations, are part of the construct of today's extractive capitalism. They have failed time and again to hold corporate power to account, and simply missed the financial problems in a range of failing companies from Patisserie Valerie to Thomas Cooke.

Claims about the overriding benefits of the outsourcing of public services to private companies have been exposed by the collapse of giant multi-billion-pound behemoths – the UK construction company Carillion and the public-service supplier Interserve (which employed 45,000 people in areas from hospital cleaning to school meals) – and by damning reports of the consequences of outsourcing in the NHS, the probation service and army recruitment.[33] In the ten years to 2016, Carillion – another company sunk by self-serving executive behaviour and mismanagement – liked to boast about how it raised dividend payments to shareholders every year, with such payments absorbing most of the annual cash generation.[34]

It is the winners from these power games that like to descend on Davos. On display is not just corporate and political muscle but the outward trappings of the new wealth. In 2019, an estimated 1500 private jets landed at local airports during the forum. Davos provides a venue for the world's global elite to share views, outside the formal sessions, on the latest ways to defend their wealth. The former World Bank chief economist Branko Milanović described the 'real agenda' as 'the ability to play one jurisdiction against another in order to avoid taxes, how to ban organized labor in their companies ... how to save on labor protection standards, or how to buy privatized companies for a song'.[35]

In 2019, as in earlier years, the forum was full of talk about the risks of outsized inequality. 'The social contracts that hold societies together are fraying', wrote Børge Brende, the president of the World Economic Forum – which organises the annual event – in the preface to the annual report.[36] The concern about inequality, however, arose less from moral outrage than personal risk. 'The pitchforks are coming for us plutocrats', as the wealthy American entrepreneur Nick Hanauer described it.[37] In the organiser's annual survey of business leaders, 59 per cent said they expected 'public anger against elites' to increase.[38] Howard Schultz, the former billionaire boss of Starbucks, told a television interviewer that he didn't want to be seen as a billionaire anymore and asked to be called "a person of means".[39]

Doublespeak is there in abundance at Davos. Despite the talk and the evidence of the impact of the immense wealth concentrations on economic stability and social resilience, the Davos community, beyond token gestures such as grand plutocratic benevolence, have shown little willingness to take any responsibility that challenged their own self-interest. As Milanović wrote of the attendees, they 'are loath to pay a living wage, but they will fund a philharmonic orchestra. They will ban unions, but they will organise a workshop on transparency in government'.[40]

Breaking the high-inequality, high-poverty cycle

For most of the last two hundred years, Britain has been a high-poverty, high-inequality nation. With the exception of the immediate post-war era, the struggles for share have been won by the richest and most affluent sections of society. In 2020 there were few signs that this norm was about to be broken.

Measured simply in absolute terms, capitalism's dynamism, along with state-supported innovation, the expansion of public services and social pressure, has brought remarkable progress, more fulfilling lives, better health and longer life spans. Conservative thinkers have used this progress to claim that poverty in wealthy countries has been banished. For Deirdre McCloskey, for example, once people have 'a roof over their heads and enough to eat, and the opportunity to read and vote and get equal treatment by the police and courts', their needs have been sufficiently met. On this basis, it is not a requirement that the poorest should share fully in rising national income.[1]

While the past is an essential reference point, there is a fatal flaw in the notion of the most basic of past standards as the key measure of social advance. Should, for example, progress be judged today on the basis of Rowntree's 1950 line, or even his 1936 line, rather than the updated versions by contemporary researchers? On past standards, poverty in Britain has been almost, but far from fully eliminated. But is it acceptable to adopt a contemporary minimum based on an ancient benchmark? And what are the implications of such an approach for policy? The adoption of a pure absolute line, as many still advocate, suggests that benefit levels should be held in a time warp, raised only enough to compensate for inflation. This happened through the 1980s, while working-age benefit levels were lowered in real terms from 2010. Absolute measures of progress imply that sections of society have no right to share in social and economic advance.

Material progress is also a partial measure of advance, while social progress has rarely followed a conventional linear theory of history. The idea of continuous upward progress may be true for some, but for many it has been a much more mixed picture. For a significant minority, the wider improvement in living standards in recent times, as in the pre-war era, has been patchy and erratic, often accompanied by a diminished quality of life, weakened opportunities, qualifications and skills that count for little, the loss of a place in society and a deepening sense of powerlessness. That the poorest half of the UK population together own a lower share of national assets than their equivalents four decades earlier is at odds with the claim of universal progress.

Establishing the level and nature of poverty requires the adoption of a dividing line between the acceptable and unacceptable. Such a line is a matter of judgement, but few would draw up such a minimum by the standards of the distant past. Once it is accepted that all have a right to a standard of living that is linked to contemporary standards, trends in poverty depend crucially on how the cake is shared. If the poor fail to share proportionately in growth over time, even though their absolute material living standards may have improved, poverty levels will rise. On this basis, social progress has been much more limited. With many of the mechanisms that deliver wealth at the top also the source of squeezed incomes at the bottom, periods of high inequality have been strongly associated with high rates of impoverishment. Models of capitalism with high levels of wealth extraction and thus a bias to inequality are incompatible with low levels of poverty. They over-empower and over-reward elites, and have a loose relationship with social priorities.

The ghosts of the past

In recent years, history has been repeating itself. Poverty, as in the pre-war era, has been normalised. As Leonard Cohen puts it, 'The poor stay poor, the rich get rich. That's how it goes, everybody knows.'[2] At least three of Beveridge's five giants – want, ignorance and squalor – have yet to be banished. Work, as in the nineteenth and early twentieth centuries, has stopped offering a guaranteed route out of poverty, or the most basic of rights in an advanced economy, a secure life. Today's tax laws barely differ from the lax approach to tax avoidance initiated a hundred years ago, while a plethora of charities and a small army of volunteers have emerged to prop up an enfeebled welfare system. Today's extractive capitalism is the latest incarnation of the 'collective monopoly power' of the nineteenth century. Once again, inequality is widely seen as natural.

After rising for a century and longer, average life expectancies began to stall from 2015, and even fall in the most deprived areas.[3] It's a trend 'that is telling us something particularly important about how well society is distributing its benefits', argues the leading epidemiologist Sir Michael Marmot.[4] The world's richest nation – the United States – has already experienced an epidemic of mortality, one attributed, according to the economists Anne Case and Angus Deaton, to 'deaths of despair' from rising rates of suicide, overdose and alcoholism, especially among the poorly educated white population, the product of deprivation, the loss of livelihoods and social isolation.[5]

With the exception of the post-war years, few governments have set out to build a national consensus on tackling poverty or level the unequal treatment of rich and poor. There have been no serious attempts to address the intense concentration of both business power and the ownership of capital. A blind eye has long been turned to the predatory business methods and carefully concealed instruments of wealth extraction that have been bad news for livelihoods, resilience and the environment, while big business has mostly eschewed any sense of wider responsibility to society, the workforce or the planet.

For four decades, Britain has been locked in a second long wave of 'high poverty' and 'bad inequality'. Poverty and inequality levels are ultimately rooted in the outcome of the political and economic power games that play out in company boardrooms, plush City offices and the corridors of Whitehall, and in the extent of popular resistance and the strength of Polanyi's 'double movement'. Just as your chance of being in poverty depends on where you are born – by country and region – the risk of being poor in the UK has been an accident of timing. That risk – so much a matter of fate – has had much less to do with personal effort than the era in which you were born, and has been consistently much higher for those born in periods of high inequality.

In the nineteenth century, immense personal fortunes depended on weak factory regulation, limited democracy and minimal social rights. The extension of the vote, war and rising popular demands eventually brought a squeeze on moneyed elites and a rise in the share of economic output going to the poorest third. The step back by the social state after 1980, with the downgrading of post-war anti-inequality countermeasures, along with the jolts of deindustrialisation, automation and globalisation, returned Britain at some pace to the prolonged high inequality, high poverty wave of the past.

What of the opportunities that might have meant a very different direction? Could the post-war Attlee governments have seized the opportunity to further weaken the 'cycle of privilege', by, for example, reform of the public school system and the recruitment practices of public institutions? Should the ongoing post-war reform of the system of social security, along with the various attempts to devise a 'new Beveridge' plan, have taken the idea of a guaranteed basic social floor more seriously? Could post-war governments have done more to cut tax avoidance, harness wealth and institute ways of sharing the gains from capital accumulation?

What if more effective measures had been taken to share the gains from decades of land and natural resource development across society? What if, rather than handing over housing supply almost entirely to the market, Britain had maintained a steady supply of affordable social housing from the early 1980s? Instead of being seduced by a fuzzy politics of the 'third way', what if New Labour had used its huge majority to build an updated and progressive model of social democracy? What if the billions poured into supporting big companies over decades had come with much firmer conditions, including equity stakes used to build greater social ownership?

While there were undoubtedly problems with the managed model of capitalism by the 1970s, the full-blooded market experiment was not the answer. Market purists have defended corporate capitalism as the central driver of progress, yet have failed to explain how the most successful and stable period of capitalist development, from the end of the war until the mid-1970s, was also the most equal and most regulated. The political responses to the global problems of recent decades, from the growing concentration of financial power to the impact of climate change, have been consistently inadequate, nationally and globally. Despite the long-standing debate about the need to upgrade Beveridge – his model was designed for a world of full and secure employment for the male breadwinner, decent and buoyant wages and subsidised housing – such a plan has yet to be devised.

The experiment in free markets and hyper-individualism, twin tested to destruction over the past four decades, has been an exercise in national self-harm. The downgrading of the state's contract with its poorest citizens has been a key cause of the erosion of the values and institutions of liberal democracy and the recent waves of populism across many parts of the globe.

Breaking the intertwined poverty and inequality cycle depends on the kind of progressive political earthquake that shook the system in 1945. The upheavals of the post-millennium decades have demonstrated that history did not end in 1989. States need to play a bigger role than as enablers of markets. Governments should ignore Tony Blair's advice to simply ride with the direction of history.[6] The shockwaves from 2008 had the potential to trigger a third post-war turning point. Some of the conditions for such a shift were in place. Yet a severe economic shock, the multiple flaws in the market experiment and a growing public impatience with a system that delivered, for many, weakening opportunities and stagnant living standards failed to usher in a more pro-equality political economy.

That the current capitalist model is on trial has been acknowledged by at least some figures at the heart of the global business establishment. For Henry Blodget, a former leading Wall Street analyst, shareholder capitalism has turned America into a 'nation of overlords and serfs', while IMF staff have asked if neoliberalism has been 'oversold'.[7] Some corporate leaders have already questioned the mantra of shareholder value by signing up to new corporate goals that include 'improving our society' and taking account of employees and the environment. With speculation as to whether such statements are little more than a token gesture to head off more thorough going reform, such a commitment needs to be formalised.[8]

In Britain, more companies have been committing themselves to socially and environmentally responsible investing and improved carbon-emission targets. Since 2020, larger UK-listed companies have had to disclose the pay ratio between executives and other staff, while there have been several legal judgments that workers in the gig economy, including uber drivers, must be treated not as self-employed workers with minimal rights but as employees with the rights that go with that status.

While even mild attempts to redistribute power and wealth have always been marked by opposition and conflict, there are examples of ruling elites adapting, if reluctantly, to change, if only to ensure their survival. In the nineteenth and early twentieth century they accommodated, if weakly, to the demands for democracy and social reform. After 1945, they had to bend to a more antipathetic public and a seismic shift in political ideology before springing back to dominance in the pro-rich climate from 1980. A decade after the 2008 crash, the new plutocracy has shown few signs that it is willing to acquiesce to anything other than a token erosion of its muscle, privileges and wealth. As George Orwell warned in 1941, 'The bankers and the larger businessmen, the landowners and dividend-drawers, the officials with their prehensile bottoms, will obstruct for all they are worth.'[9]

One study of the attitudes of a thousand business executives around the world to 'distributive justice' has found a diversity of views, roughly divided equally between those wedded to the status quo and those accepting a need for at least some change. A quarter recognised they live in societies that are lacking in justice, while another quarter believed that all members of a community should have an income that is sufficient for them to lead a dignified life. The other half were a mix of 'meritocrats', who claimed that justice in pay is primarily a matter of desert, and 'free marketeers', who believe that economic efficiency should be the main criterion for determining how income should be allocated.[10]

Despite the hopes of a 'great reckoning' for market capitalism, and a number of blueprints for a post-neoliberal political economy, there have been few attempts to make corporate and financial leaders share the burden of retrenchment.[11] There has been minimal official recognition of just how fragile market economies have become. Many of the problems that helped trigger the financial crisis, including the excessive scale of financial assets, the use of lucrative financial instruments and the level of global debt, were, by 2019, almost back to or even above the levels of 2008.[12]

As the Italian writer and political theorist Antonio Gramsci said of the 1930s, 'The old is dying and the new cannot be born.'[13] The central political story of the post-crash decade was one of 'neo-austerity'.[14] Among the causes of this political failure was the mixed record of centre-left parties in office and their lack of attempts to uproot an unsustainable economic system. They largely 'accepted the institutional and ideological settlement of mid-20th-century social democracy as the horizon of their ambitions', argued the Brazilian political thinker Roberto Unger.[15] Partly in consequence, social democratic parties ceded power. In 2000, social democrats or socialists were part of the government in two-thirds of the countries that made up the European Union. In 2017, that number had fallen to a fifth.[16]

More than patching

Creating a low-poverty, low-inequality society requires, as Beveridge declared in 1942, much more than 'patching'. Abolishing poverty, as New Labour discovered, would be a daunting task, and one no advanced government has achieved. But it is possible to do much better than Britain's recent record. To do so requires a determined plan for a new model of social democracy built on a set of new anti-poverty and pro-equality instruments, institutions and values.

An impartial assessment would surely rule that Britain's democracy has been failing its poorest citizens and that recent ministerial pledges to tackle injustice and inequality have been less than frank. After he became prime minister in December 2019, Boris Johnson made successive promises to 'level up' Britain by rebuilding neglected towns and regions. But levelling up must also be about improving the lot of ordinary people across Britain, not just reallocating limited state resources from London's Hackney to North Yorkshire's Richmond.

Tackling inequality would have significant and beneficial side effects. It would switch demand away from luxury spending. By cutting speculative financial behaviour, it would contribute to greater economic stability. As the academics Richard Wilkinson and Kate Pickett have shown, more equal societies are also associated with fewer social ills as well as better health outcomes, higher life expectancy and lower rates of crime.[17]

A serious strategy on inequality should set out clearly stated goals and targets, along with proper and realistic tests of progress. A primary target should be a lowering of Britain's high inequality index for both wealth and income as measured by the Palma ratio. A starting point for a new target-based approach might be to reduce the ratio for incomes from 1.5 to 1.25 over a ten-year period. History shows that this is achievable. The comparable Palma income ratio was less than 1.0 in the UK in the mid-1970s.[18] A comparable proportionate reduction could be set for the ratio for wealth. Meeting such targets would require a mix of comprehensive 'levelling up' and targeted 'levelling down'.

The targets set by the Blair government for lowering poverty had only short-term success, largely because they were overambitious and lacked a simultaneous strategy for the wider distribution question. An initial and realistic target for poverty might therefore be based on the average level of poverty achieved by other comparable rich countries along with the historic lows achieved in Britain in the 1970s.

The success of such a strategy should also be tested by progress on other fronts, including the narrowing of cross-class rates of child mortality, life expectancy and educational achievement, lower corporate and gender pay differentials and a more balanced division of the cake between profits and wages. Progress should also be monitored by an independent and permanent national commission, whose members should range from experts and practitioners to ordinary citizens. Its role should be to measure progress, assess the effectiveness of different strategies, identify policy gaps and improve our understanding of the mechanisms that link inequality and poverty. The commission could incorporate feedback from society through, for example, the use of regular citizens' juries and membership.

Such an approach would require a reappraisal of the role that growth and consumerism plays in improving the quality of life and the priorities that govern the way the economy is currently run. Britain needs new, and widely accepted, measures of progress based on indicators other than average material gain. This could draw on the example set by other countries including Finland, Iceland and New Zealand. In 2019, New Zealand's Treasury announced new priority to be given to sustainability, well-being and social growth over traditional financial measures.[19]

Meeting new poverty and inequality targets would require integrating new pro-equality and anti-poverty instruments into the economic and social system. Their aim should be to counter the current bias towards inequality in Britain's institutional structures, from its tax system to large chunks of corporate activity. These instruments should build on current pro-equality, inclusive and popular mechanisms such as the National Health Service, child benefit and the national minimum wage. These highly progressive measures were hard won and highly controversial when introduced, but are now largely politically untouchable.

A set of new instruments should include a guaranteed, automatic and non-means-tested social minimum, a more progressive tax and benefit system that brings benefit levels closer to those in low-poverty countries, a greater emphasis on universalism, including the extension of the principle of free services, the spread of asset ownership and new forms of 'people's capital', and a new politics of reciprocity for all that includes new rights and obligations across society, including reforms to tackle extractive corporate behaviour.

Beveridge and Attlee hoped that their post-war changes would deliver a guaranteed social minimum for all, enough to ensure a decent if modest life. But while their reforms lifted the income floor for many, Britain has yet to create a robust social minimum sufficient to ensure a decent standard of living. Any plan for building a better future needs to finish the job started in 1945, but also go a good deal further. Inequality was a blind spot for Beveridge, as it was for Blair. Ignoring what is happening at the top would derail plans to raise the income share at the bottom. Such a social guarantee should be built around a modest income floor that would lift all those on the lowest incomes. Constructing a floor to be grafted onto the existing social security system, financed through a more progressive tax and benefit system, and with modest starting rates, has been shown to be feasible and affordable. Such a scheme would create, for the first time, an 'income Plimsoll Line' that would boost the incomes of the poorest families, cut poverty levels and strengthen universalism. With a series of tax adjustments to pay for the floor and claw back the payments from high-income households, the gains could be concentrated among low-income households.[20] Achieving a social minimum would also require a boost to the 'social wage' through the rebuilding of depleted public services and the introduction of new ones, such as free child care.

Ensuring such a guaranteed social minimum would extend the enabling role of the state, but through the direct empowerment of citizens that simultaneously builds individual, household and community resilience. It would offer greater security in an increasingly uncertain world, enhanced choice over key decisions on education, training and work and lower the risk of poverty. It would be non-judgemental and thus come without the need for current levels of conditionality and coercion. As after the War, it is time to accept as given the contributions made by wider society. Because it would automatically boost lower incomes, such a social floor would steer resources towards poorer communities, thereby helping to re-energise areas suffering from a depletion of demand, while boosting the opportunity for social caring and volunteering.

Creating a fairer and more robust future also depends on the deconcentration of the mountain of privately owned wealth. Britain is an asset-rich nation, yet these lightly taxed assets are a largely untapped resource that could be used to release significant funds for social reconstruction. Measures to spread the asset base would lower the Palma ratio for wealth. Such measures should include reformed taxation on wealth, the promotion of alternative but greatly under-represented business models – from partnerships to mutually owned and social enterprises – that create wealth, improve well-being and distribute primary economic gains more equally. They should also encourage the greater common ownership of natural and created resources through national and local citizen-owned wealth funds. Such a strategy would return, over time, large chunks of natural and created wealth back to 'the commons'. Such is the size of the national wealth pool, now close to £15 trillion, that even modest taxes on assets could deliver potentially large tax yields. The Office of Tax Simplification, for example, has shown that changes to the taxation of capital gains could raise up to an extra £14 billion annually, while a wealth tax commission found that a one-off tax on the richest households could raise much larger sums.[21]

These reforms should aim to build a closer fit between economic activity and the common good, while the bloated financial sector also needs to be realigned with the wider needs and priorities of society, innovation and the ecosystem. Ensuring the gains from growth are more equally shared depends on a more socially responsible model of capitalism, a rethinking of the limits to sustainability and a re-evaluation of the role of economic activity. Such a plan also requires a more concerted and global effort to tackle tax havens and the structures of immense global corporate power that have enabled a rolling process of wealth extraction. While some progress can be made by tougher domestic policies, further advance would require a new age of global co-operation and common purpose, a Bretton Woods for the twenty-first century.

Such a plan is challenging and would need to be implemented in stages. While some of the proposed reforms would be more controversial than others, none are utopian. Other countries have a much better record on inequality and limiting poverty. A significant reduction in poverty from its currently inflated levels is a perfectly attainable goal, while giving priority to greater equality would bring significant social and economic gains.

The future hangs in the balance. Without a fundamental change in direction, poverty and inequality levels will stay at, near or above today's record levels, with the short post-war period as good as it gets for Britain's poorest citizens.

Afterword: COVID-19 and 'the polo season'

At least initially, COVID-19 had a galvanising impact on the national mood. A pandemic is one of Walter Scheidel's 'Four Horsemen', associated historically with a shift towards equalisation. While earlier jolts, including the 2008 crisis and a decade of austerity, had largely failed to ignite a '1945 moment', the sacrifices from COVID-19 certainly created, at least initially, a momentum for change. 'The present crisis seems destined again to change the face of Britain, unleashing demands for social, political and economic reform unprecedented in our memories', declared the former editor of the *Daily Telegraph* Max Hastings. 'The polo season, figuratively speaking, is over.'[1]

An initial and important side-effect of COVID-19 was a change in the terms of the debate about how society should function. The pandemic exposed the flaws in Britain's social protection system, while within a matter of weeks, views on who the most valuable workers are and which activities count were being overturned. Simon Henderson, the headmaster of Eton, told the *Times*: 'Many of those who work in the lowest-paid roles are in fact the key to our survival, and these people who have been undervalued for so long have shown astonishing dedication when we have needed them the most. That can't just be forgotten.'[2] *British Vogue*, on its July covers, featured not models but a train driver, a midwife and a supermarket shop assistant.[3]

As the pandemic took hold, key pillars of neoliberal orthodoxy began to crumble. New questions emerged about the nature and purpose of economic activity. The epidemic challenged a decade of fiscal conservatism, while a new consensus emerged that despite the growing national budget deficit, there should be no return to austerity. The midst of a pandemic 'is no time for Britain's government to worry about a spiralling deficit', declared the *Financial Times*.[4] Despite the Conservative Party's dislike of the state, the Johnson government responded with a series of widely welcomed measures, from the furlough scheme aimed at preserving jobs to a slightly more generous universal credit. Unlike the 1930s and 2010, ministers accepted the need to improve the protective role of the state and cushion the impact of the virus on households. At the height of the first phase of the pandemic, in May 2020, in an unprecedented move, around a third of UK employees were paid 80 per cent of their salaries through the state Job Retention Scheme.[5] This was a return of activist government driven by the need to prevent a near total collapse of the economy. Balancing the books had to take a back seat at least for a while.

The most significant sign of the possibility of a fundamental shift in direction came from the new American president, Joe Biden, who – in a clear sign of a return to distributional politics – launched the largest fiscal package in history aimed at economic recovery, creating jobs and tackling social polarisation.[6] 'Bidenomics' – a modern equivalent of Roosevelt's New Deal – has included a boost to family benefits and a $2 trillion infrastructure programme paid for by a rise in corporation tax, a strategy that would begin to reverse the long-run fall in the corporate tax take.[7] The new president has also called for a global minimum corporation tax rate aimed at preventing the shift of profits between jurisdictions, an extensively used route for avoiding tax, a move subsequently endorsed by the G20 group of nations and a significant step in international tax rules aimed at curbing tax avoidance and boosting state revenues.

The exposed poor, the shielded rich

Despite these grounds for optimism, a spontaneous rise in grassroots community organising, and new expectations of government, the pandemic magnified existing social and economic disparities and exposed, again, the negative impact of inequality on health and social well-being. New gaps emerged between those travelling to work (typically the low-paid and insecure) and those able to work from home (mostly higher-paid professionals), between those with secure and insecure employment, and by age, ethnicity, income and wealth. There was growing concern that past gains for women were being threatened by the impact of the disease.

It was no accident that infection rates were the highest among the already disadvantaged, while existing regional divides were intensified.[8] Official data showed significant differences in COVID-19 mortality rates by occupation, social class and ethnicity, with those of working age in low-paid manual jobs – from machine operators to taxi drivers, security guards and care workers – facing the highest risk.[9] As the *Financial Times* put it, 'This crisis has broadly separated us into the exposed poor and the shielded rich.'[10]

Job losses were concentrated in areas already scarred by high unemployment from the hollowing out of manufacturing and the decline in retailing over the previous decade. A sure sign of what was in store was the close to one million new applications for Universal Credit in the first two weeks of the pandemic alone. This was five times the rate of new claims made during the peak of the 2008 crisis, while at the beginning of 2021, the number receiving the benefit had doubled.[11]

The new support measures, vital as they were, turned out to be poorly targeted, with many of those losing their jobs missing out altogether. During

2020, some four million people lost income but were excluded from any of the government income support schemes. Among this group some 1.8 million adults lost at least a third of their income.[12] Evidence emerged that levels of destitution were beginning to rise.[13] A new educational divide, between pupils able and unable to get support and tuition at home, also became evident.[14] What was at risk, warned Robert Halfon, the Conservative chair of the Education Select Committee, was 'an epidemic of educational poverty'.[15]

Crises, as Churchill declared just before the end of the Second World War, should not be allowed to go to waste. While the first priority for government was to manage the immense challenges of the pandemic, the opportunity could also have been seized to prepare for a new post-COVID-19 society. Yet there has been little evidence of strategic political thinking about how to move from emergency measures to build a more socially resilient and just society. The contrast with the war years could hardly be greater. The wartime coalition government commissioned the Beveridge report, enacted bipartisan social reforms, published groundbreaking plans for post-war full employment and worked with other governments to prepare for a more robust international financial system.

There are no signs of such groundwork today. The 2021 budget revealed Treasury plans to cut public spending once the pandemic had been controlled. Despite mounting pressure from campaigners, the government announced that it was to withdraw the small, temporary uplift to Universal Credit (worth up to £20 a week), while sickness and out-of-work benefit levels remained among the meanest in Europe.[16] Despite the downward pressure on low-income families, calls for even a temporary rise in the level of child benefit and the ending of the benefit cap and the two-child limit were ignored. While the system of benefit sanctions was initially suspended, it was reintroduced despite a greatly weakened jobs market and the evidence that the newly unemployed hardly needed state discipline to persuade them to search for work.[17]

In contrast to rising insecurity for many, the pandemic proved to be another bonanza for large groups of the already rich and affluent. Some 45 per cent of the net cost of the government's income support measures were found to have trickled up to wealthier members of society.[18] The wealth of the world's 2189 billionaires rose by over a quarter in the four months to July 2020, taking their joint wealth to a new peak. This surge was in large part the product of bets on the impact of the virus on stock markets.[19] The global list of billionaires and centi-billionaires also grew longer, while the two corporate groups to do best out of the crisis were 'big finance' – Goldman Sachs, JP Morgan and Citigroup all saw profit surges – and 'big tech'. The six largest tech companies, from Amazon to Facebook, saw their combined market valuations rise by $1.9 trillion in the six months following the pandemic outbreak, an increase of 38 per cent.[20]

Before the pandemic, some business leaders had acknowledged the need to exercise greater social responsibility, even if their commitment was vague and non-formalised. Government, national and global, could have used the crisis to develop such a commitment and to set out ways of rebalancing the relationship between state, society and capital. The huge crisis-related, multi-billion-pound subsidy bill to keep business alive, for example, could have come with new conditions on issues such as tax dodging and employment practice. Critically, the cash injections could have required a proportionate equity stake, opening the way to the socialisation of a small part of the economy and tackling one of the key roots of endemic inequality, the concentration of returns from economic activity.

Critically, the pandemic provided an opportunity to build a more equitable tax system. Options included the closure of tax loopholes, the proper resourcing of the investigative arm of the HMRC and a response to the growing calls for higher levels of wealth taxation, including the IMF's proposal for a temporary 'solidarity tax' to reduce social inequalities exacerbated by the pandemic, and provide new revenue streams to fund recovery.[21] Changes could also have included new taxes on digital giants which are among the most blatant of avoiders.[22]

Although public institutions responded swiftly to the crisis, vast sums of public money, bypassing normal tendering processes, were poured into large private companies and consultancies to help manage the state's response – from track-and-trace to the procurement of vital equipment – despite these companies' lack of a track record in these areas. Senior executives from Boston Consulting Group, enlisted to aid with the testing regime, were paid more than £7,000 per day, while some of the firms enjoying these handouts had close ties with senior ministers and advisers.[23] Much of this work could have been carried out at much lower cost by existing public agencies, including local authorities with extensive expertise in these areas. This is what happened with the big success story of the pandemic, the roll-out of the vaccination programme, one conceived and managed by public health service professionals.

It would be wrong to understate the task that the pandemic has posed for government, business and the public. The post-COVID-19 response will need to contend with a shrunken and more fragile economy, a huge hike in the national debt and new layers of hardship and uncertainty. These immense challenges underline the need to heed the growing calls for a 'global reset' of capitalism.[24] The pandemic has given us some glimpses of what a better society might look like, including the importance of the public realm, a renewed social empathy and the gains from greater collaboration between corporations, academia, wider society and local and national government. The joint AstraZeneca and Oxford University initiative has delivered a powerful vaccine at a cost of $3 a jab, much cheaper than its rivals. As Will

Hutton has written, 'It is a social market, stakeholder-capitalism success story, as has been the UK government's public-private vaccination policy.'[25]

While some saw the crisis as a wake-up call that would reshape society, others argued that it would simply 'accelerate history'.[26] The question Britain now faces is whether the pre-COVID-19 economic model has been suspended permanently or only partially and temporarily. A post-pandemic society can take one of two paths. It can return to its pre-crisis norm, to an out-of-control, value-sapping and high-inequality model of capitalism. Or it can be steered in a wholly new direction, one built around a different set of social values aimed at finally breaking the four-decade-long high-inequality, high-poverty cycle. Will Britain opt, metaphorically speaking, for an end to the 'polo season' or its continuation, or some fudge of the two?

Notes

Preface and acknowledgements

[1]   Department for Work and Pensions, *Households Below Average Incomes*, 1994/5–2018/ 9, March 2020: https://www.gov.uk/government/statistics/households-below-average-income-199495-to-201819. C. Kidd, *Total Wealth: Wealth in Great Britain*, Office for National Statistics, 2019; Institute for Fiscal Studies, 'Living Standards, Inequality and Poverty Spreadsheet', *Institute for Fiscal Studies*. http://www.ifs.org.uk/fiscalFacts/ povertyStats; *World Inequality Database*, Paris School of Economics. http://wid.world/. Thomas Piketty data sets available at: http://piketty.pse.ens.fr/en/ideology.
[2]   T. Piketty, *Capital and Ideology*, Harvard University Press, 2020, p 1.
[3]   M. Dean, *Democracy Under Attack*, Policy Press, 2013, p 253.

Introduction

[1]   D. Watkins and Y. Brook, *Equal is Unfair, America's Misguided Fight Against Income Inequality*, St Martin's Press, 2016.
[2]   Debate on inequality between the author and Dr Brook, Eton College, 5 February 2019.
[3]   Department for Work and Pensions, *Households Below Average Incomes, 1994/5–2018/9*, DWP, 2020. (The poverty figures are based on a relative income measure set at 60 per cent of median income after deducting housing costs.) OECD, *Income Inequality Data*, OECD, 2019 (based on the summary Gini coefficient). OECD, *Better Life Index*, OECD, 2018.
[4]   R. Steiner, 'Inequality is Good says Goldman Chief', *Daily Mail*, 21 October 2009.
[5]   B. Johnson, *The Third Margaret Thatcher Lecture: Boris Johnson*, Centre for Policy Studies, 2013.
[6]   J.M. Keynes, *The Economic Consequences of the Peace*, Macmillan, 1920, p 17.
[7]   *Newsnight*, BBC One, 5 June 2001.
[8]   D. Ricardo, *The Principles of Taxation and Political Economy*, John Murray, 1817.
[9]   A.B. Atkinson, *Inequality: What Can Be Done?*, Harvard University Press, 2015, p 25.
[10] J. Hills et al, *Poverty and Inequality*, Centre for Analysis of Social Exclusion, London School of Economics, 2019.
[11] R.H. Tawney, 'Poverty as an Industrial Problem', inaugural lecture, reproduced in *Memoranda on the Problems of Poverty*, William Morris Press, 1913.
[12] G. Orwell, *1984*, Secker & Warburg, 1949, p 112.
[13] R.E. Lucas, 'The Industrial Revolution: Past and Future,' *Economic Education Bulletin*, XLIV(8), 2004, pp 1–8.
[14] P. Golding, 'Prejudice Against the Poor', *New Internationalist*, 1 September 1982.

Chapter 1

[1]   G.W.E. Russell, *Collections and Recollections*, Outlook Verlag, 2018, p 66.
[2]   A. Ponsonby, *The Decline of Aristocracy*, TF Unwin, 2012, p 24.
[3]   R. Rhodes-James (ed), *'Chips', The Diaries of Sir Henry Channon*, Phoenix, 1996, p 224.
[4]   R. McKibbin, *Classes and Cultures: England 1918–1951*, Oxford University Press, 1998, p 2.
[5]   W.L. Guttsman, 'The British Political Elite and their Class Structure', in P. Stanworth and A. Giddens (eds), *Elites and Power in British Society*, Cambridge University Press, 1974, p 36.
[6]   W.L. Guttsman, *The British Political Elite*, MacGibbon & Kee, 1963, ch 2.
[7]   D. Cannadine, *Class in Britain*, Penguin, 2000, p 87.

8   For two different views, see J.G. Williamson, *Did British Capitalism Breed Inequality?*, Allen and Unwin, 1985; and C.H. Feinstein, 'The rise and fall of the Williamson Curve', *Journal of Economic History*, 48(3), 1988, pp 699–729. See also J. Freeman, *A History of the Factory and the Making of the Modern World*, Norton, 2019; E.P. Thompson, *The Making of the English Working Class*, Penguin, 2013; and E. Griffin, *Liberty's Dawn*, Yale University Press, 2013.

9   Quoted in R. Ashcraft, 'Lockean Ideas, Poverty and the Development of Liberal Political Theory', in J. Brewer and S. Staves (eds), *Early Modern Concepts of Property*, Routledge, 1996, p 26.

10 Quoted in B. Geremek, *Poverty: A History*, Blackwell, 1994, p 232.

11 P. Colquhoun, *Treatise on Indigence,* Hatchard, 1806, pp 7–8.

12 S. Heffer, *High Minds*, Windmill Books, 2014, p 14; G. Stedman Jones, *Outcast London*, Oxford University Press, 1971, part III.

13 J. Harris, 'From Poor Law to Welfare State? A European Perspective', in D. Winch and P.K. O'Brien (eds), *The Political Economy of British Historical Experience, 1688–1914*, Oxford University Press, 2002, pp 409–37.

14 J. Cobden Unwin, *The Hungry Forties*, Fisher Unwin, 1904, pp 82–3, 107–11.

15 E.J. Hobsbawm, *The Age of Capital, 1848–1875,* Abacus, 1988.

16 C. Kollmeyer, 'Income Inequality in Advanced Capitalism: How Protective Institutions can Promote Egalitarian Societies', *Comparative Sociology*, 13(4), 2014, pp 419–44.

17 T. Piketty, *Capital in the Twenty-First Century*, Harvard University Press, 2014, p 200.

18 B. Christophers, *The New Enclosure,* Verso, 2018, ch 3; G. Standing, *Plunder of the Commons,* Pelican, 2019.

19 K. Cahill, *Who Owns Britain,* Canongate, 2001.

20 J. Prebble, *The Highland Clearances*, Penguin, 1963.

21 K. Polanyi, *The Great Transformation*, 2nd edn, Beacon Press, 2002, p 164.

22 D. Philipsen, 'Economics for the people', *Aeon,* 22 October 2020.

23 J.G. Williamson, *Did British Capitalism Breed Inequality?*, Allen and Unwin, 1985.

24 E.P. Thompson, *The Making of the English Working Class*, Penguin, 2013, p 351.

25 I. Gazeley and A. Newell, 'No Room to Live: Urban Overcrowding in Edwardian Britain', IZA Discussion Paper 4209, 2009.

26 S.E. Finer, *The Life and Times of Sir Edwin Chadwick*, Methuen, 1970, p 9.

27 S. Heffer, *High Minds*, Windmill Books, 2014, pp 77–7.

28 J. Bradshaw, 'Preface', in B.S. Rowntree, *Poverty: A Study of Town Life*, centennial edn, Policy Press, 2000.

29 House of Commons, *Hansard*, vol 186, 18 March 1867, col 7.

30 W. Guttsman, *The British Political Elite*, MacGibbon and Kee, 1963, p 41.

31 P. Thane, *The Foundations of the Welfare State*, Longmans, 1996, p 14.

32 P. Thane, *The Foundations of the Welfare State*, 1996, p 34–5.

33 R. Floud, 'High and Mighty', *New Statesman*, 27 May 1983.

Chapter 2

1   R. Sugg, 'An American's Verdict on Victorian Britain', *BBC History Magazine*, February, 2019.

2   J.G. Williamson, *Did British Capitalism Breed Inequality?*, Allen and Unwin, 1985.

3   W.D. Rubenstein, 'Introduction' in W.D. Rubenstein (ed), *Wealth and The Wealthy in the Modern World*, Croom Helm, 1980, p 35.

4   T. Piketty, *Capital and Ideology*, Harvard University Press, 1919, p 194–5. For details, see http://piketty.pse.ens.fr/en/ideology; J. Harris, *Private Lives, Public Spirit, 1870–1914*, Oxford University Press, 1993, pp 99–100.

Notes

5   T. Piketty, *Capital in the 21st Century*, Harvard University Press, 2014, fig 10.3 and 10.5, pp 342 and 348.

6   F.C. Jaher, 'The Gilded Elite', in W.D. Rubinstein (ed), *Wealth and the Wealthy in the Modern World*, Croom Helm, 1980, p 193.

7   W.D. Rubenstein, 'Introduction' in W.D. Rubinstein (ed), *Wealth and the Wealthy in the Modern World*, Croom Helm, 1980, p 20–21.

8   W. Whitman, *Complete Prose Works,* New York University Press, 1892, p 1065.

9   G.G. Acheson, G. Campbell and J.D. Turner, 'Active Controllers or Wealthy Rentiers? Large Shareholders in Victorian Public Companies', *Business History Review*, 89(4), 2015, pp 661–91; R.H. Tawney, *The Acquisitive Society*, 1920, republished by BiblioLife, 2008, p 34.

10 R.H. Tawney, *The Acquisitive Society*, 1920, republished by BiblioLife, 2008, pp 76–7.

11 A. Smith, *An Inquiry into the Nature and Causes of the Wealth of Nations*, Brown, Green, & Longmans, 1850 (ed. J.R. McCulloch), book I, ch VI, p 23.

12 D. Ricardo, *The Principles of Taxation and Political Economy*, John Murray, 1917.

13 J.S. Mill, *Principles of Political Economy,* 1848, book V, ch II, p 492.

14 V. Pareto, *Manual of Political Economy*, Augustus M. Kelley, 1896.

15 G. Standing, *The Corruption of Capitalism*, Biteback, 2016; M. Mazzucato, *The Value of Everything*, Penguin, 2018; B. Christophers, *Rentier Capitalism*, Verso, 2020; M. Mazzucato, J. Ryan-Collins and G. Gouzoulis, 'Theorising and Mapping Modern Economic Rents', *Working Paper Series, 2020–13*, UCL Institute for Innovation and Public Purpose, 2020; S. Lansley, *The Cost of Inequality*, Gibson Square, 2011.

16 G. Himmelfarb, 'The Idea of Poverty', *History Today*, 4 April 1984.

17 J. Bates Clark, *The Distribution of Wealth: A Theory of Wages, Interest and Profits*, Macmillan & Co, 1899.

18 K. Polanyi, *The Great Transformation*, Beacon Press, 2002, pp 117–18.

19 M. Arnold, *The Miscellaneous works of Matthew Arnold*, B. Fellows, 1845, p 459.

20 T. Carlyle, *The Works of Thomas Carlyle*, centenary edn, vol XXIX, Chapman and Hall, 1899, p 118.

21 W.S. Sanders, 'The Welfare of the Workers', in H. Tracey (ed), *The Book of the Labour Party* vol II, Caxton, 1926, p 71.

22 M. Merrill, 'Interview with EP Thompson', *Radical History Review*, 12, 1976, p 24.

23 J.M. Keynes, *The Economic Consequences of the Peace*, Macmillan, 1920, p 17.

24 R. Skidelsky, *John Maynard Keynes, 1883–1946*, Pan Books, 2003, p 238.

25 K. Polanyi, *The Great Transformation*, 2nd edn, Beacon Press, 2002, p 87.

26 K. Marx, *Capital,* Vol. 1, Part 7, Pelican, 1981, pp 400–53.

27 B. Jackson, *Equality and the British Left, A Study in Progressive Political Thought, 1900–1964*, Manchester University Press, 2007, p 93.

28 J. Ruskin, 'The Veins of Wealth: Four Essays on the Principles of Political Economy', *Cornhill Magazine*, 1860.

29 A. Smith, *The Theory of Moral Sentiments*, Penguin, 2010.

30 R.H. Tawney, *The Acquisitive Society*, 1920, republished by BiblioLife, 2008, pp 241–2.

31 A. Marshall, *Principles of Economics*, 8th edn, Macmillan, 1920, p 2.

32 'Letter to the editor', *The Times*, 19 August 1905.

33 'Letter to the editor', *The Times*, 9 November 1905.

34 P. Spicker, 'Charles Booth: The Examination of Poverty', *Social Policy & Administration*, 24(1), 1990, pp 21–38.

35 P. Spicker, 'Charles Booth, the Examination of Poverty', *Social Policy and Administration*, 24(1), 1990, pp 21–38.

36 C. Booth, *Life and Labour of the People in London, First Series: Poverty*, Macmillan, 1902.

37 B.S. Rowntree, *Poverty: A Study of Town Life*, new edn, Longman, 1922.

38 J. Bradshaw, 'Preface', in BS Rowntree, *Poverty: A Study of Town Life*, centennial edn, Policy Press, 2000.
39 R. Jenkins, *Churchill,* Pan, 2001, p 81.
40 P. Molander, *The Anatomy of Inequality*, Melville House, 2017, p 183.

Chapter 3

1   J. London, *The People of the Abyss*, George N Morang & Co, 1903.
2   B.S. Rowntree, *Poverty: A Study of Town Life*, new edn, Longman, 1922, p 145.
3   K. Harris, *Attlee*, Weidenfeld and Nicolson, 1995, p 20.
4   K. Harris, *Attlee*, 1995, p 55.
5   C. Attlee, 'Blue Stocking in Action', *The Times*, 22 January 1958.
6   HMSO, *Report of the Royal Commission on the Poor Laws and Relief of Distress*, Cd 4499. HMSO, 1909, pt IV, ch 5, p 132.
7   National Committee to Promote the Break-Up of the Poor Law, *The Minority Report*, 1909, part I, p 732.
8   C. Masterman, *The Condition of England*, Hardpress Publishing, 2013.
9   H. George, *Progress and Poverty,* Cosimo Inc, 2006, p 12.
10 *Report of the Royal Commission on the Poor Law*, appendix, vol I, 'Minutes of Evidence', HMSO, 1909, p xxxvii, Q 2230.
11 S. Webb and B. Webb, *English Poor Law History, Part II: The Last Hundred Years*, vol 2, Longmans, 1929, p 546.
12 B. Jackson, *Equality and the British Left: A Study in Progressive Political Thought, 1900–1964*, Manchester University Press, 2007, pp 67–70.
13 'Report on the annual meeting of the Charity Organisation Society', *The Times*, 8 March 1899.
14 A. Briggs, 'Towards the Welfare State', in P. Barker (ed), *Founders of the Welfare State*, Gower, 1985, p 6.
15 D. Cannadine, *The Decline and Fall of the British Aristocracy*, Papermac, 1996, p 49.
16 J. Meadowcroft (ed), *Hobhouse: Liberalism and Other Writings*, Cambridge University Press, 1994, p 90.
17 Quoted in J. Camplin, *The Rise of the Rich*, St Martin's Press, 1979, p 38.
18 F.C. Jaher, 'The Gilded Elite', in W.D. Rubinstein, *Wealth and the Wealthy in the Modern World*, Croom Helm, 1980, p 194.
19 T. Veblen, *The Theory of the Leisured Classes*, The Modern Library, 1899; T. Veblen, *The Engineers and the Price System*, B.W. Huebsch, 1921; A. Nesvetailova and R. Palan, *Sabotage, the Business of Finance*, Allen Lane, 2020.
20 R.S. Churchill, *Winston S. Churchill,* Heinemann, 1967, p 263.
21 J.K. Hardie, 'The compliments of the Season', *Labour Leader*, 1 January 1909, p 9.
22 A.B. Atkinson, *Unequal Shares: Wealth in Britain*, Pelican, 1974, p 115.
23 D. Cannadine, *The Decline and Fall of the British Aristocracy*, Papermac, 1996, p 48.
24 A.W. Fitzroy, 'Report of the Inter-Departmental Committee on Physical Deterioration', HMSO, 1904.
25 W.D. Rubenstein, *Men of Property*, Croom Helm, 1981, tables 3.3–3.7, p 62–6.
26 D. Cannadine, *The Decline and Fall of the British Aristocracy*, 1996, p 342.
27 D. Cannadine, *The Decline and Fall of the British Aristocracy*, 1996, p 111.
28 R. McKibbin, *Class and Culture: England 1918–1951*, Oxford University Press, 2000, p 17.
29 D. Cannadine, *The Decline and Fall of the British Aristocracy*, 1996, p 407.
30 A.L. Bowley, *Some Economic Consequences of the Great War*, Butterworth, 1930, p 139.
31 M. Craig, *When the Clyde Ran Red,* Birlinn, 2018.

[32]   T. Piketty, *Capital and Ideology,* Harvard University Press, 2019, p 195.

[33]   N. Cohen, 'How Britain Paid for the War', *BankUnderground,* Bank of England, January, 2021. Available online from: https://bankunderground.co.uk/2021/01/18/how-britain-paid-for-war-bond-holders-in-the-great-war-1914-32/amp/?mc_cid=c26e5461bf&mc_eid=8980345f8b

Chapter 4

[1]   D.K. Benjamin and L.A. Kochin, 'Searching for an Explanation of Unemployment in Interwar Britain', *Journal of Political Economy,* 87(3), 1979, pp 441–78.

[2]   Cabinet paper, 24/107/91: *Report on revolutionary organisations,* 59, 17 June 1920. Available online from: https://discovery.nationalarchives.gov.uk/details/r/D7735977

[3]   N. Jones, 'How Tory leaders should emulate Stanley Baldwin', *Conservative Home,* 13 April, 2010.

[4]   'Mr Ben Tillett's warning', *The Times,* 26 July 1915.

[5]   F.C. Jaher, 'The Gilded Elite', in W.D. Rubinstein, *Wealth and the Wealthy in the Modern World,* Croom Helm, 1980, p 195.

[6]   Quoted in M. Daunton, *Just Taxes: The Politics of Taxation in Britain, 1914–1979,* Cambridge University Press, 2008, p 79.

[7]   B.G. Gilbert, *British Social Policy 1914–39,* BT Batsford Ltd, 1973, pp 29–30.

[8]   G.A. Riddell, *Intimate Diary of the Peace Conference, 1918–1923,* Reynal & Hitchcock, 1934, p 179.

[9]   S. Todd, *The People: The Rise and Fall of the Working Class,* John Murray, 2015, p 52.

[10]   S. Heffer (ed), Henry 'Chips' Channon, *The Diaries, 1918–38,* Hutchinson, 2021, entry for 8 October, 1923, p 131.

[11]   H. Dalton, 'Taxation, income and inherited wealth' in H. Tracey (ed), *The Book of the Labour Party,* vol II, Caxton, 1926, p 293.

[12]   D. Fraser, *The Evolution of the British Welfare State,* Macmillan, 1973, p172.

[13]   Ministry of Health, *Poor Law. Report of a Special Inquiry into Various Forms of Work Test,* HMSO, Cmd. 3585, 1930.

[14]   A. Deacon, *In Search of the Scrounger,* Occasional Papers on Social Administration, 60, G. Bell and Sons, 1976.

[15]   M. Pugh, *We Danced All Night,* Vintage Books, 2008, p 80.

[16]   C.M. Lloyd, 'The Poor Law', in H. Tracey (ed), *The Book of the Labour Party,* vol II, Caxton, 1926, p 18.

[17]   R. Skidelsky, *Politicians and the Slump,* Penguin, 1967, p 31.

[18]   P. Scott, 'The Anatomy of Britain's Inter-War Super-Rich, Reconstructing the 1928/9 "Millionaire" population', *Economic History Review,* 2020 (online).

[19]   P. Scott, 'The Anatomy of Britain's Inter-War Super-Rich', 2020 (online).

[20]   'Tax avoidance', *The Times,* 24 March 1938.

[21]   House of Commons, *Hansard,* vol 166, 19 July 1923, cols 2514–2515.

[22]   P. Scott, 'A Fiscal, Constitutional Crisis, Tax Avoidance and Evasion in Inter-War Britain', *English History Review,* (forthcoming).

[23]   J.M. Keynes, *The General Theory of Employment, Interest and Money,* Harcourt, Brace and World, 1936, p 159.

[24]   F.S. Fitzgerald, 'Echoes of the Jazz Age', *Scribner's,* 90(5), p 8.

[25]   J.K. Galbraith, *The Great Crash, 1929,* Penguin, 2009, p 194–5.

[26]   M.S. Eccles, *Beckoning Frontiers,* Alfred A Knopf, 1951.

[27]   J.A. Hobson, *The Industrial System,* AM Kelly, 1909.

[28]   C. Attlee, *As It Happened,* Odhams Press, 1954, p 74.

[29]   R. Skidelsky, *Politicians and the Slump,* Penguin, 1967, p 12.

30 The Pilgrim Trust, *Enquiry into Causes and Effects of Long-term Unemployment*, The National Archives, 1936–8, AST 7/255.

31 J. Seabrook, *Pauperland*, Hurst and Co, 2013, p 135.

32 J. Garside, *The Thirties*, HarperPress, 2011, p 446.

33 J.B. Priestly, *English Journey*, Mandarin, 1994, p 314.

34 R. Blythe, *The Age of Illusion*, Oxford University Press, 1983, p 165.

35 'Letter to the editor', *The Times*, 22 August 1931.

36 Cabinet Papers, CAB 23/85/10, *March of the Unemployed on London*, 14 October, Cabinet Office, 1936, p 4.

37 F. Calder, 'The Reporter who Marched with the men from Jarrow', *New Statesman*, 7 November 1986.

38 N. Chamberlain, 'Letter to Ida Chamberlain, 22 November, 1936', in R. Self (ed), *The Neville Chamberlain Diary Letters, Volume IV, The Downing Street Years, 1934–40*, Ashgate, 2005.

39 G. Orwell, *The Road to Wigan Pier*, Penguin, 1962, p 131.

40 J.B. Priestly, *English Journey*, Mandarin, 1994, p 310.

41 F. D. Roosevelt, 'Second Inaugural Address', Washington, DC, 20 January, 1937.

42 P. Temin, *Lessons from the Great Depression*, MIT Press, 1991, p 97.

43 R. Cutforth, *Later Than We Thought*, David and Charles, 1976, p 20.

44 'Trouble on the Road', *The Manchester Guardian*, 27 October 1932

45 J. Stevenson, *British Society, 1914–45*, Penguin, 1984, p 119.

46 See, for example, J. Gardiner, *The Thirties*, Harper Press, 2011, pp 67–79.

47 J.B. Orr, *Food, Health and Income*, Macmillan, 1937; C.L. Mowat, *Britain Between the Wars*, Methuen, 1955, pp 480–501.

48 R.M. Titmuss, 'Man-power and Health', *The Spectator*, 26 May 1939, pp 896–7.

49 M. Mayhew, 'The 1930s Nutrition Controversy', *Journal of Contemporary History*, 25(3) 1988, pp 445–64.

50 B.S. Rowntree, *Poverty and progress: A Second Social Survey of York*, Longmans, 1941, p 461.

51 P. Scott, 'The Anatomy of Britain's Inter-War Super-Rich, English Historical Review', *Economic History Review*, 2020 (online).

52 T. Piketty, *Capital and Ideology*, Harvard University Press, 2019, p 195; A.B. Atkinson, *The Economics of Inequality*, 2nd edn, Oxford University Press, 1989, pp 157–78.

53 B.G. Gilbert, *British Social Policy 1914–39*, BT Batsford Ltd, 1973, p 306.

54 P. Thane, *The Foundations of the Welfare State*, Longmans, 1996, p 171.

55 S. Todd, *The People: The Rise and Fall of the Working Class*, John Murray, 2015, p 62.

Chapter 5

1 R. Rhodes-James, (ed), *'Chips', The Diaries of Sir Henry Channon*, Phoenix, 1996, p 224.

2 L. Stone and J.C. Fawtier Stone, *An Open Elite?, England 1540–1880*, Oxford University Press, 1984, p 425.

3 R. Rhodes-James, (ed), *'Chips', The Diaries of Sir Henry Channon*, 1996, p 222

4 J.R. Hicks, U.K. Hicks and L. Rostas, *The Taxation of War Wealth*, Oxford University Press, 1942, chs 11 and 12.

5 For full lyrics, see https://www.lyrics.com/lyric/34887921/No%C3%ABl+Coward/The+Stately+Homes+of+England

6 F. Raphael, *There and Then, Personal Terms, 6*, Carcanet Press, 2013, p 193.

7 James Lees-Milne, *Diaries, 1942–1954*, John Murray, 2007, p 188.

8 F. MacCarthy, *Last Curtsey*, Faber and Faber, 2006, p 120; B Robertson, *I saw England*, New York, 1941, p 153.

9 C. Attlee, 'Uncle Fred Looks Back', *The Observer*, 25 October 1959.

10 'Profile: C.R. Attlee', *The Observer*, 7 May 1944, p 6.

11 'Editorial: The New Europe', *The Times*, 1 July 1940, p 5.

12 J.B. Priestley, *Postscripts*, Heinemann, 1940, p 90.

13 A. Heuser (ed), *Selected Prose of Louis MacNeice*, Oxford, 1990, p 101.

14 M. Kennedy, *Where Stands a Wingèd Sentry*, Yale University Press, 1941, p 232.

15 S. Todd, *The People: The Rise and Fall of the Working Class*, John Murray, 2015, p 134–5.

16 Mass Observation Archive, *The Mass-Observation Diaries*, The Mass-Observation Archive (University of Sussex Library) and the Centre for Continuing Education University of Sussex, 1991, p 10.

17 D. Donnison, *80th Birthday Lecture*, Glasgow, 26 October 2005.

18 P. Piratin, *Our Flag Stays Red*, Lawrence and Wishart, 2006, p 73.

19 Past Tense, *Crowds Force Entry to Liverpool Street Station to Use as Air Raid Shelter*, Past Tense Blog, 8 September 2016. https://pasttenseblog.wordpress.com/2016/09/08/today-in-londons-radical-history-crowd-force-entry-to-liverpool-street-station-to-use-it-as-air-raid-shelter-1940/

20 N. Nicolson, (ed), *H Nicolson, Diaries and Letters, 1939–1945*, Collins, 1967, entry for 17 September, 1940.

21 T. Harrison, *Living Through the Blitz*, Collins, 1976, pp 314–15.

22 J.B. Priestly, *Out of the People*, Collins, 1941, p 130.

23 W. Beveridge, *Social Insurance and Allied Services*, Cmnd 6404, HMSO, 1942, pp 6–7.

24 Ministry of Information, *Ministry of Information Home Intelligence Report*, HMSO, 1942. Catalogue reference: INF 1/292.

25 British Institute of Public Opinion, *The Beveridge Report and the Public,* British Institute for Public Opinion, 1943.

26 Warwick Digital Collection, 'What they say about the Beveridge Report', *Left*, 76, January 1943: archive ref 172/BE/7.

Chapter 6

1 R. Rhodes-James, (ed), *'Chips', The Diaries of Sir Henry Channon*, Phoenix, 1996, p 414.

2 This image has been converted to black and white. The original colour image can be found here: https://flashbak.com/greet-the-dawn-labour-party-election-posters-from-the-20thcentury-380018/

3 Quoted in A. Howard, 'We Are The Masters Now', in M. Sissons and P. French (eds), *The Age of Austerity 1945–51*, Penguin, 1964, p 16.

4 R. Rhodes-James, (ed), *'Chips', The Diaries of Sir Henry Channon*, 1996, p 409.

5 P. Worsthorne, *The Politics of Manners and the Uses of Inequality*, Centre for Policy Studies, 1988, p 5.

6 *The Manchester Guardian*, 27 July 1945.

7 Labour Party, *Annual Conference Report*, Labour Party, 1945, p 114.

8 D. Kynaston, *The City of London Volume III, Illusions of Gold 1914–1945*, Pimlico, 2000, p 509.

9 H. Macmillan, *Tides of Fortune, 1945–55*, Harper and Row, 1969, p 32.

10 K. Harris, *Attlee*, Weidenfeld and Nicolson, 1984, p 281.

11 D. Moggridge, (ed), *The Collected Writing of JM Keynes, Vol XXIV, Activities 1944–46*, Macmillan, 1979, p 410.

12 E. Rathbone, *The Disinherited Family*, Yale University Press, 1924.

13 Ministry of Health, 'The development of the health services', memorandum, The National Archive, MH 79/409, 6 April 1938.

14 Quoted in J. Bew, *Citizen Clem*, Riverrun, 2017, p 403.

15 R.M. Titmuss, *Problems of Social Policy*, HMSO and Longmans, Green & Co, 1950, p 506.
16 T.H. Marshall, *Citizenship and Social Class*, Cambridge University Press, 1950.
17 W. Beveridge, *Social Insurance and Allied Services,* Cmnd 6404, HMSO, 1942, p 122, para 307.
18 D. Todman, *Britain's War, Into Battle, 1937–41*, Penguin, 2017, p 85.
19 W. Temple, *Christianity and the Social Order*, Harmondsworth, 1942, p 65.
20 T. Rogan, *The Moral Economists*, Princeton University Press, 2017, p 134.
21 A. Crosland, 'The transition from capitalism', in R.H.S. Crossman (ed), *New Fabian Essays*, Turnstile Press, 1952.
22 See, for example, P. Collier, *The Future of Capitalism*, Penguin, 2019.
23 B. Milanović, 'Nostalgia for the past that never was', *Global Inequality*, 8 August 2019.
24 T. Piketty, *Capital in the Twenty-First Century*, Harvard University Press, 2014, p 275.
25 W. Scheidel, *The Great Leveler: Violence and the History of Inequality from the Stone Age to the Twenty-First Century*, Princeton University Press, 2017.
26 P. Malcolmson and R. Malcolmson, *Nella Last's Peace*, Profile, 2008, p 5.

Chapter 7
1 B.S. Rowntree and G.R. Lavers, *Poverty and the Welfare State*, Longmans, 1951, p 40.
2 *News Chronicle,* 12 October 1951.
3 'Poverty To-day', *The Times*, 15 October 1951.
4 A. Crosland, *The Future of Socialism*, Jonathan Cape, 1956, p 59.
5 Labour Party, *Annual Conference Report*, Labour Party, 1959, p 84.
6 S. Pollard, *The Development of the British Economy, 1914–1967*, Edward Arnold, 1969, p 408.
7 A.B. Atkinson, *Poverty in Britain and the Reform of Social Security*, Cambridge University Press, 1970, p 21.
8 S. Pollard, *The Development of the British Economy, 1914–1967*, 1969, p 500.
9 D. Kynaston, *Family Britain*, Bloomsbury, 2010 p 32.
10 K. Harris, *Attlee*, Weidenfeld and Nicolson, 1984, p 533.
11 A.H. Halsey (ed), *British Social Trends since 1900*, Macmillan, 1988, pp 402–3.
12 D. Bell, *The End of Ideology*, Free Press of Glencoe, 1960.
13 See, for example, 'Crisis in the Welfare State', *The Times*, 25 February 1952.
14 BBC News, *Was Britain Better in the 50s?*, BBC News, 24 May 2007.
15 A.H. Halsey (ed), *British Social Trends since 1900*, Macmillan, 1988, p 427.
16 T. Phillips, *Report of the Committee on the Economic and Financial Problems of Provision for Old Age*, Cmnd 9333, HMSO, 1954, para 109.
17 P. Townsend, *The Family Life of Old People*, Routledge & Kegan Paul, 1957, p 183.
18 P. Marris, *Widows and Their Families*, Routledge, 1958, p 112.
19 A. Harvey, *Casualties of the Welfare State*, Fabian Tract 321, 1960, p 31.
20 BBC, *Waiting For Work*, 12 February 1963, 21:25.
21 A.B. Atkinson, J. Corlyon, A.K. Maynard, H. Sutherland and C.G. Trinder, 'Poverty in York: A Re-Analysis of Rowntree's 1950 Survey', *Bulletin of Economic Research*, 33, 1981, pp 59–71.
22 D. Edgerton, *The Rise and Fall of the British Nation,* Penguin, 2018, pp 244–5.
23 E. Abbott and K. Bompas, *The Woman Citizen and Social Security*, Wadsworth and Co, 1943, p 20.
24 P. Townsend, 'Poverty: ten years after Beveridge', *Political and Economic Planning*, vol XIX, 344, 1952, pp 21–40.
25 A.B. Atkinson, *Poverty in Britain and the Reform of Social Security*, Cambridge University Press, 1970, p 24.

26 G. Fiegehen, P.S. Lansley and A.D. Smith, *Poverty and Progress in Britain, 1953–73*, Cambridge University Press, 1977, p 134.

27 A. Marwick, *Britain in the Century of Total War: War, Peace and Social Change, 1900–1967*, Bodley Head, 1970, p 345.

28 W. Beveridge, *Social Insurance and Allied Services,* Cmnd 6404, HMSO, 1942, para 23, p 14.

29 A.B. Atkinson, *Poverty in Britain and the Reform of Social Security*, Cambridge University Press, 1970, Figure 1.2, p 25; Ministry of Pensions and National Insurance, *Financial and Other Circumstances of Retirement Pensioners*, HMSO, 1966, p108.

30 N. Whiteside, 'The Beveridge Report and Its Implementation, a Revolutionary Project?', *Histoire@Politique*, 24, 2014, p 19.

31 Author's interview with Roger Brown, February 2020.

32 Author's interview with a North East Aberdeen fishing community, 1987.

33 P. Townsend, 'Poverty: ten years after Beveridge', *Political and Economic Planning*, vol XIX, 344, 1952, pp 21–40.

34 A. Sinfield, A. Walker and C. Walker, 'The Legacy of Peter Townsend', in A. Walker, A. Sinfield and C. Walker, *Fighting Poverty, Inequality and Injustice*, Policy Press, 2011, p 3.

35 P. Townsend, 'Measuring Poverty', *British Journal of Sociology*, 5(2), 1954, pp 130–7.

36 P. Townsend, 'The meaning of poverty', *British Journal of Sociology*, 13(3), 1962, p 225

37 A. Smith, *An Inquiry into the Nature and Causes of the Wealth of Nations*, Brown, Green, & Longmans, 1850 (ed J.R. McCulloch), book V, ch II, p 393.

38 J.H. Veit-Wilson, 'Paradigm of poverty: a rehabilitation of B.S. Rowntree', *Journal of Social Policy*, 15(4), 1986, pp 69–99.

39 H. Glennerster, *British Social Policy Since 1945*, Blackwell, 1995, p 115.

40 P. Townsend, *Poverty in the United Kingdom*, Penguin, 1979, p 31.

41 J. Bradshaw, 'Poverty', in A. Walker, A. Sinfield and C. Walker, *Fighting Poverty, Inequality and Injustice*, Policy Press, 2011, p 92.

42 P. Townsend, 'Poverty as Relative Deprivation' in D. Wedderburn (ed), *Poverty, Inequality and Class Structure*, Cambridge University Press, 1974, p 16.

43 A. Sen, *Development as Freedom*, Alfred Knopf, 1999.

44 W. Beveridge, *Power and Influence*, Hodder and Stoughton, 1953, pp 360–1.

45 V. Bogdanor and R. Skidelsky (eds) *The Age of Affluence, 1951–1964*, Macmillan, 1970, p 7.

Chapter 8

1 Phillips Committee, *State Provision for Social Need, The Beveridge Committee Report on the Welfare State*, HMSO, 1943, National Archive, PIN 8/115–116.

2 E. Wilson, *Europe Without Baedeker*, Secker and Warburg, 1945, p 186.

3 D. Cannadine, *Class in Britain*, Penguin, 1998, p 148.

4 F. Raphael, *The Glittering Prizes*, Penguin, 1976, p 50.

5 L. Robbins, 'Notes on Public Finances', *Lloyds Bank Review*, 38, 1955, p 8.

6 H. Nicolson, *Diaries and Letters, 1939–1945*, Collins, 1967, p 465.

7 R. Rhodes-James (ed), *'Chips', The Diaries of Sir Henry Channon*, Phoenix, 1996, p 423.

8 D. Kynaston, 'How the Class War was Won', *New Statesman*, 13 April 2018.

9 T. Rogan, *The Moral Economists*, Princeton University Press, 2017, p 110.

10 H. Thomas, *The Establishment,* Antony Blond, 1959.

11 G. Orwell, 'The Lion and the Unicorn', in *George Orwell Essays*, Penguin, 2000, pp 166–7.

12 E. Waugh, *Brideshead Revisited*, Penguin, 2000, p 8.

13 J. Derbyshire, 'Who Was Ralph Miliband?', *New Statesman*, 30 August 2010.

14 R. Miliband, *Parliamentary Socialism*, 2nd edn, Merlin Press, 1991.
15 See, for example, Labour Party, *Labour and the New Social Order, A Report on Reconstruction*, Labour Party, 1918.
16 R. Hattersley, 'How My Support for Labour Turned from Tribal to Ideological', *The Guardian*, 14 August 2013.
17 B. Jackson, *Equality and the British Left: A Study in Progressive Political Thought, 1900–1964*, Manchester University Press, 2007, p2.
18 H. Wilson, *The New Britain: Selected Speeches*, Penguin, 1964, p 9.
19 D. Edgerton, 'Labour has to Free Itself from the Shackles of its Own Invented Histories', *Prospect*, 5 April 2020.
20 S. Kuznets, 'Economic Growth and Income Inequality', *American Economic Review*, 65, 1955, pp 1–28.
21 Quoted in P. Sloman, *Transfer State*, Oxford University Press, 2019, p 39.
22 J.K. Galbraith, *The Affluent Society*, Houghton Mifflin, 1958, p 82.
23 P. Thane, *Foundations of the Welfare State*, Longman, 1982, p 299.
24 D. Donnison, 'Drawing conclusions', in P. Barker, *Founders of the Welfare State*, Gower, 1985, p 127.
25 J.M. Winter, 'RH Tawney' in P. Barker, *Founders of the Welfare State*, Gower, 1985, p 104.
26 J.H. Veit-Wilson, 'Paradigm of Poverty: a Rehabilitation of B.S. Rowntree', *Journal of Social Policy*, 15(4), 1986, pp 69–99.
27 N. Annan, *Our Age*, Harper Collins, 1995, p 7.
28 R. Skidelsky, *Keynes*, Oxford University Press, 1996, pp 43–8.
29 R. Harrod, 'Review of the General Theory of Employment, Interest and Money', *Political Quarterly*, 7, 1936, pp 297–8.
30 L. Klein, *The Keynesian Revolution*, Macmillan, 1947, p 131.
31 H. Glennerster, *Why Did the Post-War Welfare State Fail to Prevent the Growth of Inequality*, Institute of Historical Research, 2008.
32 J. Hills, *Good Times, Bad Times*, Policy Press, 2015.
33 B. Jackson, *Equality and the British Left*, Manchester University Press, 2007, p 140.
34 D. Marquand, 'Passion and Politics', *Encounter*, December 1961.

Chapter 9

1 A.H. Halsey, 'Titmuss, Richard Morris', *Oxford Dictionary of National Biography*, Oxford University Press, 2004.
2 'The Impact of Taxes and Social Service Benefits on Different Groups of Households', *Economic Trends*, Central Statistical Office, 1962.
3 B. Able-Smith and P. Townsend, *The Poor and the Poorest*, Occasional Papers in Social Administration, No 17, G. Bell and Sons, 1965.
4 B. Abel-Smith and P. Townsend, *The Poor and the Poorest*, 1965, p 17. See also J. Veit-Wilson, 'Condemned to Deprivation?' in J. Hills, J. Ditch and H. Glennerster, *Beveridge and Social Security: An International Retrospective*, Oxford University Press, 1994, pp 97–117.
5 G.C. Fiegehen, P.S. Lansley, and A.D. Smith, *Poverty and Progress in Britain, 1953–73*, Cambridge University Press, 1977, table II.2, p 131.
6 To allow for the additional payments for social needs, especially for the sick and disabled, such as help with fuel and a special diet or clothing, the researchers set the poverty line as National Assistance plus 40 per cent, though in some ways this uplift was essentially arbitrary.
7 I. Gazeley, H.G. Rufrancos, A. Newell, K. Reynolds and R. Searle, 'The Poor and the Poorest, Fifty Years On: Evidence from British Household Expenditure Surveys of the 1950s and 1960s', *Journal of the Royal Statistical Society*, series A, 180(2), 2017, pp 455–74.

8   J. Seabrook, *Pauperland*, Hurst and Co, 2013, p 154.
9   J.K. Galbraith, *The Affluent Society*, Houghton Mifflin, 1958, ch 23.
10 M. Harrington, *The Other America*, Penguin, 1963, p 10 and 156. See also G. Myrdal, *Challenge to Affluence*, Random House, 1963.
11 D. Torstensson, *America's War on Poverty and the Building of the Welfare State*, Oxford Research Encyclopedia, American History, 2019; S. Babones, *Absolute Poverty in America Higher than in 1969*, Poverty and Social Exclusion, 2013, https://www.poverty.ac.uk/
12 A. Sinfield, 'Poverty research in Britain and Europe', lecture at Conference on Poverty Research, Bureau of Social Science Research, Washington, 1967; C. Reinecke, 'Localising the Social: The Rediscovery of Urban Poverty in Western European "Affluent Societies"', *Contemporary European History*, 24(04), 2015, pp 555–76.
13 M. Ravallion, *The Economics of Poverty*, Oxford University Press, 2016, p 85.
14 See, for example, A.B. Atkinson, 'On the Measurement of Inequality', *Journal of Economic Theory*, 2, 1970, pp 244–63; O. Giovannoni, 'Functional Distribution of Income, Inequality and Incidence of Poverty', University of Texas Inequality Project, *Working Paper No 58*, 2010.
15 P. Thane and R. Davidson, *The Child Poverty Action Group, 1965–2015*, CPAG, 2016.
16 D. Marsden, *Mothers Alone*, Pelican, 1973, pp 66, 43, 333.
17 F. Field, 'A Pressure Group for the Poor', in D. Bull (ed), *Family Poverty*, Gerald Duckworth & Co, 1971, p 146.
18 A. Sinfield, 'Obituary: John Veit-Wilson', *The Guardian*, 3 June 2020.
19 J. Bradshaw, 'Remembering Tony Lynes', *CPAG Blog*, 20 October 2014.
20 R. Williams (ed), *May Day Manifesto, 1968*, Penguin, 1968, p 28.
21 R. Crossman, *The Crossman Diaries*, Hamish Hamilton, 1979, entry for 19 July 1967.
22 G. Brown, *In My Way*, Gollancz, 1971, p 270.

Chapter 10

1   F. Field, *Poverty and Politics*, Heinemann, 1982, p 33.
2   M. Meyer-Kelly and M.D. Kandiah (eds), *The Poor Get Poorer Under Labour. The Validity and Effects of CPAG's Campaign in the 1970s*, witness seminar, Institute of Contemporary British History, 2000.
3   'Interview with Frank Field', *Poverty and Social Exclusion*, 14 November 2016.
4   M. Meyer-Kelly and M.D. Kandiah, (eds), *The Poor Get Poorer Under Labour*, 2000.
5   F. Field, *Poverty and Politics*, Heinemann, 1982, pp 38–9.
6   A. Oakley, *Father and Daughter*, Policy Press, 2014, p 185.
7   K.O. Morgan, *The People's Peace*, Oxford University Press, 1992, p 323.
8   See, for example, R. Lewes and A. Maude, *Professional People*, Phoenix House, 1952; B. De Jouvenel, *The Ethics of Redistribution*, Cambridge University Press, 1951.
9   F. von Hayek, *The Road to Serfdom*, Chicago University Press, 1944.
10 K. Polanyi, *The Great Transformation*, Beacon Press, 2002.
11 Institute of Economic Affairs, 'A Conversation with Harris and Seldon', *Occasional Papers*, 116, 2001, p 25.
12 M. Friedman and R. Friedman, *Capitalism and Freedom: Fortieth Anniversary Edition*, University of Chicago Press, 2002, p xiv.
13 J. Robinson, *The Economics of Imperfect Competition*, Macmillan, 1933. See also Council of Economic Advisers, 'Labour Market Monopsony', *Issue Brief*, October, 2016.
14 A. Offer and G. Söderberg, *The Nobel Factor*, Princeton University Press, 2016.
15 Labour Party, *Now Britain's Strong – Let's Make it Great to Live In*, election manifesto, Labour Party, 1970; Conservative Party, *A Better Tomorrow*, election manifesto, Conservative Party, 1970.

[16]   M. Halcrow, *Keith Joseph, A Single Mind*, Macmillan, 1989, p 43.

[17]   N. Timmins, *The Five Giants*, William Collins, 2017, p 283.

[18]   Quoted in S. MacGregor, *The Politics of Poverty*, Longman, 1981, p 137.

[19]   D. Houghton, *Paying for the Social Services*, Institute for Economic Affairs, 1967.

[20]   J.C. Kincaid, *Poverty and Equality in Britain*, Pelican, 1973, p 12.

[21]   'Major Change in Social Services', *The Times*, 19 June 1967, p 2.

[22]   P. Sloman, *The Transfer State*, Cambridge University Press, 2019; G. Standing, *Basic Income*, Penguin, 2017, ch 1.

[23]   P. Sloman, *Beveridge's rival: Juliet Rhys-Williams and the Campaign for Basic Income, 1942–55*, University of Oxford, 2016; J. Rhys-Williams, *Something to Look Forward To*, MacDonald, 1943.

[24]   P. Sloman, *The Transfer State*, Cambridge University Press, 2019, ch 9.

[25]   N. Timmins, *The Five Giants*, William Collins, 2017, p 287.

[26]   A. Glyn, *Capitalism Unleashed*, Oxford University Press, 2006, p 5.

Chapter 11

[1]   Labour Party, *Let Us Work Together*, election manifesto, Labour Party, 1974.

[2]   Labour Party, *Let Us Face the Future*, election manifesto, Labour Party, 1945.

[3]   G. Esping-Andersen, *The Three Worlds of Welfare Capitalism*, Princeton University Press, 1990.

[4]   W.D. Rubinstein, *Men of Property*, Croom Helm, 1982, p 232–3.

[5]   A. Crosland, *The Future of Socialism*, Jonathan Cape, 1956, p 214.

[6]   W.D. Rubenstein, *Capitalism, Culture and Decline in Britain, 1750–1990*, Routledge, 1993, p 82.

[7]   F. Römer, 'The Politics of Measurement: Knowledge about Economic Inequality in the United Kingdom and Beyond since 1945', *History of Knowledge*, 2, 2019.

[8]   H.F. Lydall, 'The Long-Term Trend in the Size Distribution of Income' *Journal of the Royal Statistical Society*, series A, 122(1), 1959, pp 1–46; R.J. Nicholson, 'The Distribution of Personal Income', *Lloyds Bank Review*, January, 1967, pp 11–21; A.R. Thatcher, 'The Distribution of Earnings of Employees in Great Britain', *Journal of the Royal Statistical Society*, series A, 31(2), 1968, pp 133–81; A.B. Atkinson, 'Poverty and Income Inequality in Britain', in D. Wedderburn (ed), *Poverty, Inequality and Class Structure*, Cambridge University Press, 1974, pp 43–70.

[9]   The Royal Commission on the Distribution of Income and Wealth, *Report no 7, Fourth Report on the Standing Reference*, Cmnd 7595, HMSO, 1979, p 17; A.B. Atkinson, *The Economics of Inequality*, 2nd edn, Oxford University Press, 1983, pp 62–4.

[10]   T. Piketty, *Capital and Ideology*, Harvard University Press, 2020, p 195.

[11]   N. Cummins, *Hidden Wealth*, 2021, figure 6.1 p 37.

[12]   Department of the Environment, *Housing Policy: Technical Volume Part I*, HMSO, 1977, tables IV.33, IV.34, pp 210–11.

[13]   R.M. Titmuss, 'The Social Division of Welfare: Some Reflections on the Search for Equity', in R.M. Titmuss, *Essays on 'The Welfare State'*, Allen and Unwin, London, 1958, pp. 34–55.

[14]   Quoted in A. Sampson, *The Midas Touch: Money, People and Power from West to East*, Hodder and Stoughton, 1989, p 56.

[15]   W.D. Rubinstein, *Men of Property*, Croom Helm, 1982, p 233–4.

[16]   L.T. Hobhouse, *Property: Its Rights and Duties*, Macmillan, 1913, p 31.

[17]   S. Webb and B. Webb, *A Constitution for the Socialist Commonwealth of Great Britain*, Longmans Green, 1920, p xii.

18 C. Pierson, 'Lost property: What the Third Way Lacks', *Journal of Political Ideologies*, 10(2), 2005, pp 145–63.
19 B. Jackson, 'Revisionism Reconsidered: 'Property-owning Democracy and Egalitarian Strategy in Post-War Britain', *Twentieth Century British History*, 16(4), 2005, pp 416–40.
20 J. Meade, 'Next Steps to Domestic Economic Policy', Labour Party Research Department, RD201, 1948.
21 J. Meade, *Efficiency, Equality and the Ownership of Property*, Allen and Unwin, 1964, p 38. See also S. White, 'Revolutionary liberalism? The Philosophy and Politics of Ownership in the Post-War Liberal Party', *British Politics*, 4(2), 2009, p 179.
22 Labour Party, *Capital and Equality*, Opposition Green Paper, Labour Party, 1973.
23 Labour Party, *Capital and Equality*, 1973, p 31.
24 Labour Party, *Towards Equality*, 1956; S. White, 'Citizen Ownership: the Lost Radicalism of the Centre?', *Open Democracy*, 8 November 2013.
25 R.L. Heilbroner, 'The Swedish Promise', *New York Review of Books*, 4 December 1980.
26 HMSO, *Wealth Tax*, Cmnd 5704, HMSO, 1974.
27 C.T. Sandford, 'The Wealth Tax Debate', in F. Field (ed), *The Wealth Report*, Routledge and Kegan Paul, 1978; House of Commons, *House of Commons Select Committee on a Wealth Tax, Report and Proceedings*, HC 696, HMSO 1975.
28 D. Healey, *The Time of My Life*, Penguin, 1990, p 404.
29 M. Meacher, 'Wealth' in N. Bosanquet and P. Townsend (eds), *Labour and Equality*, Heinemann, 1980, pp 121–34.
30 'Diamond Wants the Facts', *Sunday Telegraph*, 8 September 1974.
31 D. Healey, *The Time of My Life*, Penguin, 1990, p 404.
32 G. Stedman Jones, 'Tawneyism is not enough', *New Statesman,* 21 December 1984.

Chapter 12

1   R. Lister, 'Family Policy' in N. Bosanquet and P. Townsend, *Labour and Equality*, Heinemann, 1980, p188.
2   J. Jones, 'Wages and Social Security', *New Statesman,* 7 January 1972, p 7.
3   F. Field, 'Killing a Commitment: the Cabinet v the Children', *New Society*, 17 June 1976.
4   F. Field, *Poverty and Politics*, Heinemann, 1982, p 108.
5   R. Lister, 'Family Policy' in N. Bosanquet and P. Townsend, *Labour and Equality*, 1980, p 196.
6   M. Wicks, *My Life*, Troubador Publishing, 2013.
7   N. Bosanquet, 'Labour and Public Expenditure', in N. Bosanquet and P. Townsend, *Labour and Equality*, 1980, p 33.
8   'After 30 years…the gardener who gets £58 a week', *Evening Standard*, 22 January 1979.
9   Royal Commission on the Distribution of Income and Wealth, *Selected Evidence For Report No 6, Lower Incomes*, HMSO, 1978, p 61.
10 T. Kelsey, *An Unexpected Cut: Revisiting the Diamond Commission and Assessing Inequality in Post-War Britain*, Resolution Foundation, 2018, p 8.
11 Royal Commission on the Distribution of Income and Wealth, *Selected Evidence to the Commission,* HMSO, 1976, p 207.
12 Royal Commission on the Distribution of Income and Wealth, *Report No 3, Higher incomes from employment*, HMSO, 1976, pp 50–6; 'Two faces of capitalism', *The Daily Mail*, 30 November 1976.
13 T. Kelsey, *An Unexpected Cut: Revisiting the Diamond Commission and Assessing Inequality in Post-War Britain*, Resolution Foundation, 2018, pp 6, 20.
14 National Archive, *Halley to Butler*, Treasury, 1977, T 371/505, available online from: https://discovery.nationalarchives.gov.uk/details/r/C11534775

[15] F. Römer, 'The Politics of Measurement: Knowledge about Economic Inequality in the United Kingdom and Beyond since 1945', *History of Knowledge*, 2 June 2019.

[16] Royal Commission on the Distribution of Income and Wealth, *Report No 6, Lower Incomes*, HMSO, Cmnd 7175, 1978, ch 4.

[17] HMSO, *The Government's Expenditure Plans, 1979/80–1982/3*, Cmnd 7439, HMSO, 1979; P. Townsend, 'Social Planning and the Treasury', in N. Bosanquet and P. Townsend, *Labour and Equality*, 1980, p 15.

[18] Such a set, for a variety of poverty measures, has been compiled by the Institute for Fiscal Studies, starting from 1961. This confirms that during the 1960s and 1970s there were only small changes in the relative poverty rate.

[19] As measured by several indicators including the share of national income taken by the top 1 per cent. A.B. Atkinson, J. Hasell, S. Morelli and M. Roser, *Chartbook of Economic Inequality*, Institute for New Economic Thinking, University of Oxford, 1917, p 55.

[20] D. Edgerton, *The Rise and Fall of the British Nation*, Penguin, 2018, p 407.

[21] T. Piketty, *Capital and Ideology*, Harvard University Press, 2020, ch 11.

[22] A. Crosland, *The Future of Socialism*, Constable and Robinson, 2006, p 143.

[23] H. Glennerster, *British Social Policy Since 1945*, Blackwell, 1995, p 172.

[24] B. Jagger, *Mail on Sunday*, 18 July 1999.

[25] K.O. Morgan, *The People's Peace*, Oxford University Press, 1992, p 354.

[26] Cited in P. Diamond, *The Crosland Legacy*, Policy Press, 2016, p 74.

[27] J. O'Connor, *The Fiscal Crisis of the State*, Transaction Publishers, 2001.

[28] C. Offe, *Disorganised Capitalism*, Polity Press, 1985.

[29] R. Mishra, *The Welfare State in Crisis*, Wheatsheaf, 1984, p 127; E. Robinson, C. Schofield, F. Sutcliffe-Braithwaite and N. Thomlinson, 'Telling Stories about Post-war Britain: Popular Individualism and the "Crisis" of the 1970s', *Twentieth Century British History*, 28(2), 2017, pp 268–304.

[30] F. Hirsch, *The Social Limits to Growth*, Routledge and Kegan Paul, 1977, p 190.

[31] R. Bacon and W. Eltis, *Britain's Economic Problem: Too Few Producers*, Macmillan, 1975.

[32] R. Middleton, *Britain's Economic Problems, Too Small A Public Sector?*, University of Bristol, 1997, p 30.

[33] C. Warman, 'Councils are told to curb rise in spending', *The Times,* 10 May 1975, p 1.

[34] P. Hall, *Governing the Economy*, Polity, 1986, p 95.

Chapter 13

[1] Margaret Thatcher Foundation, 'Thatcher, Hayek & Friedman', *Margaret Thatcher Foundation*, available online from: https://www.margaretthatcher.org/archive/Hayek

[2] K. Joseph, 'Notes Towards the Definition of Policy', memorandum to Leader's Consultative Committee, 4 April 1975, LCC/75/71.

[3] A. Travis, 'Letters of congratulations to Margaret Thatcher on becoming prime minister', *The Guardian*, 30 January 2010.

[4] M. Anderson, *Welfare: The Political Economy of Welfare Reform in the United States*, Hoover Press, 1978, p 37.

[5] 'The Quality of Life', *Yes, Minister*, Series 2(6), BBC 30 March 1981.

[6] B. Donoughue, *Prime Minister: The Conduct of Policy Under Harold Wilson and James Callaghan, 1974–1979*, Jonathan Cape, 1987, p 191.

[7] M. and R. Friedman, *Capitalism and Freedom: Fortieth Anniversary Edition*, University of Chicago Press, 2002, p xiv.

[8] R. Skidelsky, 'The Crowding-Out Myth', *Project Syndicate*, 24 August 2020.

[9] House of Commons, *Hansard,* vol 968, 12 June 1979, col 246.

[10] M. Thatcher, *The Downing Street Years*, Harper Collins, 1993, p 8.

11 H. Young, *One of Us, A Biography of Mrs. Thatcher*, Pan, 2013, p 201.

12 H. Macmillan, interviewed by Robert McKenzie, *The Way Ahead*, BBC One, 14 October 1980.

13 Quoted in Y. Roberts, 'If you've got it, flaunt it', *New Statesman*, 18 December 1987.

14 P. Townsend and N. Davidson, *Inequalities in Health: The Black Report and the Health Divide*, Penguin, 1988.

15 'Letter by Alan Healey', *The Guardian*, 25 August 2018.

16 P. Townsend and N. Davidson, *Inequalities in Health*, 1988, pp 1–13.

17 'Leader column', *British Medical Journal*, 293, 1986, p 91.

18 D. Acheson, *Independent Inquiry into Inequalities in Health*, HMSO, 1998; M. Marmot, *Fair Society, Healthy Lives: Strategic Review of Health Inequalities in England Post-2010*, Department for International Development, 2010.

19 P. Townsend, *Poverty in the United Kingdom*, Penguin, 1979.

20 D. Wedderburn, 'Introduction', in D. Wedderburn (ed), *Poverty, Inequality and Class Structure*, Cambridge University Press, 1974; S. Miller, D. Tomaskovic-Devey and D. Wedderburn, 'Review Symposium', *The British Journal of Sociology, 32*(2), 1981, pp 266–78.

21 D. Piachaud, 'Peter Townsend and the Holy Grail', *New Society*, 10 September 1981; D. Piachaud, 'Interview with David Piachaud', *Poverty and Social Exclusion*, 14 November 2016.

22 A.K. Sen, *Three Notes on the Concept of Poverty*, International Labour Office, 1978.

23 K. Joseph and J. Sumption, *Equality*, John Murray, 1979, pp 27–8.

24 H. Frankfurt, 'Equality as a Moral Ideal', *Ethics*, 98, 1987, p 31.

25 L. von Mises, 'Inequality of Wealth and Income', *Ideas on Liberty*, May 1955.

26 A. Okun, *Equality and Efficiency: The Big Trade Off*, The Brookings Institute, 1975.

27 K. Joseph, *Stranded on the Middle Ground?*, Centre for Policy Studies, 1976.

28 C. Attlee, House of Commons, vol 419, 27 February, 1946, col 1952.

29 J. Rawls, *A Theory of Justice*, Harvard University Press, 1971, p 302.

30 D. McCloskey, 'Growth, not forced equality, saves the poor', *New York Times*, 23 December 2016.

31 R.H. Tawney, *Equality*, 4th edn, Allen and Unwin, 1964, p 50.

32 Quoted in J. Bew, *Citizen Clem*, Riverrun, 2017, p 401.

33 *Director*, 18 January 1977; D. Sambrook, *Seasons in the Sun*, Penguin, 2013, p 629.

34 W. Beckerman, *Growth, Equality and Poverty*, British Association Lecture, Bath, 1978.

35 F. von Hayek, *Economic Freedom and Representative Government*, Institute of Economic Affairs, 1973, pp 13.

36 M. Thatcher, 'interview', BBC Radio, 1 March 1980.

37 House of Commons, *Hansard*, written answer, vol 968, 11 June 1979, col 75W.

38 D. Walker, *Spurious Orthodoxies: The ESRC, 50 Years On*, Sage, 2016, p 36.

39 D. Walker, 'UK Social Science, Past Imperfect, Future Tense', *Discover Society*, 3, 2016.

40 'Diary: K. Joseph', *New Statesman*, 6 July 1984.

41 D. Hope and J. Limberg, 'The Economic Consequences of Tax Cuts for the Rich', *International Inequalities Institute Working Paper 55*, London School of Economics, 2020; T. Piketty, E. Saez and S. Stantcheva, 'Taxing the 1%', *Vox*, 8 December 2011.

42 See, for example, D. Card and A.B. Krueger, 'Minimum Wages and Employment: A case-study of the fast-food industry', *American Economic Review*, 84(4), 1994, pp 772–93; J. Komlos, *The Foundations of Real World Economics*, Routledge, 2019.

43 P. Krugman, *Arguing with Zombies*, WW Norton, 2020.

Chapter 14

[1] A. McSmith, *No Such Thing As Society*, Constable and Robinson, 2010, p 25.

[2] J. Ditch, 'The Undeserving Poor', in M. Loney (ed), *The State or the Market*, Sage, 1987, p 33.

[3] P. Dunn, 'Birmingham's Dispossessed', *New Society*, 18 April 1986.

[4] M. Kitson and J. Michie, 'The Deindustrial Revolution: the rise and fall of UK Manufacturing, 1870–2010', *Working Paper No. 459*, Centre for Business Research, University of Cambridge, 2014, table 2, p 15.

[5] D. Edgerton, *The Rise and Fall of the British Nation*, Penguin, 2019, p 486.

[6] H. Hoover, *The Memoirs of Herbert Hoover, vol 3, The Great Depression, 1929–1941*, Macmillan, 1951, p 30.

[7] *Business Week,* 22 May 1994.

[8] *The Times*, 5 August 1974.

[9] A. Posen, 'Interview with Adam Posen', *Challenge*, 51(4), 2008, pp 5–22.

[10] K. MacNeill and C. Pond (eds), *Britain Can't Afford Low Pay*, Low Pay Unit, 1988.

[11] M. Friedman and R. Friedman, *Capitalism and Freedom: Fortieth Anniversary Edition*, University of Chicago Press, 2002, p 133.

[12] A. Glyn and B. Sutcliffe, *British Capitalism, Workers and the Profits Squeeze*, Penguin, 1972, p 46.

[13] S. Lansley, *The Cost of Inequality*, Gibson Square, 2012, ch 2; O. Giovannoni, 'Functional Distribution of Income, Inequality and Incidence of Poverty', University of Texas Inequality Project, *Working Paper No 58*, University of Texas, 2010.

[14] Alan Budd, interviewed in *The League of Gentlemen*, BBC Two, 25 June 1992.

[15] T. Nairn, *The Break Up of Britain*, Verso, 1981, p 392.

[16] R. Davenport-Hines, *Universal Man: the Seven Lives of John Maynard Keynes*, William Collins, 2015, pp 146–8.

[17] R.W. Johnson, *The Politics of Recession*, Palgrave Macmillan, 1985, p 29.

[18] R. Ramsey, 'How Labour Embraced the City', *Open Democracy*, 18'December 2012.

[19] R. Reich, *Supercapitalism*, Alfred A. Knopf, 2009, p 72.

[20] W. Hutton, 'In 1986 monetarists ran up the white flag', *New Statesman*, 19 December 1986.

[21] S. Lansley, *The Cost of Inequality*, Gibson Square, 2011, p 142. See also K. Coutts and G. Gudgin, *The Macroeconomic Impact of Liberal Economic Policies in the UK*, Centre for Business Research, Judge Business School, 2015.

[22] P. Edwards, *Non-Standard Work and Labour-Market Restructuring in the UK*, Warwick Business School, 2006.

[23] K. Clark, 'Brexit is a Parody Version of Student Politics', interviewed by J. Freedland, *The Guardian*, 16 April 2019.

[24] P. Townsend, 'Politics and the Statistics of Poverty', *Political Quarterly*, January–March 1972.

[25] V. George and I. Howards, *Poverty Amidst Affluence*, Edward Elgar, 1991, table 2.1 p 26.

[26] House of Commons, *Hansard*, vol 51, 22 December 1983, col 561.

[27] P. Johnson and S. Webb, *Poverty in Official Statistics*, Institute for Fiscal Studies, 1990, pp 19–20.

[28] J.C. Kincaid, *Poverty and Equality*, Pelican, 1973, p 179.

[29] L. Burghes, *Living from Hand to Mouth*, Family Services Unit and CPAG, 1980, p 71–3.

[30] Social Security Advisory Committee, *Benefits for Disabled People, A Strategy for Change*, HMSO, 1983.

[31] D. Piachaud, 'Peter Townsend and the Holy Grail', *New Society*, 10 September 1981.

[32] See, for example, J. Flaherty, *Getting By, Getting Heard*, report for the Scottish Borders Commission, 2008.

33 C. Pantazis, D. Gordon and R. Levitas, *Poverty and Social Exclusion in Britain*, Policy Press, 2006; S. Lansley and J. Mack, *Breadline Britain*, Oneworld, 2015, pp 23–4.
34 J. Mack and S. Lansley, *Poor Britain*, Allen and Unwin, 1985, ch 2.
35 'Editorial', *The Sunday Times*, 21 August 1983.
36 *The Sunday Times,* 28 August 1983.
37 House of Commons, *Hansard,* vol 62, 28 June 1984, col 1241.
38 See, for example, C. Snowdon, 'Poverty, Taxes and the Cost of Living', *Prospect*, 19 November 2013, pp 26–9.

Chapter 15
1 P. Pierson, 'The New Politics of the Welfare State', *World Politics*, 48(2), 1996, pp 143–79; D. Piachaud, 'Social Security: Past, Present and Future', *LSE Public Policy Review*, 1(2), 2020, p 2.
2 A. Travis, 'Ministers Feared 1980 Plan to Cut State Pension Would Cause Riots', *The Guardian*, 30 December 2010.
3 D. Donnison, *The Politics of Poverty*, Martin Robertson, 1982, p 168; House of Commons, *Hansard*, vol 698, 13 June, 1979, col 439.
4 T. Rutherford, *Historical Rates of Social Security Benefits*, House of Commons Library, 2013, Note SN/SG 6762.
5 R. Lister, 'Behind the Lace Curtains', *New Statesman*, 7 August 1987.
6 F. Sutcliffe-Braithwaite, 'Margaret Thatcher, Individualism and the Welfare State', *History and Policy*, 15 April 2013.
7 N. Lawson, *The View from No 11,* Bantam Press, 1992, p 588.
8 D. Hencke, 'Fowler's Future', *Marxism Today*, December 1985.
9 R.M. Titmuss, 'The Irresponsible Society', *Fabian Tract*, 323, 1959, p 1.
10 Royal Society for the Arts, *Collective Pensions in the UK II,* RSA, 2013.
11 A. Brummer, *The Great Pensions Robbery*, Random House, 2010, pp 39–40.
12 A.H. Halsey, 'A Crisis in the Welfare State', *The Listener*, 22 March 1984.
13 J. Hudson, N. Lunt, C. Hamilton, S. Mackinder, J. Meers and C. Swift, 'Nostalgia narratives? Pejorative Attitudes to Welfare in Historical Perspective: Survey Evidence from Beveridge to the British Social Attitudes Survey', *Journal of Poverty and Social Justice*, 24(3), 2016, pp 227–43.
14 P. Spicker, *Stigma and Social Welfare*, Croom Helm, 1984, ch 5.
15 The Fisher Committee, *Report of the Committee on Abuse of Social Security Benefits*, Cmnd 5228, HMSO, 1973, p 12.
16 R. Page, *The Benefits Racket*, Temple Smith, 1971.
17 'MP's attack on horrifying social-security scrounging', *The Times*, 12 July 1976.
18 D. Donnison, *The Politics of Poverty*, Martin Robertson, 1982, pp 63–5.
19 The Fisher Committee, *Report of the Committee of Enquiry into the Abuse of Social Security Benefits,* Cmnd 5228, HMSO, 1973, p 209, para 446.
20 F. Field, M. Meacher and C. Pond, *To Him Who Hath*, Penguin, 1977, ch 8. See also O. Stevenson, *Claimant or Client, A Social Worker's View of The Supplementary Benefits Commission*, Allen and Unwin, 1973.
21 House of Commons, *Hansard*, vol 912, 24 May, 1976, col 79W; F. Field, M. Meacher, C. Pond, *To Him Who Hath*, Penguin, 1977, p 155.
22 S. MacGregor, *The Politics of Poverty*, Longman, 1981, p 159.
23 The Fisher Committee, *Report of the Committee of Enquiry into the Abuse of Social Security Benefits*, p 168.
24 F. Field, M. Meacher and C. Pond, *To Him Who Hath*, Penguin, 1977, p 150.

25 The Fisher Committee, *Report of the Committee of Enquiry into the Abuse of Social Security Benefits*, 1973.

26 P. Golding, 'Prejudice Against the Poor', *New Internationalist*, issue 115, 1 September 1982.

27 P. Golding and S. Middleton, *Images of Welfare*, Martin Robertson, 1982.

28 J. Ditch, 'The Undeserving Poor' in M. Loney (ed), *The State or the Market*, Sage, 1987, p 37.

29 C. Crouch, *Post-Democracy*, Polity, 2004, p 23.

30 M. Flinders, 'Low voter turnout is clearly a problem, but a much greater worry is the growing inequality of that turnout', *LSE Politics and Policy*, 13 March 2014.

31 D. Acemoglu and J. Robinson, *Why Nations Fail. The Origins of Power, Prosperity and Poverty*, Profile Books, 2013.

32 Z. Bauman, 'Fighting the Wrong Shadow', *New Statesman*, 25 September 1987, p21.

33 A. Dilnot, J. Kay and C. Morris, *The Reform of Social Security*, Oxford University Press, 1984, p 59.

34 R.H. Tawney, *Equality*, 4th edn, Allen & Unwin, 1964, pp 150, 233.

35 B. Jackson, *Equality and the British Left*, Manchester University Press, 2007, p 139.

36 A.B. Atkinson and J. Micklewright *Turning the Screw, Benefits for the Unemployed, 1979–88*, Suntory-Toyota International Centre for Economics and Related Disciplines, London School of Economics, 1988.

37 P. Spicker, 'Our Budget Under Attack: Estimating Social Security Fraud', *Radical Statistics*, 1999.

38 CHAR, *Fraud and Operation Major*, CHAR, 1983; House of Commons, *Hansard*, 36, 7 February 1983, cols 798–811.

39 K. Andrews and J. Jacobs, *Punishing the Poor*, Macmillan, 1990, p 165. See also R. Berthoud, *Selective Social Security*, Policy Studies Institute, 1986.

40 K. Andrews and J. Jacobs, *Punishing the Poor*, p 166–7.

41 R.A. Hasson, 'Tax Evasion and Social Security Abuse – Some Tentative Observations', *Canadian Taxation*, 2(2), 1980, pp 98–108.

42 K. Andrews and J Jacobs, *Punishing the Poor*, pp 164–5; D. Donnison, *The Politics of Poverty*, pp 69–71.

43 Author's calculations from Central Statistical Office, 'The effects of taxes and benefits on household income', *Economic Trends*, March 1991 and January 1994.

44 P. Bourquin and T. Waters, *The Tax System Reduces Inequality – But Benefits Do Most of the Heavy Lifting*, Institute for Fiscal Studies, 2019; A. Advani and A. Summers, 'How Much Tax Do the Rich Really Pay?', *CASE Policy Paper*, No 27, London School of Economics and University of Warwick, June 2020; D. Byrne and S. Ruane, *Paying for the Welfare State in the 21st Century*, Policy Press, 2017.

45 Ontario Fair Tax Commission, *Fair Taxation in a Changing World*, University of Toronto Press, 1993, p 45.

46 T. Piketty, E. Saez and S. Stantcheva, 'Taxing the 1%', *Vox*, 8 December 2011.

47 D. Hope and J. Limberg, 'The Economic Consequences of Higher Rate Tax Cuts on the Rich', *International Inequality Institute Working Paper, 55,* London School of Economics and Political Science, 2020.

48 P. Golding, 'Rich Man, Poor Man', *New Society*, 18 April 1986; C. Bromley, 'Has Britain become immune to inequality?', in A. Park and J. Curtice, *British Social Attitudes, The 20th Report*, NatCen, 2003, pp 76–89.

49 B. Jackson and R. Saunders, *Making Thatcher's Britain*, Cambridge University Press, 2012, p 47.

50 Quoted in J. Lawrence, 'The 21 Year War Still Rages', *New Society*, 18 April 1986.

51 J. Hoskyns, 'An End to Patchwork', *The Times*, 12 February, 1985, p 14.

52 Datablog, 'UK Public Spending Since 1963', *The Guardian*, 18 March 2013.

53 A. Hood and L. Oakley, 'The Social Security System', *Briefing no. BN156*, Institute for Fiscal Studies, 2014.

54 Department of Health and Social Security, *Reform of Social Security*, Cmnd 9517, HMSO, 1985; Department of Health and Social Security, *Reform of Social Security, Programme for Action*, Cmnd 9691, HMSO, 1985.

55 P. Sloman, *Transfer State,* Oxford University Press, 2019, figure 1.4, p 16.

56 D. Piachaud, 'The Growth of Means Testing', in A. Walker and C. Walker, *Britain Divided*, CPAG, 1997, pp 76–7.

57 C. Beatty and S. Fothergill, 'The Diversion from Unemployment to Sickness Benefit Across British Regions and Districts', *Regional Studies*, 39(7), 2005, pp 837–54.

58 R. Rowthorn and D. Webster, 'Male Worklessness and the Rise of Lone Parenthood in Great Britain', *Cambridge Journal of Regions, Economy and Society*, 1(1), 2007, pp 69–88.

59 N. Timmins and G. Tetlow, *Jobs and Benefits, the Covid-19 Challenge*, Institute for Government, 2021, p 14.

Chapter 16

1 Department of Social Security, Internal note: Williams to Allsop, October 13, 1989, The National Archive, JB 4/178/2.

2 House of Commons, *Hansard,* 174, col 543, 1990.

3 Based on the 50 per cent of average income measure and after adjusting for housing costs. Department of Social Security, *Households Below Average Incomes, 1981–87*, HMSO, 1990; and *Households Below Average Incomes, 1979–1993/4*, HMSO, 1996.

4 J. Moore, *Speech to Conservative Party Conference*, Blackpool, 8 Oct 1987.

5 Child Poverty Action Group, *Poverty*, Spring 1987, p 8.

6 J. Moore, *The End of Poverty*, Conservative Political Centre, 1989.

7 Shelter, 'From Care to Nowhere', *Roof*, July/August, 1984.

8 Quoted in J. Sweeney, 'Welcome to Cardboard City', *New Statesman*, 18 December 1987.

9 P. Bradley, 'Westminster, A tale of two cities', *New Statesman*, 2 October 1987; 'Letter from Chair of Housing Committee, Reading', *New Statesman*, 16 October, 1987.

10 A. Dilnot, *The Independent*, 13 May 1989.

11 J. Halliday, 'Capitalism is inherently unstable', 7 *DAYS*, 10 November 1971.

12 S. Pearlstein, 'When Shareholder Capitalism Came to Town', *The American Prospect*, 19 April 2014.

13 J.K. Galbraith, *The New Industrial State*, Princeton University Press, 1967, p 146.

14 A. Bailey, *Transforming Culture in Financial Services*, Financial Conduct Authority, 2018.

15 T. Faber, *Faber & Faber: The Untold Story*, Faber, 2019.

16 K. Phillips, *Wealth and Democracy*, Broadway Books, 2002, p 109.

17 *The Sunday Times*, 'Rich List', 2 April 1989.

18 J. Rentoul, 'The Real Shift', *New Statesman*, 16 October 1987.

19 I. Erturk, J. Froud, S. Johal and K. Williams, 'Pay for Corporate Performance or Pay as Social Division?', *Competition and Change*, 9(1), 2005, pp 49–74.

20 F. Partnoy, *F.I.A.S.C.O.: Blood in the Water on Wall Street*, Profile, 1997, p 40; M. Brewer, L. Sibieta and L. Wren-Lewis, 'Racing Away? Inequality and the Evolution of Top Incomes', *IFS Briefing Note No 76,* Institute for Fiscal Studies, 2008 p 25.

21 L. Parramore, 'Interview with William Lazonick', *Institute for New Economic Thinking Blog*.

22 D. Kynaston, *The City of London, vol 1V: A Club No More*, Pimlico, 2002, p 634.

23 H. Roberts and D. Kynaston, *City State*, Penguin, 2001, p 153.

24 Quoted in L. Parramore, 'Interview with William Lazonick', *Institute for New Economic Thinking Blog*, 2019.

[25] B. Cournède, O. Denk and P. Hoeller, 'Finance and Inclusive Growth', *OECD Economic Policy Papers*, 14, 2015.

[26] C. Mayer, *Prosperity*, Oxford University Press, 2018.

[27] H. Williams, 'How the City of London came to power', *Financial Times*, 21 March 2006.

[28] N. Shaxson, *Treasure Islands*, Bodley Head, 2011, p 78.

[29] M. King, *From Bagehot to Basel and Back Again*, Bank of England, 25 October, 2010, Table 1, p 23.

Chapter 17

[1] B. Burrough and J. Helyar, *Barbarians at the Gate: The Fall of RJR Nabisco*, Random House, 1990, pp 615–20.

[2] B. Burrough, 'The 00's finale of the 80's tycoons', *New York Times*, 5 June 2000.

[3] M. Savage and K. Williams, 'Elites: remembered in capitalism and forgotten in social science', *The Sociological Review*, 56(1), 2008, pp 1–24.

[4] Quoted in S. Lansley, *Rich Britain*, Politico, 2006, p 65.

[5] Quoted in W. Hutton, *The State We're In*, Jonathan Cape, 1995, p 163.

[6] D. Edgerton, *The Rise and Fall of the British Nation*, Penguin, 2018, p 463.

[7] A. Sampson, *The Midas Touch: Money, People and Power from West to East*, Hodder and Stoughton, 1989, p 24.

[8] M. Wicks, 'The Decade of Inequality', *New Society*, 6 February 1987.

[9] H. Young, *New Statesman*, 2 November 1984.

[10] G. Greig, 'Welcome to the Flashocracy', *Observer*, 6 June 2004.

[11] J. Norman, *Adam Smith: What He Thought and Why It Matters*, Allen Lane, 2018.

[12] A. Smith, *The Theory of Moral Sentiments*, Penguin, 2010, p 73.

[13] B. Pimlott, 'What Now for the Get-Rich-Quick Mood of the Mid-Eighties?', *New Statesman*, 30 October 1987.

[14] B. Williamson, *The Temper of the Times*, Blackwell, 1990, p 230.

[15] After taking account of inflation and housing costs. Joseph Rowntree Foundation, *Inquiry Into Income and Wealth*, Joseph Rowntree Foundation, 1995, figure 3, p 16.

[16] Joseph Rowntree Foundation, *Inquiry Into Income and Wealth*, Joseph Rowntree Foundation, 1995, pp 13–31.

[17] S. Lansley, 'Unfair to Middling', *TUC Touchstone Report*, TUC, 2009.

[18] S. Lansley and H. Reed, 'How to Boost the Wage-Share', *TUC Touchstone Report*, TUC, 2013, chs 3, 5; C. Oppenheim and L. Harker, *Poverty; The Facts*, CPAG, 1993, chs 5, 6.

[19] Joseph Rowntree Foundation, *Inquiry Into Income and Wealth*, 1995, figure 2, p 14.

[20] House of Commons, *Hansard*, 254, 1995, col 802–902.

[21] House of Lords, *Hansard*, 561, 1995, col 1485–556.

[22] N. Timmins, 'A Powerful Indictment of the Eighties', *The Independent*, 10 February 1995.

[23] Leader, 'The New Levellers', *The Times*, 2 February 1995.

[24] *The Sunday Telegraph*, 5 February 1995.

[25] D. Edgerton, *The Rise and Fall of the British Nation*, pp 488–91.

[26] R. McWilliam, *Making Labour Renewal Happen: Policy Options in The Light of Labour's History*, Labour History Research Unit, 2020.

[27] F. Mort, 'The Politics of Consumption' in S. Hall and M. Jaques (eds), *New Times*, Lawrence and Wishart, 1989, p 160.

[28] D. Marquand, *The Progressive Dilemma*, Heinemann, 1991.

[29] J.K. Galbraith, *A Culture of Contentment*, Houghton Mifflin, 1993.

[30] P. Glotz, *Die Arbeit der Zuspitzung*, Deutsche Verlag Anstalt, 1984.

[31] R. McKibbin, 'On the Defensive', *London Review of Books*, 17(2), 1995, pp 6–7.

[32] Commission on Social Justice, *Social Justice: Strategies for National Renewal*, Vintage, 1994.

Chapter 18

1. E. Hobsbawm, 'The Death of Neo-Liberalism', *Marxism Today*, Nov/Dec, 1998, p 14.
2. Labour Party, *New Labour Because Britain Deserves Better*, election manifesto, Labour Party, 1997.
3. C. Atkins, 'The Third Way International', *Jacobin*, 2 November 2016.
4. D. Sainsbury, 'Progressive Capitalism', *Progress*, 30 May 2013.
5. S. Brittan, 'Better than you deserve', *Financial Times*, 3 May 1997.
6. A. Giddens, *Beyond Left and Right*, Polity, 1994, p 149.
7. A. Giddens and P. Diamond (eds), *The New Egalitarianism*, Polity, 2005, p.106.
8. A.B. Atkinson, 'Equality in a Cold Climate', *New Statesman*, 15 April 1983.
9. R. Titmuss, 'Poverty vs. inequality diagnosis', *The Nation*, 8 February 1965, pp 130–3.
10. Labour Party, *New Labour Because Britain Deserves Better*, 1997.
11. B. Jackson and P. Segal, *Why Inequality Matters*, Catalyst, 2004.
12. 'Special Report: Brown's Britain', *The Sunday Times*, 17 November 2002.
13. H. Harman, *A Woman's Work*, Penguin, 2018, p 206.
14. 'Affluence exam for benefits', *The Daily Telegraph*, 12 January 1998.
15. H. Harman, *A Woman's Work*, 2018, p 195.
16. T. Blair, *A Journey*, Hutchinson, 2010, p 217.
17. R. Walker (ed), *Ending Child Poverty, Popular welfare for the 21st Century*, Policy Press, 1999, p 7.
18. See R. Lupton with J. Hills, K. Stewart and P. Vizard, *Labour's Social Policy Record: Policy, Spending and Outcomes, 1997–2010*, CASE, London School of Economics, 2013, pp 12–13; Department of Social Security, *Opportunity for All*, 2000, figure 2.1, p 29.
19. 'Interview with David Piachaud', *Poverty and Social Exclusion*, 14 November 2016.
20. Private correspondence with government statisticians. See also M. Dean, *Democracy Under Attack*, Policy Press, 2013, p 249.
21. Department for Work and Pensions, *Households Below Average Incomes*, 1999–2000, DWP, 2000.
22. Private correspondence with government statisticians; Department of Social Security, *Opportunity for All*, 1999, p17. Available from: http://webarchive.nationalarchives.gov.uk/20050301194710/http://dwp.gov.uk/publications/dss/1999/poverty/indicators/povind.pdf
23. Private correspondence with government statisticians.
24. 'Report of the Workshop Organised by Department of Social Security and Centre for Analysis of Social Exclusion, London School of Economics, 2001.
25. See, for example, P. Spicker, 'Why Refer to Poverty as a Proportion of Median Income?', *Journal of Poverty and Social Justice*, 20(2), 2012; D. Hirsch, A. Davis and N. Smith, *A Minimum Income Standard for Britain 2009*, Joseph Rowntree Foundation, 2009.
26. P. Adamson, 'Measuring Child Poverty: New league tables of child poverty in the world's rich countries', *Innocenti Report Card 10*, UNICEF, 2012.
27. The number earning below the level of the minimum wage fell from 1.28 million (5.6 per cent of the workforce) in 1998 to 242,000 (0.9 per cent of the workforce) in 2009.
28. M. Torry, 'Speenhamland, Automation and Basic Income: A Response', *Renewal*, 26(1), 2018, pp 32–5.
29. R. Lupton, J. Hills, K. Stewart and P. Vizard, *Labour's Social Policy Record: Policy, Spending and Outcomes, 1997–2010*, CASE, London School of Economics, 2013, pp 49–57.
30. B. Knight (ed), *A Minority View*, Webb Memorial Trust, 2011, p 15.
31. N. Pearce, 'Child poverty: time for honesty and a new approach', *The Guardian*, 13 May 2013

[32] R. Joyce and L. Sibieta, 'An Assessment of Labour's Record on Income Inequality and Poverty, 1997–2010', *Oxford Review of Economic Policy*, 29(1), 2013, pp 178–202.

[33] D. Hirsch, *What Will it Take to End Child Poverty?*, Joseph Rowntree Foundation, 2006.

[34] J. Tomlinson, 'Distributional Politics', in P. Hudson and K. Tribe (eds), *The Contradictions of Capital in the Twenty-First Century*, Agenda Publishing, 2016, p 183.

[35] *Newsnight*, BBC, 5 June 2001.

[36] Quoted in P. Toynbee, 'The Minister for Fatcats is Stuck in a Blairite Timewarp', *The Guardian*, 11 March 2008.

[37] L. Goodall, *Left for Dead*, William Collins, 2019, p 40.

[38] R. Lister, 'The irresponsibility of the rich', *Red Pepper*, 18 September 2008.

[39] Paris School of Economics, *The World Inequality Data Base*, Paris School of Economics. http://wid.world/; *Squeezed Britain*, Resolution Foundation, 2010, p 24; Department for Work and Pensions, 'Households Below Average Incomes, 2012/13', DWP, 2013, chart 2.3, p 29.

[40] B. Bell and J. Van Reenen, *Bankers' Pay and Extreme Wage Inequality in the UK*, Centre for Economic Performance, London School of Economics, 2010, p 9. The top 1 per cent in 2008 were mostly middle-aged men, with a concentration of company directors and those working in financial services and property, or in senior positions in law, medicine and accountancy. M. Brewer, L. Sibieta and L. Wren-Lewis, 'Racing away: inequality and the evolution of top incomes', *IFS briefing note 76*, 2008.

[41] R. Lister, 'Social Justice: Meanings and Politics', *Benefits*, 15(2), 2007, pp 113–25

[42] D. Donnison, *80th Birthday Lecture*, Glasgow, 2006.

[43] J. Kay, 'Redistributive Market Liberalism', *New Statesman*, 5 February 1997.

[44] P. Sloman, *Transfer State*, Oxford University Press, 2019, pp 3–28.

[45] Office for National Statistics, *Economic Trends*, 594, May 2003, p 33–79, and earlier editions.

Chapter 19

[1] J. Littler, *Against Meritocracy*, Routledge, 2017, p 3.

[2] A. Crosland, *The Future of Socialism*, Jonathan Cape, 1956, p 235.

[3] M. Young, 'Down with Meritocracy', *The Guardian*, 29 June 2001.

[4] P. Saunders, *Unequal But Fair*, Institute of Economic Affairs, 1996, p 7.

[5] Quoted in R. Breen and J.H. Goldthorpe, 'Class, Mobility and Merit: The Experience of Two British Birth Cohorts', *European Sociological Review*, 17, 2001, pp 81–101.

[6] L. Elliott Major and S. Machin, *Social Mobility and Its Enemies*, Pelican, 2018, p 16.

[7] S. Lansley, 'Life in the Middle', *TUC Touchstone Report*, TUC, 2009, Appendix 2.

[8] R. Hoggart, 'Introduction', in G. Orwell, *The Road to Wigan Pier*, Penguin, 2001.

[9] R. Breen and J.H. Goldthorpe, 'Class, Mobility and Merit: The Experience of Two British Birth Cohorts', *European Sociological Review*, 17, 2001, pp 81–101.

[10] J. Blanden, A. Goodman, P. Gregg and S. Machin, *Changes in Intergenerational Mobility in Britain*, Centre for Economic Performance, LSE, 2003; J. Blanden, P. Gregg and S. Machin, *Intergenerational Mobility in Europe and North America*, Centre for Economic Performance, LSE, 2005.

[11] Tom Nicholas, *The Myth of Meritocracy: An Inquiry Into the Social Origins of Britain's Business Leaders Since 1850*, London School of Economics, 1999, p 26.

[12] C.D. Harbury and D. Hitchens, *Inheritance and Wealth Inequality in Britain*, George Allen and Unwin, 1979, p 13; W.D. Rubenstein, 'Study for the Television Series *Fortune*', *London Weekend Television*, 1985.

[13] Commission on Social Mobility and Child Poverty, *Elitist Britain*, 2014.

[14] Office for National Statistics, *Life Expectancy by Birth and at Age 65 by Local Areas in the UK, 2006/8–2010/12*, ONS, 2019.

15 L.E. Major and S. Machin, *Social Mobility and Its Enemies*, Pelican, 2018, p 122.
16 A.B. Atkinson and F. Bourguignon, *Handbook of Income Distribution*, Elsevier, 2000, p 3.
17 A. Corlett, *Unequal Results*, Resolution Foundation, 2017.
18 See, for example, S. Aldridge, *Life Chances and Social Mobility*, paper to Prime Minister's Strategy Unit, 2004.
19 *Analysis*, BBC Radio 4, 20 February 2012.
20 G. Kelly and N. Pearce, 'Wanted: An Old, New Left', *Prospect*, September 2010.
21 R.H. Tawney, *Equality* (4th edn), Allen and Unwin, 1964, p 108.
22 A.B. Atkinson, *Inequality: what can be done?*, Harvard University Press, 2015, p 11.
23 A.B. Krueger, *The Rise and Consequences of Inequality in the United States*, White House, 2012. The graph was first produced by Miles Corack: M. Corack, 'Income Inequality, Equality of Opportunity, and Intergenerational Mobility', *Journal of Economic Perspectives*, 27(3), 2013, pp 79–102, fig 1.

Chapter 20

1   W. Li and S. Young, *An Analysis of CEO Pay Arrangements and Value Creation for FTSE-350 Companies*, CFA Society UK, 2016.
2   'Rich List, 2007', *Sunday Times*, 29 April 2007.
3   S. Tatton, 'Executive Pay: Fat Cats or Hungry Tigers?', Presentation on IDS executive compensation to Royal Statistical Society, 15 November 2007.
4   A. Giddens, *The Third Way and Its Critics*, Polity, 2000, p 35.
5   T. Blair, *Let Us Face the Future—the 1945 Anniversary Lecture*, Fabian Society, 1995.
6   *BBC Panorama*, BBC One, 7 November 2004.
7   A. Davis, *Reckless Opportunists: Elites at the End of the Establishment*, Manchester University Press, 2019.
8   R. Pahl, D. Rose and L. Spencer, 'Inequality and Quiescence: A Continuing Conundrum', *Institute for Social and Economic Research Working Paper Series*, 22, University of Essex, 2007.
9   K. Coutts and G. Gudgin, *The Macroeconomic Impact of Liberal Economic Policies in the UK*, *Economic and Labour Relations Review*, 27(2) 2015, pp 139–46.
10 J. Cassidy, 'The Greed Cycle', *New Yorker*, 23 September 2002.
11 F. Fukuyama, *The End of History and the Last Man*. Free Press, 1992.
12 R. Lucas, 'Macroeconomic Priorities', *Presidential Address to the American Economic Association*, 4 January 2003.
13 R. Putnam, *Bowling Alone*, Simon and Schuster, 2001.
14 L. Fioramonti, *The Well-Being Economy*, Macmillan, 2017, p 7.
15 W. Hutton 'Death of Community Spirit', *The Observer*, 16 November 2003, p 30.
16 C. Gardiner and J. Sheppard, *Consuming Passion*, Unwin Hyman, 1989, p 63.
17 J.K. Galbraith, 'Power and the useful economist', *American Economic Review*, 63(1), 1973, pp 1–11.
18 J. Ghosh, *Science and Subterfuge in Economics*, Institute for New Economic Thinking, 2019.
19 T. Piketty, 'Brahmin Left v Merchant Right', *WID Working Paper*, World Inequality Database, 2018/7, 2018.
20 N. Haring and N. Douglas, *Economists and the Powerful*, Anthem Press, 2012, p ix.
21 D. Byrne and S. Ruane, *Paying for the Welfare State in the 21st Century*, Policy Press, 2017, ch 5.
22 S. Jenkins, 'The Revolving Door Between City banks and Westminster is Distorting Our Economy', *The Guardian*, 20 August 2020.
23 A. Persaud, 'Lecture: Regulatory Capture', Gresham College, 28 June 2005.
24 M. Olson, *The Rise and Decline of Nations*, Yale University Press, 1984.
25 P. Turchin, 'Return of the Oppressed', *Aeon*, 13 February 2013.

[26] D. Runciman, 'The Crisis of British Democracy', *Juncture*, IPPR, 6 December 2013.

[27] See, for example, L. Lessig, *Republic Lost,* Twelve, 2016; and J. Mayer, *Dark Money*, Scribe Publications, 2016.

[28] T. Ferguson, 'Affluent Authoritarianism', *Institute for New Economic Thinking*, 2 November 2020

[29] G.A. Epstein and A. Jayadev, 'The Rise of Rentier Incomes in OECD countries: Financialization, Central Bank Policy and Labor Solidarity', in G.A. Epstein (ed), *Financialization and the World Economy*, Edward Elgar, 2005; M. Mazzucato, *The Value of Everything*, Allen Lane, 2018.

[30] G.W. Domhoff, *The Corporate Rich and the Power Elite in the Twentieth Century*, Routledge, 2019; L. Sklair, 'Social Movements for Global Capitalism: The Transnational Capitalist Class in Action', *Review of International Political Economy*, 4(3), 1997, pp 514–38.

[31] Quoted in O. Jones, 'A Partisan Civil Service is a Threat to us All', *The Guardian*, 4 July 2019.

[32] 'The Elite That Failed', *The Economist,* 22 December 2018.

[33] A. Haldane, *Labour's Share*, Bank of England, 12 November 2015, chart 7, p 25.

[34] A. O'Hear, 'Equality', *New Statesman*, 23 April 2001.

[35] D. Aaronovitch, 'Size Doesn't Matter', *The Observer*, 25 May 2003

[36] M. Feldstein, 'Is Income Inequality Really a Problem?', in Address to conference: *Income Inequality Issues and Policy Options*, Federal Reserve Bank of Kansas City, 27 August 1998.

[37] P. Johnson, 'When Are You Seriously Rich?', *Forbes*, 10 November 2004.

[38] F. Partnoy, *F.I.A.S.C.O.: Blood in the Water on Wall Street*, Profile, 1997, p 51.

[39] J. Prynn, '£13 billion? I'm worth much more than that', *Evening Standard*, 5 March 2013.

[40] D. Goodhart, 'The Wealth Gap Doesn't Matter', *The Guardian*, 29 July 1999.

[41] W. Hutton, 'Why the Poor Remain Silent', *The Guardian*, 13 February 1997.

[42] E. Chancellor, 'The Croupier Takes Too Much', *Prospect*, February 2003

[43] A. Monaghan 'City is Too Big and Socially Useless', *Daily Telegraph*, 26 August 2009.

[44] H. Williams, *Britain's Power Elites*, Constable, 2006, p 164.

[45] R. Larson, *Bleakonomics,* Pluto Press, 2012, p 5.

[46] C. Bromley, 'Has Britain Become Immune to Inequality?' in A. Park, J. Curtice, K. Thomson, L. Jarvis and C. Bromley (eds), *British Social Attitudes 20th Report: Continuity and Change Over Two Decades*, Sage, 2003, pp 71–92.

[47] R. Pahl, D. Rose and L. Spencer, 'Inequality and Quiescence: A Continuing Conundrum', *Institute for Social and Economic Research Working Paper Series*, 22, University of Essex, 2007, p 1.

[48] Quoted in P. Toynbee, 'The Public Worry More About Spanish Donkeys than Child Poverty', *The Guardian*, 30 March 2007.

[49] P. Taylor-Gooby, 'Why do People Stigmatise the Poor at a Time of Rapidly Increasing Inequality?', *The Political Quarterly*, 84(1), 2013, pp 31–41.

[50] S. Lansley, 'We All Think We're in the Middle', in T. Hampson and J. Olchawski, (eds), *Is Equality Fair*, Fabian Society, 2009, p 25.

[51] *Daily Telegraph*, 13 August 2009; S. Sacker, 'Boris Johnson interviewed by Stephen Sacker', *HardTalk*, BBC 14 July 2009.

[52] J. Hills et al (eds), *Poverty and Inequality*, CASE, London School of Economics, 2019.

[53] See, for example, H. Williams, *Britain's Power Elites*, Constable, 2006; S. Lansley, *Rich Britain*, Politico, 2006; M. Orton and K. Rowlingson, 'A Problem of Riches: Towards a New Social Policy Agenda on the Distribution of Economic Resources', *Journal of Social Policy*, 36(1), 2007, pp 59–77; K. Rowlingson, 'Wealth' in T. Ridge and S. Wright, *Understanding Inequality, Poverty and Wealth,* Policy Press, 2008; G. Irvin, *Super Rich*, Policy Press, 2008.

[54] Though see M. Ravallion, 'Inequality is Bad for the Poor', *World Bank Policy Research Working Paper Series*, 3677, 2005.

[55] P. Beresford, 'Endless Reports on Rising Poverty Do Little to Change Government Policy', *The Conversation,* 11 December 2017.

[56] B. Knight, 'If Knowing the Facts Reduced Poverty, it Would Be All Over by Now', *Rethinking Poverty*, 24 July 2018.

[57] Quoted in T. Rogan, *The Moral Economists*, Princeton University Press, 2017, p 20.

[58] F. Field, 'Poverty Close-Up', *New Society*, 7 March 1974.

[59] K. Green, 'Labour's Reform Programme Owes More to Authoritarianism than Enlightenment', *Chartist,* May 2011.

[60] M. Savage and K. Williams, 'Elites: Remembered in Capitalism and Forgotten in Social Science', *The Sociological Review*, 56 (1), 2008, p 4.

[61] A. Chakraborty, 'Economics Has Failed Us?', *The Guardian*, 16 April 2012.

[62] A. Sayer, 'Facing the Challenge of the Return of the Rich', in W. Atkinson, S. Roberts, and M. Savage, (eds), *Class Inequality in Austerity Britain*, Palgrave, Macmillan, 2012, pp 163–79.

[63] See, for example, B. Milanović, 'Interview with Branko Milanović', *Social Europe*, 18 March 2016.

[64] D. Walker, 'Is the ESRC Flying Below the Radar – or Left Out of the Loop?' *Times Higher Education*, 7 April 2016.

[65] A. Goodman and S. Webb, *For Richer, For Poorer: The Changing Distribution of Income in the UK, 1961–91*, Institute for Fiscal Studies, 1994.

[66] In the event, there was a later study of whether there is a public consensus on a 'rich line'. A. Davies et al, 'Living on Different Incomes in London: Can Public Consensus Identify a Riches Line?', *CASE Report*, 127, 2020.

[67] Quoted in B. Christophers, 'Making Finance Productive', *New Political Economy and Society*, 40(1), 2011, pp 112–40.

Chapter 21

[1] A. Haldane, *Unfair Shares*, speech to Bristol Festival of Ideas, 21 May 2014.

[2] R. Lupton, J. Hills, K. Stewart and P. Vizard, *Labour's Social Policy Record: Policy, Spending and Outcomes, 1997–2010*, LSE Centre for Social Exclusion, 2013, pp 50–1.

[3] R. Burkhauser, N. Hérault, S. Jenkins and R. Wilkins, *Survey Under-Coverage of Top Incomes and Estimation of Inequality: What Is the Role of the UK's SPI Adjustment?'*, *Fiscal Studies*, 39(2), pp 213–40.

[4] A.B. Atkinson, 'Top Incomes in the UK over the 20th Century', *Journal of the Royal Statistical Society, Series A*, 168(2), 2005, pp 325–43; A.B. Atkinson, J. Hasell, S. Morelli and M. Roser, *Chartbook of Economic Inequality*, Institute for New Economic Thinking, University of Oxford, 1917, p 55.

[5] P. Krugman, 'Why We're in a New Gilded Age', *New York Review of Books*, 8 May 2014. Up to this point, inequality trends had been taken mostly from official surveys. The use of tax returns offered a new and distinct perspective on what had been happening and over a longer period, while enabling improved coverage of what had been happening at the top.

[6] *The World Inequality Data Base*, Paris School of Economics. http://wid.world/

[7] G. Bellafante, 'Gunning for Wall Street', *New York Times*, 23 September 2011.

[8] Quoted in A. Tooze, 'The Forgotten History of the Financial Crisis', *Foreign Affairs*, 97(5), September/October, 2018.

[9] E. Andrews, 'Greenspan Concedes Error Over Regulation', *New York Times*, 23 October 2008.

[10] H. Minsky, *Stabilising an Unstable Economy*, Yale University Press, 1986.

[11] M. Wolf, 'The Fed is Right to Turn on the Tap', *Financial Times*, 9 November 2010.

[12] IMF, *Global Financial Stability Report*, 2009, tables 3–6, pp 177–8.

[13] S. Lansley, *The Cost of Inequality*, Gibson Square, 2011, Figure 9.1, p 207.

[14] P.R. Keefe, *The Secret History of the Sackler Dynasty*, Picador, 2021, p 135.

[15] Private Eye, 'Selling England (and Wales) by the Pound', *Private Eye*, September 2015.

[16] P. Moore, *Crash, Bang, Wallop*, New Wilberforce, 2016.

[17] Quoted in A. Tooze, *Crashed*, Penguin Books, 2019, p 64.

[18] IMF, *Global Financial Stability Report*, 2014. See also T. Philippon and A. Reshef, *Wages and Human Capital in US Financial Services,1909–2006*, NBER, 2012.

[19] S. Johnson, 'Ship of Knaves', *The New York Times*, 10 February 2011.

[20] T. Padoa-Schioppa, 'Markets and Government Before, During and After the 2007 Crisis', *Per Jacobsen Lecture, Bank for International Settlements*, Basel, Switzerland, 27 June 2010.

[21] P. Krugman, 'The Rise of the Robots', *New York Times Blog*, 8 December 2012.

[22] L. Pollack, 'Central Cankers: Pursued by a Bear', *Financial Times,* 22 November 2011.

[23] M. Somerset Webb, 'Editorial', *MoneyWeek,* 3 September 2016.

[24] J.K. Galbraith, *The Great Crash, 1929*, Penguin, 2009, p 32.

[25] C.R. Morris, *The Trillion Dollar Meltdown*, Public Affairs, 2008 p 54.

[26] G. Tett, *Fool's Gold*, Little Brown, p 46.

[27] I. Collier, 'Galbraith's Proposal to Split the Economics Department', in *Economics in the Rear-View Mirror*, 2020.

[28] P. Toynbee and D. Walker, *Unjust Rewards*, Granta, 2008; R. Wilkinson and K. Pickett, *The Spirit Level,* Penguin, 2009; D. Dorling, *Injustice*, Policy Press, 2011; S. Lansley, *The Cost of Inequality*, Gibson Square, 2011; J. Stiglitz, *The Price of Inequality*, Allen Lane, 2012.

[29] World Economic Forum, *Global Risks 2012*, 7th edn, WEF, 2012.

[30] G. Tett, 'Income inequality comes out of the igloo at Davos', *Financial Times*, 25 January 2012.

[31] G. Sargent, 'The Defining Issue of our Time', *Washington Post,* 4 December 2013.

[32] 'Rich List', *Sunday Times*, 26 May 2011.

[33] E. Shaw, 'The Labour Party and the Egalitarian Project', in D. Fée and A. Kober-Smith, *Inequalities in the UK*, Emerald, 2018, pp 149–66; M. O'Neill and T. Williamson, 'Philosophical Foundations for "good capitalism"', *Renewal*, 20(1), 2012, pp 20–32.

[34] R. Blackburn, 'The Corbyn Project', *New Left Review*, 111(2), 2018.

[35] A. Harrop, 'We Need an Honest Post-Mortem', *Labour List*, 17 January 2020.

[36] M. Marriage, 'Why the UK's Uber-Wealthy Voters fear a Corbyn-Led Government', *Financial Times*, 6 October 2018.

[37] C. Lagarde, 'A New Global Economy for a New Generation', *International Monetary Fund*, 23 January 2013.

[38] J.D. Ostry, A. Berg and C.G. Tsangarides, 'Redistribution, Inequality and Growth', *IMF Discussion Paper*, 2014; ILO, 'Wage-led growth: Concept, theories and policies', *Conditions of Work and Employment Series*, 41, 2012; R. Hockett and D. Dillon, 'Income Inequality and Market Fragility: A Model and Some Empirics in the Political Economy of Finance', *Challenge*, 62 (6), 2019, pp 354–74.

[39] D. Acemoglu and J. Robinson, *Why Nations Fail. The Origins of Power, Prosperity and Poverty*, Profile Books, 2013.

[40] OECD Ministerial Council, *Update on Inclusive Growth Project*, OECD, 2015, 3–4 June.

[41] S. Lansley, *The Cost of Inequality*, Gibson Square, fig 7.2, p 175; J.D.G. Wood, 'Can Household Debt Influence Income Inequality? Evidence from Britain: 1966–2016', *British Journal of Politics and International Relations*, 22(1) 2019, pp 24–46.

[42] See, for example, P. Augar, *The Greed Merchants*, Allen Lane, 2005.

43 A. Smith, *An Inquiry into the Nature and Causes of the Wealth of Nations*, Longman, Brown, Green, & Longmans, 1850 (ed J.R. McCulloch), book 1, ch VIII, pp 29–40.

44 R.F. Kennedy, 'Remarks at the University of Kansas', address given at University of Kansas, 18 March 1968.

45 D. Coyle, 'Progress Can no Longer be Measured by Growth in GDP', *Wired,* 16 October 2020.

46 L. Chiozza Money, *Riches and Poverty,* Methuen, 1905, pp 41–3; L. Chiozza Money, 'The Distribution of Wealth', in H. Tracey (ed), *The Book of the Labour Party*, vol II, Caxton, 1926, p 263.

47 F. Hirsch, *The Social Limits to Growth*, Routledge and Kegan Paul, 1977, p 5.

48 G. Adams and S. Harris, 'The Super-rich: Britain's Billionaires', *Independent on Sunday*, 17 December 2010.

49 B. Lindsay and S. Teles, *The Captured Economy*, Oxford University Press, 2017.

50 S. Bowles and A. Jayadev, 'Garrison America', *Economist's Voice*, April 2007.

51 B. Kachka, 'On Tour With Rock-Star Economist Thomas Piketty', *New York Magazine*, 21 April 2014.

52 T. Piketty, *Capital in the Twenty-First Century*, Harvard University Press, 2014.

53 See, for example, Y. Varoufakis, 'Egalitarianism's latest foe: a critical review of Thomas Piketty's Capital in the Twenty-First Century', *Real-World Economics Review*, 69, 2014, pp 18–35.

54 L. Adkins, M. Cooper and M. Konings, *The Asset Economy,* Polity, 2020.

55 S. Lansley, 'Unfair to Middling', *TUC Touchstone Report*, TUC, 2009, table 1, p 13.

56 B. Christopher, *Rentier Capitalism*, Verso, 2012, fig 0.7, p 42.

57 Author's calculations from C. Kidd, *Total Wealth: Wealth in Great Britain*, Office for National Statistics, 2019, table 2.2.

Chapter 22

1 A. Smith, *An Inquiry into the Nature and Causes of the Wealth of Nations*, Brown, Green, & Longmans, 1850 (ed. J.R. McCulloch), book II, ch IV, p 159.

2 B. Milanović , *The Haves and Have-Nots,* Basic Books, 2011.

3 For the US, see B. Harrison, *Lean and Mean: The Changing Landscape of Corporate Power in the Age of Flexibility*, Basic Books, 1994.

4 A. Smithers, *Productivity and the Bonus Culture*, Oxford University Press, 2019.

5 High Pay Centre/TUC, *How the Shareholder-first Model Contributes to Poverty, Inequality and Climate Change*, TUC, 2019.

6 Janus Henderson Investors, *Global Dividends Surge to New Record in 2018*, Press Release, 18 February 2020.

7 T. Panza de Paula, 'Why Bailing out Companies Doesn't Help People Recover from Economic Shocks', *World Economic Forum*, 12 October 2020.

8 R. Reich, 'The Rich Simply Can't Lose in Today's Rigged Economy', *Salon*, 3 May 2016.

9 A. Baker, G. Epstein and J. Montecino, *The UK's Finance Curse?*, SPERI, University of Sheffield, 2019.

10 B. Christophers, *Rentier Capitalism*, Verso, 2020; B. Bell, P. Bukowski and S. Machin, 'Rent Sharing and Inclusive Growth', *Working Paper*, 29, International Inequalities Institute, The London School of Economics and Political Science, 2019: T. Philippon and A. Reshef, *Wages and Human Capital in US Financial Services, 1909–2006*, The Quarterly Journal of Economics, 127(4), 2012, pp 1551–609.

11 J. Hamilton-Peterson, *What We Have Lost: the Dismantling of Great Britain*, Head of Zeus, 2018.

[12] *The Economist*, 25 November 2004. D. Roberts, 'Hyper-capitalism', *Financial Times*, 2 May 2006.

[13] J. Domenichini, *Public to Private Transactions, A Case of Debenhams*, Mimeo, 2009.

[14] K. Yearwood, *The Private Water Industry in the UK*, University of Greenwich, 2019.

[15] A. Hilton, 'Time to do Away with Tax Relief on Debt', *Evening Standard*, 13 November 2012.

[16] J. Ford, 'Private Equity Fees have Become a Rentier's Bonanza', *Financial Times*, 30 August 2020.

[17] A. Freeman, *WeWork Showed Us How Badly Start-up Bros Suck—But Shareholder Rule Isn't Better*, Institute for New Economic Thinking, 2019.

[18] G. Orwell, 'The Lion and the Unicorn', in *George Orwell Essays*, Penguin, 2000, p 150.

[19] D. Miles, 'What is the Half-life of Economic Injustice?', *Vox,* 6 December 2018; G. Shrubsole, *Who Owns England?*, William Collins, 2019.

[20] J. Meek, 'Robin Hood in a Time of Austerity', *London Review of Books*, 38(4), 2016.

[21] J. Hills, *Good Times, Bad Times,* Policy Press, 2015, pp 6–7, 45; Office for National Statistics, *The Effect of Taxes and Benefits on UK Household Incomes*, ONS, 2018.

[22] S. Lansley, *Rich Britain*, Politico, 2006, ch 10; K. Rowlingson and K.S. Connor, 'The "deserving" rich? Inequality, morality and social policy', *Journal of Social Policy*, 40(3), 2011, pp 437–52.

[23] O. Jones, *Chavs*, Verso, 2011, p 89–91.

[24] D. Webster, 'Benefit Sanctions, Social Citizenship and the Economy', *Local Economy*, 2019, pp 1–11.

[25] Department for Work and Pensions, *No One Written off, Reforming Welfare to Reward Responsibility*, Cmnd 7363, DWP, 2008.

[26] S. Johnsen and J. Blekinsorp, 'Lone Parents', *Welfare Conditionality,* Economic and Social Research Council, 2018.

[27] D. Sage, 'The Quiet Revolution', *Political Quarterly*, 90(1), January–March 2019, pp 99–106; T. O'Grady, 'How politics created rather than reacted to negative political opinion on benefits', *LSE Politics and Policy,* 7 November 2017; B. Geiger and B. Meueleman, 'Beyond 'mythbusting': How to respond to myths and perceived undeservingness in the British benefits system', *Journal of Poverty and Social Justice*, 24(3), 2016, pp 291–306.

[28] K. Green, 'Labour's Reform Programme Owes More to Authoritarianism than Enlightenment', *Chartist,* May 2011.

[29] O. Jones, *Chavs*, Verso, 2011, p 94–5.

[30] J. Purnell, 'Interview with James Purnell', interviewed by M. Bright, *New Statesman*, 18 September 2008.

[31] M. Hill, 'Social Justice and Employment', in G. Craig (ed), *Handbook on Global Social Justice*, Edward Elgar, 2018, p 387.

[32] The Labour Party, *Personal Freedom: Labour's Policy for Social Justice*, 1956.

[33] D. Piachaud, 'Revitalising Social Policy', *Political Quarterly*, 62(2), 1991, p 224.

[34] R. Lister, 'The Irresponsibility of the Rich', *Red Pepper*, 18 September 2008.

[35] S. White, 'The Left and Reciprocity', in J. Rutherford and A. Lockey (eds), *Labour's Future*, Soundings, 2010, p 39; S. White, *The Civic Minimum: On the Rights and Obligations of Economic Citizenship*, Oxford University Press, 2003.

[36] Runnymede Trust, *We Are Ghosts: Race, Class and Institutional Prejudice,* Runnymede Trust and CLASS, 2019.

[37] G. Standing, *The Plunder of the Commons,* Penguin, 2019, p 58.

[38] A. Tooze, *Crashed,* Penguin, 2018, p 166.

[39] K. Farnsworth, 'There's Not Just Five Giants', *Social Policy Association Blog*, 22 March 2019.

[40] Office for Budget Responsibility, *Fiscal Risks Report*, OBR, 2019, p 95.

41 National Audit Office, *The management of tax expenditures*, NAO, 2020.
42 National Audit Office, *The management of tax expenditures*, 2020; HMRC, *Estimated Costs of Tax Reliefs*, HMRC, 2020.
43 A. Sinfield, 'Fiscal Welfare and its Contribution to Inequality', *Social Policy Review*, 30, 2018, pp 91–110.
44 J. Hobhouse, *The Labour Movement*, 3rd edn, Macmillan, 1912, p 17.
45 A. Sampson 'We are in Danger of Remembering the First World War but Forgetting its Lessons', *The Independent*, 7 August 2004.

Chapter 23

1 D. Cameron, *Scarman Lecture*, 24 November 2006.
2 Quoted in J. Chapman, 'Benefits can do More Harm than Good for Child Poverty', *Daily Mail*, 2 December 2011.
3 Centre for Social Justice, *Dynamic Benefits*, CSJ, 2009, p 4.
4 Department for Work and Pensions, *Measuring Child Poverty, A Consultation on Better Measures of Child Poverty*, Cmnd 8483, DWP, 2012.
5 J. Bradshaw et al, 'Consultation on Child Poverty Measurement', *Poverty and Social Exclusion Policy Response Working Paper*, 8, 2013, p 2.
6 Interview with Iain Duncan Smith by Nicholas Watt and Patrick Wintour, 'I will tackle poverty', *The Guardian*, 26 May 2010.
7 F. Field, 'Poverty is About Much More than Money', *The Daily Telegraph*, 5 June 2010.
8 J. Veit-Wilson, 'Can Relative Poverty Be Abolished?', *Poverty and Social Exclusion*, 12 June 2013.
9 I. Duncan Smith and G. Osborne, 'The Conservatives' Child Poverty Plan Tackles Poverty at Source', *The Guardian*, 26 February 2014.
10 Innocenti Research Centre, 'Measuring Child Poverty: New league tables of child poverty in the world's rich countries', UNICEF, 2012, fig 5, p 12.
11 The 60 per cent measure can, in some situations, lead to seemingly distorted trends. On this basis, poverty might fall during recessions even if real incomes among the poor decline, largely because the median income, and thus the bar against which poverty is measured, has fallen. The official measure would thus understate the change in the poverty rate based on actual living standards. This is what happened after the 2008 crash, when levels of poverty on the 60 per cent measure fell for a few years. With benefit levels initially protected and real wages falling, incomes in the middle fell in relation to those lower down the income scale, thus lowering the level of relative poverty.
12 Interviewed for the Poverty and Social Exclusion UK Study. S. Pemberton, E. Sutton, E. Fahmy and K. Bell, 'Endless Pressure, Life on a Low Income in Austere Times', *Social Policy and Administration*, 51(7), 2017, pp 1156–73.
13 Interviewed for the Poverty and Social Exclusion UK Study, 'A young jobseeker', *Poverty and Social Exclusion*, February 2011. https://www.poverty.ac.uk/living-poverty/personal-experiences/marcs-story-north-east-england
14 D. Cameron, 'Troubled Families Speech', 15 December 2011.(www.gov.uk).
15 R. Levitas, *There May Be 'Trouble' Ahead*, Poverty and Social Exclusion, 2012.
16 J. Hacker, *The Great Risk Shift*, Oxford University Press, 2008, p 166.
17 J. Welshman, *Underclass, a History of the Excluded Since 1880*, Bloomsbury, 2013.
18 See, for example, M. Rutter and N. Madge, *Cycles of Disadvantage*, Heinemann, 1976, p 255; S.A. Black and P.J. Devereux, 'Recent Developments in Intergenerational Mobility', in *Handbook of Labor Economics*, Elsevier, vol 4, part B, 2011, pp 1487–541.
19 R. McDonald, *Youth, the 'Underclass' and Social Exclusion*, Routledge, 1997, p 172.

20 D. Gordon, 'Consultation Response, Social Mobility and the Child Poverty Review', *Poverty and Social Exclusion*, 2011, p 5.

21 Y.N. Harari, *21 Lessons for the 21st Century*, Jonathan Cape, 2018, p 170.

22 HM Government, *An Evidence Review of the Drivers of Child Poverty for Families in Poverty Now and for Poor Children Growing Up to Be Poor Adults*, Cmnd 8781, Stationery Office, 2014

23 N. Stevens and S. Fitzpatrick, *Country Level Devolution – Scotland*, CASE, London School of Economics, 2018. Social Security (Scotland) Act 2018 (legislation.gov.uk)

24 F. McGuiness, *Child Poverty in the UK*, House of Commons Library, 2017.

25 G. Osborne, *Speech to Conservative Party Conference,* Birmingham, 8 October 2012.

26 P. Taylor-Gooby, *A Left Trilemma: Progressive Public Policy in the Age of Austerity*, Policy Network, 2012, fig 2, p 10.

27 H. Grant and C. Michael, 'Too Poor to Play: Children in Social Housing Blocked from Communal Playground', *The Guardian*, 25 March 2019.

28 'Life Stories for Austere Times', *Poverty and Social Exclusion*, 2014; see also S. Pemberton, E. Sutton, E. Fahmy, K. Bell, 'Endless Pressure: Life on a Low Income in Austere Times', *Social Policy and Administration,* 51(7), 2017, pp 1156–73.

29 'Voices', North East Child Poverty Commission, 2021. VOICES_April_21_COVID_Disruption_and_the_Resource_Divide.pdf (children-ne.org.uk)

30 Quoted in *Moraene Robert (1953–2020) – Campaigning in a 'Banner Made of Silk',* ATD Fourth World, 15 January 2020.

Chapter 24

1   R. Chote, *Post-Budget Presentation*, Institute for Fiscal Studies, 23 June 2010.

2   R. Skidelsky, 'George Osborne's Cunning Plan', *New Statesman*, 24 April 2015.

3   D. Blanchflower, *Not Working*, Princeton University Press, 2019, p 172. See also, Office for Budget Responsibility, *Forecast Evaluation Report,* OBR, 2014; S. Wren-Lewis, 'The graph George Osborne doesn't want you to see', *The Conversation,* 17 March 2015.

4   A. Stirling, 'Austerity is Subduing UK economy by More than £3600 per Household this Year', New Economics Foundation, 2019; S. Wren-Lewis, 'The Austerity Con', *London Review of Books*, 37(4), 2015.

5   J. Gingrich and D. King, 'Americanising Brexit Britain's Welfare State?', *Political Quarterly*, 90(1), 2019, pp 89–98.

6   I. Duncan Smith, 'I'm Proud of our Welfare Reforms', *The Guardian*, 28 July 2013.

7   D. Cameron, *Prime Minister's Speech to the Lord Mayor's Banquet*, 11 November 2013.

8   P. Brien, *Public Spending*, House of Commons Library, 2020.

9   A. Gentleman, '400 in Protest at Clampdown on Council Tax Arrears', *The Guardian*, 19 October 2013.

10 C. McNeil, D. Hochlaf and H. Quilter-Pinner, *Social (In)security*, Institute for Public Policy Research, 2019, pp 17–20.

11 R. Lupton, J. Hills, K. Stewart and P. Vizard, *Labour's Social Policy Record: Policy, Spending and Outcomes, 1997–2010,* LSE Centre for Social Exclusion, 2013, fig 6, p 42.

12 A. McCarron and L. Purcell, *The Blame Game Must Stop: Challenging the Stigmatisation of People Experiencing Poverty*, Church Action on Poverty, 2013.

13 L. Gregory, 'Review of "D Edmiston, Welfare, Inequality and Social Citizenship"', Policy Press, 2018' in *Journal of Social Policy*, 48(2), 2019, pp 423–5.

14 D. Webster, Briefing on *Benefit Sanctions Statistics,* May 2019, Figure 3, p 19. Posted on David Webster (University of Glasgow) briefings on benefit sanctions, CPAG.

15 D. Webster, 'Benefit Sanctions, Social Citizenship and the Economy', *Local Economy*, 34(3), 2019, p 4.

16 'Editorial, The State Should Keep an Eye on the Rich and not Just the Poor', *The Guardian*, 14 April 2016.

17 Manchester CAB, *Punishing Poverty? A Review of Benefits Sanctions and their Impacts on Clients and Claimants*, Manchester CAB Service, 2013. See also House of Commons: Work and Pensions Committee, 'Benefit Sanctions', 31 October 2018.

18 M. Oakley, *Independent Review of the Operation of Jobseeker's Allowance Sanctions*, Department for Work and Pensions, 2014.

19 Institute for Government, *Jobs and Benefits, the Covid-19 Challenge*, Institute for Government, 2021, p 12.

20 D. Webster, *The DWP's JSA/ESA Sanctions, Statistics Release*, 2014, fig 5, p 10. Posted on David Webster (University of Glasgow) briefings on benefit sanctions, CPAG.

21 S. Duffy, *A Fairer Society*, The Centre for Welfare Reform, 2013.

22 The Centre for Welfare Reform, *The People's Review of the Work Capablility Assessment*, November 2012.

23 Welfare Conditionality Project, *Final Findings Report,* Economic and Social Research Council, 2018.

24 National Audit Office, *Universal Credit, Early Progress*, NAO, 2013.

25 T. Bell, A. Corlett and K. Handscomb, *Death by a £1000 cuts*, Resolution Foundation, 2020.

26 N. Cohen, 'Our Children go Hungry', *The Observer*, 9 September 2012.

27 Rethinking Economics – Home (rethinkeconomics.org).

28 W. Olsen, V. Gash, S. Kim and M. Zhang, *The Gender Pay Gap in the UK*, Government Equalities Office, 2018.

29 K. Polanyi, *The Great Transformation*, 2nd edn, Beacon Press, 2002, p 137.

30 G. Kent, 'We are sitting with the big people now', final report of the PSE's pilot community engagement project in Northern Ireland, *Poverty and Social Exclusion*, 2013.

31 K. Cooper and K. Stewart, *Does Money Affect Children's Outcomes?,* Centre for Analysis of Social Exclusion, London School of Economics, 2017.

32 OECD, *Labour Share in G20 Economies*, OECD, 2015; P. Bukowski, 'Globalisation and the Labour Share', *Rebuilding Macroeconomics*, 28 January 2019.

33 J. Hills, A. McKnight, and I. Bucelli, *Understanding the Relationship Between Poverty and Inequality*, Centre for Analysis of Social Exclusion, London School of Economics, 2019, p viii; Economic Policy Institute, *The State of Working America, 12th Edition*, Cornell University Press, 2014.

34 G. Osborne, *Budget Speech*, House of Commons, 8 July 2015.

35 D. Mabbett, 'Social Policy through the Looking Glass', *The Political Quarterly*, 86(4), 2015, pp 465–7.

36 J. Portes and H. Reed, *The Cumulative Impact of Tax and Benefit Reforms*, Equality and Human Rights Commission, 2018, p 183; HM Treasury, *Budget 2012*, Treasury, Annex B.

Chapter 25

1 M. Gove, 'Tories Must Win over "Hearts" to get Re-elected', *Daily Telegraph*, 12 March, 2015; D Cameron, *Speech to Conservative Party Conference*, Manchester, 7 October 2015.

2 'Britain on course for longest fall in living standards since records began over 60 years ago', *Resolution Foundation*, 23 November 2017.

3 A. Barth, 'Precarious scheduling at work affects over four million people in UK – far more than just zero-hours', *University of Cambridge*, 16 August, 2017; G. Standing, *The Precariat*, Bloomsbury, 2010.

4 D.B. Autor, 'Why Are There Still So Many Jobs? The History and Future of Workplace Automation', *Journal of Economic Perspectives*, 29(3), 2015, pp 3–30; M. Orton, *Something's Not Right*, Compass, 2015.

5 House of Commons: Committee on Business, Innovation and Skills, *Employment Practices at Sports Direct*, 2016.

6 L. Judge, *The Good, the Bad, and the Ugly*, Resolution Foundation, 2018; D. Tomlinson, *Irregular Payments*, Resolution Foundation, 2018.

7 M. Carney, 'The Spectre of Monetarism', speech given by the Governor of the Bank of England, Bank of England, 5 December 2016.

8 S. Clark and P. Gregg, 'The Prospects for the UK Labour Market in the Post-Brexit Era', *Political Quarterly*, March, 2019; G. Tiley, 'Wage growth but only for the few', TUC, 19 March 2019.

9 C. Bellfield, J. Cribb, A. Hood and T. Joyce, *Living Standards, Poverty and Inequality*, Institute for Fiscal Studies, 2015; F. Rahman, *The Generation of Poverty*, Resolution Foundation, 2019.

10 10 Downing Street, *Statement from the New Prime Minster*, Press Office, 13 July 2016.

11 R. O'Connell, A. Knight and J. Brannen, *Living Hand-to-Mouth*, CPAG, 2019.

12 S. and B. Webb, *The Prevention of Destitution*, Longmans, 1916.

13 E. Burke, *Reflections on the French Revolution*, Everyman, 1955, p 44.

14 Trussell Trust, 'Record 1.6m food bank parcels given to people in past year as the Trussell Trust calls for end to Universal Credit five week wait', *The Trussell Trust*, 15 April 2019.

15 Public Health England, *Health Matters: Rough Sleeping*, PHE, 2020.

16 Office of National Statistics, *Deaths of Homeless People in England and Wales, 2019*, ONS 2020.

17 J. Crown, 'Should the Homeless Be Protected by Hate Crime Law?', *Hodge, Jones and Allen*, October 2020.

18 D. Bentley and A. McCallum, *Rise and Fall: The Shift in Household Growth rates Since the 1990s*, Civitas, 2019; Press release, 'The generosity of the bank of Mum and Dad', *Legal & General*, May 2018.

19 Rethinking Poverty, 'Talking Points', *Webb Memorial Trust*, February 2020; *Poverty and Child Health, Views from the Frontline*, Royal College of Paediatrics and Child Health and CPAG, May, 2017; P. Alston, 'Statement on Visit to the United Kingdom', *UN Human Rights*, Resolution Foundation, 15 November 2018; *Child Poverty Risks Hitting Record Levels*, 20 February 2019; *Hidden Hunger and Malnutrition in the Elderly*, All-Party Parliamentary Group on Hunger, 2018.

20 A. Knight, J. Brannen, R. O'Connell, and L. Hamilton, 'How do children and their families experience food poverty according to UK newspaper media 2006–15?', *Journal of Poverty and Social Justice*, 26(2), 2018, pp 207–23.

21 Money Advice Trust, *Stop The Knock*, Money Advice Trust, 2017.

22 N. Woolcock, 'Schools Ask Parents to Pay for Staff and Books', *The Times*, 5 March 2019.

23 G. Davies, C. Boutaud, H. Sheffield and E. Youle, 'Revealed: the 1000s of public spaces lost in the council funding crisis', *Bureau for Investigative Journalism*, 4 March 2019.

24 Centre for Cities, 'A Decade of Austerity', *Centre for Cities*, 28 January 2019; C. Beatty and S. Fothergill, 'Recovery or Stagnation?', *Regional Studies*, 54(9), 2020, pp 1238–49.

25 C. Guilluy, *Twilight of the Elites*, Yale University Press, 2019.

26 R. Bourne and C. Snowdon, *Never Mind the Gap: Why We Shouldn't Worry about Inequality*, IEA Discussion Paper, 70, IEA, 2016.

27 T. Clark, C. Crouch, F. Nelson, A. Phillips and Z. Williams, 'Can Reversing Inequality Revive Politics?', Panel Discussion, The Royal Society, 19 October 2016.

28 B. Losse, 'Mugging up on Marxist drivel', *WirtschaftsWoche* , 26 July 2019.

29 M. Steinbaum, 'Why are Economists giving Piketty the Cold Shoulder?', *Boston Review*, 12 May 2017.

30 J. Schuessler, 'Hayek: The Back Story', *New York Times*, 9 July 2010.

[31] Z. Beauchamp, 'Why Rich People Hate Talking About Inequality', *ThinkProgress*, 29 March, 2013.

[32] J. Burns, *Goddess of the Market: Ayn Rand and the American Right*, Oxford University Press, 2019.

[33] The Student Room, 'Bringing Ayn Rand to the UK', *The Student Room*, 11 February 2017.

[34] S. Lansley, 'The Distribution Question: Measuring and Evaluating Trends in Inequality', in J. Evans, S. Ruane and H. Southall, (eds), *Data in Society*, Policy Press, 2019, pp 187–98.

[35] A. Bridge-Wilkinson, 'Johnson under fire for inaccurate use of statistics', *The Parliamentary Review*, 30 July 2020.

[36] D. Webber and J. O'Neill, *Household Income Inequality, UK, 2020*, ONS, 2021, fig 1. The main official sources for broad income trends – the HBAI series published by the Department for Work and Pensions and the series published by the Office for National Statistics – are poor at measuring the full distance between the extremes. Even though the DWP series adjusts for missing high-income households, this is only a partial adjustment. For example, by failing to take account of inheritance or capital gains, it understates high-income levels. See, for example, R.V. Burkhauser, N. Hérault, S.P. Jenkins and R. Wilkins, 'Top incomes and inequality in the UK: reconciling estimates from household survey and tax return data', *Oxford Economic Papers*, 70(2), 2018, pp 301–26; and A. Corlett and S. Clarke, *Living Standards: the Past, Present and Possible Future of UK Incomes*, Resolution Foundation, 2017. There is also some evidence that the under-reporting of benefits in household surveys may lead to an overstatement of poverty estimates. See A. Corlett, S. Clarke, C. D'Arcy and J. Wood, *The Living Standards Audit 2018*, Resolution Foundation, July 2018.

[37] M. Brewer and C. Sámano-Robles, 'Top Income in the UK', *ISER Working Papers, 2019–06*, 2019; A. Summers, *The Missing Billions*, Seminar, London School of Economics, 5 February 2019.

[38] A. Deaton and A. Case, 'Rebottling the Gini', *Prospect*, March 2020; N. Galassio, 'Why we Need to Rethink how we Measure Inequality', *Oxfam Blog*, 11 March 2016; A. Cobham, L. Schlogl and A. Sumner, *Inequality and the Tails: The Palma Revisited*, Department of Economic and Social Affairs, United Nations, July 2014.

[39] M. Doyle, and J. Stiglitz, 'Eliminating Extreme Inequality: A Sustainable Development Goal, 2015–2030', *Ethics and International Affairs*, 28(10), 2014, pp 1–7; T. Pogge and M. Sengupta, 'The Sustainable Development Goals as Drafted, Nice Idea, Poor Execution', *Washington International Law Journal*, 4(3), 2015, pp 571–87; L. Engberg-Pedersen, *Development Goals Post-2015*, Danish Institute for International Studies, Policy Brief, 2013.

[40] OECD, *Palma Ratio for OECD countries*, OECD, 2014; D. Webber and J. O'Neill, *Household Income Inequality, UK, 2020*, ONS, 2021.

[41] Author's estimates from D. Webber and J. O'Neill, *Household Income Inequality, UK, 2020*, ONS, 2021.

Chapter 26

[1] House of Commons: Business, Energy and Industrial Strategy Committee, *Executive Rewards, Paying for Success*, Stationery Office, 2019.

[2] F. Alvarado, L. Chancel, T. Piketty, E. Saez and G. Zucman, *The World Inequality Report, 2018*, World Inequality Lab, 2018, fig E6, p 14.

[3] T. Crossley and C. O'Dea, 'Household Wealth Data and Public Policy', *Fiscal Studies*, 37(1), 2016, pp 5–11; T. Piketty, *Capital and Ideology*, Harvard University Press, 2020, p 195.

[4] T. Bell and L. Gardiner, 'My Generation, Baby: The Politics of Age in Brexit Britain', *The Political Quarterly*, 90(S2), 2019, fig 8, pp 128–41.

5   A. Alstadsæter, N. Johannesen and G. Zucman, 'Who Owns the Wealth in Tax Havens? Macro Evidence and Implications for Global Inequality', *Journal of Public Economics*, 162, 2018, pp 89–100.

6   See, for example, T. Lee, J. Lee and K. Coldiron, *The Rise of Carry*, McGraw Hill, 2019.

7   D. Miles, 'What is the Half-life of Economic Injustice?', *Vox*, 6 December 2018.

8   J. Leslie, *The Missing Billions*, Resolution Foundation, 2021. See also R. Rowthorne, 'A Note on Piketty's *Capital in the Twenty-first Century*', Centre for Business Research, University of Cambridge Working Paper No. 462, 2014.

9   S. Jenkins, *A Short History of London: The Creation of a World Capital*, Viking, 2019.

10   T. Aubrey, 'Gathering the Windfall', *Centre for Progressive Policy*, 19 September 2018.

11   S. Lansley, D. McCann and S. Schifferes, *Remodelling Capitalism, How Social Wealth Funds Could Transform Britain*, City University, Friends Provident Foundation, 2018.

12   F. Alvaredo, et al, *The World Inequality Report, 2018*, fig E6, p 14; Fiscal Monitor, *Managing Public Wealth*, IMF, 2018; A.B. Atkinson, *Inequality*, Harvard University Press, 2015, p 173.

13   W. Streek, 'How Will Capitalism End?', *New Left Review*, 87(2), 2014.

14   D. Lipsey, 'Labour and Land', *Fabian Tract 422*, 1973.

15   H. Wheatley, 'Mass Sell-off of Public Land Failed to Deliver Social Housing', *New Economics Foundation*, 20 September 2019.

16   Bank of England's Independent Evaluation Office, *Evaluating the Bank of England's Approach to Quantitative Easing*, January 2021.

17   H. Simon, 'UBI and the Flat Tax', *Boston Review*, 1 October 2000.

18   T. Paine, 'Agrarian Justice', in *Common Sense and Other Writings*, Barnes and Noble, 2005, pp 332–6. J. Meade, *Agathotopia: The Economics of Partnership*, Aberdeen University Press, 1989.

19   Author's calculation from C. Kidd, *Total Wealth: Wealth in Great Britain*, Office for National Statistics, 2019, table 2.2.

20   R. Harrod, 'The Possibility of Economic Satiety – Use of Economic Growth for Improving Quality of Education and Leisure', in *Problems of United States Economic Development*, Committee for Economic Development, 1958, pp 207–13.

21   S. Lansley and H. Reed, *Basic Income for All: From Desirability to Feasibility*, Compass, 2009; S. Lansley and D. McCann, 'Citizens' Wealth Funds, a Citizen's Dividend and Basic Income', *Renewal*, 27(1), 2019, pp 72–83.

22   E. Saez and G. Zucman, *A Wealth Tax on Corporations' Stock*, University of California, 2021.

23   S. Brittan and B. Riley, 'A People's Stake in North Sea Oil', *Lloyds Bank Review*, 128, 1980, pp 1–18.

24   R. Michels, *Political Parties: A Sociological Study of the Oligarchical Tendencies of Modern Democracy*, Jarrold, 1916.

25   M.S. Webb, 'Editorial', *MoneyWeek*, 8 February 2019.

26   F. Norrestad, 'Leading Banks in UK by Total Assets', *Statistica*, November 2020.

27   A. Buller, '"Doing Well by Doing Good"? Examining the Rise of Environmental, Social, Governance (ESG) Investing', *CommonWealth*, 21 December 2020.

28   L. Halligan, 'Amazon's Success is Stifling Future Innovators', *The Telegraph,* 12 October 2019.

29   I. Stelzer, 'Malcontents put Capitalism on Trial', *Sunday Times*, 13 October 2019.

30   I. Cairo and J. Sim, *Market Power, Inequality and Financial Instability*, Federal Reserve, 2020; T. Philippon, *The Great Reversal*, Harvard University Press, 2019.

31   A. Deaton and A. Case, 'Rebottling the Gini', *Prospect*, March 2020.

32   N. Mathiason, 'Thousands of Affordable Homes Axed', The Bureau of Investigative Journalism, September 2013.

33   See, for example, National Audit Office, 'Transforming Rehabilitation: Progress Review', National Audit Office, 1 March 2019.

34   C. Higson, *Two Lessons from the Failure of Carillion*, London Business School, 6 February 2018.

35 B. Milanović, 'Dutiful Dirges of Davos', *global inequality*, 19 January 2018.
36 World Economic Forum, *The Global Risks Report, 2019*, 14th edn, WEF, 2019, p 5.
37 N. Hanauer, 'The Pitchforks are Coming for us Plutocrats', *Politico Magazine*, July 2014.
38 World Economic Forum, *The Global Risks Report, 2019*, 2019.
39 A. Caine, 'Howard Schultz Doesn't Want People Calling Him a "Billionaire"', *Business Insider*, 6 February 2019.
40 B. Milanović, 'Dutiful Dirges of Davos', *global inequality*, 19 December 2018.

Chapter 27

1   D. McCloskey, 'Growth, not Forced Equality, Saves the Poor', *New York Times*, 23 December 2016.
2   L. Cohen, 'Everybody Knows', *I'm Your Man*, Columbia Records, 1988.
3   Office for National Statistics, *Health State Life Expectancies by National Deprivation Deciles, England and Wales, 2016 to 2018*, ONS, 2020; D. Taylor-Robinson et al, 'Assessing the Impact of Rising Child Poverty on the Unprecedented Rise in Infant Mortality in England, 2000–2017: time trend analysis', *BMJ Open*, 9(10), 2019, pp 1–6.
4   Quoted in R. McKie, 'Why is Life Expectancy Faltering?', *The Observer*, 23 June 2019.
5   A. Case and A. Deaton, *Deaths of Despair and the Future of American Capitalism*, Princeton University Press, 2020.
6   J. Cowley, 'Tony Blair's Unfinished Business', *New Statesman*, 24 November 2016.
7   H. Blodget, 'Better Capitalism', *Business Insider*, 7 December 2018; J.D. Ostry, P. Loungani and D. Furceri, 'Neoliberalism: Oversold?', *Finance & Development*, IMF, 53(2), June 2016, pp 38–41.
8   Business Roundtable, 'Business Roundtable Redefines the Purpose of a Corporation to Promote "An Economy That Serves All Americans"', *Business Roundtable*, 19 August 2019; M. S. Webb, 'Editorial', *MoneyWeek*, 23 August 2019
9   G. Orwell, 'The Lion and the Unicorn', in *George Orwell Essays*, Penguin, 2000, p 175.
10 S. Burri, D. Lup and A. Pepper, 'What Do Business Executives Think About Distributive Justice?' *Journal of Business Ethics* (online), 2020.
11 See, for example, Institute for Public Policy Research, *Prosperity and Justice*, IPPR, 2018; L. Macfarlane, *New Thinking for the British Economy*, Open Democracy, 2018; A.B. Atkinson, *Inequality*, Harvard University Press, 2015; N. Abernathy, D. Hamilton and J.M. Morgan, *New Rules for the 21st Century*, The Roosevelt Institute, 2019; S. Naidu, D. Rodrick and G. Zucman, 'Economics After Neoliberalism', *Boston Review*, 15 February 2019; M. Meagher, *Competition Is Killing Us*, Penguin, 2020; T. Philippon, *The Great Reversal*, Belknap Press, 2019.
12 D. Tischer and A. Leaver, 'Attack of the Clones', *Open Democracy*, 3 April, 2019; M. Gerner, 'Are we Facing Another Subprime Crisis?', *MoneyWeek*, 25 January 2019; R. Dobbs, S. Lund, J. Woetzel and M. Mutafchieva, *Debt and (Not-Much) Deleveraging*, McKinsey Global Institute, 2015.
13 A. Gramsci, *Prison Notebooks Volume II*, Columbia University Press, 2011, pp 32–3.
14 K. Farnsworth and Z. Irving, 'Austerity Politics, Global Neoliberalism, and the Official Discourse Within the IMF, *LSE Politics and Policy*, 29 January 2019.
15 S. Wood, 'Interview with Roberto Unger', *Juncture*, IPPR, 2014.
16 W. Mayr, D. Pieper, T. Rapp, M. von Rohr, J. Schindler and H. Zuber, 'The Slow Death of Europe's Social Democrats', *Der Spiegel*, 22 September 2017.
17 R. Wilkinson and K. Pickett, *The Spirit Level*, Penguin, 2009.
18 D. Webber and J. O'Neill, *Household Income Inequality, UK, 2020*, ONS, 2021, fig 3, p 5.
19 E. Charlton, 'New Zealand has unveiled its first "well-being" budget'; *World Economic Forum,* 30 May 2019; Ministry of Business, Innovation and Employment, *Fair Pay Agreements*, January 2021.

20 S. Lansley and H. Reed, *Basic Income for All, from Desirability to Feasibility*, Compass, 2019.

21 Office of Tax Simplification, 'OTS Capital Gains Tax Review', *Gov.uk*, 11 November, 2020; A. Advani, E. Chamberlain and A. Summers, *A Wealth Tax for the UK, Final Report of the Wealth Tax Commission*, London School of Economics, 2021.

Afterword

1 M. Hastings, 'The Joy of VE Day Masked a Huge Hunger for Change', *The Times*, 7 May 2020.

2 A. Thomas, 'Interview with Simon Henderson', *The Times*, 2 May, 2020.

3 O. Marks, 'Meet the 3 Essential Workers on the Cover', *Vogue*, June 2020.

4 'Editorial: Now is Not The Time to Worry About The UK Debt Burden', *The Financial Times*, 13 May 2020.

5 Office for National Statistics, *Comparison of Furloughed Jobs Data, UK*, ONS, 2021.

6 Council for Economic Advisers, 'Building Back Better: The American Jobs Plan and the American Families Plan', *Issue Brief*, May 2021.

7 S. Leiser, 'Biden Wants Companies to Pay', *The Conversation US*, 2 April 2021.

8 See, for example, P. Turchin, 'Coronavirus and the Age of Discord', *Cliodynamica*, 8 April 2020.

9 Office for National Statistics, *Covid-19 Related Deaths by Occupation, England and Wales*, ONS, 2021.

10 A. Ahuja, 'Covid-19 is Really a Syndemic', *Financial Times*, 9 October 2020.

11 Official Statistics, *Universal Credit Statistics*, Department for Work and Pensions, 23 February 2021.

12 Standard Life Foundation, *Half of those Excluded from Government Support Lost at Least a third of their Household Income During Pandemic*, 22 February 2021. Who are the excluded? (standardlifefoundation.org.uk)

13 BBC, 'Dame Louise Casey: Families "face period of destitution"', *BBC News*, 15 October 2020.

14 L.E. Major and S. Machin, *Covid-19 and Social Mobility*, Centre for Economic Performance, London School of Economics, 2020.

15 R. Halfon, 'Our Country Faces an Epidemic of Educational Poverty', *inews*, 9 September 2020; K. Handscomb and J. Leslie, *The Covid State*, Resolution Foundation, 2020.

16 K. Handscomb, *Safe Harbour*, Resolution Foundation, 2020.

17 D. Edmiston, B.B. Geiger, L. Scullion, J. Ingold and K. Summers, 'Despite the Suspension of Conditionality, Benefit Claimants are Already Looking for Work', Policy and Politics Blog, *London School of Economics*, 29 June 2020.

18 C. Berry, L. Macfarlane and S. Nanda, *Who Wins and Who Pays*, IPPR, 13 May 2020.

19 PwC/UBS, *Riding the Storm: Billionaire Insights*, PwC/UBS, 2020.

20 J. Meadway, 'Creating a Digital Commons', *IPPR*, 6 August 2020.

21 C. Giles, 'IMF Proposes "Solidarity" Tax on Pandemic Winners and Wealthy', *Financial Times*, 7 April 2021.

22 J. A. Ocampo, J.E. Stiglitz and J. Ghosh, 'Open Letter to Joe Biden', *ICRICT*, 26 February 2021, available from: https://www.icrict.com/press-release/2021/2/26/an-open-letter-to-joe-biden-on-international-corporate-taxation.

23 J. Freedland, 'It's taken just 12 months for Boris Johnson to Create a Government of Sleaze', *The Guardian*, 7 August 2020.

24 K. Schwab, 'Now is the Time for a "Great Reset"', *World Economic Forum*, 3 June 2020.

25 W. Hutton, 'Britain's Vaccine Rollout is a Triumph', *The Observer*, 7 February 2021.

26 R Haass, 'The Pandemic Will Accelerate History Rather than Reshape it', *Foreign Affairs*, 7 April 2020.

Index